In the Shadow of the Miracle

In the Shadow of the Miracle

The Japanese Economy Since the
End of High-Speed Growth

Arthur J. Alexander

LEXINGTON BOOKS
Lanham • Boulder • New York • Oxford

LEXINGTON BOOKS

Published in the United States of America
by Lexington Books
A Member of the Rowman & Littlefield Publishing Group
4720 Boston Way, Lanham, Maryland 20706

PO Box 317
Oxford
OX2 9RU, UK

British Library Cataloguing in Publication Information Available

Library of Congress Control Number: 2002110169

ISBN 0-7391-0127-7 (cloth : alk. paper)

Printed in the United States of America

♾™ The paper used in this publication meets the minimum requirements of American
National Standard for Information Sciences—Permanence of Paper for Printed Library
Materials, ANSI/NISO Z39.48–1992.

I first wrote the chapters in this book at the Japan Economic Institute in Washington, D.C., as research articles for the institute's weekly report on Japan. Those original texts, plus considerable updates and revisions, benefited in countless ways from my JEI colleagues. I wish to acknowledge my debt by dedicating this book to them.

Contents

Figures

Tables

Preface

Japan is living in the shadow of its economic miracle. Its stagnation and decline relative to other advanced economies since the early 1990s is a consequence of business and government difficulty in breaking away from once-successful practices.

The Japanese economic miracle following World War II created the world's second largest capitalist economy. Double-digit growth over several decades also made the Japanese people among the richest in the world. This remarkable performance, following military defeat, physical destruction, and rampant hunger in 1945, gave Japan a new definition of itself. Such undeniable success in the face of such enormous obstacles helped to solidify and even sanctify the institutions, methods, habits, rules of thumb, and political arrangements that were associated with the economic miracle.

Even more, several of the customary practices that had become synonymous with Japan—lifetime employment, long-term business relations, subsidies and protection for disadvantaged industries and groups, political protection for favored clients—conformed to underlying Japanese values. Not only did the system work, it was comfortable and comforting to most Japanese people.

However, many of the practices and institutions of the miracle era had negative side effects, even during the period of high-speed growth. Their persistence and embedded quality are inappropriate and downright dangerous for an inevitably maturing and slower growing economy. While seeming to soften the transition to a more dynamic future, the habits and institutions of the miracle era drag out the process, spread the discomfort, and intensify the pain.

The changes necessary to break out of stagnation strike at many of the foundations of the post-1945 system. Delays in addressing the problems of too much capital, too many employees, bankrupt corporate borrowers, a fragile banking system, and an unresponsive political process have multiplied and intensified the problems that were becoming apparent as early as the 1970s.

The list of well-known problems facing Japan, however, is only one side of the miracle's shadow. In order to develop and get rich, Japan had to have institutions that worked; these institutions continue to give strength to the nation. The country is a market-oriented, capitalist democracy. It responds to shifting pressures, even if only slowly.

Japan is not the only advanced country to fall on hard times. Nevertheless, despite their difficulties, rich countries do not collapse. For the ten years ending in 2001, Japan's growth of real per capita gross domestic product was just under 1 percent annually. According to World Bank data, countries as diverse as Canada, Denmark, Finland, Iceland, the Netherlands, New Zealand, Spain, and Switzerland also have fallen below the 1 percent mark for at least a decade. Indeed, Switzerland's growth rate for the thirty years from 1970 to 2000 was less than Japan's in the 1990s. The lesson to draw from this example is that Switzerland is not a failed state, and neither is Japan.

The positive side of life in the shadow of the miracle is that Japan's economic future ranges from mediocre to good. One-percent per capita growth would be comparative failure; 2 percent would be a considerable achievement. Nevertheless, despite the auspicious examples of other rich nations that have managed to dig themselves out of economic stagnation, success is not guaranteed. The Japanese people, their bosses, and their politicians have to make appropriate and tough choices. The nation's demonstrated ability to overcome obstacles suggests a bright future, but it's no sure thing.

Chapter 1

An Economy in Transition

The Move to Greater Profit Orientation

Economists often use the word "transition" to describe countries whose economies are moving from planned, socialist methods to more capitalistic, market-driven ones. Japan's economy also is making a transition, perhaps not as radical as that of the former communist states but, to the Japanese, almost as dramatic.

To be sure, Japan has had a capitalist, market-oriented economy at least since the period following the Meiji Restoration of the 1860s. The reference to Japan's present course as a transition in the same sense as the former communist regimes may be stretching the definition of the word. Yet, the world's second-largest economy is acquiring a more profit-oriented thrust with a new focus on such capitalistic norms as returns on assets and the bottom line. Describing it in terms of transition helps to dramatize the point that in embarking on such a major transformation, Japan—like Eastern Europe and Russia—is hobbled by institutions, laws, regulations, habits, and a pervasive psychology, all of which are more appropriate to the old ways than to the present trajectory of economic life.

Several fundamental difficulties hamstring the Japanese economy today. Long-term growth has slowed to a rate that is typical of other advanced countries—around 2 percent or less annually. Overall productivity is relatively low and is lagging seriously in many manufacturing industries and services. Business has overinvested. Given the combination of overinvestment and low productivity, rates of return are well below those of the United States and major European countries. Finally, the financial system remains saddled with the bad loans and the wrecked balance sheets generated by the collapse of the asset-price bubble at the start of the 1990s.

All but the last of these problems existed years before the bubble burst. Eventually, Japan would have had to confront the economic complications arising from slow growth, skimpy productivity gains, and too much capital tied up in low-return investments. The financial collapse brought about by falling asset prices forced attention to all problems at once—hence, an economy in transition.

This chapter focuses on two key issues. First, what is driving the changes now underway in Japan? Second, why did it take so long for Tokyo and corporate Japan to recognize the nature of the problems hobbling the economy and to begin dealing with them?

Slowing Growth

Rich nations always grow at a slower pace than high-flying, poorer countries. All fast-expanding countries are poor, although not all poor countries experience rapid economic growth. Growth depends primarily on the productive investment of capital in physical and human resources. As investment proceeds and the capital intensity of production and technology catch up with that of the more advanced economies, the rate of expansion tends to decelerate.

These observations are illustrated in figure 1.1, plotted from data collected by the Center for International Comparisons at the University of Pennsylvania as reported in the Penn World Table, a compilation of national economic accounts for 152 countries from 1950 to 1992.[1] Expenditures are denominated in a common set of prices in a common currency so that real quantity comparisons can be made, both between countries and over time. The relationship between growth and income shown in figure 1.1 plots ten-year growth on the vertical axis and real GDP per capita at the beginning of each ten-year span on the horizontal axis. For clarity, the figure shows only those 1,700 observations with real incomes above $2,000 per person, ignoring the 50 percent of the data that falls below that cutoff. Dropping half the observations at the lower end does not change the qualitative picture in the slightest. Decade-long periods were used to reduce the effects of such short-term shocks and fluctuations as business cycles. The reason for using income levels at the beginning of each ten-year period is to avoid biased observations. Fast growing countries might be expected to have higher incomes at the end of the period than would slower growing countries precisely because of the growth experience. The reverse would be true for laggards. Looking at income levels at the beginning of the period eliminates such biases.

**Figure 1.1: Ten-Year Real GDP/Capita Growth and GDP/Capita
(percent and 1985 dollars at purchasing power parity)**

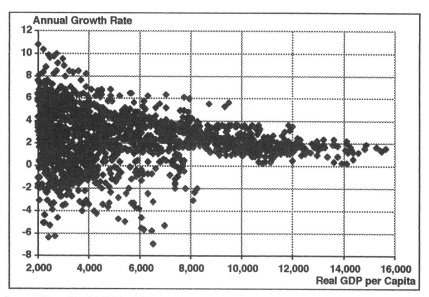

Source: Penn World Table 5.6

Growth rates converge among richer countries. The variance of growth declines as we move to the right. It is a common observation that variance declines as the unit of observation increases in size. For example, the variability of growth among large firms is smaller than for small ones. The reason for this regularity is that large units often can be thought of as incorporating many smaller ones, whose individual experiences average out, thereby reducing variability. However, the relationship revealed in figure 1.1 is not like that. We are looking at output per capita, not total output. There is no reason to expect variability to fall as relative income increases. In fact, GDP per capita has close to a zero correlation with measures of size like population and aggregate GDP. The low variability among rich countries is not a story about size but about success.

Figure 1.2: Average Annual Growth Rate of Real GDP Per Capita Over Preceding Ten Years, Japan and United States, 1960-2000 (percent)

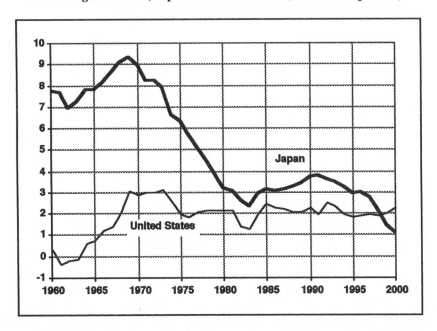

Source: Statistics Bureau, Management and Coordination Agency; Department of Commerce.

Among the nineteen economies that had attained real per capita outputs greater than $10,000 in 1985 dollars, annual expansion rates over ten-year periods averaged 1.75 percent, with a range between 0.2 percent and 3.7 percent.[2] New Zealand's 1980s stagnation was at the low end and Japan itself accounted for the high figure the year it entered the big leagues of countries above the $10,000 GDP per capita cutoff. Japan's own postwar experience has followed the pattern of other rich countries as it marched steadily down its growth curve until it fell below the average in the 1990s (see figure 1.2). Although scatter plots do not determine destiny, these observations do show the historical experience.

Since the "miracle" expansion of the 1950s and 1960s, Japan's march toward the 2 percent level has been relentless, broken only by a spurt during the asset-bubble experience of the late 1980s. Most econometric studies conclude that given the growth of the labor force, the projected rate of profitable investment, and the expected increases in productivity, growth will settle sooner or later in the range of 2 percent a year, plus or minus half a percentage point.

To many Japanese business executives and government leaders, not to mention ordinary people, the slowdown from the go-go years of the 1950s and 1960s is a disappointment. However, for a rich country, 2 percent per capita growth is a miracle in its own right. It leads to a doubling of real incomes every thirty-five years. For one of the world's richest countries to continue improving the economic welfare of its citizens at such a pace is almost without precedent. It is very much a twentieth-century phenomenon, and it certainly is not automatic. Some relatively rich countries like Brazil and Argentina lost their big-league status in the early part of the last century when their policies and business practices failed to sustain their economic promise. Current initiatives will determine whether Japan can make stable economic gains a twenty-first-century experience.

Capital Stock Too High, Returns Too Low

As mentioned, investment is the source of economic growth. The question of why some countries are able to marshal the savings of individuals and businesses and direct them to productive uses still is studied intensely. Some research indicates that education, income equality, price stability, and government competence are preconditions for high investment rates and subsequent economic development.[3] Japan has been a standout on all these requirements.

What remains to be explained is why Japanese companies continued to invest at prodigious rates after returns fell well below the levels achieved in other advanced countries. Even after Japan's ratio of capital to GDP topped that of the United States in the 1970s, capital intensity continued to increase. According to one survey, by the mid-1980s, before Japan's bubble-induced investment binge, the ratio of nonresidential capital stock to economic output was some 40 percent greater than the U.S. figure.[4]

As capital accumulated, returns fell. First, the increased use of capital relative to such other inputs as labor led to decreasing returns. Not surprisingly, businesses slid down their yield curves. However, the second reason behind the reduced profitability of capital was low productivity in the way it was used. Detailed examinations of specific industries and production processes by the McKinsey Global Institute, the research arm of management consultant McKinsey & Co., Inc., found that inefficiency, rather than diminishing returns, explained most of Japan's pattern of declining returns.[5]

Figure 1.3: Return on Business Capital in Japan and the United States, 1970-1998

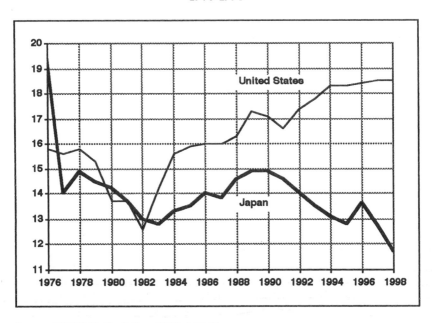

Source: OECD *Outlook*, June 1996, A80-81.
Note: The figures for 1976 are the average for the years 1970-1976.

According to the Paris-based Organization for Cooperation and Development, and consistent with other studies, business returns in Japan fell sharply from the high-growth period and dropped below U.S. levels in the 1980s (see figure 1.3). (The return to business capital is defined as the ratio of the gross operating surplus of enterprises to nonresidential gross fixed capital valued at replacement cost. Gross operating surplus is the difference between value-added calculated at factor cost and labor income.) Since 1982, the gap between the two countries widened almost every year..

A low rate of return on capital is symptomatic of insufficient attention to profitability. Corporate Japan assigned profits a low priority for a number of reasons, many of which now are changing. Regulation of the nonfinancial and financial sectors alike blunted the focus on the bottom line. Many firms in the vast nontradable goods part of the economy operated under the consensus-producing aegis of industry associations or under government rules and guidance. These companies were assured that competitors would not introduce new products or lower prices without the consent of most members of the particular industry. Government-condoned collusion and cartels that controlled prices and allocated market shares reinforced this approach to doing business.

An explicit Ministry of Finance commitment to the so-called convoy system assured that no bank would fail and that all banks would make at least some money. In the rare instances of insolvency, MOF engineered a takeover by a healthier bank or organized loans from the government and private financial institutions to assist the ailing bank. For example, in July 1991 when loans to a bankrupt shipping company crippled Toho Sogo Bank, Ltd. it was taken over by Iyo Bank, Ltd. in an "assisted merger," with funds provided by the Deposit Insurance Corp., the Bank of Japan and the Second Association of Regional Banks.[6] The no-failure guarantee for banks extended to depositors and, by implication, to creditors and major borrowers. The reasoning was that if a bank could not fail, neither could a major borrower be allowed to go under because that would threaten the solvency of the lender.

In addition to regulating interest rates and the products offered by banks, Tokyo limited the entry of new competitors into the industry and protected banks from the pressures of a more open capital market by imposing strict limits on how corporations raised funds. Banks, therefore, were at the center of finance. Japanese companies typically had much higher debt/equity ratios than would be comfortable for an American company, bank, or shareholder. For the past twenty-five years in the United States, the ratio of debt to the market value of equity has tended to be just below 1.0. In the 1970s, the ratio was 3.5 in Japan, falling gradually to around 1.5 as capital markets were deregulated and as the stock market boomed in the late 1980s. With the breaking of the bubble, however, the debt/equity ratio jumped back to 2.0.[7]

Japan's high levels of debt have been explained in part by the so-called main bank system, under which one bank has a long-term, close relationship with a company. Such ties presumably give the bank an inside view of company activities as well as confer on the banks the responsibility for guaranteeing the firm's financial dealings with others. However, a downturn in business can leave an overleveraged firm with

an insufficient cash flow to cover interest and debt repayment obliga-
tions.

In the past, the main bank was expected to arrange a salvage operation, much as the MOF rescued troubled banks. In fact, this system
seemed to work for blue-chip firms, but small companies were not so
well protected by their main bank relationships.[8] Therefore, because
highly leveraged firms were vulnerable to slower growth, the central position of banks in corporate finance has been associated with elevated
rates of business failure. In the 1970s and 1980s, the ratio of liabilities to
GDP of failed Japanese companies was about twice the American number. As the Japanese economy has weakened during the 1990s, liabilities
as a share of GDP have been four to five times greater than the U.S. rate.

Shifting Perceptions and Policies

Not until well into the 1990s did the reality of protracted slower growth
begin to permeate the Japanese psychology. Although GDP gains had
begun to drop off in the early 1970s, it took until the end of that decade
for the Economic Planning Agency to recognize the slowdown in its official projections. Authorities could point to other plausible causes, including the two oil shocks of the 1970s and the costs of reconfiguring
much of Japanese industry to accommodate higher petroleum prices, for
what they persisted in believing was a temporary phenomenon. In the
1980s, slow growth was linked to a strong yen or to other external
causes. The boom of the late 1980s was not seen as abnormal but rather
as a return to the golden times of the past. Similarly, it has taken the better part of the 1990s for business and government plans to incorporate
the idea that slower growth is here to stay.

Another shock to the Japanese psyche was the decline in the government's willingness and ability to prop up the banking system. This
shift in policy has been quite explicit: MOF has announced that it will
not feel compelled to come to the rescue of small banks or to bail out
large ones after April 2001. In fact, though, by 2000 one major bank already had gone under and two others were taken over by the government.
Tokyo's guarantee that the financial system will remain whole may not
yet be dead, but in both rhetoric and reality, this promise is dying.

Today's altered reality for banks is illustrated by the fact that no
bank failed from 1950 to 1992. In late 1993, a small *shinkin* (credit association) became insolvent. In 1994, crippling bad loans forced three more

shinkin to shut their doors. The following year, a "real" bank, Hyogo Bank, Ltd., suspended operations and subsequently was liquidated. By the end of 1999, 11 banks had closed or had been taken over by the government for disposal or liquidation. Between fiscal 1995 and 1999, the number of banks fell by 35 from 421 and 82 of Japan's 373 credit cooperatives had ceased operations, with about 53 going bankrupt.[9]

The Big Bang also is changing the banking industry. This deregulatory effort, which promises to make Japan's financial markets "free, fair, and global" by the end of FY 2001 is liberalizing the introduction of new products, freeing the pricing of financial products and services, and eliminating the walls that separate banks, securities brokers, and insurers.

Capitalizing on the deregulation process, foreign firms are moving into the Tokyo market, bringing with them experience and competitive instincts developed in New York, London, Hong Kong, and other markets that liberalized a decade or more earlier. In 1980, for example, only two foreign securities companies operated in Japan. In a 1984 interview, the head of Merrill Lynch & Co., Inc.'s Tokyo office noted that his company sold hundreds of products in New York but only two in Japan—stocks and bonds. By 1985, 12 more foreign brokers had opened securities offices; in 1995, at least 50 such companies were in business. Further liberalization in 1999 simplified entry by requiring only registration instead of MOF's laborious approval process. The foreign incursion can be expected to continue.

Foreign banks, too, have increased in both number and in terms of market share. In the mid-1980s, 74 foreign banks operated in Tokyo, but they controlled just 3 percent of total banking assets. By 1998, offshore banks numbered 91 and held 8 percent of all banking assets.

The simultaneous deregulation and globalization of financial markets, combined with fading bank guarantees, is forcing corporate Japan to pay new attention to profitability and the return on invested capital. As part of this process, both bankruptcies and mergers and acquisitions reached new highs every year in the late 1990s.

Although the government expanded its credit-guarantee program for small businesses in 1999 in an attempt to curb bankruptcies among these companies, the liabilities of failed firms continued to climb, indicating that larger operations were facing insolvency. An important feature of the new M&A situation is that foreign acquisitions of Japanese companies broke all records in 1999 and again in 2000. However, despite the unprecedented number of takeovers by domestic and foreign companies alike, M&A activity in Japan is still only a fraction of what occurs in either the United States or Great Britain.

Why Did Japan Take So Long to Respond?

Slowing growth, overinvestment, low returns, and lagging productivity have been features of the Japanese economy for decades. Over that time, the problems grew worse. Bank lending based on asset values continued well after stock market and property prices had begun to fall. (See figure 1.4.) Moreover, banks lent into their nonperforming loans, providing credit for distressed borrowers to cover interest and principal, which worsened the scale of the problem. Note in figure 1.4 that real estate lending continued to rise even as asset prices declined sharply. The bubble-induced bad-loan situation existed for at least six years before the government began to consider it a threat to the stability of Japan's financial system. It took even longer for banks to confront their problems. Action on other economic issues looming on the horizon has been put off indefinitely, resulting in underfunded private and public pensions, public corporations with excessive liabilities, and as-yet-undisclosed financial weaknesses in manufacturing and services companies.

Despite what seems at times to be an unwillingness to do anything, policymakers in Tokyo have not been sitting on their hands. The Big Bang, orchestrated in 1996 by then-Prime Minister Ryutaro Hashimoto, was designed to address many of the problems just mentioned. The public recapitalization of major banks in 1999 and the year before, along with stricter official auditing and tighter oversight, was an attempt to clean up the bad loans and the shady practices of earlier times. The massive fiscal deficits that the government began running up in 1991 were intended to boost the economy and get it moving on its own so that the transfusions eventually could be discontinued. However, some experts have characterized these policies as too little, too late.

Real estate related lending is an example of how slowly banks and government agencies dealt with a situation that was bad in 1992 and worsened in subsequent years before any actions other than cover-ups were undertaken. Property-related loans were about one-quarter of all bank lending in Japan. Since the value of property typically is the basis for borrowers' collateral, bank lending rose rapidly along with the run-up in real estate prices during the latter part of the 1980s. When the property market began to collapse in 1991, however, banks increased their lending in order to cover borrowers' missed interest and principal repayments.

**Figure 1.4: Real Estate Loans and Asset Prices in Japan, 1970-2000
(1980=100)**

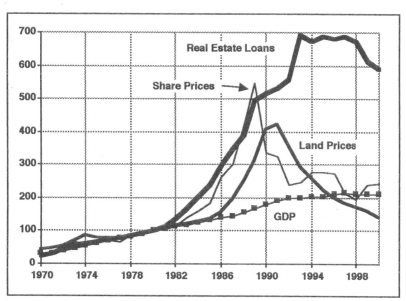

Source: Bank of Japan and Japan Real Estate Institute
Note: Real estate loans comprise loans to real estate companies, construction firms, and nonbank financial companies. Property prices are the average for Japan's six largest urban areas.

The book value of real estate loans plateaued in 1993 and did not begin to fall until 1998. For several years, banks reserved against the mounting volume of their obviously bad loans, but they did not take them off their books or renegotiate the terms. Finally, in 1998, as the process of renegotiation, securitization, and selling off bad loans to a government collection organization began in earnest, the outstanding book value of real estate-related loans started to drop. However, while property prices in Japan's six largest metropolitan areas were off 60 percent from their peak in 2000, lending was down only 9.5 percent.

Explanations for Slow Response

Japan is a rich country with institutions generally befitting that status. Nonetheless, certain of its government-business relationships, legal structures, habits, and rules of thumb are holdovers from an earlier period. These vestigial institutions, practices, and processes—which resemble those of certain other Asian countries today, especially South Korea—contributed to Japan's current problems and to the delay in recognizing the scale of the economy's troubles and in developing policies to contain the fallout. Given a good deal of overlap, these impediments to action on the policy front can be grouped into two categories: as coming either from the government or from the business community. However, one factor had a pervasive effect—the persistent Japanese belief that a return to rapid growth was just around the corner.

When the bubble burst at the start of the 1990s, the natural reaction was to wait out the decline. Policymakers made their "crossed-fingers" stance almost official, hoping for a pickup in the economy that would solve all the problems without anyone having to do anything. They maintained that do-nothing approach for the better part of five years. Finally, both corporate executives and government leaders began to understand that Japan's mature economy was on a permanently slower growth trajectory and that even if a revival occurred, it would not solve banks' bad-loan problems. This lag in recognizing the true nature of the situation was compounded by other features of the government and the business environment.

MOF's pledge that no bank would be allowed to fail was perhaps the main cause of the overinvestment and the low returns to capital that characterize Japan's economy. It also contributed greatly to the delay in recognizing the scale of the troubles coming from the collapse of the asset-price bubble of the late 1980s.

Much of the government's intervention in the economy in the early decades of the postwar era was in credit markets in an attempt to channel household savings to industry for investment purposes. A regulated, stable banking system was considered necessary to give people confidence that their money would be safe in the hands of bankers. The protection of banks from failure and the provision of guarantees to depositors were integral to Tokyo's strategy for mobilizing savings. In short, a controlled, nonmarket banking system supported high rates of investment, which, in turn, generated the miracle of sustained, rapid growth.

Unfortunately, this method of mobilizing savings and promoting investment also created the conditions that led to the eventual financial breakdown. Even without a collapsing asset market, many banks and other types of companies would have failed sooner or later because of overinvestment and low returns. The side effects of a failure-proof banking system turned routine economic shocks into crises.

As nonperforming loans to real estate and construction interests piled up in the early 1990s and as it became evident that other companies were unable to generate adequate profits with which to repay their loans, the prevailing expectation in financial circles continued to be that the government would work out some kind of solution. Indeed, such confidence was supported by concrete evidence, as MOF found saviors for failing banks and did its utmost to shield even the weakest institutions from full exposure to the consequences of their conditions. The fact that several executives from Nippon Credit Bank, Ltd. and the Long-Term Credit Bank, Ltd. of Japan later faced criminal prosecution for the illegal window-dressing of their books and other acts to cover up the true condition of their banks—apparently with the collusion and encouragement of Finance officials—suggests that the ministry found it difficult to abandon its successful postwar policies.

By the late 1990s, however, the credibility of Tokyo's guarantee was evaporating quickly. Indications were spreading that the government no longer could be counted on to save insolvent lenders, especially with the failures of three giants—Hokkaido Takushoku Bank, Ltd., LTCB and NCB—which had occurred despite the best attempts of the government. Nevertheless, old practices and habits persisted long after Tokyo had lost its ability to preserve or resurrect zombie financial institutions.

Many Japanese officials now say that it was the back-to-back collapses in late 1997 of Hokkaido Takushoku Bank and Yamaichi Securities Co., Ltd. that shocked the political leadership into the realization that the crisis engulfing the financial sector could not be solved by the traditional means of waiting, administrative guidance, and discrete, behind-the-scenes tactics. A more direct policy response was required—one that involved a government takeover of some portion of corporate Japan's unpayable debt and that accepted the government bureaucracy's inability to engineer solutions in an increasingly deregulated and complex financial system.

The governing Liberal Democratic Party owes a good deal of its electoral success to the support of and by specific industries. Accordingly, policies that might harm these constituents have not been well received. Construction companies, for example, are an important source of political contributions, even though the property-based investments made by contractors have left many of them close to insolvency. That the LDP strongly supports the industry is indicated by the fact that Japan spent 10 percent of GDP on public works projects and related land acquisitions in 1996; the comparable figure for the United States and European countries was just over 2 percent.[10] Were banks to get serious about cleaning up their bad loans and cutting lending to unprofitable companies, the construction industry would be at the top of the list. The LDP, however, has been extremely reluctant to promote a strict assessment by banks of business profitability that would have the effect of undermining the construction industry.

An even more telling example of the LDP's reluctance to allow weak firms to fail is the ¥30 trillion ($166.7 billion at ¥120=$1.00) that the government contributed in 1998 to a credit-guarantee program for small companies. Total business failures had climbed to 16,500 in 1997 and were marching to a postwar record in 1998 when the government intervened. This move enabled banks to continue to support companies that may have looked less than creditworthy without a guarantee of repayment. The credit-guarantee program had the desired effect as business failures fell sharply after the infusion of new funds.

The government's fiscal condition deteriorated badly in the 1970s as a recession triggered by the surge in oil prices drove the budget into persistent deficit. Declaring the 1980s to be a decade of recovery, MOF took radical steps to achieve a balanced budget. That goal was reached in 1990, and politicians and bureaucrats alike fervently tried to remain on the path of fiscal rectitude. However, as early as 1993, experts had concluded that public funds would be needed to help clean up the bad-loan problem. The only questions were when, how much, and in what manner? MOF policymakers, though, desperately fought the idea of nationalizing the losses incurred by the banking system as they attempted to adhere to their no-deficit policy.

In 1995, after seven *jusen* (housing finance companies) that were affiliates of large banks got into trouble, the administration of then-Prime Minister Tomiichi Murayama came up with a plan to bail them out. Aside from the ramifications for the founding banks, the major motivation for this policy shift was to assist agricultural cooperatives that had invested heavily in these companies and that were about to lose much of their money.

Losses at the cooperatives meant that farmers, another LDP constituency, would lose their deposits. Politically, the bailout was particularly clumsy. It appeared to taxpayers that their money was being used to protect a small number of the LDP's friends. The political opposition seized on the issue and organized rallies at the Diet, holding up consideration of other legislation for months. This experience made the LDP leaders extremely skittish about any new program to deal with the bad-loan situation that involved a public bailout.

Business Sources of Delayed Response

Thirty years of rapid growth left corporate Japan with business practices that hampered its ability to respond to a permanent economic slowdown. Investment and expansion had been the primary objective of business. In the 1950s and the 1960s, growth was so rapid that the main problem facing business leaders was how to manage the process.

Bringing new, productive capacity on stream was a constant challenge. Profits for the most part were invested rather than distributed to shareholders as dividends since such a move would have required firms to go into the capital market or to borrow from banks to raise the money for expansion. Moreover, it made little sense for businesses to make fine-tuned calculations of internal rates of return when economywide returns averaged 35 percent or more in the 1950s. However, as growth slowed, established business practices diverged from profitmaking rationality.

Recruitment, retention, and training were persistent problems during Japan's high-growth years. One development to cope with these challenges was the entrenchment and the refinement of lifetime employment among large companies. The spread of this feature of Japanese business practice largely was a product of the 1950s. Before that, labor relations had been turbulent. Lifetime employment and the accompanying practice of promoting people based on age and tenure served several critical purposes. They encouraged investment in human capital, produced cadres of new managers knowledgeable about the intricacies of fast-growing big companies, and tied scarce labor to the firm. The fact that the employer had a commitment to its employees for their entire careers was not seen as a problem.

Although lifetime employment formally applied only to some 25 percent of the labor force, most firms tried to follow the practice. Of course, not all companies could afford to do so. It was especially difficult for smaller firms in competitive industries. Nevertheless, the norm of lifetime employment had a noticeable effect on nationwide statistics. Japan's employment variation in response to changes in output is roughly a quarter of the fluctuation in the comparable U.S. statistic.

A corporate practice in Japan that has been widely cited as worthy of emulation is the effort to build long-term relationships among companies that do business with each other. Such ties can have many positive effects: supplier firms can make investments confident of demand for the resulting product; and companies can coordinate their activities more closely than if they engaged in arm's-length transactions. On the downside, however, if a business partner becomes less competitive than other potential partners, the relationship is maintained at a price.

While corporate America learned many lessons from Japanese inter-company relations, firms in Japan now are learning to end relationships that no longer make economic sense. Such a radical change in the business environment takes time to implement, however. Many Japanese executives consider it a matter of honor to continue to support alliances as long as possible. That loyalty drags out the adjustment process.

Changes in corporate control represent one of the main means for forcing business discipline on American firms. Underperforming companies become targets for mergers or takeovers. Moreover, insolvent companies can be reorganized through bankruptcy to reestablish their underlying value. Corporate governance in Japan, however, has been particularly weak. In part, this situation is an outgrowth of an explicit policy dating back to the early 1970s when corporate cross-shareholding relationships were promoted to foster long-term ties and to thwart unwanted takeovers. The absence of outside directors on company boards and the high price of underlying assets, particularly land, are other impediments to more profit-oriented corporate governance in Japan.

Many of the conditions that have discouraged strong corporate governance in Japan are changing. Companies are selling shares that do not yield adequate returns. Boards of directors are becoming more open. Property prices have fallen for a decade, and share prices declined to levels that are more attractive. Most importantly, corporate financial officers must pay greater attention to returns on capital. That requirement opens up possibilities for greater competition for the control of underperforming companies and for the restructuring that would be the likely result.

The Turnpike Theorem and Its Side Effects

The policies and attitudes just mentioned originally were innovative, rational, and profit-maximizing approaches to attaining high-speed growth. On a broader front, Japanese policymakers were ahead of economic theoreticians in their growth policies. Economists developed the so-called turnpike theorem in the 1950s. Under certain conditions, they posited, it would make sense for a nation to reconfigure its economic structure to emphasize rapid investment and production growth while sacrificing current consumption. It might pay to take a detour to get on the turnpike and zoom along at high speed before taking the exit ramp marked "increasing consumption." For developing economies, an emphasis on investment and production often is an appropriate policy for achieving the ultimate goal of consumer welfare.

Japan is living proof of the turnpike theorem's validity. What the economists formulating this idea did not foresee, however, was that the highway to growth easily might become a road to nowhere, with the exit ramps blocked by structural inertia and political barriers protecting the status quo.

Another barrier to change is economic obsolescence—an unwelcome fact of life that policymakers understandably try to avoid, especially when resources still are quite capable of performing their former tasks. Markets are the usual means for assessing the value of assets in changing circumstances, but the results often are troublesome if they imply hardship. Adjustment inevitably imposes economic and political costs. When government is involved in a hard-hit industry or when firms and workers are regionally concentrated or have enjoyed excessive benefits (often from protection or regulation), the political pressures to provide "good jobs for good people" become particularly difficult to resist.

In addition, the routines of business decisionmaking that had been consistent with economic rationality under past conditions block adaptation when it is not patently obvious that conditions have changed sufficiently or permanently so as to make old methods obsolete. The combination of this natural tendency to persist with successful strategies and the conservatism of institutions developed to respond to rapid growth is a recipe for delayed response.

However, countermeasures to inertia do exist. One aspect of recent Japanese experience that has promoted greater sensitivity to shifting patterns of demand is the deregulation of the financial services sector and the increasing role in the economy of foreign businesses that are not burdened with the obsolete lessons and methods of Japan's past. In particular, liberalized financial markets and the loss of the government guarantee to protect banks from their bad decisions have introduced an appreciation for profitability that was missing before.

The seemingly wasteful destruction of firms and the dissipation of their resources, including career employees, by the mysterious actions of market forces often appear to be a high price to pay for growth and productivity. However, although it can buy several years' time, failing to make needed changes is not a sustainable long-term policy.

Ultimately, the choices are deeply political. The promotion of vigorous financial markets—itself a political choice—can go a long way toward bringing economic forces to bear on business and political judgments. This is happening in Japan today. Business is restructuring at a rate that, from an American perspective, looks slow but that cumulatively could change the landscape of Japanese society.

Notes

1.   The Penn World Table is described in Alan Heston & Robert Summers, "The Penn World Table (Mark 5): An Expanded Set of International Comparisons, 1950-1988," *Quarterly Journal of Economics* 106, no. 2 (May 1991): 327-68.

2.   Figure 1.1 and the summary statistics exclude the oil countries of Bahrain, Saudi Arabia, and Trinidad and Tobago.

3.   Dani Rodrik, "Understanding Economic Policy Reform," *Journal of Economic Literature* 34, no. 1 (March 1996): 20-21.

4.   Angus Maddison, "Standardised Estimates of Fixed Capital Stock: A Six-Country Comparison," in *Explaining the Economic Performance of Nations* (Brookfield, Vt.: Edward Elgar Publishing Co., 1995).

5.   McKinsey Global Institute, *Capital Productivity* (Washington, D.C.: 1996), 3.

6.   Maximilian J. B. Hall, *Financial Reform in Japan: Causes and Consequences* (Northampton, Mass.: Edward Elgar Publishing Co., 1998), 160.

7.   R. N. McCauley and S. A. Zimmer, "Explaining International Differences in the Cost of Capital," *Quarterly Review*, Federal Reserve Bank of New York (Summer 1992).

8.   Takeo Hoshi, Anil Kashyap, David Scharfstein, "The Role of Banks in Reducing the Costs of Financial Distress in Japan," *Journal of Financial Economics* (1990): 75.

9.   "Credit Co-Op Failures Soar Over Past Five Years," *Nihon Keizai Shimbun*, October 20, 2000.

10.   Organization for Economic Cooperation and Development, *OECD Economic Surveys: Japan, 1996-1997* (Paris: 1997): 67.

Chapter 2

The Economy in the Twentieth Century

Overview

By almost any definition, Japan's economy turned in a remarkable performance starting in the last quarter of the nineteenth century and continuing through most of the twentieth. To cite just one statistic, annual output grew a massive seventy-fold between 1885 and the end of 1999. The American economy, in comparison, expanded at less than half that rate.

This absolute increase in the sheer size of economic production in Japan brought with it an immense multiplication of the standard measures for gauging economic welfare. For example, the average value of national income per person expanded by a factor of almost twenty-one.

With its stellar performance by this and other yardsticks, Japan demonstrated to the world that it was not necessary to be European or North American to get rich. The more recent takeoff of economies in Asia and elsewhere in the developing world owes much to this example and to the lessons, learned and mislearned, from the Japanese experience.

This chapter outlines the main trends of Japan's economy over the twentieth century. Before proceeding, though, a word needs to be said about the data that were used to calculate the long-term trends discussed here. To construct more or less consistent information spanning a century-plus, several shorter time series that had been compiled on different occasions had to be strung together. The need to convert monetary values into quantities that reflect general price changes introduced additional complications. Therefore, the analysis should carry a large, bold-faced warning: Read with caution. To say, for instance, that real gross national product per capita in 1885 was ¥188,000 in 1990 prices compared with a 1999 figure of ¥3,866,000 is, at best, a gross characterization—although not necessarily a mischaracterization. Fine distinctions are not warranted by the quality of the data.

Pre-Meiji Foundations of the Modern Japanese Economy

The rapid industrialization of Japan following the Meiji restoration in 1868 surprised most contemporary observers. Japan's military defeat of China in 1895 and Russia ten years later demonstrated a mastery of modern technology and industrial practice that could be brought to bear in a compelling fashion. According to figures compiled by growth economist Angus Maddison, Japan's economic performance over the years 1870 to 1913 was exceeded by only seven countries out of the twenty-nine examined.[1] From 1950 to 1973, no other country did as well as Japan. Such an amazing track record raises the question of its foundations. What was happening inside Japan before its economic prowess startled the world?

For the 250 years that ran from the beginning of the 1600s to the middle of the nineteenth century, Japan's leaders cut the nation off from contact with other countries. The Tokugawa shoguns who ruled during this period from their capital in Edo—now Tokyo—prohibited the construction of oceangoing ships and severely punished unauthorized contact with foreigners. In 1600, the largely peasant Japanese economy was not that different from most of the rest of the world in terms of technology and living standards. In the intervening years, however, the industrial revolution in Great Britain and then in North America created technology, growth, wealth, and capabilities that far surpassed what was happening in the isolated islands of Japan.

Despite the absence of the fruits of the industrial revolution that were transforming the West, Japan was not undeveloped. It boasted three of the largest cities in the world; Edo alone had more than one million inhabitants. With this urbanization came the creation of craft industries and merchant classes that processed the food and other materials of the countryside and catered to society's elites as well as to the tastes and the incomes of the masses. Sophisticated as well as popular arts flourished. When Japan began to open in the 1850s, the West was astounded by the creativity that had thrived there out of sight. Western artists and manufacturers quickly incorporated Japanese ideas into their own products.

Although most Japanese production was in small craft shops that used little capital, several mining establishments employed more than one thousand full-time laborers apiece. Spread around the country were eighty to ninety iron mines, each of which had around three hundred workers. The growth of an iron industry promoted the beginnings of a factory system, with the attendant accumulation of capital and the organization of paid work.[2]

The production and marketing of products for urban centers and the taxes-in-kind imposed on feudal lords based on rice output led to the growth of sophisticated financial practices and markets. Osaka was the main financial center. A small group of bankers performed many of the functions of a central bank, acting as lenders of last resort, making loans to local governments, controlling the level of bank credits, and establishing a market between gold and bank money. A rice market in Osaka featured such modern activities as futures trading.[3]

The population was relatively well fed, housed, clothed, and educated. About 40 percent to 50 percent of all males and about half as many females benefited from some formal schooling. Temple schools in rural areas spread literacy, with 30 percent to 40 percent of males able to read and write.[4] According to World Bank estimates, that level of literacy in Japan in the middle of the nineteenth century was greater than that found today in some forty countries.[5]

One peculiar feature of the Tokugawa shogunate was the practice known as alternate attendance. Feudal lords were required to spend every other year in Edo. When they returned to their lands, their families remained in the capital—essentially as hostages of the shogun. This policy was meant to restrict the ability of the lords to plan uprisings against the central authorities by keeping them under the direct gaze of the shogun when they were in Edo and by breaking up their periods away from the capital when they could engage in plotting. But it had unintended consequences that were important for long-term economic growth; the movement every year of several hundred feudal masters with up to several thousand retainers required roads, means of transportation, post houses, feeding and supplying of people and animals, and considerable planning.[6]

When, in 1861, the emperor's younger sister traveled from Kyoto to

Edo to marry the shogun, some twenty-five thousand court retainers accompanied the royal party. Planning for this movement took several months and involved thousands of porters, animal tenders, and other staff at each of the sixty-nine posts along the Kiso road. It required administrative competence in the capital, but local initiative and energy made the whole thing work.

Smaller versions of this once-in-a-millennium event took place almost on a daily basis. The movement of people from their native villages to metropolitan areas across the breadth of Japan educated generations of minor officials and peasants who otherwise would have known little more than the fields around their villages. At the same time that peasants were learning the ways of the big city, local methods, ideas, and arts were being introduced to Edo. This two-way flow nurtured the notion of a greater Japan.[7]

Economic growth was slow but positive in the eighteenth century and the first half of the nineteenth. Living standards even in a poor district like the Morioka region examined by University of Washington professor Kozo Yamamura rose by roughly 0.5 percent a year from the early 1700s to the end of Tokugawa rule. Nutrition, clothing, and housing improved steadily throughout the period.[8]

Thus, when the leaders of the Meiji Restoration decided to seek Western technology and institutions and to adapt them to national purposes, Japan already had a society that worked—and worked well. Mr. Maddison has estimated that Japan's 1820 per capita output was about $609 in 1985 purchasing power dollars, or roughly $750 at 1995 purchasing power parity prices. According to World Bank estimates, that level of economic output would have placed Japan ahead of about fifteen countries in 1995, making it underdeveloped but not at the bottom of the economic league tables.

In the words of Kazushi Ohkawa of Hitotsubashi University and Henry Rosovsky of Harvard University, Japan "was a vigorous, advanced, and effective traditional society. In many ways, it was more advanced than many countries in Africa or Latin America today. . . . We tend to inevitably associate low income per capita with poor organization, corruption, lethargy, and undernourishment. And, this gives a false picture of Japan before the Restoration."[9] In short, Japan, on the eve of its coming out, was in a good position to absorb the lessons that the West had for it.

The Growth of National Economic Output

Although Japan began to move toward economic modernity in the last decades of the Tokugawa shogunate, this transition became a burning national priority only after the installation of the new regime in 1868. The years until 1885 or so were ones of change as such traditional institutions as clans, feudal domains, and state support for samurai were disestablished and new institutions were created.

By 1885, the contours of the modern Japanese state and economy were evident. From that year through 1930, the growth of the economy was fairly steady, averaging 2.8 percent annually. However, since the population was increasing at a pace of slightly more than 1 percent a year, average individual welfare improved more slowly than the expansion of the overall economy. Real GNP per capita doubled over this period, rising by roughly 1.6 percent a year.

The ups and downs in the pre-1940 economy were affected by events in the global economy. For instance, a doubling of growth from 2 percent to 4 percent between 1915 and the 1920s was fueled at least in part by a surge in European orders due to World War I and by the economic boom that followed. A decline from the 1920s to the early 1930s reflected the effects of the Great Depression on Japan. A subsequent spurt in the late 1930s was caused largely by stepped-up production in preparation for World War II.

Despite the fluctuations in growth in the half-century preceding World War II, the Japanese economy demonstrated considerable momentum after the Meiji Restoration. Wartime destruction ended that phase of industrialization and growth. Total output failed to reach 1939's level until 1955. However, after that point, Japan's economy took off in an unprecedented fashion. Indeed, to borrow from the poet, Samuel Taylor Coleridge, it was a "miracle of rare device." It would not be an exaggeration to assert that the economy's performance between 1956 and the early 1970s continues to color our views and understanding of Japan.

The postwar period can be divided into several phases. The first one was the immediate aftermath of the surrender, when Japan struggled with shortages of virtually every kind. Not only had domestic production capacity been destroyed by the war, but Japan also lost many of its suppliers because they were either former colonies whose ties had been broken or other Asian nations that had suffered similar destruction.

Inflation of more than 100 percent annually raged from 1946 through 1948. The following year, the occupation authorities implemented a stabilization program crafted by Joseph Dodge, a Detroit banker who had undertaken a similar job in war-torn Germany. The fiscal and monetary policies known as the Dodge line stabilized the economy and set the stage for a revival of investment and growth.

The onset of the Korean War in 1950 generated large-scale equipment orders from the American military that helped to revive the Japanese industrial sector and brought the economy out of a deep, stabilization-induced recession. From that base, the economy's expansion became self-sustaining. As early as 1960, growth over the preceding ten years was nearly 8 percent, although, admittedly, it was from a low postwar level. From the late 1950s to 1970, the rise in GDP accelerated to double-digit rates. In the Tokugawa era, output had doubled in one hundred fifty years; after the Meiji Restoration, the same increase had taken forty-five years. The postwar doubling was accomplished between 1963 and 1970!

Deceleration then set in. The economy's expansion during the 1970s fell to 4 percent a year, where it remained until the 1990s. Since the end of its high-speed growth, Japan has marched toward a long-term growth rate of roughly 2 percent. Although there is nothing magical about that figure, it is the maximum sustained rate that rich countries have managed to attain in the past twenty-five years.

The methods, institutions, habits, and psychology that were instrumental in producing the miracle growth of the postwar era had to be adjusted to a new reality. The necessity to revise expectations and to recast standard operating procedures and assumptions is the problem facing the world's second-biggest economy at the beginning of a new century as it attempts to deregulate and restructure business operations in response to permanently slower growth.

Chasing the United States

Not only did the economy's surge transform the very nature of Japan's global role, but it also produced a level of per capita income that is among the highest in the world today. One measure of the gain in personal welfare is obtained by dividing GNP by population. Figure 2.1 shows real GNP per capita for Japan and the United States converted into 1990 dollars by using that year's estimated purchasing power parity of ¥196=$1.00. Note that the vertical axis is a logarithmic scale such that each division is double the previous one and that the slopes of the curves indicate rates of growth.

In 1890, the first year of comparable data, American output per capita was 3.7 times the Japanese figure. The United States was not quite the richest country in the world at the turn of the twentieth century but according to Mr. Maddison, then at the University of Groningen, the Netherlands, it would be in just a few years.[10] Despite steady growth in Japan, the relative situations of the two countries had not changed much by 1930 because the United States also was experiencing a vigorous expansion.

**Figure 2.1: Real GNP per Capita, Japan, United States, 1890-2000
(1990 Dollars at Purchasing Power Parity of ¥196=$1.00)**

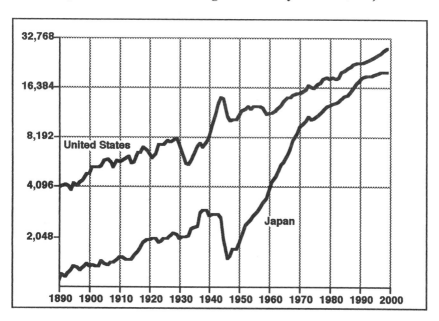

Sources: Historical Statistics of Japan on CD-ROM, (Tokyo: Japan Statistical Association, 1999); U.S. Bureau of the Census, Historical Statistics of the United States, Colonial Times to 1970, Bicentennial Edition, Washington, D.C., 1975; Survey of Current Business, various.

Although the American economy continued to increase in size after 1945, the exceptional experience of Japan pushed its average output closer to the U.S. figure. However, even in 1970, American per capita output still was 80 percent larger than Japan's. Nevertheless, Japan's faster growth gradually drew the two curves closer together, with the nearest approach reached in 1992, when the U.S. economy in per capita terms was only 24 percent bigger. The 1990s were not good to Japan, and outputs moved apart in the remaining years of the decade. The 2000 figure showed that, per person, America produced some 40 percent more per person than Japan.

It sometimes was said in the 1980s that Japan's GNP per capita would overtake that of the United States before the end of the century. Rasher voices extended the prediction to GNP itself. A little arithmetic would have shown that neither possibility was likely over the forecast span of years. If, starting in 1992, Japan had maintained its 2 percent growth differential, it would have taken eleven more years for that country's GNP per capita (measured by 1990 purchasing power parity) to catch up with the United States. In terms of the absolute size of the two economies, Japan's 1992 GNP was only 40 percent as large as America's. Again, with a 2-point expansion differential, convergence would have required another forty-six years.[11] In fact, the gap has swung in the other direction. By 2000, America's economy was three times larger than Japan's.

Investment in Physical Capital

It is a commonplace of development economics to note that nations grow through investment in physical and human capital, through increased efficiency, and through the absorption of more productive technologies, which generally occurs in conjunction with investment. In the latter part of the 1800s, a good deal of Japan's productivity advances came from the internal diffusion of best practice, mainly in agriculture.

As industry and finance developed and as personal incomes rose, retained earnings and individual savings became available to fund an increasing share of investment out of total output. The long-term trend of investment is captured in a data series on gross domestic fixed capital formation, which covers the entire century. This information includes government infrastructure investment, business investment, and residential housing investment. For purposes of describing the capital accumulation that made Japanese industry more productive, however, it is too inclusive. It is better to exclude residential investment.

Mr. Maddison has produced standardized estimates of nonresidential investment and accumulated capital for the world's major economies.[12] However, his data do not include the government's contribution to infrastructure, which represented the largest and most productive share of investment in Japan in the late 1800s.

Both investment measures are plotted in figure 2.2 as ratios of GNP, all in 1990 prices. The pattern is similar in both curves. Investment started at low levels in the nineteenth century, rose gradually as a share of total output, and reached high points in 1920 and then again in the wartime buildup of the late 1930s. Mr. Maddison estimated that one-quarter of the capital stock subsequently was destroyed in the war.

Figure 2.2: Ratio of Investment to GNP, 1990 Prices, 1890-1999 (Percent)

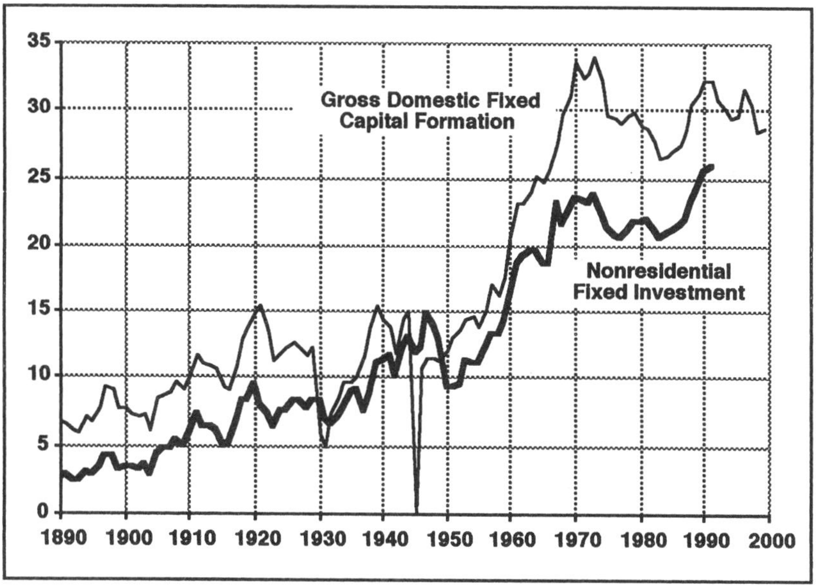

Sources: Nonresidential fixed investment: Angus Maddison, "Standardised Estimates of Fixed Capital Stock: A Six Country Comparison," in *Explaining the Economic Performance of Nations* (Brookfield, Vermont: Edward Elgar Publishing Co., 1995); gross domestic fixed capital investment: *Historical Statistics of Japan on CD-ROM*, Japan Statistical Association, 1999.

It was in the postwar period that investment took off in Japan. Gross fixed capital formation soared to more than one-third of GNP in 1970. Even the narrower measure shows that more than 20 percent of the nation's product was plowed back into private plant and equipment. With the slowdown in growth in the 1970s, the pace of capital accumulation slowed—but not by as much as might have been expected by the falling rate of GNP increase. The "bubble economy" of the late 1980s stimulated a resumption of high investment reminiscent of Japan's economic glory days.

Investment has several important effects. Since new technology typically is incorporated in new equipment, not only does investment expand productive capacity, but it also increases the productivity of capital itself as well as that of other inputs. Moreover, labor productivity rises as the capital stock increases relative to the number of employees—even without new technology. Investment, therefore, is the key ingredient for growth.

Figure 2.3: Ratio of Capital Stock to GNP in 1990 Prices, Japan and United States, 1890-1997

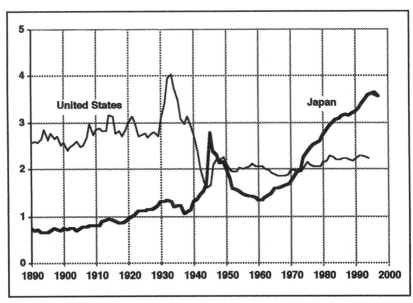

Sources: Angus Maddison, "Standardised Estimates of Fixed Capital Stock: A Six Country Comparison," in *Explaining the Economic Performance of Nations* (Brookfield, Vt: Edward Elgar Publishing Co., 1995).

The capital intensity of the Japanese and the American economies is shown in figure 2.3. As one of the fastest-growing and richest economies of the late nineteenth and early twentieth centuries, the United States already had a large capital base relative to output in the 1890s. The Great Depression of the 1930s caused investment to collapse as depreciation eroded the value of the capital stock faster than the dwindling additions could increase it. During World War II, little nonmilitary investment was undertaken, and the capital stock continued to deteriorate. However, sharp increases in productivity in the postwar period allowed the U.S. economy to prosper with a lower capital intensity of production than in the prewar period.

Japan's capital stock increased gradually relative to output from 1890 to 1930, with only a shallow dip during the Great Depression, followed by a wartime surge. By 1960, the very high rate of investment caused the capital-to-output ratio to resume its prewar trend, but at an accelerated pace. In the 1970s, the capital intensity of production in Japan exceeded that in the United States. Moreover, the capital stock continued to expand faster than output itself. By 1995, the capital intensity of production in Japan was 60 percent higher than in the United States. By then, the apparent excess of capital was an increasing problem for Japan. It was indicative of the economy's low productivity and inadequate rates of return on investment.

Investment in Human Capital

A high priority of the government after the Meiji Restoration was to promote universal education. The education law of 1872 established a three-tiered structure of primary schools, middle schools, and universities. Enrollment rates for six to twelve year olds increased gradually from the 1875 level of 50 percent for boys and less than 20 percent for girls to near universality by 1905 (see table 2.1)

In 1947, the educational system was changed to six years of elementary school, three years of lower secondary school, and three years of upper secondary school. Although the population was almost 100 percent literate and had basic mathematical abilities, advancement to upper secondary school was not automatic. In 1950, less than half the graduates of lower secondary schools continued their education. It was not until 1975 that more than 90 percent of those completing their ninth year of schooling moved on to the next stage of education (see table 2.2).

The relatively rapid spread of literacy and basic educational skills admirably suited the needs of an industrializing economy. Since most technology came from abroad, either embodied in investment goods or licensed directly from foreign firms, there was little need for an extensive university system to train engineers and scientists. Recent research on the impact of education on development emphasizes the importance of basic schooling, especially for women, rather than university training for an

Table 2.1: Elementary School Enrollment,
Percent of 6-12 Year Olds, 1875-1920

Year	Male	Female
1875	50.8	18.7
1880	58.7	21.9
1885	65.8	32.1
1890	65.1	31.1
1895	76.7	43.9
1900	90.4	71.7
1905	97.7	93.3
1910	98.8	97.4
1915	98.9	98.0
1920	99.2	98.8

Source: *Historical Statistics of Japan on CD-ROM* (Tokyo: Japan Statistical Association, 1999).

elite class.

As an economy matures, a greater share of the increase in productivity flows from technology that is not incorporated in machines but rather produced by targeted research and directed productivity-enhancing efforts. To make the transition to a phase that is more oriented to research and development, university and graduate education becomes more important. As shown in table 2.2, the advancement rate for males from upper secondary schools plateaued in the 1970s. Female advancement, however, continued to increase, partly because of the popularity of women's junior colleges.

The proportion of nineteen to twenty-four year olds enrolled in four-year colleges and universities accelerated from 1890 to 1980 and then leveled off for ten years, only to rise again in the 1990s (see figure 2.4). Increases in college and graduate school enrollments have been typical reactions to difficult employment markets in the United States. Perhaps the sharp fall in the availability of jobs for high school graduates in Japan had the same effect there.

Table 2.2: Advancement Rates from Lower and Upper Secondary Schools to Higher Grade, 1950-1999 (percent)

Year	Lower Secondary		Upper Secondary	
	Male	Female	Male	Female
1950	48	36.7	n.a.	n.a.
1955	55.5	47.4	20.9	14.9
1960	59.6	55.9	19.7	14.2
1965	71.7	69.6	30.1	20.4
1970	81.6	82.7	25.0	23.5
1975	91.0	93.0	33.8	34.6
1980	93.1	95.4	30.3	33.5
1985	92.8	94.9	27.0	33.9
1990	95.1		23.8	37.3
1995	96.7		29.7	45.4
1999	96.9		40.2	48.1

Source: Management and Coordination Agency, Statistics Bureau, *Japan Statistical Yearbook*, various years.

Enrollment in Japanese graduate schools was very low until the late 1950s. Even between 1965 and 1980, only about 3 percent of the people who graduated from four-year colleges and universities continued with graduate education. In the 1990s, the rate almost doubled at the same time that the share of nineteen to twenty-four year olds going to college also rose. By 1998, the number of graduate students was twice as high as in 1990 and triple the 1980 level.

The growth of undergraduate and graduate education in Japan over the past twenty years has helped to equip the country with a more flexible workforce that has the capability to learn new skills on a continuing basis. Compared with the United States, however, Japan still has room for improvement. Approximately 50 percent more of the U.S. college-age cohort is enrolled in four-year educational institutions and 23 percent of the undergraduate student body goes on to graduate studies—roughly four times the Japanese ratio. Enhancing the role of higher education remains on Japan's agenda for the future.

**Figure 2.4: Ratios of Four-Year University Students to 19-24 Year Olds
(1890-1998) and Graduate Students to Undergraduates (1951-1998)
(percent)**

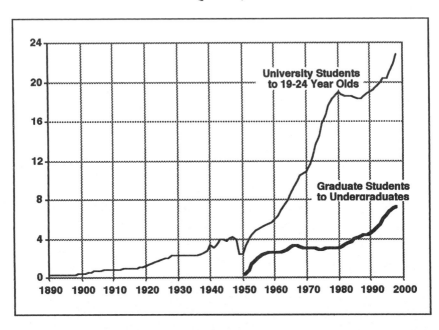

Source: Statistics Bureau, Management and Coordination Agency, *Historical Statistics of Japan on CD-ROM*, Japan Statistical Association, 1999. Management and Coordination Agency, Statistics Bureau, *Japan Statistical Yearbook*, various.

Trade and Exchange Rates

Japan depended on imports of raw materials and machinery for its development. Imports from the West allowed the nation's new businesses to access advanced technologies and products that were unavailable at home. At first, Japan paid for its purchases from abroad by exporting such traditional goods as silk and silk products. However, as industrialization occurred, it was able to sell overseas the output of its new mills and factories, particularly nonsilk textiles. Actually, exports played a critical role in Japan's development since they earned the foreign exchange to pay for essential imports. Throughout the period before World War II, imports and exports alike were a large fraction of total economic production, much more than they would be in the postwar period.

On a ten-year moving average basis, exports and imports as shares of

GNP rose steadily from the end of the nineteenth century, peaking at 20 percent of national output in the 1920s and 1930s (see figure 2.5). The effects of the Great Depression, the widespread imposition of tariffs, and the onset of war combined to drive down trade in Japan, as they did in other countries as well.

Figure 2.5: Ratio of Exports and Imports to GNP, 1890-2000 (percent)

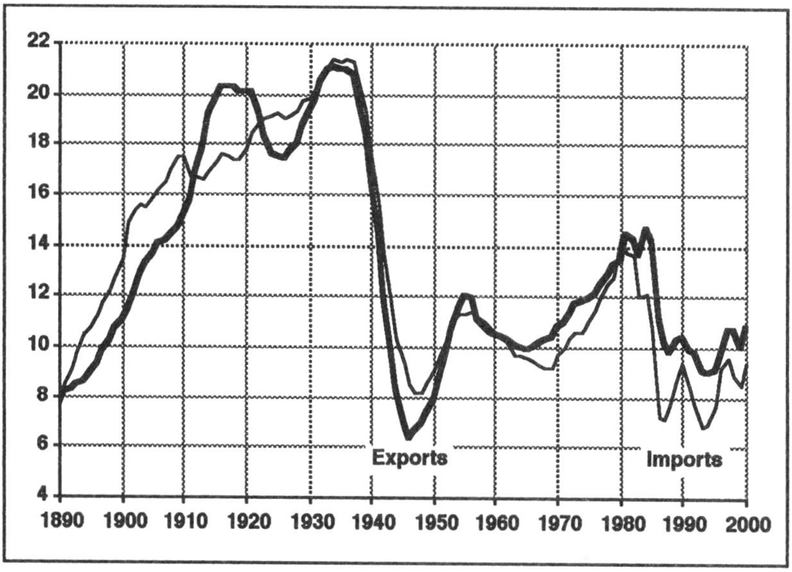

Source: 1890-1954: *Historical Statistics of Japan on CD-ROM*, (Tokyo: Japan Statistical Association, 1999): 1955-1999: Statistics Bureau.

In 1945, Japanese industry was destitute and unable to produce for export. The American occupation authorities managed trade on an item-by-item basis, making up differences in export earnings and import bills through subsidies provided by the U.S. government. Since many import items were deliberately subsidized to keep prices low, Japan's trade deficit turned into a burden for American taxpayers.

Occupation economists saw a clear need to resume trade based on market principles, but rampant inflation complicated the calculation of an exchange rate. An exchange rate of ¥360=$1.00 was introduced in April 1949, and inflation was tamed through the implementation of the Dodge line. Those developments positioned the Japanese economy to resume unsubsidized trade. However, trade never returned to its prewar levels. During the fifteen years of maximum growth from 1955 to 1970, exports averaged less than 10.5 percent of GNP. The peak export year was 1981 when sales abroad represented 13.6 percent of total output. In the 1990s, exports and imports both were equivalent to less than 10 percent of the economy.

The notion that Japan's economy is export-driven even today is hard to shake because of the visibility of Japanese products to the world's consumers as well as to most Japanese. The real importance of exports, as economists have noted ever since 1776 when Adam Smith developed the logic in *The Wealth of Nations*, is that they provide payment for imported goods and services. Based on the numbers, it is hard to understand why the idea of export-driven growth has received such prominent attention in economic histories of Japan. If anything, the discussion should be about import-driven growth, since the essential ingredients of life, economic development, and economic welfare were all supported by foreign goods and services.

The yen-dollar exchange rate has varied from parity in 1875 to ¥360=$1.00 in 1949 to ¥80 briefly in the spring of 1995. What accounts for these fluctuations? As a good first approximation, variations in the relative prices of so-called tradable goods explain most of the changes in the exchange rate. Such other influences as interest rates and capital flows account for the remaining movement. However, the difference between inflation rates in Japan and the United States is a good place to begin.

The theory that relative prices drive exchange rates follows from the notion of the "law of one price." That is, if a product is sold at different prices in different places, it pays arbitrageurs to buy it at the lower price and resell it at the higher one, thereby driving the gap to zero.

A technical issue in estimating the effects of relative inflation rates is the choice of a price index for tradable goods. Not all goods are traded, as demonstrated by the fact that only 10 percent of Japan's output enter export channels. Thus, a broad measure like the GNP price deflator would include too many items that are unaffected by the international law of one price. Surprisingly perhaps, export and import price indexes also are inappropriate. They respond to the exchange rate at the same time that they influence it. If they did not adjust to exchange rate changes, either it would be impossible to sell a product because its international price was too high, or the product would be so cheap that the seller would face excess demand and probably would have an inadequate profit margin.

**Figure 2.6: Actual and Estimated Values of the Yen/Dollar
Exchange Rate, 1890-1940**

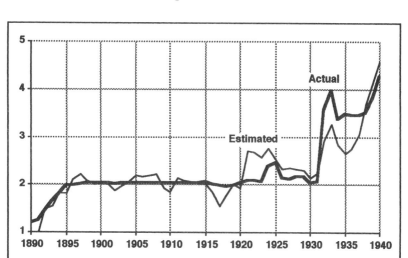

Sources: Japan: *Historical Statistics of Japan on CD-ROM*, (Tokyo: Japan Statistical Association, 1999);

The price index chosen here to implement the concept is the wholesale price index for Japan and the comparable producer price index for the United States. These indexes mainly reflect the prices of manufactured products and bulk commodities that potentially could enter international trade.

To estimate the effect of these price series on the exchange rate, a simple equation was constructed with the yen-dollar exchange rate as the dependent variable and the two price indexes as independent variables, all in natural logarithms. If the strict version of the law of one price holds such that purchasing power parity determines exchange rates, the Japanese price variable would have a coefficient of 1.0 and the U.S. price variable a coefficient of minus 1.0. In fact, the coefficients are 1.02 and minus 1.30, respectively. Actual and predicted yen-dollar values are shown in two panels in figures 2.6 and 2.7 to separate the very different values of the prewar and postwar eras.

The simple, relative-price explanation of the exchange rate does remarkably well over the entire 1892-1999 period. Figure 2.7 indicates that analysts did a pretty good job in 1948 in estimating an equilibrium exchange rate, given the inflation raging at the time and the absence of reliable trade data. The occupation economists working for Gen. Douglas MacArthur kept track of the individual exchange rates implicit in the negotiated prices of each trade deal. They also measured the rate of inflation to determine how fast relative prices were moving. Exchange rates for specific products varied from ¥100=$1.00 for agar to ¥600=$1.00 for flat glass.

Figure 2.7: Actual and Estimated Values of the Yen/Dollar Exchange Rate, 1960-2000

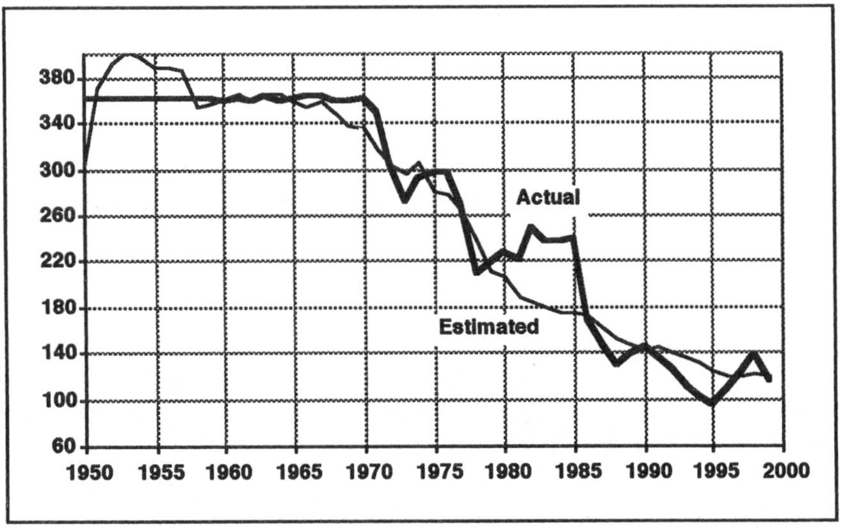

Sources: Bank of Japan; United States: Bureau of Labor Statistics

In May 1948, Ralph Young, a Federal Reserve Board economist, suggested an exchange rate of ¥300=$1.00, which he thought would undervalue the yen to encourage exports. An October 1948 Ministry of Finance report recommended that exports be priced at ¥350=$1.00. Analysts running a price computing system proposed a rate of ¥450=$1.00 in February 1949. The final decision, announced in April 1949, was ¥360=$1.00.

According to the estimate shown in figure 2.7, the yen seemed to be overvalued for several years in the 1950s, but it then became undervalued as U.S. inflation rose faster than the increase in prices in Japan. The generally excessive strength of the dollar in the late 1960s and early 1970s led to the replacement of the fixed exchange rate regime by a system of floating rates. The other period of an overly strong dollar in the first half of the 1980s also is obvious. On the same basis, it is possible to argue that the yen was overvalued in the 1990s. However, as noted, enough other forces act on exchange rates that conclusions based simply on relative prices are not fully warranted, although a currency's long-term movement certainly responds to the price differentials of tradable goods.

The Shadow of the Miracle

Japan faced enormous challenges in developing the modern, affluent, and technologically advanced economy that it is today. It was the first nation to set out deliberately to change itself in fundamental ways for the express purpose of modernizing the economy and society along Western lines. The risk-taking creativity of that endeavor left little untouched. Growth itself wrought continuing mutations and permutations in techniques, technologies, and relationships. In fact, breathtaking change has been an integral part of Japanese economic history.

Ironically, the lingering effects of one particular phase of this history—the so-called miracle years—bound Japanese psychology and policy to inappropriate routines that once had economic logic behind them but that became unproductive. As Japan makes the transition to a permanently slower growth trajectory, a move that requires greater attention to the mundane objectives of rates of return and profitability, the nation again is being forced to change. History leaves little doubt about Japan's capacity to adapt to a new environment. Nevertheless, the legacy of the past can handicap the race to the future, however sure the eventual results may be.

Notes

1.   Angus Maddison, "Ultimate and Proximate Growth Causality," in *Explaining the Economic Performance of Nations* (Brookfield, Vt.: Edward Elgar Publishing Co., 1995), 97.

2.   Kozo Yamamura, "Toward a Reexamination of the Economic History of To-kugawa Japan, 1600-1867," *The Journal of Economic History* (September 1973): 533.

3.   Sydney Crawcour, "Economic Change in the Nineteenth Century," in Marius Jansen (ed.), *The Cambridge History of Japan, Vol. 5, The Nineteenth Century* (Cambridge, England and New York: Cambridge University Press, 1989), 585.

4.   Kazushi Ohkawa and Henry Rosovsky, *Japanese Economic Growth* (Stanford, California: Stanford University Press, 1973), 8.

5.   World Bank, *World Development Report, 1999* (Washington, D.C.: 1999).

6.   For a good description of the transportation and post-house system and for a flavor of the changes occurring during the second half of the nineteenth century, see the novel by Toson Shimazaki, *Before the Dawn (Yo-ake Mae)*, trans. William Naff (Honolulu, Hawaii: University of Hawaii Press, 1987).

7.   Constantine Vaporis, "To Edo and Back: Alternate Attendance and Japanese Culture in the Early Modern Period," *Journal of Japanese Studies* 23, no. 1 (1997).

8.   Yamamura, "Toward a Reexamination of the Economic History of Tokugawa Japan, 1600-1867," 535.

9.   Ohkawa and Rosovsky, *Japanese Economic Growth*, 7.

10.   Maddison, "Ultimate and Proximate Growth Causality," 93.

11.   The period of convergence depends on the current ratio of the two countries' GNPs and the difference in the rate of growth. The convergence period n is: n = (ln U/J)/(j-u), where U is American GNP in the base year, J is Japanese GNP, j and u are the Japanese and American growth rates (a 1.5 percent growth rate is stated as 0.015), and ln is the natural logarithm.

12.   Angus Maddison, "Standardised Estimates of Fixed Capital Stock: A Six-Country Comparison," in *Explaining the Economic Performance of Nations* (Brookfield, Vt.: Edward Elgar Publishing Co., 1995).

Chapter 3

Japan as Number Three:
Long-Term Productivity Problems

The Side-Effects of Success

In 1979, Harvard University's Ezra Vogel published *Japan as Number One: Lessons for Americans*, which subsequently became the most popular nonfiction book in Japan.[1] The title alludes to the possibility that Japanese policies had worked so well that the nation could become the largest in the world and that the United States might profitably follow some of the policies that were asserted to have worked so well in Japan.

Professor Vogel's book appeared as the Japanese economy was experiencing its first major postwar deceleration. Later decades produced further slowdown. As a consequence of Japan's inevitable normalization, the American economy will continue to be number one in absolute size and near number one in per capita output well into the twenty-first century. Using purchasing power parities to convert national currencies to common dollar values, China—according to World Bank estimates—is the world's second largest economy, 40 percent bigger than Japan. Just a few years ago Japan had been projected for the top spot; in 1999 it was third in size and even further back in productivity levels—the World Bank ranked it in fourteenth place.[2]

Policies and behavior associated with Japan's post-World War II economic success are endangering its transformation into a successful, mature twenty-first century economy. Moreover, its position in the international league tables is not automatically assured. If stagnation rather than vigor characterizes Japan's economic future, its role as an economic power and political leader would be in jeopardy.

Some of Japan's problems derive from its very success. For example, high investment rates in physical capital and R&D have driven down rates of return; one of the twentieth century's most significant innovations, the Toyota system of production, is now globally disseminated (often by Japanese companies) and is transforming the way the world makes things, thereby reducing Japan's competitive advantage.

Elements of Japan's industrial policies intended to promote economic development carried negative side effects that would later retard growth and productivity. For example, the regulated system of finance that favored heavy industry and manufacturing also starved light industry and services. The controlled banking sector that was the model of stability and that financed much of Japan's economic miracle was of little help in supporting innovative companies seeking venture capital. The regulatory framework that protected consumers and producers from financial irresponsibility or defective products also protected the inefficient behavior of politically favored groups.

Lifetime employment bred a close alliance between employee and company, promoted training and personal development, and motivated managers to outstanding levels of effort. However, it also encouraged conservative corporate decisionmaking. An R&D system mainly financed by the private sector was widely and correctly regarded as a model of effectiveness because of its close attention to business objectives rather than to the technological choices of government bureaucrats; now, that same system is criticized rightly for insufficient support of basic research—the source of tomorrow's innovations and industries.

Policies whose negative effects could be safely ignored during the rapid growth period are now seen to be placing a drag on the welfare of the Japanese people as a whole and dampening the growth of the economy. Dealing with the accumulated problems of the past requires a substantial reordering of priorities—a political as well as an economic and managerial task.

Although Japan's economic structure has been one of the most adaptive of all the industrial countries in the past 100 years, many of its most profound changes have been precipitated by external forces and events. The changes required now have to be self-imposed in both the political and economic spheres.

The Role of Openness and Competition: The Automobile as Metaphor

Between 1903 and 1926, close to two hundred companies produced automobiles in the United States. At that time, the very concept of the automobile was clouded in technological and market uncertainty. Steam, electric, and internal combustion engines had their merits and were incorporated in popular production models. Designers attacked the steering problem with handlebars, wheels, and ship-like tillers. Two, three, four, and more wheels were used. Some producers favored lightweight, flexible designs derived from bicycles while others based their concepts on the rigid structures of the horse-drawn wagon or the massive iron and steel assemblies of the locomotive. Production methods were as varied as the technological approaches: from the one-by-one method favored by the locomotive industry to the batch process of mass production.

The use of automobiles was as ambiguous as the technology. Would they be purchased by rich city buyers, by farmers, by commerce and industry? Would they run on roads, rails, or be driven cross-country like tractors? Would they be used for moving people or goods, for business or pleasure, for long or short distances?

Each of the companies entering this market believed that it had the answers to all of the questions surrounding the design, production, and use of automobiles. Of course, most were wrong; 20 percent lasted three years or less while half disappeared within six years of their founding.[3] The top ten producers in 1903 lost eight of their members within six years. However, out of the turmoil of market experimentation, the modern automobile was born as well as an industry and production system that dominated manufacturing for the better part of a century.

As the concept of the automobile evolved and as the scale of production increased by orders of magnitude, the number of players in the American market gradually dwindled. Three companies comprised virtually the entire industry by the 1970s.

In 1955, nine Japanese automobile producers shared a domestic market whose annual output was less than a single day's production of the American industry. Although protected from foreign competitors, entry was open to domestic firms. Engaged in vicious domestic competition, the Japanese companies were compelled to seek greater efficiency in order to reduce their costs and prices, increase their sales, and generate profits. They gradually developed a production method that drastically reduced costs and improved quality. By 1965, Toyota was estimated to be 50 percent more productive than the average U.S. company was and Nissan was producing at the American level. A decade later, the Japanese companies had substantially increased their lead over their American competitors. Meanwhile, the Toyota production system had been adopted throughout the Japanese automobile industry and its parts and machinery suppliers. As the name of Henry Ford represented the essence of the assembly line and the transforming quality of the American automobile saga, Toyota's production manager, Taiichi Ohno, was the symbol of Japan's manufacturing genius and productivity advance.

These quite different automobile stories capture several of the distinguishing characteristics of the American and Japanese approaches to innovation and productivity. The American style emphasized wholly new products and wild entrepreneurial behavior whereas the Japanese approach focused on production methods and creative product improvements. Both cases depended on the motivation and selection effects of market forces and competition. Competitive conditions provided the incentive to play the game with skill and passion. Market experimentation by large numbers of participants increased the probability of coming up with winners, of recognizing genius. Competition established a method for identifying successful ideas and a requirement to adopt the best ones developed by others. Companies that were slow to respond to the new techniques were driven out of the industry.

The Productivity Gap

A fact that surprises many Americans is that average Japanese productivity levels are considerably below American levels. According to the broadest comparative productivity measure, gross domestic product per capita converted at purchasing power parity, Japan's level was 73 percent of the United States in 2000. However, this method does not take into account the inputs used to produce the national output. Japanese producers actually use relatively more inputs to yield a smaller quantity of output.

Since productivity measures of nonmarket activities are severely flawed, many analysts prefer to focus on the market sector. Japan's GDP per equivalent full-time employee in the market economy, which accounts for 87 percent of employment, is only 61 percent of the U.S. value and falls below the productivity of France, Germany, and the United Kingdom. In manufacturing, where Japan's reputation was established in the 1970s, productivity estimates for recent years range from 60 percent to 83 percent of the American rate. Industry estimates for 1990 by the McKinsey Global Institute confirm the popular impression that Japan does especially well in automobiles and parts, metalworking, steel, and consumer electronics, in all of which Japanese productivity is greater than American.[4] On the other hand, food processing in Japan is only 33 percent as productive. Moreover, more Japanese are employed in the food-processing industry than in steel, cars, auto parts, and metalworking combined.[5]

Productivity measures for services are more difficult to compile than for manufacturing, but one study found a 56 percent gap between Japan and the United States in merchandise retailing and a 23 percent gap in telecommunication.[6] Evidence that is more impressionistic suggests gaps of around 50 percent for airlines, road transportation, and many other producer and consumer services.

Studies by the management consulting firm Bain & Company in Japan showed low white-collar worker productivity relative to manufacturing, which the author attributed to a traditional Japanese concentration on efficiency in production rather than office work. White-collar overhead as a percentage of total costs had grown by more than one-third from 1981 to 1992, from 12.5 percent to 17 percent.[7] Across service and manufacturing industries, the number of excess workers was estimated at a minimum of 15-20 percent of the white-collar labor force.

The productivity of services is critical to the overall efficiency of manufacturing because at least half of the sales value of manufactured goods comes from service inputs such as R&D, accounting, computing, and post-production distribution costs such as advertising or transportation.[8] Thus, the low productivity of in-house and purchased services contributes to lowered efficiency in manufacturing, not to speak of the service sector itself, which includes close to two-thirds of all economic activity.

Estimating the Scale of Adjustment

Over the past century, Japan's economic structure has demonstrated great adaptability. The shares of output across industries and the structure of trade have been more variable than those of any of the other OECD countries.[9] Closing the productivity gap will require the same kind of structural change in the future.

A potential gold mine of productivity gains is the very fact that many companies and industries in Japan lag the productivity leaders, both at home and abroad. For example, benchmark studies of several Japanese service industries compared each industry's most efficient firm with a representative domestic industry sample; the evaluations found differences of more than 20 percent in supermarkets, department stores, hotels, and airlines.[10]

If we assume that Japan takes the necessary steps to deregulate its economy and fully open itself to foreign competition and investment, what may be some of the consequences? The average productivity of Japan's market economy is 60 percent of the American level; manufacturing performs at the 80 percent level. If the productivity of the total market sector rose to the manufacturing level, from 60 percent to 80 percent of the U.S. figure, one-quarter of the affected workforce could be released for activities that are more productive. However, a transition to a more productive economy over a twenty-year period would create redundancies amounting to almost one million people annually.[11]

In a well-functioning economy, these people would not remain idle but would find jobs in new or expanded activities in other parts of the economy. Ideally, total output would expand, efficiencies would spread, and living standards would rise. However, all of these positive benefits would come at the cost of short-term individual distress and probably a permanent increase in uncertainty.

Forces for Change

The simple presence of inefficiency does not by itself create a demand to do something about it. However, several forces are at work in Japan that reduce the support for the status quo and militate for change. The Japanese people, as consumers rather than as employees, are the principal agents of change. Through their political choices, people are questioning the policies that favor the narrow interests of specific groups of producers and the special interests of politically favored sectors over those of consumers. Partly, this arises from shifting demographics. Relatively fewer people work in the sectors formerly favored by the government in its pursuit of political patronage and economic growth. Agriculture, small-scale retailing, and heavy industry employ smaller shares of the workforce than in the past. The professional service sector is growing, as is large-scale retailing. Urbanization and the increased labor force participation of women motivate a demand for more efficient utilization of time in household chores, including shopping. Added to this latent demand for efficiency and lower prices is the knowledge, brought about by the immense growth of international travel, that alternatives are feasible.

Companies participating in international markets are also agents for change as they find themselves saddled with the excessive costs of inefficient, protected suppliers. Even if a manufacturer can produce at a 50 percent cost advantage over foreign rivals, plant investment may be more expensive because of collusion among construction firms. Transportation of materials and supplies into the plant and of finished products to the port will add to costs unnecessarily because of excessive regulation of road transport. Regulated insurance policy prices in the 1980s were an estimated 30 percent higher than competition would dictate; and telecommunications services up through at least 2000 were at a minimum 30 percent more expensive—with fewer services available than to foreign competitors. Lower priced consumer products would also benefit business because employees' real incomes would rise without the need to increase salaries. Representatives of big business, such as *Keidanren* (Japan Federation of Economic Organizations), have been urging the government to deregulate the economy with the aim of enhancing efficiency and driving down costs.

Finally, the international community is pushing Japan to continue the deregulation and opening process begun in the late 1970s. Foreign companies that believe that their products and services would be highly competitive in Japan if markets were deregulated and opened are pressuring their own governments, which need little additional incentive, to negotiate market-opening measures.

Sources of Japan's Productivity Gap

Despite economists' predictions that capital accumulation eventually would drive capital's rate of return to zero, returns to investment continue to be positive for even the most mature economies. The reason that yields have not fallen as far as predicted is that productivity gains have managed to more than make up for diminishing returns. Of the ten industrial countries with the highest per capita incomes over the period

1969-1989, productivity growth across all inputs or factors of production—so-called total factor productivity—was in the low but positive 1-2 percent range.[12] Explaining the variation of productivity growth across countries and over time has not been wholly successful, but an accumulated collection of clues point to such factors as the growth process itself, domestic competition, international openness, and scientific research (especially basic research).[13]

Slower economic growth and sluggish productivity gains are related. Investment was the locomotive of the Japanese economy. Investment also stimulated productivity because new equipment and technology embodied the most advanced capabilities.[14] Therefore, as investment fell, both productivity and overall economic growth slowed.

Another source of sluggishness is the end of the catch-up phenomenon whereby economies that are behind the productivity leaders appear to gain an extra boost from their investment. The greater the initial lag, the more that investment contributes to productivity gains; an economy with 1950s technology will get a bigger kick from investing in the latest machine than an economy with a more modern 1990s vintage capital stock. Japan's manufacturing productivity seemed to have stopped benefiting from being a laggard in the 1970s when its capital stock was the youngest of the industrial countries.[15]

According to a series of McKinsey Global Institute studies on productivity, the principal explanations for lagging sectors and firms in Japan is overt regulation or other forms of noncompetitive behavior condoned and sanctioned by government, either through formal laws and regulations or through informal and customary practices. Many of these practices were established for sound regulatory reasons: to protect the public from financial instability in the case of banking and insurance; to guard against unsafe products in the case of numerous specification requirements; or to control the prices of monopoly producers in the case of telecommunications and transport. In other instances, regulation was explicitly designed to protect important political supporters: agriculture and small-scale retailing are examples. The main conclusion of the McKinsey study on manufacturing was: "The intensity of competition to which managers are exposed and, more specifically, the degree to which they are faced by direct competition from producers on the leading edge matter a great deal."[16] The notoriously inefficient food production industry in Japan, for example, was sheltered from the most competitive foreign producers and had failed to modernize.

Several of the most dynamic new industries are in areas that formerly were subject to traditional methods of regulation. For example, the coming together of telecommunications, entertainment, computers, broadcasting, cable, and Internet creates vast new opportunities embedded in uncertainties as profound as those facing the budding automobile industry in 1905. Despite the initial stab at privatizing the monopoly telephone company Nippon Telegraph and Telephone in 1985, Japan's telecommunications industry remained constrained by bureaucratic sluggishness and residual regulation for the next fifteen years. Although NTT shed almost 100,000 jobs or 25 percent of its workforce after privatization in an attempt to become more efficient, regulation prevented it from playing a more significant role in the evolving industry.

A breakthrough in 1994 substantially deregulated cellular telephone service, which subsequently took off as the number of cellular telephone subscribers rose from 2.1 million in 1993 to 50 million in 1999. NTT's mobile telephone subsidiary DoCoMo became one of the most highly valued companies in the world as measured by market capitalization. DoCoMo went on to lead a dramatic shift of Internet usage away from computers and onto the telephone.

McKinsey found that in Japan, Germany, and the United States, foreign direct investment had a more powerful impact on improving local productivity than the competitive pressures from trade. It was the United States that benefited most from foreign-owned plants operating in the domestic economy. The analysts constructed a global exposure index by combining exports and imports, the scale of foreign direct investment, and the penetration of foreign investment in domestic production. This index was computed for each of nine industries to test the relationship between international competition and productivity. In every variable that went into the index, the United States was the most exposed; furthermore, a high correlation existed between globalization and relative productivity.[17]

These conclusions are consistent with other studies that find an orientation toward trade and external competition strongly related to productivity growth. According to World Bank research, international trade was important in all the high-performing Asian economies and was the factor most consistently correlated with their success. However, these conclusions about the effects of trade on growth and productivity have not gone unchallenged. The chief criticism is that the cause and effect relationship may be in the other direction: countries may engage in more trade because they are more efficient rather than become efficient because they trade more. Possible reasons why income may affect trade include improved transportation infrastructure that allows more efficient access to distant markets and superior managerial skills that enable firms to compete effectively in world markets that are more complex than local ones.

A study by economists from Harvard University and the University of California at Berkeley confront this criticism directly. Their conclusions reinforce the importance of trade on productivity and income. When the issue of cause and effect is dealt with explicitly, trade appears to be even more important than it was in earlier studies. Their analysis indicates that trade increases the previously identified effects of investment and schooling on income. Most importantly, it has a powerful effect on productivity growth.[18]

Examination of the possibility that the widespread productivity slowdown of the 1970s and 1980s was attributable to diminishing returns to science and technology has not been supported by subsequent research. In fact, as will be discussed in chapter 5, the reverse was found: the productivity gains from R&D seemed to increase over time. Accumulating evidence suggests that science and research maintain the returns to investment above zero. Although the case is by no means fully proven, studies of the American economy show that private R&D has a dollar-for-dollar impact on productivity several times greater than investment in plant and equipment. More importantly, the returns to basic research are several times higher than to applied research. Cross-national studies are consistent with the findings based on the American experience. One study of fifty-three countries over the 1964-1988 period found that fundamental research had more than three times the impact on output than nonfundamental research.[19] This strong showing indicates that cross-border spillovers are not so prevalent as to wipe out the returns to this kind of research, as some policy analysts had feared; the country performing the research gets a high return from it.

Most of the studies examining the effects of R&D on the economy focus on the productivity gains—a social good that affects the general welfare. Companies, though, take profits to the bank, not productivity. The potential for a wedge between private and social returns is the basis for the argument that government should support basic research.

Given the apparent role of basic or fundamental research in productivity growth and especially in the development of science-based new products, how well does Japan do? Many analysts observe that Japanese research across the board tends to be more applied than American. Japan's total R&D expenditures rose by 50 percent between 1986 and 1991; the returns to this massive increase in spending were not commensurate with the volume. The chief villains behind this disappointing performance seem to be the same as observed in capital investment: Japanese R&D performers were moving down their yield curves and they were operating inefficiently.

Although the available knowledge does not permit unqualified assertions, the evidence clearly suggests that Japan may be suffering (relatively speaking) from a weakness in basic research and science. As its economy matures and the returns to investment decline, a stronger science and graduate education base may be required to stimulate innovation and productivity. Stated government policy has placed priority on these areas for several years, but little in the way of implementation has been seen as budget allocations and institutional structures appear to be stuck in a rigid mold.

Closing the Productivity Gap

Can an economy like Japan's, where business and social norms place great stress on employment stability, accommodate the flow of workers demanded by a more flexible economy, especially when aggregate growth will be slow? Most of Japan's earlier restructuring took place during rapid economic growth, which considerably eased the transition process. Since the early 1950s, the unemployment rate in Japan was considerably below that in the United States. That situation changed in 1999 when the combination of a decade of slow growth in Japan and almost a decade of continuous U.S. expansion reversed the usual positions.

Nevertheless, the Japanese labor force has demonstrated much more mobility than the popular myths admit. For example, the annual rate at which regular employees leave a job (excluding transfers within a corporate family) has been around 15 percent for many years; this overall average includes a rate of 11-12 percent for males and 20 percent for females.[20] Moreover, for industries other than large-scale manufacturing, the mobility rate often is considerably higher than the average.

Even for manufacturing establishments with more than thirty employees, among the most stable groups of workers in Japan, annual turnover is more than 16 percent. These figures underestimate mobility because they do not include part-time or short-term contract workers. In services, in particular, nonregular workers represent 14 percent of the labor force and in wholesale and retail trade 26 percent; these employees are less tied to a place of employment than regular workers. The industries outside of manufacturing, construction, and mining now account for more than 60 percent of all employment and are the fastest growing part of the economy. The traditional notion of stable, male, manufacturing employment no longer represents the average experience of Japanese workers.

Although mobility data indicate that substantial fractions of Japanese workers leave their jobs each year, job tenure is longer, separation rates are lower, and there is less geographical movement than in the United States. Yet, on a broader comparison, Japan falls closer to the American experience than the European. For example, in 1980, Japan was second only to the United States among the member countries of the Organization for Economic Cooperation and Development in terms of changing residence across state or prefecture boundaries.[21]

Lifetime employment has been a goal of most firms since the 1950s, but only the largest have had the ability to implement it fully. This system of employment encompassed several features: promotion from within the firm; low starting salaries with steeply rising earnings as experience was accumulated; and investment in training and experience that was specific to the individual firm. In combination, these features tied individuals to a firm for most of their careers, provided strong incentives for training, and created powerful motivations for intense effort.

Despite the outward appearance of continuity, substantial changes occurred in the employment system because of the growth slowdown beginning in the early 1970s. The effect of firm-specific experience on wages weakened from 1971 to 1988, especially among large firms.[22] At the same time, the returns to experience gained outside a specific firm increased at large firms, as did the mobility of mid-career workers. These findings suggest that a worker's experience outside the firm was having an increasing payoff relative to the internal rewards as viewed against comparable data from before the early 1970s.[23]

Just such findings were predicted by research on Japanese internal labor markets. Using promotion as an incentive has many advantages over straight monetary compensation. The promise of better pay tomorrow through promotion plus other rewards such as pensions that are tilted toward longevity produce an incentive for young fast flyers to ignore better paying jobs elsewhere. Compared to payment schemes that reward performance immediately, the greater assurance of stability that comes from delayed rewards encourages employers and employees to invest in training, especially of the kind that has a payoff mainly within a given firm.

The typical large Japanese firm's practice of limiting mid-level appointments to incumbents rather than opening jobs to the external market is highly dependent on rapid growth. Tenure-related wage profiles are steeper with higher growth; incentives related to promotion probabilities depend on fast growth; and higher growth rates enhance the incentives for investments in skill formation. Moreover, all of these growth-related effects leading to lifetime employment patterns are stronger for larger firms. As a result of the Japanese growth slowdown in the 1970s, large companies did, in fact, adjust their promotion patterns: they reduced promotion probabilities; flattened wage profiles; and created alternative job ladders and grading systems to detach compensation from managerial rank.[24]

Such changes, largely, were modifications to the old system. As growth slowed even more in the 1990s and further eroded the rationale for lifetime employment, large firms found themselves in a severe dilemma. Business and social norms accepted by most large companies and by the public curbed the potential for rapid adjustments.

In addition to the difficulties of maintaining the lifetime employment system in the face of slower growth, its side effects created other problems—especially in a time of rapid change. Detailed examinations of promotion patterns in six major, typical firms in representative industries reveal a standard practice of selecting people for promotion based on their not failing at previous tasks. Where failure is penalized more than success is rewarded, managers soon absorb the lessons for getting ahead: "Outstanding action will be punished while going along with others becomes important. In an organization where one can be promoted with 80 percent certainty if one does not fail and can successfully avoid being labeled a loser, there will not be many who will be adventurous if it involves a risk of failing. A climate develops where failure is feared and aggressiveness is inhibited."[25]

This conservative pattern, though, was not uniform across all the companies. In one of the studied firms, the personnel system gave a second chance to losers; positive achievement rather than the avoidance of failure was the criterion for promotion. In this company, a "go for broke" attitude was favored and innovative behavior rewarded. The very existence of such a firm demonstrates its feasibility, even when fully embedded in the norms and practices of Japanese society.

Lifetime employment, promotion from within the firm, and conservative corporate decisionmaking were creative adaptations to the conditions of high-growth. Indeed, millions of Japanese change jobs every year and these figures are increasing. At least some Japanese firms are adopting systems of management and personnel that favor innovation and risk-taking. They are hiring new employees under term contracts and are offering them higher cash earnings today rather than fringe benefits and future promotions and pensions. Nevertheless, the transition to new forms of management will be long and difficult as firms struggle to deal with systems designed under different conditions and as employees come to grips with expectations that may not be borne out.

Diversification as an Adjustment Response

One way out of the dilemma facing large firms as they move away from the lifetime employment system is to diversify their activities, both to preserve profitability and to create opportunities for redundant workers and excess capacity. In fact, the creation of a large number of small subsidiaries by large firms has been one of the chief means for allocating excess managers to new positions when promotion slots dried up in the core firm. This escape valve was especially attractive when *keiretsu* (corporate groups) had deep pockets that could sustain unprofitable subsidiaries over extended periods. The possibilities for duplicating this behavior in the future, though, will be more difficult for several reasons: the greater importance of explicit profit criterion in corporate investment decisions, *keiretsu* pockets are not as deep as they once were, and new accounting standards require consolidated statements under which inefficiencies in subsidiaries cannot be hidden.

Within American establishments, diversification has a low success rate. Entry into an industry can be accomplished three ways: diversification of an existing plant; diversification by building a new plant; or entry of a new company. In-plant diversification is the least successful of these methods and new-plant construction by an existing firm the most successful. Within ten years of entering a new industry, more than 80 percent of the firms diversifying at the plant level exited, compared to 66 percent for firms that entered through new plants.[26] The diversification efforts of even the largest American companies, those in the *Fortune* magazine list of the 200 largest, experienced severe losses through the first four years of operation in a new industry. On average, they needed at least eight years to achieve positive returns, and ten to twelve years to establish profit rates comparable to those enjoyed by incumbents.[27]

The American experience with diversification indicates that expanding the variety of operations within a single establishment is generally unprofitable. Organizations are very difficult to move in new directions. Establishment diversification has been on a downward trend in the United States since the 1960s. On the average, American establishments produced fewer than two products in a single industry.[28]

The evidence from the American experience is that establishments are specialized and that it is difficult to move resources profitably as a package to other activities. When American companies desire to move into new fields, they tend to unpackage and repackage resources. Most of all, when they face declining demand, they tend to get smaller by closing plants and downsizing their operations.

The diversification experience of American companies provides some guides for large Japanese companies, but smaller firms may have to face more unpalatable choices. The small amount of evidence from Japan does not bring good news for a slow-growth future: it suggests that diversification in large firms rises during expansions and actually falls rather than increases in recessions.[29] It looks as though Japanese companies, especially small, inefficient, formerly protected ones with poor access to capital, will face hard times in the future.

Indeed, according to the five-year Establishment and Enterprise Census conducted by the Management and Coordination Agency, the number of all establishments fell in 1996 for the first time since the original census was undertaken in 1947. Although the overall decline was a bare 0.5 percent from the 1991 census, the decrease in some industries was sharper. Between 1991 and 1996, the number of manufacturing establishments fell by 10 percent—a loss of 86,000 production locations. Employment in manufacturing contracted by 1.2 million, or 8.3 percent, over the same period. Despite the norms, myths, and structural impediments, change is occurring in the Japanese economy. Public and private policy can facilitate or retard this adjustment.

Policy Conclusions

It is possible for Japan to accelerate its growth just by bringing its inefficient industries up to 80 percent of current American levels. If a transition were to last for twenty years, growth of 1.4 percent annually could be captured from a renewed effort at playing catch-up. The advantage that Japanese government and private policymakers possess is that the objective already has been demonstrated to be feasible. Achieving this, however, will require an increased flexibility and mobility of the Japanese worker on whom much of the burden of adjustment will fall. Government policy can assist this process by reducing the penalties to mobility now paid by many workers. Pensions, for example, could be made more portable so that they are not lost when an employee moves from one job to another. In fact, the government in 1999 adopted just such a policy.

Currently, thin housing markets make it difficult for a moving employee to sell a residence or purchase a new home. Tax laws that favor nonmonetary rewards such as company-provided automobiles or subsidized housing tie an employee to the firm. Corporate and personal tax reforms under consideration could make the tax advantages to nonpecuniary rewards more neutral. Labor law currently provides incentives for companies to retain excess workers during recessions. This policy may be appropriate when underlying economic growth is strong and recessions are expected to be short. However, when an economy is undergoing major restructuring, it retards the adjustment process and drags out the transition. Creation of new jobs through the introduction of new products and services is probably the chief means by which vitality can be regained.

Workers, management, and capital tied up in unproductive enterprise are a drag on the entire economy. However, in order to accommodate greater business flexibility, the ongoing liberalization of the financial sector would have to be continued and strengthened. In particular, the ability of small, new firms to raise capital would have to be enhanced. The creation in 2000 of several new stock exchanges with less burdensome listing requirements than those imposed by the Tokyo Stock Exchange could prove to be important in channeling capital to innovative entrepreneurs.

In the end, economic reform is profoundly political. Many groups benefit from the status quo and are likely to fight against change. Inefficient firms facing new competitors, workers facing job loss, cities and prefectures whose fortunes are affected by local business declines, and government ministries giving up their authority and control all face real loss. However, the gains from increased productivity and growth should make it possible to reduce the severity of many of these losses.

Countering the political opposition to change are the political forces—long bottled up—that push in the other direction. Reforms passed in the early 1990s that rebalanced electoral districts could work toward shifting political forces to favor urban and consumer interests and away from the traditional supporters of the old power structure represented by the Liberal Democratic Party. However, this process could take several electoral cycles spanning a decade or more to work itself out.

Still, voices will certainly be heard warning against the "chaos and confusion of unregulated markets" or suggesting that Japanese people have a cultural preference for the comfortable certainty of past practices. Such statements can be translated to mean that the speaker prefers the economic rents and quiet life afforded by regulated markets or collusive activity to the hard work and uncertainties of competition. If such voices influence policy, Japan could drop from number three to number four—or more.

Notes

1.   Ezra Vogel, *Japan as Number One: Lessons for Americans* (Cambridge, Mass.: Harvard University Press, 1979).

2.   World Bank, *World Development Indicators*, (Washington, D.C.: World Bank, 2000). Liechtenstein and Luxembourg have greater levels of GDP per capita than the United States.

3.   Burton F. Klein, *Dynamic Economics* (Cambridge, Mass.: Harvard University Press, 1977), 99.

4.   McKinsey Global Institute, *Manufacturing Productivity* (Washington, D.C.: McKinsey Global Institute, 1993).

5.   Similar figures were estimated by Bart van Ark and Dirk Pilat, "Cross-Country Productivity Levels: Differences and Causes," *Brookings Papers on Economic Activity: Microeconomics*, no. 2 (1993).

6.   McKinsey Global Institute, *Service Sector Productivity* (Washington, D.C.: McKinsey Global Institute, 1992).

7.   Shintaro Hori, "Fixing Japan's White-Collar Economy," *Harvard Business Review* (November-December 1993): 161.

8.   McKinsey, *Manufacturing Productivity*, Exhibit 1-11; van Ark and Pilat, "Cross Country Productivity Levels," 11.

9.   Gary Saxonhouse, "What Does Japanese Trade Structure Tell Us About Japanese Trade Policy," *Journal of Economic Perspectives* 7, no. 3 (summer, 1993).

10.   Hori, "Fixing Japan's White-Collar Economy," 160-61.

11.   To say that Japan is only 60 percent as productive means that it requires 167 people to produce the same output as 100 people in the United States. An efficiency level of 80 percent would require 125 people. Moving from 60 percent to 80 percent relative productivity would free up one-quarter of the workforce or 1.45 percent annually if done over twenty years.

12.   The World Bank, *The East Asian Miracle: Economic Growth and Public Policy* (New York: Oxford University Press, 1993), 56.

13.   Paul M. Romer, "The Origins of Endogenous Growth," and Howard Pack, "Endogenous Growth Theory: Intellectual Appeal and Empirical Shortcomings," *Journal of Economic Perspectives* 8, no. 1 (winter 1994).

14.   J. Bradford De Long and Lawrence H. Summers, "Equipment Investment and Economic Growth," *Quarterly Journal of Economics* 106, no. 2 (May 1991).

15.   Edward N. Wolff, "Capital Formation and Productivity Convergence Over the Long Term," *American Economic Review* 81, no. 2 (June 1991).

16. McKinsey, *Manufacturing Productivity*, Summary, 3.

17. McKinsey, Manufacturing Productivity, 3-20.

18. Jeffrey Frankel and David Romer, "Does Trade Cause Growth?" *American Economic Review* 89, no. 3 (June 1999): 390.

19. Frank Lichtenberg, *R&D Investment and International Productivity Differences*, Working Paper No. 4161, (Cambridge, Mass.: National Bureau of Economic Research, 1992).

20. Management and Coordination Agency, Statistics Bureau, *Japan Statistical Yearbook* (Tokyo: Management and Coordination Agency, 1999), tables 3-9, 3-10.

21. Organization for Economic Cooperation and Development, *Structural Adjustment and Economic Performance* (Paris: OECD, 1987), 136.

22. Robert L. Clark and Naohiro Ogawa, "Employment Tenure and Earnings Profiles in Japan and the United States: Comment," *American Economic Review* 82, no. 1 (March 1992).

23. Masanori Hashimoto and John Raisian, "Employment Tenure and Earnings Profiles in Japan and the United States: Reply," *American Economic Review* 82, no. 1 (March 1992), 349-51.

24. Kenn Ariga, Giorgio Brunello, Yasushi Ohkusa, and Yoshihiko Nishiyama, "Corporate Hierarchy, Promotion, and Firm Growth: Japanese Internal Labor Market in Transition," *Journal of the Japanese and International Economies* 6, no. 6 (December 1992).

25. Mitsuyo Hanada, "The Principle of Competition in Japan's Personnel System," *Japanese Economic Studies*, (winter 1988-89), 19.

26. Timothy Dunne, Mark Roberts, and Larry Samuelson, "Patterns of Firm Entry and Exit in U.S. Manufacturing Industries," *RAND Journal of Economics* 19, no. 4 (winter 1988), 503.

27. E. Biggadike, cited by P. A. Geroski, *Market Dynamics and Entry* (Cambridge, Mass.: Blackwell, 1991), 34.

28. Frank M. Gollop and James L. Monahan, "A Generalized Index of Diversification: Trends in U.S. Manufacturing," *Review of Economics and Statistics* 73 (1991), 328-29.

29. Akita Goto, "Statistical Evidence on the Diversification of Japanese Large Firms," *Journal of Industrial Economics* 29 (March 1981), 271-78.

Chapter 4

Investment

Investment and Economic Growth

Investment has been the most important means for improving economic welfare for most people, in most countries, most of the time. Japan is no exception. Investment increased economic capacity, it stimulated growth by contributing to aggregate demand, and it advanced productivity through the introduction of the newest production technologies and methods.

An economy also can grow if other productive inputs, mainly labor, expand, or if the efficiency in the use of these various inputs increases. For economies far from the technological frontier of the most advanced nations, as Japan was for most of its modern history, investment has been the primary source of per capita income growth.

Investing in industrial plant and equipment, social infrastructure, research and development, and in human potential through education, training, and improved health requires that current output be diverted from current consumption. A portion of national income must be saved and devoted to expenditures that will have a future payoff. The Japanese economy channeled more than one-third of its output into gross capital investment in the peak years of the postwar economic miracle.

However, as capital accumulates, the returns from such investment tend to decline. Mature economies must look more toward increased productivity as the source of improved economic welfare. Unfortunately for Japan, productivity has not kept up with the pace of investment. The admirable qualities of discipline and patience undergirding a nation of savers and investors are less valuable to an economy when productivity improvements are the main source of growth. When productive levels are high and the frontier is near, risk-taking and impatience seem to be the necessary qualities for an economy to prosper.

The Role of Capital in Economic Development

The World Bank published a major study in 1993 on the sources of growth of high-performing Asian economies. This volume, *The East Asian Miracle*, built on decades of work on economic development. The researchers concluded that investment in human and physical capital was among the most significant contributors to real per capita income growth. According to the statistical analysis for Japan, 38 percent of that country's growth from 1960 to 1985 could be attributed to investment in plant, equipment, and infrastructure over the period. Investment in primary and secondary school education was just as important a contributor.[1]

However, these inputs do not tell the whole growth story. After accounting for physical capital accumulation, human capital investment, and labor force growth, a significant fraction of growth remains unexplained. That residual is the growth in the effectiveness of using resources, otherwise known as total factor productivity (TFP). The World Bank's calculations put Japan's TFP growth near the top of the rankings for eighty-seven countries in the 1960-1985 period, with a value of approximately 3.5 percent annually.

One question implied by the importance of investment in economic growth is why some countries invest heavily with all the positive consequences whereas others do not do so. Economics ministers in developing economies, many of whom have advanced economic degrees from the leading universities of the advanced countries, are quick to acknowledge their understanding of the investment-growth nexus. Achieving the necessary savings and stimulating the desire to invest by local businesses is the problem, they say.

Examinations of the East Asia experience and comparisons with other regions provide some clues about why Japan and its Asian neighbors were able to enter the virtuous circle of savings, investment, growth, productivity gains, higher incomes, and more savings and growth. Dani Rodrik of Harvard University notes that the Asian high flyers by the late 1950s had a much better educated labor force than would have been expected based on their income levels. In addition, the distribution of income and wealth was exceptionally equal in international comparison. These two features may not have been independent since a wide distribution of educational achievement also provides the chief means by which people can improve their incomes. Quality and equality of education produce a more even division of capabilities and income. The third characteristic possessed by Japan and the Asian fast-growth countries was a higher quality of governance and official bureaucracy than might have been expected on the basis of original income levels.[2]

Rodrik notes that investment and growth tended to vary both within the Asian economies and between Asia and other regions according to the strengths of these three characteristics. Although he attempts to come up with compelling stories about why these broad features of national life may be related to economic growth, he acknowledges that they are not fully supported explanations. In any event, Japan possessed all of the features in good measure from the Meiji period onward, but especially after World War II when changes in education and land redistribution by the occupation authorities increased both income equality and education levels of all Japanese.

In addition to investment, the other important variable in the World Bank analysis—and most others of this genre—is a nation's per capita income relative to the world leader: the United States for most of the twentieth century. The more a country lags behind the frontier, the greater the impact of investment on economic growth. This effect sometimes is called conditional convergence. Backwardness yields positive benefits to investment, as advanced economies provide technology, ideas, experience, investment goods, and tutelage; but these benefits only flow through the pipeline of investment. Hence the term conditional convergence: no investment, no gain.

The sources of growth for more advanced economies are less heavily weighted toward investment and more toward productivity gains. For example, in a study that compared growth trends in East Asia with the advanced economies, capital accumulation yielded an estimated 24 to 26 percent of U.S. growth, while productivity gains produced 49 percent of this expansion. The remaining one-quarter of the increase in real GDP in the United States over the period from 1948 to 1990 came from a larger labor force.[3]

Examination of the investment process suggests that investment and productivity growth are related. Indeed, several scholars have hypothesized that positive interactions exist between capital accumulation and technological advance. This can come about from several different processes.[4]

• Investment may be required to embody new inventions and knowledge in production. New capital is likely to be more productive than older vintages because of technical progress in the capital goods-producing sector.

• New capital also may require better organization and management.

• An economy that experiences a high rate of investment may benefit because of the learning experience gained in production and investment—so-called learning by doing.

• An economy with low levels of capital and low productivity likely will experience high rates of return to investment because capital is so scarce, leading to more investment and subsequent gains in productivity.

• High investment leads to strong growth in demand and a business climate generally favorable to further investment and innovation.

These arguments seem particularly appropriate to the Japanese experience. Compared to the advanced economies over the period from 1880 to 1979, Japan had both the biggest rise in the ratio of capital to labor and the highest TFP growth rate—as well as the lowest absolute level of productivity.[5] Statistical analysis of one hundred years of data showed that TFP growth was related strongly to the variation in the capital-labor ratio. This relationship strengthened in the 1950-1979 period, the years of Japan's powerful catch-up with other leading economies.

The high rates of investment in Japan in the postwar period can be seen as part of a virtuous circle of growth: high investment plus backwardness led to high returns and fast productivity increases, which, in turn, stimulated demand and even higher rates of investment. This very process, however, brought about the conditions leading to its own decay.

Long-Term Capital Trends

Figure 4.1 portrays the 1910-1995 pattern of Japan's gross domestic capital formation, which includes all new investment by both private business actors and the public sector as well as households. ("Gross" in this context means that depreciation is not subtracted from the quantities.) Piecing together several time series to provide a consistent view over ninety years generated this particular measure.[6]

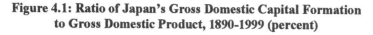

**Figure 4.1: Ratio of Japan's Gross Domestic Capital Formation
to Gross Domestic Product, 1890-1999 (percent)**

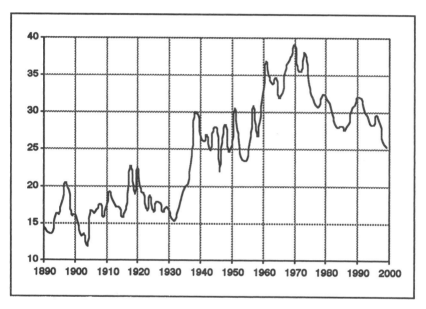

Source: Japan, Economic Planning Agency, *Historical Statistics of Japan on CD-ROM* (Tokyo: Japan Statistical Association, 1999).

In the forty years from 1890 to 1930, gross investment drifted upward accompanied by many shocks to investment spending. It then shot up to support the strengthening of military industry for the ten years between 1935 and 1945. The destruction of World War II left Japan's heavy industry in disarray; economic output fell even faster than investment, leaving the ratio of gross investment to GDP at a higher level than in the prewar years. As energy supplies, transportation, and machinery-producing industries recovered, supported in part by Korean War-inspired demand from the United States, investment began to move upward in 1955. Within fifteen years, it accounted for more than one-third of all output. Compared to Japan's prior experience, investment's share of total economic output reached unprecedented heights.

The resources incorporated in this expansion of the capital base were diverted from household consumption and government spending alike. In the early 1970s, families were saving more than one-fifth of their disposable income, with the diverted resources going to industry (via the banking system) for investment purposes. The government budget tended to be in surplus, which added to the funds available for investment purposes as well.

In the 1960s, the period of Japan's fastest economic development, almost three-quarters of gross investment went into industrial plant and equipment. Another 20 percent were devoted to residential construction; government spent the remainder on infrastructure. Government investment not only laid the foundations of a modern state, but economic policymakers also used investment spending as a tool for fiscal stimulus during recessions. Liberal Democratic Party politicians quickly learned that the rebuilding of Japan in the first postwar decades also gave them a powerful source of patronage in the construction industry. Even after the reconstruction of the basic infrastructure needs was completed, public construction remained close to 10 percent of GDP, about double the share of other advanced economies. The construction industry fulfilled its share of the bargain through continuing large financial contributions to the LDP.

Most economic growth studies indicate that private, nonresidential investment is the most relevant for an economy's expansion; housing, in contrast, is a form of consumer durable that does not contribute directly to productive potential. In addition to the usual infrastructure expenditures on such projects as roads, bridges, water, and sewer systems that are considered the responsibility of government, Japan's public sector also invested in plant and equipment for a variety of government-owned production operations. In 1955, this contribution represented 20 percent of plant and equipment investment, but later it declined to 10 percent.

Equipment investment is especially significant. Some studies indicate that this particular form of spending generates very high growth returns. The leading proponents of this view, former Harvard University economists J. Bradford De Long and Lawrence Summers, noted that "differences in equipment investment account for essentially all of the extraordinary growth performance of Japan relative to the sample [of the twenty five most advanced economies] as a whole."[7] In their study, equipment was defined as including electric and nonelectric machinery and excluding transportation equipment. Over the 1960-1985 period, Japan consistently devoted a greater proportion of GDP to equipment as defined in this way (12 percent) than any other country investigated.

When measured as a share of GDP, the size of Japan's capital stock overtook the American level in the mid-1970s (figure 4.2). This particular ratio measures the capital intensity of production; it expresses the quantity of capital required to produce a unit of annual output. The American stock of nonresidential fixed capital has hovered around 2.25 times GDP since the early 1980s. Japan's capital stock has grown continuously, even during the years of slowdown in the 1990s; it remained more than three times as large as annual national output. In 1995, the ratio of capital to output was 55 percent greater in Japan than in the United States.

Figure 4.2: Ratio of Nonresidential Capital Stock to GDP, Japan and United States, 1955-1995

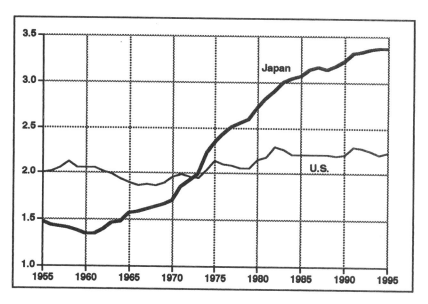

Source: Angus Maddison, "Standardised Estimates of Fixed Capital Stock: A Six-Country Comparison," in *Explaining the Economic Performance of Nations* (Brookfield, Vt.: Edward Elgar Publishing Co., 1995).

Although the added output from each new unit of investment in Japan has continued to be positive (unlike the situation in the Soviet Union in the 1980s, where the marginal product of capital was negative), the increment is declining. A not surprising consequence of this high degree of capital intensity is that the rate of return on investment has fallen steadily in the postwar era, producing important consequences for the Japanese economy.

Sectoral Composition of Investment

Substantial changes in the sectoral composition of investment have re-flected the transition of Japan from a developing economy focused on manufacturing to one more oriented toward services. Whereas in the early 1970s about 45 percent of investment went into manufacturing and 55 percent into nonmanufacturing, thirty years later the difference between the respective shares had widened to 30 percent and 70 percent (figure 4.3). The big losers in manufacturing over this stretch include the usual suspects in heavy industry. Chemicals fell 3 percentage points from 6.5 percent to 3.5 percent of total business investment, steel was down 2.3 percentage points and motor vehicles was off 2.2 points.

Figure 4.3: Investment Shares of Manufacturing and Nonmanufacturing, 1970-2000 (percent of total investment)

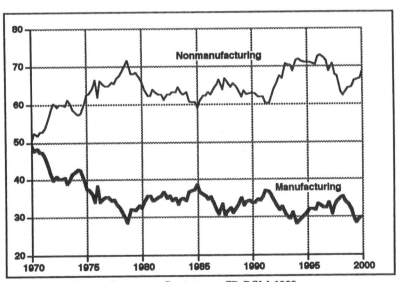

Source: Bank of Japan, *Economics Statistics on CD-ROM*, 1999

On the nonmanufacturing side, investment in electricity-generating facilities fell 6.4 percentage points from 1980 to 1997. However, transportation and communications (5.6 percentage points), real estate (3.1 points), narrowly defined services (3.1 percentage points), and finance and insurance (1.2 points) registered strong gains.

The investment shift toward nonmanufacturing from manufacturing is illustrated by a decline of almost a full percentage point for food and beverage production and a 2.4-percentage point gain for eating and drinking establishments. Japanese anxiety over the hollowing out of manufacturing seems to arise not because the changes are unexpected or unprecedented—the same process unfolded in the United States and elsewhere in the West—but because it signifies deep changes in relative importance among the different parts of the economy.

Recent Investment Trends and the Economy

Not only does investment act to expand the supply capacity of an economy over the long run; it also is a driving element of demand and stimulation in the short term. Private nonresidential investment in most economies is notoriously volatile; that is one reason John Maynard Keynes in the 1930s focused on the role of investment in creating the familiar cycle of boom and bust. Japan is not an exception to this experience. Figure 4.4 portrays that country's quarterly ratio of private plant and equipment spending to GDP for forty-five years. Since 1955, this ratio has moved more than five percentage points in just a few years, adding or subtracting a powerful impulse to the economy. Following the slowdown of the economic expansion in the early 1970s, the general trend of plant and equipment investment was downward. It fell from a postwar high of more than 21 percent of GDP in 1971 to 13.5 percent in 1978. That loss of demand, amounting to 8.5 percent of the total economy, initiated and then intensified the recession accompanying the first oil crisis.

The investment boom that characterized the bubble economy is evident in figure 4.4. Between 1986 and 1991, plant and equipment's share of GDP jumped by more than four percentage points. Fueled by price/earnings ratios on the Tokyo Stock Exchange that were as high as sixty or seventy, the nominal cost of funds was around 1.5 percent (the inverse of the price-to-earnings ratio). After subtracting the rate of inflation, the real cost of investment funds was negative by the end of the 1980s; investors literally were paying companies to take their money. With those kinds of incentives, a boom in plant and equipment investment accompanied one in real estate; the subsequent takeoff of asset prices in the late 1980s was the consequence. At that time, some analysts, citing with wonder the fact that each year domestic businesses were investing as much as the entire Canadian economy, saw Japan's fast-expanding asset base as the launching pad for the future.

**Figure 4.4: Ratio of Private Plant and Equipment Investment to GDP,
1956-2001 (percent)**

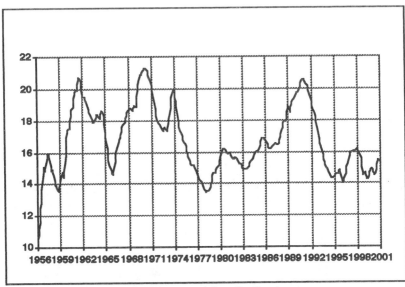

Source: Statistics Bureau, Management and Coordination Agency

With the stimulus of investment, Japan's economic growth rate surged for several years, rising from 1986's minirecession level of 2 percent to almost 7 percent only two years later. However, anyone considering the sustainability of these conditions should have taken pause. Just as the real cost of funds sank to negative levels in 1989, a shift in monetary policy began to drive up short-term interest rates, doubling them in less than two years. Equity prices peaked at the end of 1989; as shares collapsed, the cost of money raised on the stock exchange rose from a negative 2 percent to a positive 4 percent at the beginning of 1992. What had appeared to be a launching pad into the future turned out to be an anchor that would drag down the Japanese economy for more than ten years.

From its peak in 1991, business investment fell by almost 25 percent through 1994—a full 6 percent of GDP. Not surprisingly, the economy's performance slumped, crossing below the zero line in 1992. Not until plant and equipment spending began to turn up in 1995 did the GDP figures show any sustained increase.

Since business investment has been the locomotive pulling the Japanese economy for most of its modern existence, its future course is of the utmost importance in projecting economic trends. In the past, rapid productivity improvements and high rates of return provided potent incentives for Japanese investors. In addition, an extensively regulated financial sector until the 1980s supplied funds to heavy industrial borrowers at what were probably below market rates. With the deregulation and internationalization of Japan's financial markets, domestic borrowers must pay the same market interest rates as any other borrower around the world. The increased flow of funds across borders speaks to the fact that global borrowers and financial investors react to interest rates and returns with the speed of contemporary information flows. Japanese investors, therefore, no longer have any inherent advantage that may have favored them in past decades.

In addition to the cost of financial capital, the other major factor influencing Japanese business investment decisions is the expected return on projected investments. This payback is quite skimpy by international standards. The clear-cut consequence is rather low levels of investment for the future. Plant and equipment spending is unlikely to rise much above 15 percent of GDP for any sustained period and, more probably, the long-term trend will be lower.

Rates of Return on Japanese Capital

As the capital intensity of production rises and the quantity of capital per unit of labor increases, diminishing returns to capital are an expected outcome. Japan is no exception to this rule of thumb. Making use of production functions estimated by Stanford University's Kim and Lau and the standardized data on capital stock collected by the University of Gronigen's Angus Maddison, it is possible to calculate rates of return for several advanced industrial countries for the postwar period (see table 4.1).[8]

Referring back to figure 4.2, the level of capital stock relative to output in the United States in 1955 was one-third higher than in Japan. Wartime destruction combined with Japan's isolation from global trade and investment for much of the 1930s and 1940s meant that its capital was both scarce and out of date. Under such conditions, the returns on new investment were quite high. In 1955, Japan's economy-wide return on capital was 34 percent, more than twice the U.S. value. The 1960 estimates for the United Kingdom, Germany, and France were somewhat below Japan's but considerably higher than the American rate of return. Capital deepening drove down returns in all these countries. Moreover, the resumption of international capital flows in the mid-1970s worked to bring some additional convergence of returns.

Table 4.1: Real Aggregate Rates of Return on Gross Nonresidential Fixed Capital Stock in Selected Countries, 1955-1990 (percent)

Year	Japan	United States	United Kingdom	Germany	France
1955	33.9	16.0	—	—	—
1960	28.3	14.4	23.3	23.8	23.9
1970	18.0	12.4	15.1	14.0	18.0
1990	3.9	5.9	7.9	5.3	6.0

Sources: Angus Maddison, "Standardised Estimates of Fixed Capital Stock: A Six-Country Comparison," in *Explaining the Economic Performance of Nations* (Brookfield, Vt.: Edward Elgar Publishing Co., 1995); Kim and Lau, "The Sources of Economic Growth," 259.

The interesting part of the story occurred in the 1970s when the capital stock relative to output in Japan surpassed that in the United States. Returns in Japan subsequently fell below American values. It is not coincidental that 1980 also witnessed the beginning of Japan's current account surplus and its export of capital to the rest of the world, as Japanese investors sought returns higher than those available at home. By 1990, returns in the United States were an estimated 50 percent-plus above the comparable figures for Japan.

Japan's comparative investment situation is shown in figure 4.5, which plots, on a per capita basis, GDP and capital stock for Japan, the United States and the United Kingdom. It covers the critical years from 1965 through 1990, during which Japan's miracle growth ended and Prime Minister Margaret Thatcher's leadership helped transform the British economy.

Several points can be drawn from this chart. First, higher levels of income are associated with higher stocks of capital, as suggested above. However, the British and the American curves lie above the Japanese one, indicating that at all levels of capital, Japan's output has been well below America's and Great Britain's. In recent years, the United States has generated 55 percent to 60 percent more GDP than Japan with the same amount of capital. The lesson is that it requires capital to get rich, but growth can be more or less efficient. Given the experiences of the other two countries, Japan used more capital than was necessary to emerge as the world's second-largest economy.[9]

Figure 4.5: Nonresidential Capital and Gross Domestic Product per Capita, Japan, United States, United Kingdom, 1965-1990 (1985 dollars at purchasing power parity)

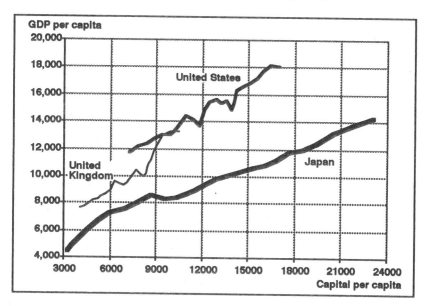

Source: Penn World Table 5.6. Available at: http://pwt.econ.upenn.edu/

Figure 4.5 also shows a distinct flattening of Japan's curve in the 1970s. From 1965 to 1970, the Japanese curve was steeper than the American one, pointing to a somewhat higher marginal return to capital. The slope of the line became less steep for several years before 1973, followed by a pause until 1976. The plateau can be attributed to the first global oil price hike and the subsequent economic disruptions. Investment continued but with little increase in output to show for it. The economy's reaction to the sharp deceleration in growth plus the reshuffling of relative prices was reflected in the temporary collapse in rates of return.

The pause was followed by a less steep slope than in previous years and flatter than the British and American trends. The drop in gains from investment was dramatic. Between 1965 and 1973 (the period up to the flattening of the curve), every extra unit of capital generated 0.75 units of output. In contrast, from 1976 to 1990, investment yields dropped by almost 40 percent to 0.46 units of output per unit of additional capital. U.S. returns over the full 1965-1990 period averaged 66 cents per dollar invested, with little indication of either an increase or a decrease.

The other dramatic shift in the yield curves was the British jump beginning in 1983 after a three-year fall in real income from a high in 1979, the first year of Mrs. Thatcher's tenure as prime minister. It has been suggested that her reforms made the British economy less regulated and more competitive. Such a transformation certainly shows up in the numbers: the average British return on capital jumped to the U.S. level. Today, the main difference between the United States and the United Kingdom is that the United States has more capital.

The greater capital intensity of production in Japan than in other countries is not the only reason that the returns to capital are lower there. The productivity of capital plays at least as great a role. The Washington, D.C.-based McKinsey Global Institute has conducted comparative studies on the productivity of specific economies as well as individual industries in several advanced countries. A central paradox was noted in its report on capital productivity. Japan used 22 percent more capital per capita than the United States and 40 percent more labor, yet Japan's GDP per capita was 23 percent less, averaged over the period from 1990 through 1993.[10]

The solution to this paradox, of course, is that Japan uses its resources less effectively than does the United States. In fact, as calculated by McKinsey, the total factor productivity of the market economy in Japan averaged only 58 percent of the American level for the 1990-1993 period. TFP was calculated from labor productivity 55 percent of the U.S. value and capital productivity that was 63 percent as large. (TFP in Germany, the other country in the comparison, was 20 percent below the American level.)

The McKinsey case study results are shown in table 4.2. The one Japanese industry with a U.S.-equivalent level of capital productivity was motor vehicles. In 1987, the figure for that industry was 25 percent higher than its American counterpart, but very heavy Japanese investment combined with little additional output over the next five years offset the underlying advantage. In food processing, the most productive Japanese product line was sugar (at 82 percent of U.S. capital productivity) and the worst was meat, which was only 38 percent as efficient.

**Table 4.2: Capital Productivity for Selected Industries in Japan and
Germany Relative to United States, 1990-1993
(United States = 100)**

Industry	Japan	Germany
Motor Vehicles	100	65
Food Production	64	70
Retail	65	110
Telecommunications	46	38
Electric Utilities	49	78
Economywide Average	63	65

Source: McKinsey Global Institute, *Capital Productivity* (Washington, D.C.: 1996)

In retailing, according to the McKinsey study, the American drive for profits created innovations that led to large productivity gains as well as to great uncertainty. Among the top ten department stores in 1982, three had disappeared a decade later; the turnover among specialty stores was even greater, with half of the 1982 members dropping out by 1992. In contrast, the Japanese top ten were the same in both years.

Accompanying the low productivity of physical capital in Japan was a lower return on invested capital. In the food industry, the gap was 35 percent: 10.9 percent versus 16.9 percent in the United States. Internal rates of return calculated for the entire corporate sector (after corporate income taxes but before personal income taxes) and averaged for the period 1974 to 1993 yielded a Japanese return that was 78 percent of the U.S. value (7.1 percent versus 9.1 percent). However, the McKinsey study also found, as was noted in table 4.1, that Japanese returns were higher in the earlier period and fell below the comparable American figures in the latter part.

The McKinsey authors noted another paradox concerning savings. From 1974 to 1993, Japanese national savings as a proportion of GDP were twice the very low American rates, while German savings rates were 60 percent greater. However, the United States accumulated more new wealth, which produced more output than in either Japan or Germany. Despite Japan's enormous stock of nonresidential capital, which had reached almost $65,000 for every person by 1995 and surpassed American wealth by almost 20 percent, Japanese income remained substantially below the American position.[11] Savings rates in the United States, though smaller than in Japan or Germany, generated more income because of higher financial returns, driven by high physical capital productivity.

Explanations for Low Returns and Lagging Productivity

After five years of research, preparing case studies on scores of companies, and drafting a half-dozen reports on labor and capital productivity, services and manufacturing industries, and labor and capital markets, the McKinsey researchers concluded that "productivity differences across countries arise because economic systems create different dynamics of innovation, improvement, and creative destruction." They went on to note that a competitive market is critical, including low entry barriers, frequent start-ups and exits, and intense price-value competition. "In all of our non-monopoly case studies, the more intense the product market competition, the higher the productivity."[12] Regulations, they concluded, were often the basic cause of differences in the nature of competition.

A political argument for the origins of this situation is made by Richard Katz and concerns the role played by the Liberal Democratic Party and its chief strategist and prime minister from 1972 to 1974, Kakuei Tanaka. As the party in power, the LDP increasingly had to deal with political discontent arising from demographic trends, declining growth, and industries left grounded in the wake of the first oil shock. Extrapolation of early 1970s electoral victories by candidates from the political left, who were helped by the rise of urbanization and industrialization, suggested the eventual downfall of the LDP. Even such party stalwarts as small shopkeepers, other small business owners, and farmers were leaving the LDP camp.[13]

The party needed a way to shore up its existing base while appealing to the new white-collar urban electorate. It responded with cheap credit for small business, instructions to the Ministry of Finance to go easy on small companies' tax returns, increased funding for construction projects, and higher price supports and subsidies for farmers. Urban voters got health insurance, social security, bullet trains, and education.

Many of these programs were draining the budget, however. To provide additional benefits to LDP supporters, the party and the government turned to off-budget methods. These included the Large Retail Store Law to protect neighborhood shopkeepers, so-called recession cartels to support the prices and the profits of hard-hit, politically connected industries, and *dango* (bid-rigging) in construction. Mr. Katz describes these moves as the origins of the "cartelized economy" that became the foundation for a less productive nation. They did not just redistribute income; their negative effects on incentives for efficiency reduced the income potential of the entire economy.

Basic materials industries, in particular, became hopelessly unprofitable in the 1970s. Excessive expansion in the period preceding the slowdown had left suppliers with unused capacity and high costs. Cement, steel, petrochemicals, aluminum, coal, and other industrial inputs could be purchased from foreign sources at prices far below what Japanese companies were quoting. Protection of these industries required webs of cartel activities that had to cross industry lines. Why else would a construction company buy Japanese cement if it could get the same product 50 percent cheaper from South Korea? Interlinked trade associations representing the cement and the construction businesses made sure that their members were kept in line by the threat of restricted supplies from other sources. A steelmaker, for example, might not sell to a construction company that bought foreign cement.[14]

Banking also was part of the cartel solution. Banks operated in a "convoy" environment of price and product regulation that preserved the profitability of the weakest bank and allowed none to fold; that implicit guarantee against failure lasted until 1997. According to one anecdote, regulatory detail went so far as to restrict to a single sheet the calendars that banks gave to customers. The thinking, apparently, was that one bank might gain an unfair advantage over the others by distributing a better calendar. Banks were expected to support the clients of the LDP—especially construction companies and agricultural cooperatives. Because a customer's risks could rebound on its lender, large borrowers also had implicit guarantees against failure to keep them from dragging down their banks. As suggested by these examples, cartels begat cartels, and guarantees begat guarantees.

According to this research, competition in product and capital markets generates pressures stimulating productivity because it gives, or does not give, managers incentives to improve financial performance; in turn, better financial performance results in more productive behavior. The McKinsey authors emphasized that the high productivity of American firms is inconsistent with the assertion that U.S. capital markets undermine the nation's economic performance by forcing firms to be too focused on short-term results. As Japanese returns fell to historically low levels, time horizons as revealed by markets lengthened almost immeasurably. Patient capital and long time horizons arose as the problem, not the solution.

Notes

1.   The World Bank, *The East Asian Miracle: Economic Growth and Public Policy* (New York: Oxford University Press, 1993), 52.

2.   Dani Rodrik, "Understanding Economic Policy Reform," *Journal of Economic Literature* 34, (March 1996), 20-21.

3.   Jong-Il Kim and Lawrence J. Lau, "The Sources of Economic Growth of the East Asian Newly Industrialized Countries," *Journal of the Japanese and International Economies* 8, no. 3 (September 1994), 259.

4.   Edward N. Wolff, "Capital Formation and Productivity Convergence Over the Long Term," *American Economic Review* 81, no. 2 (June 1991), 566.

5.   Wolff, "Capital Formation," 571. The seven countries in the sample are Canada, France, Germany, Italy, Japan, the United Kingdom, and the United States.

6.   The data through 1955 came from Kazushi Ohkawa and Henry Rosovsky, *Japanese Economic Growth* (Stanford, California: Stanford University Press, 1973), Appendix. Data for 1955 to 1995 were from Economic Planning Agency, *Annual Report on National Accounts* (CD-ROM), 1996.

7.   J. Bradford De Long and Lawrence H. Summers, "Equipment Investment and Economic Growth," *Quarterly Journal of Economics* 106, no. 2 (May 1991), 455.

8.   The elasticity of real output with respect to capital (Kim and Lau, 254) was multiplied by the ratio of output to capital stock to produce the change in output with respect to a change in capital—the rate of return.

9.   The plots do not show the rates of return as would be computed from production functions, which include such other inputs as labor and take into account the possible substitution of one input for another.

10.   McKinsey Global Institute, *Capital Productivity* (Washington, D.C.: 1996), 2.

11.   Yen were converted to dollars at the 1990 purchasing power parity of ¥195=$1.00 estimated by the Organization for Economic Cooperation and Development.

12.   McKinsey, *Capital Productivity*, Executive Summary, 4.

13.   Richard Katz, Japan, The System That Soured: The Rise and Fall of the Japanese Economic Miracle (Armonk, New York: M.E. Sharpe, 1998), 102-05.

14.   Mark Tilton, *Restrained Trade: Cartels in Japan's Basic Materials Industries* (Ithaca, New York: Cornell University Press, 1996).

Chapter 5

Basic Research and Science

The Quantity and Quality of Japanese Science

The theme of this chapter is that despite the scale and overall competence of its research and development effort, Japan is not obtaining many of the potential benefits. Japan's spending on research and development ranks second globally.[1] Based on data from the Organization for Economic Cooperation and Development shown in figure 5.1, the 1999 value of Japan's R&D was 39 percent of the U.S. total, or 45 percent of American nondefense R&D. However, as a share of the total economy, shown in figure 5.2, spending patterns in the two countries have been within a fraction of a percent of each other since the mid-1980s. Japan's business R&D in relation to sales was 20 percent below the American figure in the early 1980s, but surpassed it in 1989; since then, the two countries have moved in tandem.

Another indicator of the strength of Japan's business R&D is the proportion of the private labor force accounted for by scientific researchers. According to OECD estimates for 1999, the Japanese figure of 64 researchers per 10,000 workers was second only to the U.S. value of 70.

A constant theme of official rhetoric has focused on increasing the budget for science and basic research. Since at least the late 1980s, government officials and industry executives have expressed unease at the apparently growing lags in technology between Japanese businesses and leading-edge developments elsewhere. They pointed to the science activities of American universities and the close ties between academic researchers and industry in the United States as a pattern that deserved scrutiny—and perhaps emulation.

Strongly backed by industry, the Japanese government embraced the June 1996 recommendation of the advisory Council for Science and Technology to expand government support for science. This policy called for funding increases that would boost total research and development spending 50 percent over five years.

Figure 5.1: R&D Expenditures in the United States and Japan, 1980-1999 (billions 1996 dollars)

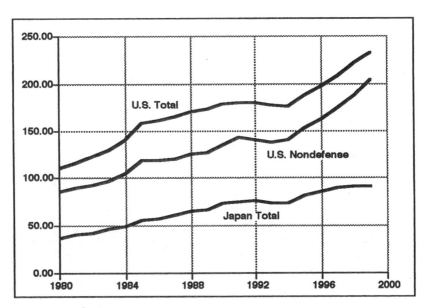

Source: Organization for Economic Cooperation and Development

Despite such repeated calls for greater attention to basic research, however, subsequent increases in budget outlays have been minimal. If anything, the share of basic research in total government-funded R&D declined. The university percentage of the basic research account, a prime indicator of government support, fell from 54.2 percent in 1987 to 52.6 percent in 1994.

Many observers suggest that a recession-induced three-year drop in private R&D spending in the first half of the 1990s, particularly the sharp decline in corporate support for basic research, drove home the significance of government R&D funding. However, according to the Science and Technology Agency's 1999 R&D survey, basic research's share of total expenditures held steady since 1980.

Although the growth of basic science kept pace with overall spending, the numerous new programs that targeted basic research did not have a visible impact. Many analysts despair of Japan's ability to close the basic research gap without a thorough overhaul of the government's methods for allocating money and selecting research projects.

Figure 5.2: Total and Business R&D Expenditures in the United States and Japan as Share of GDP and Sales, 1981-1999

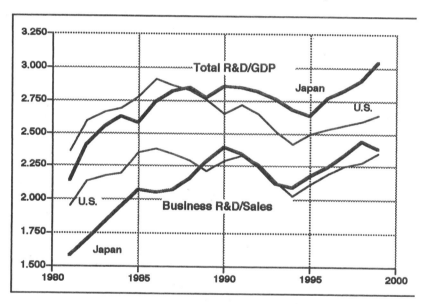

Source: Organization for Economic Cooperation and Development

The economic rationale for government support of basic research flows from the combination of two of its attributes. First, high social returns accompany basic research. Second, privately funded basic research is presumed to have low profitability because of the unpredictability of the results, the long lag between research and profitable exploitation, and the relative ease of using the results of someone else's research efforts. Given these drawbacks, companies are unlikely to make the socially desirable level of R&D investment. In this situation, government has a legitimate role in covering the difference since its responsibilities encompass the broader welfare of the entire nation.

Expenditures, however, measure inputs only. To determine R&D output, or what a country gets for its money, the number of articles authored by a nation's scientists can be used as an indicator. According to a National Science Foundation report, the United States produced 33.6 percent of the articles published in scientific and technical journals worldwide in the years 1995-1997. Japan's share was second at 8.5 percent, followed by Great Britain's 8.0 percent, and Germany's 7.7 percent.[2] The ratio of Japanese to American articles was 25 percent, considerably smaller than the 39 percent expenditure ratio. This comparison suggests that in terms of scientific output, Japanese R&D is not as productive as that of other top countries.

The value of each scientific article itself can be measured by the number of times it is cited in subsequent research. In 1994, citations per Japanese paper were half the U.S. number, placing it eighteenth in international rankings.[3]

Bringing these numbers together, a crude measure of overall scientific productivity is citations per dollar spent. Thus, with R&D spending of 40 percent of the U.S. level, scientific output of 33 percent, and citations per article of 50 percent, Japan gets only two-fifths the results of American science resources.

Counting citations, admittedly, may result in a biased indication of the scientific worth of Japanese research. First, for obvious reasons, scientists tend to cite their own work and that of their colleagues working in the same country. Second, scientists outside of Japan may be unfamiliar with the output of researchers there because of language and geography. American authors, for example, cited their colleagues 67 percent of the time. Indeed, researchers from each of the 31 countries surveyed by the NSF cited other scientists doing work in the same country to a disproportionate degree.

However, almost all countries cited U.S.-authored articles at an even higher rate than their own. Since the United States is the largest producer of scientific articles, the high citation frequency of its articles is not surprising. Foreign citations of U.S. scientific literature exceed the U.S. world share of articles in most fields. An exception was Japan, where Japanese and U.S.-authored articles each accounted for 35 percent of the citations in 1997. The only other countries to cite their own literature as much as they did the American were Pakistan, Nigeria, and Russia.[4]

These figures arguably are irrelevant. The chief feature that distinguishes Japanese R&D is neither its scale nor its considerable vigor but its orientation toward business, especially manufacturing. This characteristic can be seen in the sources of R&D funding. As shown in table 5.1, industry contributed five percentage points more to national R&D than did the American private sector. Ten years earlier, the difference was fifteen percentage points as U.S. defense was a larger contributor during the Cold War years. The contrast is even greater for R&D work performed by industry, which in Japan is paid for almost entirely by business itself.

**Table 5.1: Sources of R&D Finance
in Japan and the United States, 1999 (percent)**

	Japan	United States
Total R&D Financed by:		
Industry	72.2	66.8
Government	19.5	29.2
Industry R&D Financed by:		
Industry	98.6	81.4
Government	1.2	18.6

Source: Organization of Economic Cooperation and Development

Despite many apparent similarities in the overall distribution and performance of R&D in the two countries, the high proportion of business financing in Japan has a significant impact on the kind of work done there. A 1985 survey of two hundred matched, large, science-oriented firms in each nation by Edwin Mansfield of the University of Pennsylvania identified the activities emphasized by each company in their innovation spending. The Japanese respondents put almost two-thirds (64 percent) of their money into R&D that improved manufacturing processes. The American participants devoted only half that effort (32 percent) to process R&D. They focused 68 percent of their innovation spending instead on new products; Japanese firms earmarked just 36 percent for these activities.[5]

The business orientation of Japan's R&D was correctly identified in the past as the foundation of the country's technological strength. Now, that slant is a growing problem. In advanced countries, the linkages between science and the economy appear to have intensified to such a degree that the practical orientation of much of Japan's scientific community and the acknowledged weaknesses of its basic research and university science may retard productivity growth in the future.

Links between Science and the Economy

Many studies have linked science to economic performance. One scholar aggregated the available stock of scientific knowledge by cataloging the post-1908 worldwide dissemination and use of articles in nine scientific disciplines, assuming an annual obsolescence rate of 13 percent based on previous studies. The study estimated the effect of this measure of scientific knowledge on industrial productivity in each of eighteen U.S. manufacturing industries according to the number of scientists working in them. From 1966 to 1980, scientific knowledge was estimated to have contributed about 0.5 percent annually to productivity growth, or about two-thirds of the total increase. The time elapsed between the creation of knowledge and its peak effect on productivity averaged about twenty years. In the computer and engineering fields, however, the lags were only ten years, reflecting the more applied, less basic character of research in these areas.[6]

Another way to assess the impact of science on the economy is to examine a sample of countries whose spending on R&D varies across nations and over time. Typical of this genre is a recent study published by the National Bureau of Economic Research that included thirteen of the more affluent countries belonging to the OECD. Again, the authors focused on the effects of R&D on productivity, compiling the R&D stock from annual spending converted at purchasing power parity. The estimates for the 1971-1990 period then were changed into rates of return. The return on a country's own R&D was a substantial 51 percent in the seven largest countries and 63 percent in the smaller ones. Such a high return on research spending, much greater than the yield estimated for physical capital, is not out of line with the results of other studies. The NBER paper also examined the spillover effects of R&D performed in other countries. The impact of foreign R&D on American productivity was equal to some 40 percent of the effect from domestic R&D. The comparable Japanese figure was 20 percent.[7] This finding suggests that the United States makes greater use of foreign R&D than its competitors, an outcome that appears in several other studies.

Edwin Mansfield examined the dependence of new commercial products and production processes on academic research in a late 1980s survey of sixty-six firms randomly chosen from a larger group known to include major R&D performers. The survey asked the subject companies to list five academics whose work had contributed the most to their firms' technology. More than three hundred researchers were named, the majority of whom were on the faculties of leading U.S. research universities. Mr. Mansfield then interviewed the academics to determine the sources of their funding. Almost all had received government support, two-thirds of which came from the National Science Foundation. A statistical analysis suggested that overall faculty quality correlated well with the frequency with which the companies in the Mansfield study cited individual academics. Proximity to the company also was an important predictor of being noted by a particular firm.[8]

Some of the most compelling research on the increasingly tighter links between academic science and commercial activities has come from the work of Francis Narin, president of CHI Research. His work has focused on citations contained in corporate patents filed in the United States, almost half of which were from foreign sources. The main information extracted from the patents was the front-page citations to prior art, which the issued patent is presumed to improve on. Citations are previous patents and nonpatent references such as scientific journal articles. Experts on the use of patents believe that citations are a good source for uncovering the antecedents of invention.

In one study, Mr. Narin selected for analysis the 397,660 patents issued in the United States in the 1987-1988 and the 1993-1994 periods. These patents included references to 175,000 scientific articles in journals listed in the Science Citation Index. Researchers selected for further analysis papers published in the eleven years prior to the patent filings, a process that resulted in 40,000 papers in the earlier time span and 104,000 in the later period. The 144,000 articles were matched against the Science Citation Index to obtain information on authors and their affiliation. The number of articles was further limited to those with at least one American author. The remaining 45,000 articles formed the core for further examination.[9]

Including additional patent data from previous studies, researchers found that U.S. corporate patent citations to science articles jumped more than three times between 1985 and 1995. Patents from other countries showed similar rates of increase, but the scale of American science references was considerably greater than for other countries. Vis-à-vis Japan, the difference was almost threefold (see table 5.2).

As was noted earlier, every country tends to cite its own literature disproportionately. Thus, German-to-German patent-to-paper citations were 2.4 times as frequent as would have been expected based on the number of German publications. At 4.5 times its relative publication frequency, Japan's rate of listing its own scientific literature was the highest among the five countries studied. U.S. inventors cited the American literature less and foreign literature more than their counterparts. Such openness belies the accusation that corporate America has a "not invented here" attitude.

Table 5.2: Science Citations per U.S. Patent by Patent Country of Origin and Field, 1985 and 1995

	All Fields		Chemicals		Drugs, Medicines		Electrical Components		Scientific Instruments	
	1985	1995	1985	1995	1985	1995	1985	1995	1985	1995
United States	0.39	1.44	0.94	4.63	3.05	11.61	0.53	1.28	0.58	1.72
Great Britain	0.30	1.12	0.68	2.50	1.33	5.26	0.44	1.20	0.39	1.35
France	0.25	0.64	0.32	1.05	1.24	2.49	0.54	0.79	0.31	1.02
Germany	0.18	0.54	0.44	1.34	0.97	3.54	0.44	0.98	0.24	0.55
Japan	0.17	0.50	0.44	1.28	4.06	3.26	0.31	0.69	0.13	0.42

Source: Narin, Hamilton, and Olivastro, "The Increasing Linkage," 320-21.

The authors of cited articles published in 1988, the peak citation year for patents filed in 1993-1994, worked at the most prestigious universities and laboratories. Several corporate laboratories ranked high on the list in certain technologies, but almost three-quarters of all cited studies had been supported by public sources in the United States and other countries (see table 5.3).

Table 5.3: Institutional Origins of Scientific Papers Cited by All U.S. Industry Patents and by IBM Patents

Citation Source	All Patents	IBM Patents
U.S. Private (including IBM)	20.4	34.4 (21.0)
U.S. Public	43.9	25.1
Foreign Private	6.3	17.1
Foreign Public	29.4	14.1
Other		9.4

Source: Narin, Hamilton, and Olivastro, "The Increasing Linkage," 328-29.

The rate of citing public institutions varied by industry, but even electrical component patents, which cited industry sources the most of all industries, public sources were just under 50 percent of all citations. Even giants like International Business Machines Corp., which has its own renowned laboratories and whose scientists have received several Nobel Prizes, relied on publicly supported science. At IBM, 40 percent of its science citations were to university research. For U.S. patents as a whole as well as for IBM, foreign sources of science funding figured prominently.

Localization of Knowledge Diffusion

Japan would not have to be overly concerned about its relatively weak science base if it easily could take advantage of the best science around the world. However, the diffusion of scientific results has a very strong local affinity. What makes the problem more serious for Japan is that it seems to be more insular than many other countries in its ability to bene- fit from foreign science. Localization can be moderated by the movement of scientists across borders, but, as will be shown, Japanese scientists do not participate in this flow nearly as much as their peers in other coun- tries.

It often is asserted that the results of basic research are available at little cost to anyone in the world with access to the latest science jour- nals. This ideal, however, is not consistent with the evidence. For exam- ple, the National Science Foundation supports much of the basic research performed at U.S. universities. CHI Research's Mr. Narin selected pat- ents held by both American and foreign companies and counted the cita- tions to NSF-supported research. Table 5.4 shows the citation rates for several technologies ranging from strongly science-based biomedicine and clinical medicine to the more applied field of engineering. American inventors dominated these citations three to seven times more frequently than foreign inventors did.[10]

Adam Jaffe of Brandeis University has studied R&D spillovers to in- stitutions beyond those conducting the original research. In one study, he examined the links between universities and industry in twenty-nine states for eight years ending in 1981. In addition to considering the spill- over within the state, he constructed a more localized measure of the geographic proximity of universities and corporate labs by narrowing the scope of the analysis to metropolitan areas. The output measure he used was the corporate rate of patenting.

Mr. Jaffe found that, within a state, industrial R&D spending was closely associated with university science expenditures. The impact of universities on company laboratories at the local level was weak, how- ever. At the state level, an increase in university research of 1 percent was estimated to increase patents directly by 0.1 percent and indirectly through the impact on industry R&D by an additional 0.5 percent. The total impact of university science within the state was several times as powerful as industry's own effort.[11]

Table 5.4: U.S. and Foreign Patents Citing NSF-Supported Basic Research, 1993-1994

Scientific Field	U.S. Patents	Foreign Patents
Biomedicine and Clinical Medicine	2,659	413
Biology	144	27
Chemistry	1,698	251
Physics	1,204	386
Engineering and Technology	656	180

Source: Francis Narin, *Linkage between Basic Research and Patented Technology* (Haddon Heights, New Jersey: CHI Research, August 14, 1996).

A follow-up study to Mr. Jaffe's used a more direct output measure than patents: the innovations attributed to U.S. firms in 1982. In other respects, the two studies were similar. Substitution of corporate innovations for patents reinforced the Jaffe findings. Significantly, the geographic coincidence of universities and research labs within a metropolitan area had a much greater effect than earlier estimated. The authors concluded that the proximity of university research to industry R&D was a powerful catalyst for corporate innovation.[12]

In a later study, Mr. Jaffe and two colleagues looked at citations to patents granted to universities and corporations. They raised the following issues: "Is there any advantage to nearby firms, or even firms in the same country, or do spillovers waft into the ether, available for anyone around the globe to grab? The presumption that U.S. international competitiveness is affected by what goes on at federal laboratories and U.S. universities and the belief that universities and other research centers can stimulate regional economic growth are predicated on the existence of a geographical component to the spillover mechanism."

To address these issues, the trio created two samples: patent applications in 1975 and 1980, including all patents assigned to universities; and samples of corporate patents chosen to match the university patents by date and technology. After collecting all citations to these patents through 1989, they concluded that 1980 patents were two to six times more likely to be cited by other patents granted in the same metropolitan area than were random patents in a matched control group. Reinforcing the message from other studies, corporations cited university patents at about the same rate as they listed other companies' patents; businesses located near a university seem to gain added payoffs from innovation.[13]

International Spillovers

The studies surveyed above demonstrate a strong tendency for science to have local effects. However, this evidence is based mainly on the American experience. Several studies have examined international spillovers, taking a direct look at Japan. For instance, Mr. Jaffe and a colleague from Tel Aviv University, Manuel Trajtenberg, examined citations from patents granted in the United States, Japan, Great Britain, Germany, and France. The pair defined a "descendant" patent as one that cited an earlier "antecedent" patent.

The central question Messrs. Jaffe and Trajtenberg sought to answer was: "Is a descendant more likely to benefit from an antecedent that is nearby geographically, from within the same institutional setting, and is technologically similar?" Their data consisted of 1.5 million citable patents granted between 1963 and 1993, 1.2 million citing patents between 1977 and 1994, and five million citations. A key finding was that the countries studied tended to cite their own patents more often than would be expected, given the distribution of patents across countries. However, the United States was the most likely to cite a foreign patent; Japan was the least likely. For example, accounting for the relative frequencies of patents by country, U.S. inventors were 72 percent as likely to cite a Japanese patent as a domestic one. Japanese inventors, in contrast, were only 33 percent as likely to cite an American patent as one emanating from Japan. Perhaps the most important result relating to U.S. economic welfare was that American inventors make and receive more citations than those in other countries do. "This may be evidence confirming the view of the U.S. as the most open and interconnected economic and technological system."[14]

The effects of domestic and international spillovers on the patenting activity of Japanese and American companies have been studied by Lee Branstetter of the University of California at Davis. From the five industries with the highest ratios of R&D to sales, he chose a sample of firms with more than 10 U.S. patents granted from 1983 to 1989; that universe included 205 Japanese and 209 American firms. Mr. Branstetter then calculated the domestic and foreign R&D pools available to each firm, defined as the sum of other companies' R&D weighted according to technological distance from the specific firm. These pools constituted the potential for spillovers that might influence a firm's patenting activity. Explaining his choice of approach, Mr. Branstetter noted: "There is considerable anecdotal evidence to suggest that Japanese firms are particularly good at monitoring R&D developments abroad. If one is going to find international knowledge spillovers anywhere, one should find them here." The central conclusion of the Branstetter study was that knowledge spillovers are primarily a domestic phenomenon. He compared his statistical findings with the results of a survey distributed to American and Japanese R&D managers that asked whether foreign or domestic research was more important. The reports from both groups indicated that domestic research was "perceived to be overwhelmingly more important."[15]

Localization through Direct Links

Since localization has been shown to be a pervasive influence in the diffusion of scientific knowledge, the mechanism that underlies this process is critical. Is it a generalized osmosis from one laboratory to another, or is there a specific process at work? Researchers at the University of California at Los Angeles have performed groundbreaking research on this question by analyzing the influence of so-called star scientists on the creation of biotechnology enterprises.

The investigators defined a star scientist as the discoverer of more than forty genetic sequences or the author of twenty or more articles reporting such discoveries through early 1990. Worldwide, 327 such individuals were identified, almost all of whom held university appointments. The United States was home to 207 star scientists, Japan 52. Great Britain had the next highest number with 30.

The UCLA researchers then investigated the links between the stars and the creation of biotechnology businesses, identifying 751 enterprise births in the United States from 1976 through April 1990. Strong localization effects were found in the United States. The emergence of biotech firms in a given year was strongly influenced by the local distribution of star scientists. These start-ups were the result of scientists who remained on faculty staffs while establishing businesses on the side or engaging in close consultations with established companies. Significantly, the presence of top-flight universities and the value of federal research grants at local universities also had as strong an effect on the creation of biotech firms as the proximity of stars.[16]

The UCLA team duplicated the U.S. study in Japan and found 277 new biotechnology enterprises. (When they included secondary locations of laboratories or plants, the Japanese total came to 416.) Only 12.3 percent of the Japanese enterprises were new firms, however, compared with 77.3 percent in the United States.[17]

Until 2000, Japan's national, publicly funded universities—the institutions with sufficient resources to play a significant role in basic research—prohibited professors from profiting from their research by consultation for pay or by starting a firm as a principal. Technology transfer was supposed to be paid for out of a teacher's salary. In addition, commercialization of any research output could require permission from the relevant ministry, thus creating another barrier to the exploitation of university research. Even with government approval, ownership of the intellectual property was unlikely to be transferred to the company in question.

Nevertheless, the UCLA researchers found that the incentives were strong enough to motivate collaboration in the biotechnology field. For example, 40 percent of the Japanese stars coauthored articles with a company scientist compared with a U.S. figure of 33 percent. Typically, firms sponsor talented employees as graduate students in top academic departments. These students expand a professor's research workforce and may bring with them corporate funding for equipment or supplies. With the student as a liaison, the academic department can assume certain research tasks for the company as an exchange for in-kind research support. Similarly, the company often provides routine but costly support for the university laboratory.

Many new biotechnology enterprises indicated that it was "understood" that they would place productive professors in "extraordinarily well-paid advisory positions after the professors' mandatory retirement." At least some biotechnology firms made unreported cash payments to important professors that were the size of annual salaries. Overall, the UCLA study noted that the incentives in Japan were workable but smaller than in the United States. The report's authors also found that the opportunity for a professor to start a biotechnology firm while still in the academic environment was "nonexistent." In the United States, there was a significant net outflow of star scientists from universities to firms. No such movement occurred in Japan.[18]

According to statistical analyses performed across geographic regions, the presence of a star scientist within a prefecture increased the probability of a start-up in the same prefecture by roughly 10 percent. Comparing the effect of stars on the formation of biotechnology enterprises in Japan and the United States, the UCLA researchers discovered that the impact was about half the American effect. This quantitative gap is consistent with Japan's institutional differences: weaker incentives for scientists to be involved in commercialization, the absence of a venture capital market, and restraints that keep professors from becoming scientists-entrepreneurs.

The UCLA researchers noted that with more than twice as many patents and products on the market, American biotech firms were far ahead of their Japanese counterparts. They also pointed out, however, that despite concerns about real barriers, Japan has done more with its science base in the creation of biotech enterprises and products than any major European country. The country's scientific talent and corporate R&D competence are, by most measures (including biotechnology advancement) second in the world.

The UCLA research illustrated the importance of the reforms underway in Japan or being considered to increase support for academic basic research, to focus it on successful investigators, and to remove the legal and institutional barriers that restrict scientists from participating in the commercialization of their discoveries. The authors concluded: "The fact that the institutional differences lead to such different patterns of economic impact is strong evidence in support of the view that technology transfer in the case of major breakthroughs involves movement of extraordinarily talented people responding to economic and scientific incentives."[19] They also suggested that in slower-moving, less complex technologies, such close relations between star scientists and industry may be less critical.

Transferring Knowledge through People

One study by the UCLA team noted that the technological transformation of an established American company they examined was achieved primarily by hiring scientists familiar with the new technology and incorporating them into the existing business structure. In fact, this particular firm's cooperation with universities was designed intentionally to recruit students working in departments where the science interested the firm.[20] Likewise, the study by the University of Pennsylvania's Mr. Mansfield of the links between academic researchers and companies found that most of the academics cited as important by the firms had students who found jobs with the companies.[21]

A central question is whether scientists and companies in Japan take advantage of the openness of American science through this kind of direct contact. Such associations can arise through the training of doctoral students, postdoctoral fellowships, university appointments, and coauthorship as well as by establishing laboratories in the United States.

According to figures compiled by the National Science Foundation, 214 Japanese students earned doctoral degrees in science and engineering in the United States in 1997. Students from the People's Republic of China, Taiwan, South Korea, and India earned ten to twenty times as many U.S. doctoral degrees in that time. Hong Kong had almost as many science and engineering Ph.D.s to its credit as Japan.[22]

Moreover, the number of Japanese doctoral recipients in science receiving degrees in 1992-1993 who worked in the United States over the next three years ranked thirteenth out of seventeen on the NSF list. Japan also had the third smallest proportion of those remaining to work in American laboratories.[23]

In 1997, Japanese scientists ranked in eleventh place according to the number of foreign-born scientists working in the United States. Japan was in eighth place on the list of countries of origin of foreign-born science and engineering faculty in U.S. higher education, just below Greece.[24] Japanese science does not seem any more cosmopolitan in terms of international coauthorship, NSF data indicate. From 1995 to 1997, the ratio of internationally coauthored scientific articles to all scientific literature coming out of Japan was 15 percent. That placed it in next to last place out of seventy countries, just ahead of the former USSR[25]

By most measures, Japan is tied into the world science community relatively weakly. One might argue that the strength of Japan's science does not require it to participate in foreign education, teaching, and coauthorship at the same rates as other countries. However, excellent science centers such as the United Kingdom, Germany, France, and Canada sent about as many or more scientists to American graduate schools and faculties as Japan, despite much smaller populations. In addition, their coauthorship rates of scientific articles are twice Japan's. The main conclusion stands: Japanese science is relatively insulated from the rest of the world.

A partial deviation from this pattern is corporate R&D. Japan heads the list of countries with R&D facilities in the United States. Of 715 foreign laboratories in 1998, 35 percent were Japanese-affiliated. However, with expenditures by majority-owned affiliates of $1.5 billion, Japanese companies ranked fifth after Germany, Switzerland, the United Kingdom, and France.[26]

Indeed, the corporate lab is the main way in which Japanese industry taps into American science. Mitsubishi Electric Corp. exemplifies this strategy. According to discussions with the head of its North American operations, the company's Cambridge, Massachusetts' lab is its premier technical establishment. It remains an open question, however, whether this approach will suffice if Japanese industry and the economy as a whole are to gain the greatest benefits from the expanding scientific base at home and abroad.

Conclusions

The increasing role of basic research in advanced industrial technology, the contribution of this type of work to corporate and national productivity, and the links between academic science and high technology industry all speak to the importance of a healthy research base for economic welfare. The role of geographic proximity in the effective transmission of research also suggests that it should occur near where it is likely to be used. The comparative weakness of basic research in Japan and the institutional impediments to its use supply a rationale for the government's policy of strengthening the performance and the institutional framework of the Japanese research system.

A word of caution may be appropriate, however. Basic research, by its nature, is an uncertain undertaking. Indeed, that characteristic provides the main argument for government involvement. The implication is that results cannot be planned. Consequently, it makes little sense to try to justify basic research by assigning concrete goals. Moreover, it often takes many years, sometimes decades, for the results of research to find economic application. (In some fast-moving areas the time scale admittedly is considerably compressed.) Because of the uncertainty surrounding results and timing, patience and long time horizons are required for the economic payoffs to be realized. These are qualities often ascribed as central to Japanese planners. Accordingly, the future for basic research in Japan may be a bright one. Alternatively, if these qualities are not as strong as they are asserted to be, the future may be somewhat dimmer.

Notes

1. Organization for Economic Cooperation and Development, *Main Science and Technology Indicators*, various years. The OECD adjusts nationally reported data for comparability purposes and uses purchasing power parity to convert currencies into common dollar values. The 1998 purchasing power parity for the yen was ¥163=$1.00.

2. National Science Board, *Science & Engineering Indicators—2000* (NSB-00-1) (Arlington, Va.: National Science Foundation, 2000) appendix table 6-56.

3. Robert M. May, "The Scientific Wealth of Nations," *Science* 275 (February 7, 1997): 793.

4. National Science Board, Science & Engineering Indicators—2000, 6-53.

5. Edwin Mansfield, "Industrial Innovation in Japan and the United States," *Science* 241 (September 30, 1988): 1771.

6. James D. Adams, "Fundamental Stocks of Knowledge and Productivity Growth," *Journal of Political Economy* 98, no. 4 (August 1990): 682, 676.

7. Frank Lichtenberg and Bruno van Pottelsberghe de la Potterie, *International R&D Spillovers: A Reexamination* (Working Paper 5668) (Cambridge, Massachusetts: National Bureau of Economic Research, July 1996), 14, 21.

8. Edwin Mansfield, "Academic Research Underlying Industrial Innovation: Sources, Characteristics, and Financing," *Review of Economics and Statistics* 77, no. 1 (February 1995): 56, 59.

9. Francis Narin, Kimberly Hamilton, and Dominic Olivastro, "The Increasing Linkage between U.S. Technology and Public Science," *Research Policy* 26 (1997): 318-19.

10. Francis Narin, *Linkage between Basic Research and Patented Technology* (Haddon Heights, New Jersey: CHI Research, August 14, 1996).

11. Adam B. Jaffe, "Real Effects of Academic Research," *American Economic Review*, 79, no. 4, (December 1989): 965-968.

12. Zoltan Acs, David B. Audretsch, and Maryann P. Feldman, "Real Effects of Academic Research: Comment," *American Economic Review* 82, no. 1 (March 1992): 366.

13. Adam Jaffe, Manuel Trajtenberg, and Rebecca Henderson, "Geographic Localization of Knowledge Spillovers as Evidenced by Patent Citations," *Quarterly Journal of Economics* 108, no. 3 (August 1993): 577, 590-595.

14. Adam Jaffe and Manuel Trajtenberg, *International Knowledge Flows: Evidence from Patent Citations* (Working Paper 6507) (Cambridge, Massachusetts: National Bureau of Economic Research, April 1998), 3, 20-23.

15. Lee Branstetter, *Are Knowledge Spillovers International or Intranational in Scope? Microeconomic Evidence from the U.S. and Japan* (Working Paper 5800) (Cambridge, Massachusetts: National Bureau of Economic Research, October 1996), 16, 24-25.

16. Lynne Zucker, Michael Darby, and Marilynn Brewer, "Intellectual Human Capital and the Birth of U.S. Biotechnology Enterprises," *American Economic Review* 88, no. 1 (March 1998): 297.

17. Michael R. Darby and Lynne G. Zucker, *Star Scientists, Institutions, and the Entry of Japanese Biotechnology Enterprises* (Working Paper 5795) (Cambridge, Massa-

chusetts: National Bureau of Economic Research, October 1996), 1.

18. Darby and Zucker, *Star Scientists*, 6, 30.

19. Lynne Zucker and Michael Darby, *Capturing Technological Opportunity via Japan's Star Scientists: Evidence From Japanese Firms' Biotech Patents and Products* (Working Paper 6360) (Cambridge, Massachusetts: National Bureau of Economic Research, January 1998), 21.

20. Lynne Zucker and Michael Darby, "Present at the Biotechnological Revolution: Transformation of Technological Identity for a Large Incumbent Pharmaceutical Firm," *Research Policy* 26 (1997): 440, 444.

21. Mansfield, "Academic Research Underlying Industrial Innovation," 63.

22. National Science Board, *Science & Engineering Indicators—2000*, appendix tables 3-23, 4-44.

23. National Science Board, *Science & Engineering Indicators—2000*, appendix table 4-44.

24. National Science Board, *Science & Engineering Indicators—2000*, appendix table 4-48.

25. National Science Board, *Science & Engineering Indicators—2000*, appendix table 6-60.

26. National Science Board, *Science & Engineering Indicators—2000*, 2-66, appendix table 2-71.

Chapter 6

International Capital Flows

The Growth of International Capital Movements

Japan's net capital exports in 2000, were greater than its combined shipments of motor vehicles and computer hardware. This large—and persistent—outflow dated back to 1981. Yet, the net figures, important as they are for some purposes, are not at all informative about the multiple sources and uses of the investments, loans, and acquisitions that comprise Japan's current account surplus. Likewise, undue focus on subaccounts and particular financial flows may blind one to the overall movements that affect such critical economic variables as exchange rates and trade balances. To gain a comprehensive view of capital flows it is necessary to deconstruct and reconstruct the current account.

International capital flows have soared globally since the early 1980s; Japan's experience fits within this broader development. In the previous decade, gross capital outflows were under $10 billion a year. Subsequently, the combination of capital market liberalization, falling rates of return on investment in Japan, and domestic savings exceeding the demands of business investment at home produced rapidly expanding outward flows. By 1989, annual gross capital outflows surged to more than $200 billion. The net flow, as recorded in the current account balance, totaled more than $100 billion throughout much of the 1990s.

The growing volume of trade in assets, like trade involving goods and services, occurs because it yields benefits to the participants. Two of the principal benefits are higher returns on foreign assets than are available on domestic investments and risk reduction through portfolio diversification. Although some may question whether Japanese investors actually have made money on their foreign investments—given some spectacular losses on major transactions—simple calculations indicate an average annual return of about 10.7 percent in dollars since 1985, significantly larger than was realized on domestic investments. (See table 6.7.) Such rate of return differentials go a long way toward explaining the several decades of capital pouring out of Japan.

Transition to Capital Liberalization in the 1970s

During the period after World War II when the written and the unwritten rules of the 1945 Bretton Woods Agreement governed international economic affairs, national domestic investment was constrained to equal national savings. Since large international capital flows could create pressures on exchange rates, governments adjusted fiscal policies to keep current account imbalances small in order to preserve the currency values fixed by the Bretton Woods accord. Moreover, exchange controls that restricted capital flows were still quite severe in Japan and elsewhere in the 1950s and the 1960s. Consequently, little private capital was available to accommodate current account imbalances. Net capital transfers remained very small well into the 1970s.

U.S. inflation rates in the late 1960s that were higher than those of America's trading partners caused the dollar to be overvalued at its fixed parity. Speculative flows of "hot" money and wider concerns about the dollar's overvaluation led the U.S. government under President Richard Nixon to abandon the fixed rate exchange system in the 1971-1973 period. The new system of floating exchange rates allowed governments to pay less attention to controlling current account imbalances. Subsequently, savings and investment could depart from equality within a country and seek balance among the world's economies.[1]

Until the late 1970s, restrictions on foreign exchange and private capital flows in Japan remained tight. The two groups formally allowed to invest abroad—insurance companies and investment trusts—had to obtain permission from the Ministry of Finance to do so. Very little overseas investment took place under the restrictive rules. These policies came under pressure toward the end of the decade from the domestic financial sector as well as from American government negotiators. Outside pressure likely had less impact than the declining domestic demand for loans. In addition, growing overseas opportunities for profitable investment became evident as other countries liberalized their financial regimes. The United States undertook substantial banking deregulation in 1979 and the United Kingdom relaxed capital controls the same year. These domestic and foreign developments generated incentives for Japanese investors to seek changes in domestic regulations.

With the economic slowdown of the 1970s, Japanese business demand for domestic loans shrank; higher cost lenders, such as insurance and investment companies, were squeezed out of the market. In 1980, the Foreign Exchange and Trade Control Law was revised. Although billed at the time as representing an about-face in the regulatory environment governing international transactions, the revamped law kept many restrictions in place. For example, strict ceilings meant that most Japanese banks still were limited in their foreign operations. MOF gradually eased these restrictions and in 1986 moved to raise the ceilings sharply. This series of actions greatly expanded the opportunities for Japanese financial institutions to invest abroad. The subsequent rapid growth in Japan's foreign asset position was driven partly by adjustments toward desired levels that previously had been off limits.

Balance of Payments Accounting

The point of departure for analyzing capital flows is the balance of payments. As standardized by the International Monetary Fund, the balance of payments is a statistical statement for a given period showing transactions categorized into several accounts: goods, services, and income between an economy and the rest of the world; unrequited or unilateral transfers (such as earnings of foreign workers sent home or official development assistance); and changes of ownership involving claims on and liabilities to the rest of the world, including monetary gold and foreign currency reserves.

Most transactions involve economic values that are provided or received in exchange for other economic values. Reflecting such exchanges, international transaction gives rise to two offsetting accounting entries. For example, an import of a good may be offset by an export as in barter transactions, by a promissory note if the purchase of the good is financed by a loan, or by the reduction of a buyer's foreign bank account.

When items are given away or are otherwise one-sided, special types of entries, referred to as unilateral or unrequited transfers, furnish the required offset.

Balance of payments transactions are aggregated into two main accounts: the current account and the capital and financial accounts. In addition, an item called the statistical discrepancy is entered to balance the total so that the credits and debits sum to zero. The current account comprises the trade balance (exports and imports of goods and services), the income balance (property and wage income), and unilateral transfers. The capital account, as narrowly defined since 1993, usually is a relatively small figure reflecting such items as debt forgiveness and the transfer of title to fixed assets. The transfer of the Panama Canal, for example, from the United States to Panama in 1999 resulted in a negative $3.5 billion entry in the U.S. capital account that year.

The financial account is the primary place to examine capital flows. Its main components are direct investment (which presumes a degree of influence over the management of a business enterprise in another country), portfolio investment in stocks and bonds, and loans by banks and nonbank enterprises. The financial account also includes government monetary and reserve transactions. For example, if the Bank of Japan enters the foreign exchange market to push down the value of the yen by buying dollars, this transaction will increase the nation's dollar reserves.

The accounting structure of the balance of payments guarantees that the current account balance equals the negative of the capital and financial account balance plus the statistical discrepancy. Because the data are collected from many different sources, there are inevitable differences between credits and debits in any given period. These discrepancies reflect inaccurate valuation, timing differences, incomplete reporting, and errors from estimating procedures. The entry necessary to balance recorded credits and debits is termed in American practice the "statistical discrepancy"—formerly "errors and omissions."

Linkages across Accounts

Another way to look at the current account is that it reflects the difference between a country's production and its aggregate consumption. The current account balance is the bottom line; it shows whether the income earned in producing the economy's output is sufficient to cover all its purchases—domestic and foreign. If there is a current account surplus, the economy typically possesses both unconsumed output and the savings to finance the sale of this excess to other countries; an economy with a deficit increases its liabilities to the rest of the world in exchange for consuming more than it produces and earns. In other words, if a country consumes more than it produces, the products and services have to come from somewhere; a foreign trade deficit is the only alternative short of miracles or theft on a grand scale. When a country consumes in aggregate more than it has earned, someone, somewhere must finance this excess consumption. Therefore, a trade deficit usually is accompanied by a capital inflow because the deficit country does not earn enough abroad to pay for all its imports; other nations finance the difference by providing loans, acquiring IOUs in the form of debt, or otherwise investing in the country.

This reasoning lies behind the statement that a current account imbalance is equivalent to a net savings imbalance. That is, domestic savings are greater than investment for a surplus economy, or are insufficient to finance investment in countries with current account deficits.

This discussion can be summarized in an equation:

$$CA = GNP - C = S - I = (X - M) + (R - P) + (T - U) = CX - CM,$$

where CA is the current account balance, GNP is gross national product, C is aggregate consumption of households, business, and government, S is aggregate savings across the same sectors, I is total investment, X is export of goods and services, M is import of goods and services, R is receipt of factor income payments (mainly from assets owned abroad), P is payments of factor income (again, mainly to foreign owners of domestic assets), T is unrequited transfers abroad, and U is unrequited transfers received from foreign sources. If the sum of the items in the current account is not zero, the imbalance must be made up by a net transfer of assets between domestic and foreign owners; this equality is represented by capital exports (CX) and capital imports (CM). Hovering over this relationship, which is true by accounting definitions, are two prices: the exchange rate and the rate of return on capital. These prices transform the accounting definitions into cause and effect relations, but at the same time are influenced by the flows. Time horizon is the critical determinant of whether the prices are cause or effect.

Table 6.1 shows the balance of payments of Japan and the United States for 1999. For comparison, yen figures are converted into dollars at the average exchange rate. Several points can be drawn from the table.

Table 6.1: Balance of Payments, Japan and United States, 1999
(billions of yen and dollars)

Account	Japan Yen	Japan Dollars	United States Dollars
Current Account	12,174.0	107.2	-331.5
Exports of goods	45,794.8	403.1	684.4
Exports of services	6,935.3	61.1	271.9
Imports of goods	-31,779.4	-279.8	-1,029.9
Imports of services	-13,085.9	-115.2	-191.3
Income receipts	21,498.4	189.2	276.2
Income payments	-15,802.6	-139.1	-294.6
Unilateral current transfers, net	-1,386.7	-12.2	-48.0
Capital, Financial, Reserves Accounts	-14,192.5	-124.9	319.8
Capital account transactions, net	-1,908.7	-16.8	-3.5
Direct investment, assets	-2,590.8	-22.8	-150.9
Portfolio investment, assets	-18,969.5	-167.0	-128.6
Loans, other investments, assets	31,906.9	280.9	-162.2
Direct investment, liabilities	1,451.4	12.8	275.5
Portfolio investment, liabilities	16,515.1	145.4	333.4
Loans, other investments, liabilities	-31,800.4	-279.9	101.7
Changes in reserves	-8,796.4	-77.4	54.4
Statistical Discrepancy	2,018.4	17.8	11.6
Gross Domestic Product (reference)	495,144.5	4,358.7	9,299.2

Notes: Yen converted to dollars at 1999 average exchange rate: ¥113.6=$1.00. Minus sign indicates capital outflow (increase in assets or decrease in liabilities).
Sources: *Survey of Current Business*, October 2000; Bank of Japan (annual data summed from monthly data).

Perhaps the first item that meets the eye is the hundred billion-dollar Japanese current account surplus and the more than three hundred billion-dollar U.S. deficit. Although American companies export more than twice the amount of goods and services as their Japanese counterparts, U.S. businesses and households import three times as much as Japanese do. Similarly, American companies in aggregate are the largest sponsors of direct investment abroad, and the United States is the largest target of direct investment by the rest of the world's business community. In contrast, a large share of Japanese foreign investments is in portfolio assets rather than in business investments.

Undue focus on just the net current account figures, which show a large outflow of Japanese capital to the rest of the world, can obscure the picture revealed by closer examination of the subaccounts, particularly the separation of assets and liabilities. A case in point is Japan's loan assets for 1999. Normally this line would show a negative amount, representing bank loans to the rest of the world. The table shows, instead, a plus figure of $281 billion. As explained by the Bank of Japan, the increase in inflows to Japanese banks was due mainly to repayments of large-volume loans made to overseas branches when the Japanese premium increased in the autumn of 1998. The Japanese premium was a higher interest rate charged to Japanese banks operating in international capital markets that emerged toward the end of 1997 and into 1998 because of the lack of confidence in Japanese financial institutions caused by the collapse of several large financial companies. To avoid paying the premium, home offices lent their subsidiaries the funds to finance their foreign lending. In addition to repayment of these intra-bank loans, overseas branch closures also caused a repatriation of funds.[2]

The reason for paying attention to these disaggregated movements is that the current account portrays the net result of myriad flows. Gross flows in one direction may depart considerably from the picture conveyed by net statistics. Despite the many different ways that the separate accounts can add up to the current account imbalance, people looking at narrow sectors sometimes generalize their particular experience. A common example is the assertion that capital flows out of Japan have dried up (the flowback of bank loans noted above is an example)—despite $100 billion-plus current account surpluses. One obvious interpretation of such a statement is that the flows crossing at least one trader's desk or the areas covered by the analyst making the comment are not what they used to be; however, the current account total is the obvious number to which individual accounts must add up.

Table 6.2 illustrates the difference between gross and net purchases between the United States on one side and Japan and all foreign players on the other. Although Japanese buyers purchased $300 billion of U.S. Treasury bonds and notes in 1999, they sold almost the same amount over the course of the year. The net flow out of Japan into these instruments was $20 billion. When all of the transactions are aggregated, neglecting the direction of capital flows, the gross total of long-term securities changing hands between Japanese and American parties was $1.3 trillion! The net flow of capital into and out of these securities, the number that makes its way into the current account, came to an outflow from the United States of $270 million—a tiny fraction of the gross flows, which largely balanced out. Turning to flows between the United States and the rest of the world, the gross value of transactions was almost $19 trillion whereas the net flows added up to an American import of capital of $360 billion, about 2 percent of the gross. Which, then, is the "real" number: the net or the gross? The answer, of course, depends on why the question is asked.

Table 6.2: Foreign Transactions in Long-term Securities with U.S. Residents by Type of Security, 1999
(billion dollars)

Type of Security	Japanese Purchases	Japanese Sales	Japan Net	Total Purchases	Total Sales	Total Net
Treasury securities	303.5	283.4	20.1	4,288.1	4,298.1	-10.0
Other government bonds	44.5	32.8	11.6	486.0	393.8	92.2
U.S. corporate bonds	11.5	5.6	5.9	368.7	208.3	160.4
U.S. corporate stocks	95.9	90.1	5.7	2,340.7	2,233.1	107.5
Foreign bonds	26.2	23.7	2.5	798.3	803.9	-5.7
Foreign stocks	154.9	201.0	-46.1	1,177.3	1,161.7	15.6

Gross value of Japanese transactions:	1,273.1
Net value of Japanese transactions:	-0.3
Gross value of all transactions:	18,558.0
Net value of all transactions:	360.0

Source: United States, Department of Treasury

Components of the Savings-Investment Balance

One approach to examining the sources of capital movements is to consider the components of the savings-investment balance, especially the sectoral breakdown among households, business, and government. Care must be taken, though, when reviewing the shifting trends not to ascribe cause and effect without a compelling logic. We know that the sum of the sectoral imbalances adds up to the national total, and we know that the difference between national savings and investment equals the current account balance. What is less clear is what is driving the balances. Is it the sum of each of the individual components, or are they responding to a broader array of forces? We will return to this issue below.

The economic downturn in the 1970s caused declining business investment demand for household savings; this was counterbalanced for a time by very large government deficits (see figure 6.1). As Tokyo worked to end its use of deficit financing through the 1980s, Japan's current account gradually moved into surplus—with its excess savings flowing overseas. A torrent of business investment during the bubble period in the late 1980s was met partly by government surpluses; at the height of this period of corporate exuberance, the current account surplus declined as domestic savers served domestic demands.

**Figure 6.1: Japan's Savings-Investment Balances
as Shares of GDP, 1970-1999 (percent)**

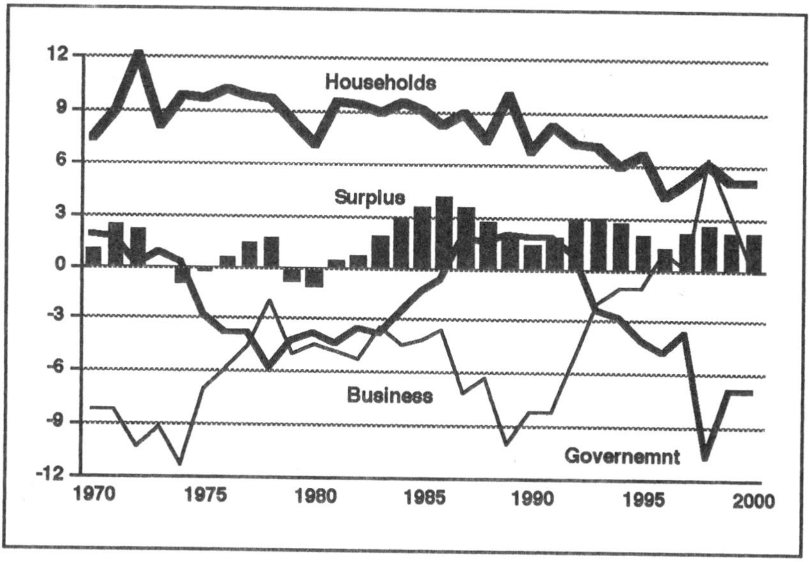

Source: Economic Planning Agency, *Annual Report on National Accounts.*

The years after the bubble saw a reversal of these trends. While net household savings as a share of GDP slowly declined, dramatic shifts occurred in the government and business accounts. As investment dried up in the 1990s, companies could finance their requirements from their own earnings, with a considerable amount left over. From being a net user of the country's savings for most of the postwar period, the business community turned into a supplier of funds to the tune of 6.5 percent of GDP in 1998. The government's balance also took a strategic turn toward larger and larger deficits, ending the decade in the red with a deficit of more than 10 percent of GDP. Despite these dramatically shifting patterns, Japan has produced a persistent savings surplus that has been available to the rest of the world for several decades. The accumulated foreign investments turned the country into the world's largest net creditor.

The shifts in the components of the American savings-investment balance have not been as extraordinary as Japan's; nevertheless, striking changes also marked the American experience. The most noticeable change was the movement of the federal government budget balance from a deficit of 4.7 percent of GDP in 1992 to a surplus of more than 2 percent in 2000. Despite this historic reversal in the demand and supply of savings, the American current account deficit has been as persistent as the Japanese surplus.

Indeed, the surplus in Japan seems to mirror the U.S. deficit, as shown in figure 6.2. The match, though, is not dollar for dollar. Japan is participating in an international game with many other players. The wave of foreign capital into the United States in the late 1990s, for example, appears to have been based on a search for safety in the wake of the 1997 Asian economic crisis plus extraordinary gains available on Wall Street.

A Closer Look at the Flows

Table 6.3 shows the breakdown since 1991 of Japan's asset flows in dollars together with its current account surplus in both dollars and yen. It is difficult to find a relationship between the current account balance and the flows of different types of capital. The main characteristic of the data is volatility. Loans, for example, gyrated as banks and other companies lent to foreign subsidiaries and customers and then liquidated these loans. The reasons given for the sharp shifts in asset movements have varied to suit the particular time and place—the Asian financial collapse and the Japan premium are examples. However, the remarkable feature of these flows is their large-scale swings while the current account aggregate remained relatively stable.

Foreign direct investment and long-term loans with a maturity greater than one year finance real business activities and are less volatile than portfolio investment and short-term loans, which can move in and out of a country with little notice. The very high ratio of outward to inward FDI has been widely cited as evidence of Japanese markets that are closed to outsiders. However, in 1999 according to the official figures, foreign business investment into Japan was more than 50 percent of the outflow.

**Figure 6.2: Current Account Balances
in Japan and United States, 1970-2000 (billion dollars)**

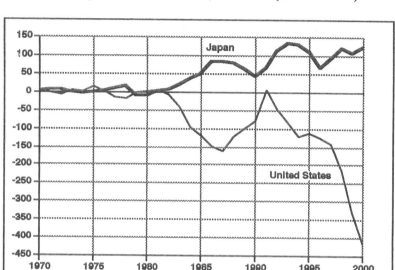

Sources: Bank of Japan; Department of Commerce, *Survey of Current Business.*

Despite the notoriety of corporate Japan's direct investment around the world, Japanese investors tend to prefer debt securities. The acquisition of debt assets is many times the volume of FDI. Over the years, some 15 to 40 percent of these investments have been placed in U.S. government bonds and notes.

Since a large share of Japanese portfolio investment has been in American securities and most of that has been placed in government debt instruments, the question has been raised: How important were Japanese buyers in financing the U.S. fiscal deficit? This issue was paraphrased by the question: What if they held a Treasury auction and the Japanese did not come?

Table 6.3: Japan's International Capital Flows, 1991-1999
(billion dollars)

Assets

Year	FDI	Portfolio		Loans	
		Equities	Debt	Long	Short
1991	-31.7	-3.7	-78.0	-15.7	32.6
1992	-16.3	3.1	-36.3	-9.5	68.1
1993	-13.9	-14.8	-46.8	-8.3	38.1
1994	-18.1	-13.8	-76.2	-8.6	-1.7
1995	-22.6	0.1	-85.1	-11.1	-155.0
1996	-23.4	-8.3	-106.6	2.4	-10.7
1997	-26.0	-13.6	-55.8	0.6	-163.2
1998	-24.2	-14.1	-101.7	24.8	-32.4
1999	-22.8	-32.1	-134.9	9.0	260.6

Liabilities

Year	FDI	Portfolio		Loans	
		Equities	Debt	Long	Short
1991	1.3	46.6	79.9	40.6	-62.3
1992	2.8	9.0	-1.1	19.4	-93.3
1993	0.2	19.7	-26.9	6.0	-16.3
1994	0.9	50.9	16.0	-6.9	3.0
1995	0.1	51.1	1.3	-0.3	104.0
1996	0.2	48.6	24.9	2.2	16.6
1997	3.2	26.4	73.7	8.0	75.3
1998	3.2	14.0	56.4	-12.1	-35.8
1999	12.8	103.3	42.1	5.7	-216.7

Net Flows

Year	Current Account		FDI	Portfolio		Loans	
	Yen	Dollars		Equities	Debt	Long	Short
1991	-9,176	-68.2	-30.4	42.9	1.9	24.9	-29.7
1992	-14,235	-112.3	-14.5	12.1	-38.4	9.9	-25.2
1993	-14,669	-131.9	-13.7	4.9	-74.7	-1.3	20.8
1994	-13,342	-130.6	-16.2	36.0	-60.2	-16.5	1.3
1995	-10,386	-110.4	-22.6	51.1	-83.8	-11.4	-51.1
1996	-7,158	-65.7	-23.2	40.3	-81.8	4.5	6.9
1997	-11,436	-94.4	-22.7	12.8	16.9	8.6	-86.9
1998	-15,785	-120.7	-21.0	-0.2	-45.3	12.7	-68.2
1999	-12,174	-106.2	-10.0	71.2	-92.8	14.7	42.8

Note: Capital outflows are negative.
Source: Bank of Japan.

However, this story line changed in 1997 when the Treasury began using a growing fiscal surplus to draw down the outstanding debt. In a period of surplus, the old question could be rephrased: What if the Japanese came and there was no Treasury auction?

**Table 6.4: Net U.S. Treasury Securities Coming to Market
and Purchases by Foreigners, 1981-2000
(billion dollars)**

Year	Net New Marketable Treasury Securities	Net Purchases by Foreigners	Net Purchases by Japanese
1981	88.7	12.7	1.3
1982	141.2	15.0	0.8
1983	199.6	3.7	2.3
1984	152.6	21.5	6.3
1985	183.6	29.8	18.9
1986	204.1	19.4	0.0
1987	111.7	25.6	0.9
1988	126.9	48.8	21.8
1989	89.9	54.2	1.7
1990	200.0	17.9	-14.8
1991	297.9	19.9	-4.1
1992	363.3	39.3	9.8
1993	235.5	23.6	17.1
1994	136.5	78.8	29.8
1995	181.2	134.1	17.0
1996	152.5	232.2	41.4
1997	-2.9	184.2	20.4
1998	-101.3	49.0	13.0
1999	-74.5	-10.0	20.1
2000	-244.3	-35.8	11.2

Source: U.S. Department of Treasury, *Foreign Purchases and Sales of Long-term Domestic and Foreign Securities by Type.*

The Treasury Department publishes statistics on net foreign purchases of marketable securities with more than a one-year maturity (see table 6.4). The volume of government debt bought by foreigners is erratic and has no obvious relationship to the amount of U.S. securities coming on the market. Foreign buyers acquired a significant share of U.S. government debt in some years—some 60 percent in 1989, for example. The average Japanese share, though, was much smaller. Japanese buyers had peaks of importance in 1988 and 1994 when they acquired around 20 percent of the U.S. government's long-term marketable instruments. In contrast, 1990 and 1991 witnessed net disinvestment by

Japanese holders. The foreign share of the Treasuries market peaked in 1996 with net foreign purchases adding up to more than the total coming onto the market that year. As the Treasury reduced the outstanding debt in subsequent years, foreigners became net sellers, although Japanese buyers continued to accumulate these assets.

By the end of 2000, foreigners held an estimated $1.2 trillion of U.S. Treasury assets. Japanese investors accounted for $335 billion. Because of the declining amount of available debt, the share of the outstanding amount owned by foreign official and private parties climbed slowly to 40 percent in 2000, about a quarter of which was in Japanese hands.

Where Do Japanese Assets Go?

The United States is the favorite parking place for Japanese assets. Since year-to-year volatility can distort broader trends, annual figures are aggregated over the five-year period 1995-1999 in table 6.5. In that period, a full 40 percent of Japan's excess savings—one-quarter of a trillion dollars—was invested in various American assets. As noted earlier, the bulk of those flows went into portfolio investments. Western Europe as a whole was more popular than the United States, with the United Kingdom the most favored investment target

Table 6.5: Japan's Asset Outflows from 1995 through 1999, by Selected Region and Country (billion dollars)

Region	Total	Direct Investment	Portfolio Investment	Loans	Other
Total	641.2	119.0	552.2	75.0	-104.9
Asia	44.1	41.2	6.9	-12.4	8.5
China	9.4	9.1	-2.8	1.3	1.9
Hong Kong	-28.0	3.8	8.3	-45.0	4.8
United States	259.2	40.1	168.6	51.1	-0.6
Western Europe	340.5	19.1	263.7	31.3	26.3
Germany	66.9	1.6	60.9	4.3	0.2
United Kingdom	154.0	6.6	80.1	46.8	20.5
France	25.7	1.3	22.3	1.9	0.2
Netherlands	40.5	11.2	26.2	-0.3	3.4
Rest of World	-2.6	18.5	113.1	4.9	-139.1

Note: Minus indicates a decrease of Japanese assets.
Source: Ministry of Finance

Despite the attention given to China, that country attracted less than ten billion dollars over the five-year period, most of it in direct investment. Hong Kong saw a decline in Japanese funds with a withdrawal of $45 billion of bank loans.

The bulk of Japanese capital placed in advanced countries was in financial assets, reflecting the highly developed capital markets in those countries. For Western Europe as a whole, less than 6 percent was placed in direct investment. For Asia and the rest of the world, however, a large proportion was directed to business investment. Economic research suggests that the possession of firm-specific assets is the most important factor driving FDI. Such specialized capabilities can yield high returns to the company possessing them, and at the same time often make it difficult to realize equivalent returns through exports or licensing other companies to produce the products.[3] Such assets include design, production, and styling know-how as well as marketing and selling skills, trademarks, and brand names, all of which give a firm's products a special cost or marketing edge.

The fact that American firms emphasize direct investment overseas whereas Japanese prefer to put their money into financial assets suggests that the motivations tend to be different in the two countries. American FDI would seem to be taking advantage of specialized skills to earn profitable returns elsewhere whereas Japanese are seeking higher returns in standardized assets than are available at home.

Japan's International Investment Position

Japan's capital exports gradually expanded the scale of the country's overseas assets. Comparisons with other major industrialized countries show Japan as holding the largest net asset position since 1991. By the end of 2000, the country's investors had accumulated gross assets abroad valued at approximately $3.2 trillion (¥346 trillion). The single largest share, almost 40 percent of the total, is in portfolio investment—equities and debt instruments such as government or corporate bonds. Bonds dominate this portion of overseas funds, accounting for almost 80 percent of Japan's portfolio investment. Somewhat less than 10 percent of the total is in direct investment.

For comparison, American foreign assets at the end of 2000 totaled $6.2 trillion at current cost (adjusting for exchange rate and price changes). As shown in table 6.6, in contrast to Japan's allocation of overseas assets, almost one-quarter of U.S. foreign capital represented direct investments. A whopping 76 percent of U.S. portfolio investment was in corporate stocks compared with only 22 percent for the more timid Japanese investor.

**Table 6.6: Distribution of Foreign Asset Stock,
Japan and United States, End of 2000 (percent)**

Type of Asset	Japan	United States
Foreign Direct Investment	9.2	23.4
Equities	8.7	29.7
Bonds	30.3	9.4
Loans	25.0	20.7
Other	26.7	16.8
Total (billion dollars)	$3,208.8	$6,167.2

Source: Bank of Japan; Harlan King, "The International Investment Position of the United States at Yearend, 2000," *Survey of Current Business*, July 2001, 13.

FDI and investments in equities depend on business profits for their returns. Since profits are more volatile and less predictable than the fixed returns of debt instruments, they generally are accompanied by higher risks. At the end of 2000, American investors had 53 percent of their foreign holdings in such relatively risky investments, whereas only 17.9 percent of Japan's total were in similar assets.

The Finance Ministry does not produce regional figures for the total stock of Japanese assets; however, it does publish regional estimates of FDI and portfolio investments, which account for about two-thirds of the total. The stock figures largely mimic the flows shown in table 6.5. The United States accounted for about one-third of the listed assets and Western Europe another 40 percent. Although low-cost countries like China or Thailand are important manufacturing centers for Japanese companies, and energy-rich countries like Indonesia have been home to large oil projects, the advanced economies have been the most important target for Japan's investments over the years.

The Profitability of Japan's Overseas Investments

Many observers have expressed doubts about whether Japanese investors have made money on their foreign holdings. The economic disasters as-

sociated with names like Rockefeller Center and Pebble Beach are buttressed by stories about Japanese-owned office buildings in Los Angeles
that were half vacant before being sold at a loss or resort properties in
Hawaii, where one hotel reputedly required 95 percent occupancy rates
at $800 per night to break even. These are potent reminders that Japanese
bankers and investors did not possess superhuman financial skills, especially during the bubble years. The fact that Japanese direct investment in
the United States did not earn positive returns until around 1990 adds to
the qualms in corporate boardrooms about the financial soundness of its
companies' overseas investment.

Anecdotes, however, do not tell the whole story. Even the bleak tale
portrayed by decades-long negative returns on Japanese direct investment in the United States is not an accurate rendition of the complete
picture. What is required for a fuller story is an estimate of rates of return
on the cumulative investments made on all types of assets in all countries. Calculations of rates of returns require two numbers: a numerator
showing income flows and a denominator describing the value of the asset stock. The choice of an income figure is relatively easy, since there is
only one. The balance-of-payments statistics report investment income
receipts from assets owned abroad and payments to foreign owners of
domestic assets. The receipts item will be the numerator for Japan's foreign earnings on its foreign assets, while the payments information will
be used to calculate the returns earned by foreign investors in Japan.

One method to measure the foreign capital stock is to accumulate the
asset side of the balance of payments. This procedure sums the gross outflow of Japanese savings to the rest of the world over an extended period.
It is a book value calculation, making no allowance for depreciation or
value changes. A potential problem with this measure is that, since it begins counting at a specific date, it ignores prior investments. However,
for Japan, this is not a serious issue because flows were quite small before the 1970s; accumulation beginning in 1970 should capture most of
the relevant information.

Another capital stock figure is the international investment position.
This measure adjusts the capital stock for price changes. It is based on
surveys rather than on the sum of earlier investments. A deficiency of
this series, however, is that Ministry of Finance data on the international
investment position are available only from 1995.

Rates of return averaged over five-year periods are shown in table
6.7. Also included is the return earned by foreigners on their investment
position in Japan. For comparison, an estimate of the rate of return on
domestic nonresidential capital is shown in the second column; these

numbers are calculated in the same way as in table 4.1, chapter 4.

Table 6.7: Estimated Rates of Return on Japan's Foreign and Domestic Assets, 1971-1999 (percent)

Period	Accumulated Foreign Assets	Nonresidential Domestic Capital	International Investment Position, Assets	International Investment Position, Liabilities
1971-74	11.3	15.9	n.a.	n.a.
1975-79	9.8	10.1	n.a.	n.a.
1980-84	11.3	6.9	n.a.	n.a.
1985-89	8.5	4.9	n.a.	n.a.
1990-94	11.4	3.8	n.a.	n.a.
1995-99	10.9	3.7	7.4	8.3

Sources: Ministry of Finance; Angus Maddison, "Standardised Estimates of Fixed Capital Stock: A Six-Country Comparison," in *Explaining the Economic Performance of Nations* (Brookfield, Vt.: Edward Elgar Publishing Co., 1995); Jong-Il Kim and Lawrence J. Lau, "The Sources of Economic Growth of the East Asian Newly Industrialized Countries," *Journal of the Japanese and International Economies* 8, no. 3 (September 1994), 259.
Note: Foreign assets were accumulated from 1970.

According to these estimates, the returns on foreign investment surpassed those in the domestic economy since the late 1970s. As the profitability of capital within Japan declined, the outside world looked like a better and better bet. By the 1990s, Japanese savers and investors could earn two to three times as much by placing their money in foreign instruments than at home.

One further item in table 6.7 deserves mention. As calculated from the international investment position, the return earned by foreigners in Japan was almost a full percentage point greater than Japanese earnings in other countries. Moreover, foreign investors generated markedly higher returns than domestic businesses did. While not reading too much into these figures, they are consistent with the contention that low profitability is not an inherent and permanent condition of the Japanese economy. When motivated by bottom-line considerations, it is possible to produce higher returns in Japan than earned by the average domestic company.

An Explanation for the Persistent Imbalances

What explains the persistence of Japan's and America's current account imbalances over several decades? Before capital flows were liberalized in the 1970s, current account imbalances often could be attributed to trade flows. The rise of imports during an economic expansion, for example, would produce a current account deficit. Attempts to preserve a fixed exchange rate, in addition to restrictions on capital flows, would then require the government to pursue a contractionary policy to cool the economy and eliminate the deficit.

Following capital liberalization, it became theoretically logical to link the current account in a cause and effect manner to the presumed sources of net capital flows: the savings-investment balance. For example, the aging of the Japanese population was projected to reduce household savings and thereby contribute to a reduction in Japan's surplus. In the United States, asserted links between the notorious double deficits of the federal government's fiscal balance and the current account in the 1980s and 1990s reinforced this line of reasoning.

However, if we try to explain either the Japanese or American savings-investment and current account imbalances by looking at their constituent components, we run into a problem. Japan's subaggregates have undergone sizeable turnabouts over the years: net household savings declined by four to five percentage points of GDP since 1980, while government and business balances each have moved a startling sixteen percentage points while reversing the direction of their flows. It is not possible to assert that any one sector has been the driving force behind Japan's trends. In the United States, despite the realignment of the government budget balance amounting to seven percentage points of GDP towards greater net savings, the American current account ballooned.

Examination of the allocation of investment flows is not much help either in explaining the current account. Japanese outward-bound foreign direct investment, for example, shot up during the bubble expansion and then fell back. Portfolio equity investment went from a small inflow (drawdown of foreign assets) in 1995 to an outflow of $32 billion in 1999. Gross long-term lending went from $11 billion inflow in 1995 (decrease in foreign lending) to a $25 billion outflow three years later. Gross short-term lending shows even larger changes: from minus to plus to minus: $68 billion outflow in 1992, $155 billion inflow in 1995, $163 billion inflow in 1997, and $261 billion outflow in 1999. No single rivulet of capital can explain adequately the tide that is rushing from Japan.

Taken together, these dramatic shifts in the savings-investment components and in the constituent parts of the financial account suggest that something else must be driving the current account imbalances. What that "something else" may be is suggested by the very notion of investment. The explanation for the movement of capital out of Japan since around 1980 most likely is due to low rates of return in Japan relative to the potential rewards elsewhere. More precisely, differences in expected risk-adjusted returns are a potent motivator for investors to move funds. Thus, despite changes in the sectoral sources of the outflow, Japanese investors have been seeking higher profitability on their assets by placing them in other countries. In the same fashion, America's persistent import of capital, despite the gyrating permutations of savings and investment behavior across households, business, and government, suggests that investors worldwide have been willingly placing their collective bets on the U.S. economy in their search for safety and high returns.

If this view is correct—namely, that differentials in rates of return on capital are the driving force behind the trans-Pacific current account imbalances—then explanations that focus on sectoral behavior or on specific types of capital or on trade flows must be deficient, if not downright wrong. Neither the aging of the Japanese population with its projected decline of household savings nor the turning around of Japanese government finances will stem the outward torrent. The only thing that would make a difference in the end is the raising of returns on domestic investment.

In the short term, trade can matter, as can price changes and a whole lot of other things as suggested by the equation previously discussed. Cause and effect can flow in any direction, and any variable can be the one to shift exogenously. However, the appropriate time horizon for these long-term trends is at least two years. Econometric analyses of capital flows find most of the action occurring at three-year horizons. Therefore, when predicting long-term capital flows and the consequent current account and domestic savings balances, look to comparative rates of return; they drive investments, which will drive the other elements of the equation. The asset price that makes all this happen is the exchange rate, which over the long run responds to the supply and demand for capital and forces the other parts of the balance of payments into alignment. The next chapter will take up this subject.

How long will differentials on expected returns continue? Forces for change can be found on both sides of the Pacific. First, the flows themselves, if unrestricted by regulation and if continued for a long enough time, would act to equilibrate the differentials. A legitimate question, then, is why they have endured for several decades? One answer is that the flows have not been unconstrained. Regulation of insurance company and pension investments, for example, places strict limits on foreign allocations. Although these limits have been loosened over the years, they continue to influence private decisions.

High returns in the United States are not necessarily ordained for all time. American businesses in the latter half of the 1990s and into the early part of the new century invested at record rates; as a percent of GDP, this capital binge approached the famously high Japanese investment rate. Some of this investment will not pay off. The literal decline of satellite telecommunications businesses together with their satellites are examples of multi-billion dollar investments burning up in thin air. How many optical fiber networks and cellular transmission towers will travel the same financial route? Meanwhile, Japanese companies entered a phase of restructuring, which means raising their returns on assets. These measures include reducing employment costs, closing excess capacity, and selling plants to other producers (at reduced prices). All of these changes to the numerator and denominator of the profits-assets ratio raise returns.

It would be imprudent to predict an imminent crossover of returns, especially across entire economies. Projections of expected risk-adjusted returns would have to take into account the profitability of real investment, the movement of exchange rates, and the relative growth prospects of two mature economies. However, massive transfers of capital across borders and the profit trends in both countries are in directions that will work to reduce a long-lasting disequilibrium in returns and the cross-border flows of capital.

Other countries have exported capital for extended periods, notably the United Kingdom in the nineteenth century and Germany, Switzerland, and the United States in the post-World War II period. Persistent exports of capital usually accompany economic maturity; historically they were associated with the world's highest living standards and productivity levels. The United Kingdom ran continuous and growing current account surpluses for more than 100 years in the nineteenth and early twentieth centuries. The continually appreciating pound sterling produced increasingly large trade deficits in the decade before World War I.[4] The British had the highest standard of living in the world at the close of the 1800s, and their economy was the most productive. They bought goods and services from the rest of the world at low prices and sold their own output at high prices. The economic welfare of the average citizen was enhanced by the ability of British investors to find investment opportunities abroad that earned higher rates of return than were available at home.[5] The only ones who suffered were exporters, since their products faced higher prices on world markets.

It could be argued that Japanese savers would be better off if their savings, which flow so freely around the world, were invested at home. Of course, the reason they are not put to work domestically is that the returns are too low. Just as the United States and other developing countries thrived because of the capital investments made in earlier centuries by the United Kingdom, the rest of the world has benefited from Japanese savings. The Japanese people, though, must wonder when they will see comparable benefits at home.

Notes

1.   Roland I. McKinnon, "The Rules of the Game: International Money in Historical Perspective," *Journal of Economic Literature* 31, no. 1 (March 1993): 24.

2.   *Bank of Japan Quarterly Bulletin*, "Japan's Balance of Payments for 1999," (May 2000): 176.

3.   Richard Caves of Harvard University, who described the concept of "firm-specific assets," notes that no single phrase captures the essence of the term. He suggests as alternatives "proprietary assets" or "intangible assets." Richard E. Caves, *Multinational Enterprise and Economic Analysis* (New York: Cambridge University Press, 1996), 3.

4.   Robert Triffin, *The Evolution of the International Monetary System: Historical Reappraisal and Future Perspectives* (Princeton Studies in International Finance No. 12) (Princeton, N. J.: Princeton University Press, 1964), 7.

5.   Barry Eichengreen, "Historical Research on International Lending and Debt," *Journal of Economic Perspectives* 5, no. 2 (spring 1991): 153.

Chapter 7

The Long-Run Behavior of the Yen

Why did the yen appreciate by more than 300 percent against the dollar between the time that floating exchange rates were introduced in 1973 and 2000? Why has the dollar depreciated? Moreover, why has neither change eliminated Japan's large, persistent trade surplus?

Exchange rates are one of the more confusing subjects of international economics—with good reason. An exchange rate is the relative price of one currency in terms of another, or the price of one country's money in terms of the other country's. It must bring into balance the supply and demand of goods as well as of assets, both monetary and real. Since financial assets exist with various future maturities, exchange rates necessarily are forward looking.

The many tasks assigned to exchange rates make their behavior complicated to explain theoretically and to predict empirically. Relationships can reverse direction over time, from being positively to negatively related. Exchange rates can mutate from cause to effect, from independent to dependent variable. In thinking about exchange rates, therefore, it is necessary to consider the context: the time horizon under consideration—a month, a year, or several years; whether exchange rates are independent or dependent; and what other factors are changing or are presumed to be remaining constant. This chapter addresses these issues in terms of the yen and the dollar.

A Postwar View of the Yen

Between 1875 and 1943, the yen traded against the dollar in single digits, depreciating gradually from 1.0 to 4.25 to the dollar. In the immediate aftermath of World War II, American occupation authorities prohibited trading in the currency. Following two years of inflation of several hundred percent, prices stabilized in 1949. As noted in chapter two, the authorities subsequently sought to place a value on the yen to enable Japan to resume foreign trade. They had only a limited number of transactions and black market prices on which to base a new exchange rate. Recognizing that any precise number was arbitrary within the broad range they had estimated as appropriate, American financial experts chose the figure of 360 yen to the dollar. This value was selected in a deliberate attempt to undervalue the currency from the best guess estimate of ¥330; but another consideration was that the number 360 would carry a symbolic significance as representative of a full circle.

The value of 360 yen per dollar lasted for more than twenty years, until the postwar fixed exchange rate regime began to break down in 1971. At a December 1971 Smithsonian Institution meeting, the Group of 10—Belgium, Canada, France, Germany, Italy, Japan, the Netherlands, Sweden, the United Kingdom, and the United States—assigned a new yen rate of 308 to the dollar. A general collapse of the fixed exchange rate regime subsequently occurred in March 1973, with the currencies of most leading economies moving to a floating system.

An exchange rate that was fixed for almost a quarter century, a period that encompassed extraordinary Japanese and European economic growth and reconstruction, could not have been the rate that free markets would have dictated, except by accident. One group of economists, for example, estimated an equilibrium exchange rate of 277 yen to the dollar for 1970, just before the end of the regime of fixed rates.[1] Alternative assumptions produced a range of estimates from ¥259 to ¥310—all considerably below the old parity. The market rate at the end of 1973 was ¥280=$1.00. Although this appreciation shocked Japan's exporters who had grown accustomed to the stability of fixed rates and the profits of an undervalued currency, in retrospect the new rate did not seem out of line with the underlying economic fundamentals.

Toward the latter part of the fixed exchange rate period, the undervalued yen contributed to the expansion of Japanese exports. However, even when floating rates came into play, the newly liberated market forces did not wholly succeed in adjusting the misalignment because Tokyo continued to exercise tight controls over capital flows into and out of the country. The distortions to the economy, however, were minimized because exports represented a relatively small proportion of national output—not exceeding 10 percent of gross national product until the mid-1970s.

The yen-dollar relationship, though, is not the only one affecting Japan's international trade. Despite the importance of the United States as a trading partner and the centrality of the dollar in the international economy, other nations and their currencies are of more than passing interest to Japan. A broader issue, therefore, is the relationship of the yen to an array of other currencies.

Figure 7.1: Nominal Trade-Weighted Exchange Rate Indices, U.S. and Japan, January 1971–December 2000 (1990 = 100)

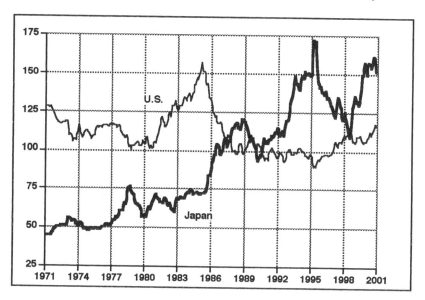

Source: J. P. Morgan

To address multilateral exchange rate issues, indices can be calculated that average the rates across a group of currencies. For example, J.P. Morgan and Co. produces trade-weighted exchange rates for many countries, using a consistent estimating method across currencies. Since its estimates are available for the United States as well as for Japan, its figures are used here (see figure 7.1). According to J. P. Morgan, from January 1971 to December 2000, the yen appreciated 343 percent or 4.2

percent annually against the currencies of eighteen other countries, close to the 3.9 percent yearly rise in value against the dollar over the same period. In contrast, the dollar depreciated against the currencies of its trading partners only by 10 percent over the entire thirty-year period. Thus, the dollar's decline against a weighted average of its major trading partners was considerably smaller than its fall against the yen.

Effect of Prices on Exchange Rates

Three relationships lie behind the theoretical and actual behavior of exchange rates over time: purchasing power parity, covered interest rate parity, and uncovered interest rate parity. The first of these describes the effects of changing price levels and the role of exchange rates in the markets for goods and services. The other two parities relate to the role of exchange rates in assets markets and will be taken up later.

Purchasing power parity (PPP) has been one of the fundamental building blocks in explaining exchange rates. It states that the value of the nominal exchange rate between two countries will vary with the ratio of the countries' price levels. The powerful reasoning behind this assertion is that, assuming zero transportation costs and no trade barriers, deviations from a PPP-based exchange rate create opportunities for riskless profits by trading in commodities. Deviations from PPP imply that the same good, after adjusting for the exchange rate, will sell at different prices in two locations. Therefore, profit-driven arbitrage—buying the good in the low-price country and selling it in the high-price one—will create pressures on the currency to adjust to the PPP value.

Of course, transportation costs, trade barriers, and inflexible prices exist in real markets. Although PPP has been deficient in explaining short-run exchange rate movements, it does describe long-term behavior quite well, with the long-term measured in periods ranging from several years to sometimes as long as centuries.[2]

In accounting for the influence of price trends on currency values, the main issue is determining just what price index or bundle of goods best reflects market forces. The price index or deflator of gross domestic product is a good place to begin. Since exchange rates measure the relative values of currencies, and currencies are used to buy the output of an economy, many analysts turn to the deflator for gross domestic product. This broad index, however, has the drawback that foreign exchange is not used to buy all of GDP, only that portion of it entering international trade. Exchange rates, therefore, are likely to be more closely related to a narrower price index than to the GDP deflator.

An index of actual export prices might seem like just what is needed. This index, though, also is deficient. It is too narrow, both theoretically and empirically. A theoretically appropriate price index recognizes that tradeable goods not only compete in foreign markets but also contend with nontradeables in the domestic market because producers of both traded and nontraded products compete for inputs like labor and capital. Both the terms of trade in international markets and the relative prices of tradeables and nontradeables at home would enter such an ideal price index.[3] In addition, narrow export price measures tell little about prices and costs of the entire tradeable goods sector—all those products that might enter world markets if the prospects were sufficiently profitable. Even if a producer is not actually participating in global markets, such potential market entrants generate competitive forces that act on prices and exchange rates.

Consequently, price indices made up from just those products that actually are exported are biased estimates of price trends among the broader class of tradeable goods. The bias is especially severe for currencies that experience persistent appreciation. Consider, for example, a country like Japan, which has experienced a more or less steady rise in the real value of its currency since around 1980. A typical industry includes producers with a range of efficiencies in the production of those goods or services entering international markets. As the yen appreciates, companies receive fewer yen for the same foreign price. Because of competitive price pressures in foreign markets, sellers are reluctant to raise their foreign prices too high for fear of losing sales. Although some companies may be able to absorb revenue reductions for a time by accepting lower profits or by tolerating the reduced sales that follow from higher foreign prices, eventually unprofitable firms would leave the market or close down their most inefficient lines. If this process continued for several years, only the most efficient producers would remain active exporters. Prices averaged across the shrinking group of surviving exporters would fall and average productivity of the survivors would rise—even though the cost structure and the productivity of the original cohort of exporting companies might have remained unchanged. Because of this selection bias, actual export prices do not fully reveal the price trends among tradeable goods. In addition, the firms remaining in the export business under such competitive pressure would be particularly well motivated to seek greater efficiencies, further skewing price indices.

Several organizations have experimented with alternative price indexes to adjust exchange rates. The type of deflator favored by many experts is based on unit labor costs in manufacturing or the price of basic manufacturing goods, partly because a large proportion of exports is of manufactured goods. Figure 7.2 shows the actual U.S.-Japan exchange rate and two adjustments to account for inflation. A base period of mid-1976, when the yen traded on average at 296 to the dollar, is used. Major trading nations went to a flexible exchange rate regime in 1973 following two years of official revaluations. The yen faced competitive pressures for the first time since the end of the immediate postwar period and was settling into market equilibrium by 1976, although restrictions still did not allow full capital mobility.

Figure 7.2: Yen/Dollar, Adjusted to July 1976 by Relative Prices, January 1974-December 2001

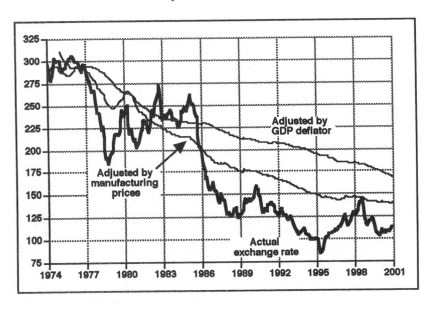

The two exchange rate estimates in figure 7.2 are produced in the same way: the July 1976 value of 296.4 yen to the dollar is multiplied by the ratio of the relevant Japanese price index to the comparable U.S. price index, both indexed to July 1976. Several points emerge from figure 7.2. The transpacific exchange rate has deviated progressively from the GDP deflator-adjusted value, primarily because of the relatively poor productivity performance of the nontradeables sector in the Japanese economy. If productivity growth is greater in the tradeable goods sector than in the nontradeables area and if these differences are not the same in other countries, GDP deflators can generate significant deviations from the actual exchange rate. One study of the years 1973 to 1983 estimated a productivity growth gap between tradeables and nontradeables of 73 percent in Japan, but only 13 percent in the United States.[4]

**Figure 7.3: Real, Trade-weighted Exchange Rates
January 1971-December 2000 (index: 1990=100)**

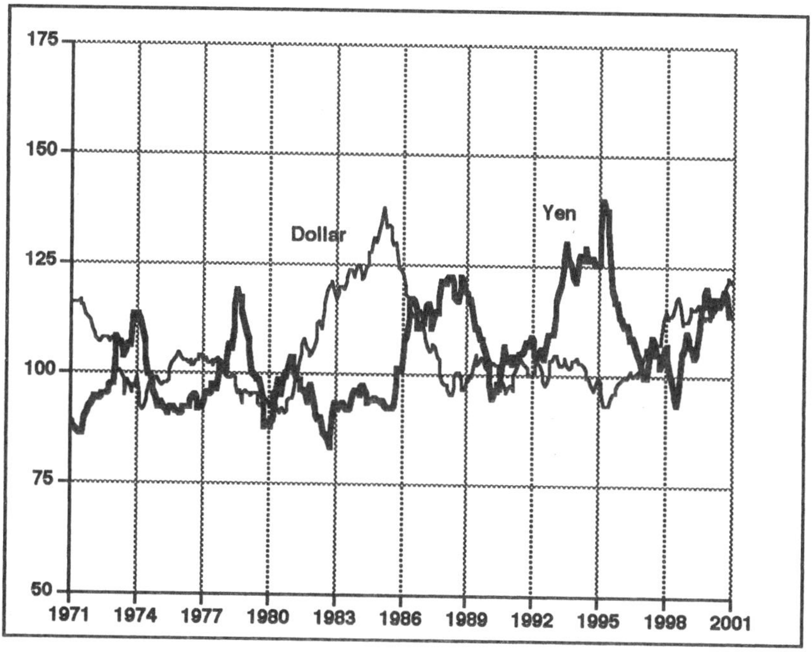

Source: J. P. Morgan

Since manufactures account for most of Japan's exports and about two-thirds of America's, the exchange rate adjusted by manufacturing prices tracks the long-run trend of the actual exchange rate. Indeed, much of the yen-dollar appreciation in the period of floating rates is accounted for by relative price inflation in manufacturing. The estimated manufacturing price-adjusted exchange rate at the end of 2001 accounts for almost 90 percent of the actual appreciation since 1976.

Figure 7.3 traces the trade-weighted real exchange rate indexes for the United States and Japan against eighteen other trading partners using core producer prices to account for aggregate price changes. A 1980s bubble in the dollar's real value shows up clearly. The yen followed with a comparable surge ten years later. However, despite considerable volatility, the longer-term trends show a slight depreciation of the dollar until the mid-1990s and a sustained appreciation of the yen, at least since 1980. From January 1980 to December 2000, the yen's trend value appreciated in real terms against the currencies of Japan's major trading partners by 1.0 percent annually on average, whereas the dollar's trend depreciation was a slight 0.17 percent.[5] The cumulative changes and volatility of the real, trade-weighted rates are significantly smaller than the movement of the nominal yen-dollar rate.

Currencies as Financial Assets

Several international financial developments have enlarged the role of currencies in capital markets in recent decades, including the gradual removal of restrictions on international capital flows, the vastly enlarged volume of global capital transactions, and the increased flexibility of exchange rates themselves.

Since a currency is a financial asset and an exchange rate is the relative value of two currencies, its value responds to the same forces that affect other assets, especially interest rates. Differences across countries in rates of return account for much of the short-term variation in real exchange rates. The reason for this linkage is that if exchange rates did not respond to changes in interest rates, arbitragers could make a lot of money. Their transactions would eliminate the arbitrage possibilities. If, for example, yen interest rates of a given maturity were lower than comparable rates on dollar assets, the value of the yen would have to appreciate over the maturity period to eliminate the arbitrage profits on the interest differential.

Two theories establish the basic relationships between interest rates and exchange rates: covered and uncovered interest rate parities (CIP and UIP). CIP states that the ratio of the forward exchange rate to the spot exchange rate equals the ratio of the home country's to foreign country's interest rates on instruments of equal risk and of the same maturity as the future contract. Spot rates are the prices of foreign currencies for immediate delivery. Forward rates are contracts for delivery at a specified future date at a price determined today.

A simple equation describes the CIP relationship:

$$F/S = (1+i)/(1+i)*$$

where F is the forward rate, S is the spot rate, (1+i) is the interest in the home market and (1+i)* is the interest in the foreign market. An important aspect of CIP is that all of the variables are current market rates. Instant arbitrage can work to remove profit opportunities.

A concrete example from the *Financial Times* (December 21, 2001) illustrates this concept. The spot rate for the yen on December 20 was ¥128.61=$1.00; the one-year future was priced at ¥125.67=$1.00, implying a 2.34 percent, one-year appreciation. In the London money market, the one-year dollar interest rate was 2.3925 percent and the interest on one-year yen instruments was 0.10438. The ratio of 1.023925 to 1.0010438 is 1.0229—a bare 0.05 percentage points from the implied appreciation in the currency futures market. Indeed, most research on covered interest parity shows that the concept has worked for the currencies of most leading economies most of the time since the mid-1980s when barriers to international capital flows were lowered.[6]

The concept behind UIP is that the ratio of the expected rate in the future to the spot rate today also should be equal to the interest ratio:

$$E/S = (1+i)/(1+i)*$$

where E is the expected exchange rate in the future. The theory of UIP asserts that today's interest rate differentials predict tomorrow's exchange rates; equivalently, the forward rate on today's market is the best predictor of the actual future value. This theory, as commonly tested, usually is inconsistent with the evidence. Not only do interest rates fail to predict future exchange rates, even the direction of predicted change often is wrong.[7]

The supposed failure of the UIP hypothesis has been so well known that a paper on the subject began: "Few propositions are more widely accepted in international economics than that UIP is at best useless—or at worst perverse—as a predictor of future exchange rate movements. This finding has been replicated in an extensive literature."[8]

This paper goes on to show, however, that most tests have been defective because the time period over which the exchange rate change was predicted and the term of the interest rate did not match. Typically, a ten-year interest rate differential is correlated with a monthly, quarterly, or annual change in exchange rates. When the authors tested ten-year exchange rate changes against ten-year government bond differentials at the beginning of the ten-year period across several currencies (including the yen), the results came much closer to those predicted by theory. For example, interest rate differentials between American and Japanese ten-year government bonds predicted 60 percent of the change in the yen's value over the subsequent ten-year period.[9]

The paper cited above explains the perverse findings of other scholars by noting that unexpected shocks to interest rates create a short-term risk premium that causes the spot exchange rate to deviate from the expected future rate. Over longer horizons, the temporary effects of the unexpected shocks fade and the results are dominated by long-term fundamentals that are consistent with the UIP hypothesis. The authors conclude, therefore, "UIP is essentially useless as a predictor of short-term movements in exchange rates."[10]

The predictive failure of the UIP hypothesis stems from an important characteristic of the short-term movement of exchange rates. Exchange rates vary according to a random walk—more or less. This last qualifier is important because if random walks completely governed behavior, no prediction or explanations of trends would be possible, which is not the case. A variable exhibits random walk properties when its change is not related to its level. The fact that a price may be high (or low) today yields no information about what it may be tomorrow. Random events and shocks hit exchange rates minute by minute, each of which is independent of what transpired minutes, days, or weeks earlier. Exchange rates are not unique in this regard; many other economic variables, including stock market prices, exhibit random walk behavior. One implication of this observation is that a random number generator predicts short-term movements as well as any analyst or economic model.

Despite the short-run unpredictability of exchange rates, a growing volume of research shows that movements over the longer run are more satisfactorily explained. Depending on the particular exchange rate and explanatory model, the long run can be one to four years before predictability emerges. In one study, the average error from a standard model used to estimate the yen-dollar rate was 20 percent less than a random number prediction over a two-year horizon, 30 percent better over three years, and more than 40 percent better over a four-year time frame. The conclusions of this study are consistent with findings from other scholars: "While short-run horizon changes tend to be dominated by noise, this noise is apparently averaged out over time, thus revealing systematic exchange-rate movements that are determined by economic fundamentals. These findings are noteworthy because it has long been thought that exchange rates are unpredictable."[11] Another study using quarterly data barely was able to beat a random model for a prediction three months ahead, but it did a much better job at one-year to two-year predictions.[12]

Jerome Stein of Brown University models the U.S. exchange rate as responding to a twelve-quarter moving average of the fundamental factors; over the moving three-year period, short-term disequilibrium effects work themselves out. Mr. Stein writes, "Although in the short run the exchange rate does not reflect the fundamentals, it does so in the longer run. As the time horizon lengthens, market pressures push the real exchange rate toward the natural real exchange rate."[13]

One class of models that has been successful in predicting exchange rates over longer periods combines two ideas mentioned above: purchasing power parity and uncovered interest rate theories. As experience with floating rates accumulated in the 1970s, scholars pulled many older ideas out of their tool chests to try to explain the recent exchange rate movements. The data forced them to modify some of their first approaches—for example, the assumption that price levels adjusted rapidly to interest rate and exchange rate changes. Instead, later theories incorporated the evidence that price levels were sticky and took time to adjust. In addition, they recognized that PPP did not describe exchange rates on a day-to-day basis. However, deviations from a PPP-determined exchange rate could be explained by real interest rate differentials between comparable instruments in two economies.[14]

Real-interest differential models find that exchange rates rise (fall in value, depreciate) as a function of price level differences between the home and the foreign country, and fall (rise in value, appreciate) with differences in real interest rates. (Remember that if it takes more yen to buy a dollar, the yen is falling in relative value, or depreciating.) Figure 7.2 was proof of the long-term applicability of PPP to the yen-dollar rate. Differences in the inflation rates in the two countries were associated with most of the rise of the yen's nominal value since floating began in the 1970s. Interest rate differentials help to explain at least some of the bubble in real dollar exchange rates in the 1980s. The U.S. budget deficit rose from 0.6 percent of GDP in 1979 to almost 5 percent three years later. The enormous demand for borrowing that was required by this deficit drove up real interest rates, which led to the appreciation of the dollar.

Some analysts have found a tendency for long-term interest rates to converge due to the ability of capital to move easily across national borders in response to rate-of-return differentials.[15] Because of the relative size of the U.S. economy and the huge stock of dollars, it turns out that interest rates in Japan and the other advanced countries are more sensitive to the American economy than vice versa.

Foreign exchange experts in Japan, however, do not seem to base their predictions on such findings as those noted above. The Ministry of Finance sponsored bimonthly surveys from 1985 to 1993 of forty-four experts working for banks, brokerage houses, and other private financial companies. Analysis of these surveys indicated that they expected recent exchange rate changes to continue for about three months and then reverse in six months to what was felt to be a long-term norm. Because of their failure to look at fundamental forces, their expectations were "spectacularly wrong" on occasion.[16]

Exchange Rates, Trade Balances, and Capital Flows

Exchange rates affect trade flows because they determine the prices of foreign goods in domestic markets. Typically, it takes from one to two years for exchange rate changes to work themselves out in product markets. At first, in fact, the effects are in the "wrong" direction because of the so-called J-curve path of adjustment. The J-curve describes the lag of a year or more that it takes for the quantities of goods that are bought and sold to respond to exchange rate shifts; long-term contracts, habit, and such other factors as product durability contribute to the persistence of past patterns and a subsequent response lag. Immediately, though, buyers in a country with a depreciated currency face higher prices; until they have time to adapt, the value of their imports increases After a while, though, when consumers have had time to adjust their purchasing decisions, the quantity of purchases declines. Thus, the J-curve: first in one direction and then in the other.

The other main influence on imports and exports in the medium term is national income. As income rises at home, imports increase; conversely, exports expand with rising foreign incomes. Thus, the chief medium-run determinants of trade are real exchange rates and income levels.

However, the factors that determine the *difference* between exports and imports, or net trade balances, are often independent of the separate export and import relationships described above, especially over time horizons of several years. Trade balances can be analyzed by considering the links between trade and capital flows as described in the balance of payments. Repeating the discussion from the previous chapter, the balance of payments and the current account balance can be described by the equation:

$$CA = GNP - C = S - I = (X - M) + (R - P) + (T - U) = CX - CM,$$

where CA is the current account balance, GNP is gross national product, C is aggregate consumption of households, business, and government, S is aggregate savings across the same sectors, I is total investment, X is export of goods and services, M is import of goods and services, R is receipt of factor income payments (mainly from assets owned abroad), P is payments of factor income (again, mainly to foreign owners of domestic assets), T is unrequited transfers abroad, and U is unrequited transfers received from foreign sources. The transfer of assets between domestic and foreign owners is represented by capital exports (CX) and capital imports (CM).

The forces determining net capital flows tend to be based on deep and slow-moving characteristics of an economy. Consequently, capital flows determine in a causal way the trade balance when considered over the course of several years. Care must be taken, therefore, when making projections of exports and imports, to assure their consistency with the longer run determinants of the capital balance.

Persistent savings shortages lead to a buildup of foreign debt or a reduction of foreign assets. Net receipts from foreign assets decline. In order to accommodate this change, the borrowing country either has to export more or import less, which implies that the value of the nation's currency must depreciate. Note that it is not necessary for a country with foreign holdings to completely reverse its position and become a net debtor for these effects to occur. It only is necessary to move in the indicated direction. Of course, the reverse of these arguments is true for a surplus country.

It may be useful to repeat this argument in a somewhat different manner. The initial assumption is that the saving-investment balance, largely independent of trade flows, generates the current account balance. The current account is allocated between trade and income from foreign assets, ignoring the other—usually small—items. If a country receives more income from the assets that it owns abroad than it pays out, as Japan has done since around 1980, these return flows can be thought of as competing with exports for the available capital flows. As estimated in table 7.1, the exchange rate responds to the incoming flow of income by appreciating, which has the effect of reducing exports and increasing imports. Trade is the balancing item in this relationship because the other elements are predetermined: domestic savings and investment respond to demography, growth, and rates of return—all of which are slow to change; net asset income is based on the cumulative value of property that has built up over decades, also a slow-moving variable.

**Table 7.1: Exchange Rate Adjustments to
Japanese and U.S. Asset Income Flows, 1980-1999**

Japan

Year	Exports (trillion ¥)	Imports (trillion ¥)	Asset Income (trillion ¥)	Yen Adjustment (percent)
1980	32.9	35.0	0.2	0.4
1999	55.0	45.9	6.4	8.6
Net Adjustment				8.2

United States

Year	Exports (billion $)	Imports (billion $)	Asset Income (billion $)	Dollar Adjustment (percent)
1980	293.9	279.2	30.1	5.8
1999	1,042.2	1,391.0	-12.3	-0.5
Net Adjustment				-6.3

The changes in exchange rate required to accommodate asset income (itemized in table 7.1) are estimated in a rough way from the following equation: $e = (I)/(aX - bM)$, where e is the percentage change in exchange rates, I is net asset income, a is the export price elasticity, X is exports, b is the import price elasticity, and M is imports. Between 1980 and 2000, the dollar depreciated an estimated 6.3 percent against its trading partners as influenced by America's changed asset position. Since the forces acting on the yen were in the other direction, that currency was pushed up in value by an estimated 8.2 percent. Putting these two estimates together, the yen's appreciation against the dollar, as driven by long-term capital flows, comes out to 14.5 percent.[17]

What Should the Yen's Value Be?

Assertions that the yen or the dollar is too low or too high imply that they ought to be different. Is there any validity to the idea that, somehow, current rates are wrong? Although economic theory presumes that markets make use of all available information in determining prices, some participants must be on the wrong side of history. Moreover, all the information appearing on traders' computer screens can move prices in bewildering and seemingly random ways. Indeed, the correlation of the value of the yen/dollar exchange rate with its change from one day to the next is 0.020 for the 2620 observations of the 1990s. This correlation is about as close to zero as one could find in a random sample. Thus, today's change in an exchange rate bears no relationship to whether it is low or high.

Table 7.2: Exchange Rate Equation, Yen per Dollar,
Monthly, January 1980-December 1999

Independent Variables	Coefficient	t statistic
Constant	0.388	4.98
Δ Yen (-1)	0.154	2.59
Yen (-2)	-0.074	4.93
Δ Price ratio	3.210	6.10
Price ratio (-1)	0.100	2.62
Δ Real interest ratio	0.097	0.40
Real interest ratio (-1)	0.178	2.94
Japan asset income adjustment (-12)	-0.125	0.76
U.S. asset income adjustment (-12)	0.320	1.90

Notes: Dependent variable: Δ yen; all variables in natural logarithms; month lags in parentheses; R^2 = 0.383; adjusted R^2 = 0.361; Durbin-Watson statistic = 1.86.

However, as has been noted, longer-term relationships seem to be able to break out of the random walk mandate of unpredictability. A simplified version of the real-interest differential models found in the literature can be used to estimate the effects of these variables. I extended this model by adding asset income flows into the standard equations. Table 7.2 shows the results of an equation using monthly data from January 1980 to December 1999. A start date of 1980 was chosen because capital markets in Japan were sufficiently liberalized by then to allow capital to flow into and out of the country. The estimation of the exchange rate included the following independent variables: the exchange rate itself lagged one and two months; current and one-month lagged values of the ratio of Japanese to U.S. manufacturing prices; current and one-month lagged values of the ratio of U.S. to Japanese real interest rates on three-month certificates of deposit; and twelve-month lagged values of the currency adjustments dictated by asset income flows for the yen and the dollar (as shown in table 7.1).[18] The natural logarithm of all the variables

was used in the estimations. In order to deal with the high degree of auto-
correlation, first differences were taken of the original lagged version of
the equation (except for the two asset income variables).

**Figure 7.4: Actual and Predicted Yen/Dollar Exchange Rate,
January 1981-December 1999**

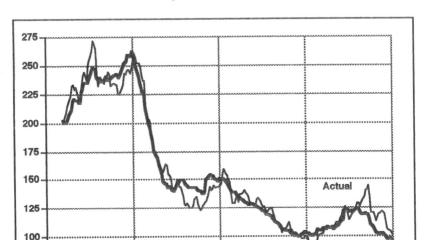

All the coefficients have the expected effects; however, the asset income adjustment factor for Japan, is not statistically significant. The estimated value of the yen shown in table 7.2 can be simplified by refor-
mulating it and combining the lagged variables:

$$Yen = 0.4 \, (yen_{t-1})^{0.9} \, (p_j/p_u)^{0.1} \, (1+r_j)/(1+r_u)^{0.2} \, (1+a_j)^{-0.1} \, (1+a_u)^{0.3},$$

where p_j and p_u are the Japanese and U.S. manufacturing price indices, r_j
and r_u are the real interest rates, and a_j and a_u are the percentage adjustments in exchange rates stemming from asset income flows as calculated
in table 7.1.

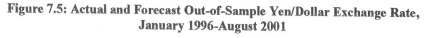

Figure 7.5: Actual and Forecast Out-of-Sample Yen/Dollar Exchange Rate, January 1996–August 2001

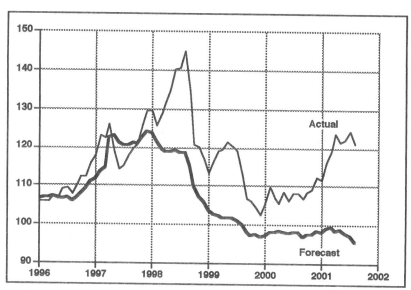

Note: Out-of-sample forecast from January 2000.

A dynamic estimation of the exchange rate from the equation in table 7.2 is shown in figure 7.4 (because of the twelve-month lags on two variables, the estimate shown in the figure started in 1981). First differences are calculated from the equation and added to the actual value of December 1980 and subsequent predicted values. Since all lagged values of the dependent variable are estimates from the equation itself, only the independent variables are involved in this projection. The figure suggests that the interest rate variable accounts for most of the dollar's bubble in the early 1980s, except for several months in 1982.

This same equation was used to make an out-of-sample forecast from January 2000 through August 2001. Figure 7.5 plots the actual value of the yen, the in-sample estimate through the end of 1999 and the out-of-sample forecast period from January 2000. The actual value of the yen was weaker than predicted from early 1998. The equation predicts that the exchange rate should have been below ¥100=$1.00 after mid-1999. What drives this forecast is the falling price level in Japan as well as burgeoning asset income flows into the country; several years of zero interest rates acted in the other direction.

The yen's weaker-than-predicted performance for the past several years is notable. Apparently, other forces than those accounted for in the equation are driving the yen's value. One commonly heard speculation is that there has been capital flight from Japan. Long-term capital movements will be picked up in the equation by real interest rate differentials; however, the estimation is likely to miss speculative flows. The data, though, are inconsistent with the view that capital flight is causing yen weakness. The most inclusive measure of capital movement—the current account surplus—moved in the other direction. From 1998 to 2001, it fell by one-third, from ¥15,800 billion to ¥10,800 billion (in then-year dollar terms, a drop of $32 billion). The components of the capital flows produce few suspects that hold up to detailed scrutiny. Some are up and others down. For example, foreign portfolio investment into Japan fell very sharply between 1999 and the end of 2000. However, Japanese portfolio investments in other countries fell by similar amounts; net portfolio flows were marked by sharp year-to-year fluctuations with little apparent trend. Therefore, despite what a Wall Street trader may find crossing his desk, there was not a net flight of capital from Japan.

Do official exchange-rate interventions explain the weak yen? A recent literature survey finds that the evidence "does suggest a significant effect of official intervention on both the level and the change of exchange rates."[19] The authors propose an explanation for intervention effectiveness: its role in remedying a coordination failure in the foreign exchange market.[20]

> The foreign exchange market may be subject to irrational speculative bubbles brought about by important noneconomic factors. . . . Once the exchange rate has moved a long way away from the fundamental equilibrium, it may be very hard for individual market agents to act to bring about a reversion of the exchange rate, even though they may strongly believe it to be misaligned, because of a coordination failure. . . . In practice, once the exchange rate gets stuck into a trend, it takes a great deal of courage for an individual trader to attempt to buck the market. Publicly announced intervention operations can here be seen as fulfilling a coordinating role in that they may organize the "smart money" to enter the market at the same time.

Japan's Ministry of Finance has been an explicit believer in this theory. This was the policy described to me in 1999 by Eisuke Sakakibara when he was the MOF official in charge of exchange rate policy. Intervention would not drive an exchange rate away from its fundamental value, he admitted. However, it could reduce overshooting, particularly if a currency were too strong. This policymaker stressed that a country on the strong side of an exchange rate could take the lead on intervention by selling its own currency, of which it has an almost unlimited quantity. At the same time, however, he acknowledged how tough it is to distinguish overshooting from warranted market reactions. The practical answer to that problem is easy, this strategist said. If markets do not react to intervention in the expected direction, then the market value was correct and the MOF was wrong. If markets respond as anticipated, then the officials were right.

The MOF has published the details of its interventions from 1991 through the end of September 2001. As revealed by the data in figure 7.6, the Japanese government's basic approach seems to have been to keep the yen at around 120 to the dollar.

Figure 7.6: MOF Exchange Rate Interventions (billion ¥) and Value of Yen (¥/$), 1991-2002

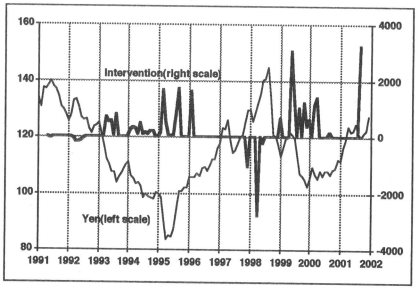

However, as time passed, the underlying fundamental rate appreciated, apparently unnoticed by the Japanese government. Looking at interventions along with the residual from the yen equation described earlier emphasizes this point. The residual can be thought of as representing departures from long-run equilibrium. The attempts by the MOF to bring the exchange rate into line with fundamentals is shown in figure 7.7, which plots monthly interventions against the residual from the equation. In 1993, 1995, and 1998, the evidence is consistent with intervention working against unsustainable market prices as the MOF attempted to correct departures from fundamentals. After 1999, however, interventions simply tried to keep the yen weak, regardless of fundamentals.

Figure 7.7: Official Interventions in Exchange Market (billion ¥) and Residual from Yen Equation (yen), 1991-2002

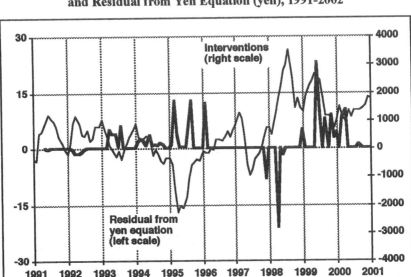

For how long can the MOF fight against the long-run appreciation of the currency? Traders seemed to have accepted the belief that the MOF had placed a floor under the yen at around ¥120=$1.00. Anything that changed this belief could send the currency moving very quickly to its long-term value. For example, the U.S. administration might suggest that the yen was undervalued and that Japan's economic policies were not moving sufficiently fast enough or in the right direction to warrant accepting a weak yen policy. We then could see traders quickly revise their expectations. If the equation has any predictive power, almost any shock could send the yen headed toward 100 to the dollar.

Closed Markets and Trade Balances

The arguments developed above to explain exchange rates and trade balances have not met with universal acceptance. While it must be true that aggregate consumption minus aggregate income (or savings minus investment) equals the current account imbalance because of accounting definitions, some writers object to the line of causation laid out above. Their argument runs in the other direction: trade imbalances cause macroeconomic distortions. Sometimes this is taken even further by the assertion that closed markets overseas and open markets in the United States have caused the American trade deficit, especially with Japan.

There are several responses to this line of reasoning. First, critics are correct to note that the aggregate macroeconomic savings-investment relationship says nothing about a bilateral trade balance. Given a shortage of savings, the United States will have a trade deficit with the rest of the world; specific countries are not identified by the theory. However, a less-than-rigorous argument suggests that if the United States has a large trade deficit, and if Japan runs a large trade surplus, and if each country is among the other's largest trade partners, then the United States is likely to have a trade deficit with Japan.

An argument against the notion that closed markets, especially in Japan, cause the American export-import gap is that, since the early 1980s, Japanese markets (and most others around the world) have opened in numerous ways even as U.S. markets became more restricted in the 1980s through a variety of protectionist measures, including the so-called voluntary restraint agreements covering cars, machine tools, and other products. Thus, U.S. trade deficits were burgeoning at the very time in the 1980s that markets were opening abroad and becoming more closed at home.

However, there may be occasions in the short run of a few months when causation runs from trade flows to savings and investment. For example, a decline in the price of petroleum will have the effect of reducing the value of Japanese imports and increasing its trade surplus. The falling prices of gasoline and other refined petroleum products will allow companies and consumers to spend less on consumption than they had anticipated and savings will increase. However, over the longer term, these savings are unlikely to persist as people recognize their good fortune. Consumption will rise to absorb the excess savings; the trade surplus will decline to its long-term equilibrium level based on the nation's desired savings-investment pattern.

The central issue of whether a trade imbalance is the cause of a savings-investment imbalance, or vice versa, is whether exchange rates affect domestic savings and investment. One survey of the research literature suggests that for the United States and other large countries, including Japan, savings and investment are "either independent of the real exchange rate or relatively unresponsive to it." Conversely, exports, imports, and the current account do respond to real exchange rate changes.[21] Another survey of the research literature found that U.S. and Japanese domestic savings and investment decisions are relatively unaffected by exchange rates over the long run.[22] This evidence indicates that the explanation for the current account balance is determined mainly by local factors and is not to be found in asserted closed markets.

Answering the Central Questions

With this background, the questions posed at the beginning of the chapter can be seen to have a web of interlocking responses. What has caused the persistent real appreciation of the yen and the parallel depreciation of the dollar and what is behind the continuing trade imbalances of the United States and Japan? Savings-investment imbalances lead to trade imbalances; these are financed by capital flows that generate holdings of foreign assets. The latter, in turn, produce property income, which requires exchange rate revaluation to induce the corresponding shifts in imports and exports and thus keep trade and capital flows in equilibrium. Rather than being paradoxical, trade imbalances and the long-run appreciation of the yen are related as cause and effect. The yen has risen in real terms and the dollar has fallen *because* of each country's respective trade surplus and deficit. Different inflation rates in the two countries account for most of the change in nominal exchange rates.

Although most people accept the idea that an appreciating currency will reduce a trade surplus by encouraging imports and by raising the price of exports, the possibility that continued surpluses will cause a belated increase in the value of a country's currency is not as familiar. Policymakers and commentators frequently fail to recognize that short-run and long-run effects may be reversed. An example of a market-opening measure in Japan, for example, illustrates the difference between the long and short run. In the mid-1980s, Tokyo removed its de facto ban on imports of satellites by the business sector. Consequently, American manufacturers have won contracts valued at several billion dollars to supply satellites to Japan. Other than making U.S. satellite producers happy, what other effects might this move have produced?

Savings and investment trends in both the United States and Japan would not be expected to vary because of these additional trade flows; the current account would therefore remain unchanged. Something though would have had to balance increased U.S. exports of satellites. The increased Japanese demand for foreign goods as reflected in higher satellite purchases would drive down the yen and make the dollar's value increase. Consequently, other American exporters would have had a slightly more difficult job selling overseas, but U.S. importers could buy at lower prices. The current account thus would have been balanced by a combination of exchange rate-driven trade adjustments little contemplated by U.S. negotiators who took pride in the results of their negotiating skills.

All of the forces affecting exchange rates can occur simultaneously; it is a multivariable world. While the yen is undervalued because Japan is exporting capital, the same currency is appreciating because of the returns from holding foreign assets. As Japanese exporters await the latest twist of the J-curve, they are responding to exchange rate changes of eighteen or more months ago. When talking about exchange rates, what is true today may be reversed tomorrow. What is cause may become effect.

Notes

1.   Tamim Bayoumi et al., "The Robustness of Equilibrium Exchange Rate Calculations to Alternative Assumptions and Methodologies," in *Estimating Equilibrium Exchange Rates*, ed. John Williamson (Washington, D.C.: Institute for International Economics, 1994), 29.

2.   This explanation ignores transportation costs, differentiated products, monopolized markets, trade barriers (visible and invisible), and other impediments to free trade.

3.   Polly Reynolds Allen, "The Economic and Policy Implications of the NATREX (Natural Real Exchange) Approach," in *Fundamental Determinants of Exchange Rates*, ed. Jerome L. Stein (Oxford, England: Oxford University Press, 1995).

4.   Richard C. Marston, "Real Exchange Rates and Productivity Growth in the United States and Japan," in *Real Financial Linkages among Open Economies*, ed. Sven W. Arndt and J. David Richardson, (Cambridge, Massachusetts: MIT Press, 1987), 80.

5.   Trend changes in currency values were measured by the regression coefficient of the real, trade-weighted exchange rate versus time.

6.   Daniel L. Thornton, "Tests of Covered Interest Rate Parity," *Federal Reserve Bank of St. Louis Review* 71, no. 4 (July-August, 1989): 65; Charles Pigott, "International Interest Rate Convergence: A Survey of the Issues and Evidence," *Federal Reserve Bank of New York Quarterly Review* 18, no. 4 (winter 1993-1994): 27.

7.   Mark Taylor, "The Economics of Exchange Rates," *Journal of Economic Literature* 32, no. 1 (March 1995): 14-15.

8.   Guy Meredith and Menzie Chinn, *Long-Horizon Uncovered Interest Rate Parity* (Working Paper 6797) (Cambridge, Massachusetts: National Bureau of Economic Re-

search, November 1998), 1.

9. Meredith and Chinn, Long-Horizon Uncovered Interest Rate Parity, 27.

10. Meredith and Chinn, Long-Horizon Uncovered Interest Rate Parity, 17.

11. Nelson C. Mark, "Exchange Rates and Fundamentals: Evidence on Long-Horizon Predictability," *American Economic Review* 85, no. 1 (March 1995): 213-15.

12. Ronald MacDonald and Jun Nagayasu, "On the Japanese Yen-U.S. Dollar Exchange Rate: A Structural Econometric Model Based on Real Interest Differentials," *Journal of the Japanese and International Economies* 12, no. 1 (March 1998): 97.

13. Stein, "The Natural Real Exchange Rate," 137.

14. One of the first proponents of this approach was Jeffrey Frankel, "On the Mark: A Theory of Floating Exchange Rates Based on Real Interest Differentials," *American Economic Review* 69, no. 4 (September 1979): 610-22.

15. Jerome L. Stein, "The Natural Real Exchange Rate of the US Dollar and Determinants of Capital Flows," in *Estimating Equilibrium Exchange Rates*, ed. John Williamson (Washington, D.C.: Institute for International Economics, 1994), 153.

16. Takatoshi Ito, "Short-Run and Long-Run Expectations of the Yen/Dollar Exchange Rate," *Journal of the Japanese and International Economies* 8, no. 2 (June 1994): 127.

17. Export elasticities for both countries are 0.71. The U.S. import elasticity is -1.1, and the Japanese figure is -0.77. Bayoumi, et al., "The Robustness of Equilibrium Exchange Rate Calculations."

18. The real interest rates are in the form 1 + r, where r is the three-month CD rate minus the previous twelve-month rate of change of manufacturing prices. The asset income adjustment figure adopted the same form, adding one to the estimated percentage change in exchange rate.

19. Lucio Sarno and Mark Taylor, "Official Intervention in the Foreign Exchange Market: Is It Effective and, If So, How Does It Work?" *Journal of Economic Literature* 39 no. 3 (September 2001): 862.

20. Lucio Sarno and Mark Taylor, "Official Intervention in the Foreign Exchange Market," 863.

21. Allen, "The Economic and Policy Implications of the NATREX Approach," 6.

22. Simon Wren-Lewis and Rebecca L. Driver, *Real Exchange Rates for the Year 2000* (Washington, D.C.: Institute for International Economics, 1998), 27.

Chapter 8

Japan's Foreign Direct Investment in the United States

Japan's Overseas Investments in Context

Japanese investors held three trillion dollars in assets abroad as of the end of March 2000. Less than 10 percent of this total—$228 billion—was in direct investments, defined as ownership of a sufficient share of a foreign company to presume some degree of managerial control.[1]

All investments expose the investor to risk. In addition to exchange rate risks, FDI incorporates the prospect of business risk or the chance that future profits will not measure up to forecasts. Foreign markets, which are likely to be less familiar to an investor than one's own, are especially vulnerable to business risk.

Not surprisingly, the main destination for Japan's FDI is the United States—the country that Japanese business people know best. At the end of fiscal year 1999, the United States accounted for 48 percent of the stock of Japan's FDI. Together with Western Europe, Canada, Australia, and New Zealand, the advanced economies were the sites of 73 percent of Japanese FDI. Almost all of the rest was in Asia. Japanese companies had nearly 3 percent of their FDI in the People's Republic of China and 18 percent in Asia as a whole (see figure 8.1 and table 8.1).

**Figure 8.1: Regional Breakdown of Japan's Foreign Direct Investment
Position, March 31, 2000**

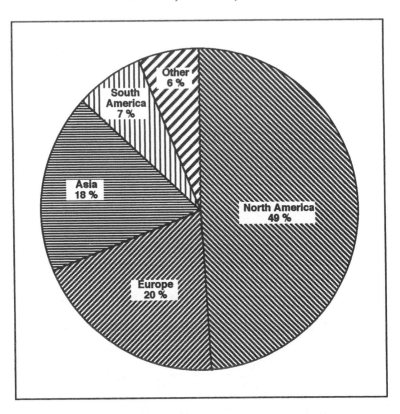

Japan's American Investments

The U.S. Department of Commerce estimated Japan's year-end 1999
stock of direct investment in the United States at $149 billion—15 per-
cent of the total for all countries and second to the United Kingdom's
18.5 percent share. In 1980, Japan ranked seventh as a direct investor in
the United States. In subsequent years it quickly moved up the standings,
reaching third in 1984 and second in 1988. A surge in Japanese investment activity in the second half of the 1980s was responsible for this
rapid ascent. However, an equally sharp slowdown in FDI in the post-
1990 period, combined with strong investment inflows into the United
States from other countries, gradually eroded Japan's share. Nonetheless,

the world's second-biggest economy still has a firm hold on the number-two position.

In order to make better sense of the official figures on FDI, it is necessary to consider the methods used to collect and define the information. Surveys and analyses from the Department of Commerce yield three ways of measuring FDI flows into the United States.

Table 8.1: Japanese and U.S. Foreign Direct Investment Position in Top 20 Countries, 1999 (billion dollars)

	Japan		United States	
Rank	Recipient	Amount	Recipient	Amount
1	United States	108.5	United Kingdom	213.1
2	United Kingdom	16.5	Canada	111.7
3	Netherlands	16.0	Netherlands	106.4
4	Australia	7.8	Switzerland	51.2
5	Singapore	7.7	Germany	49.6
6	China	6.7	Japan	47.8
7	Hong Kong	5.7	Bermuda	46.0
8	Brazil	4.3	France	40.0
9	Thailand	4.2	Brazil	35.0
10	Indonesia	4.1	Mexico	34.3
11	Taiwan	3.6	Australia	33.7
12	Malaysia	3.3	Panama	33.4
13	Germany	3.1	Singapore	24.8
14	Belgium/Luxembourg	3.1	Hong Kong	20.8
15	Canada	3.0	Caribbean	19.9
16	France	2.8	Ireland	19.8
17	Korea	2.7	Italy	17.6
18	Mexico	2.0	Belgium	17.3
19	Philippines	1.8	Luxembourg	15.3
20	New Zealand	1.2	Argentina	14.2
	Global Total	228.2	Global Total	1,132.6

Sources: Bank of Japan, U.S. Department of Commerce.

1. *Outlays for the acquisition or the establishment of U.S. businesses* incorporate investments made by foreign parents from abroad as well as those made through their existing U.S. affiliates. This measure does not cover money going into existing foreign-owned businesses. In 1999, total outlays to acquire or establish U.S. businesses were $283 billion, of

which 80 percent came from the foreign parents. The 1999 figure was four times larger than the 1997 amount. Japanese investors accounted for just 2.8 percent of the 1999 outlays.[2]

2. *Capital inflows* include net equity investments, changes in intercompany debt, and reinvested earnings. This measure incorporates outlays for the acquisition or the establishment of new businesses and adds to that figure additional investments in existing businesses. However, this measure only includes transactions with foreign sources. In 1999, total FDI capital inflows into the United States of $271 billion comprised $212 billion in equity capital, $40.2 billion in intercompany debt, and $18.8 billion of reinvested earnings.[3]

3. *Change in the historical-cost position* includes the capital inflow figure just noted, plus several valuation adjustments. One such adjustment reflects changes in exchange rates that alter the value of a U.S. affiliate's foreign assets and liabilities, which typically is quite small. The other main adjustment reflects capital gains or losses on assets that are sold during a year as well as other differences between market and book value. The change in the overall historical-cost position was $192.9 billion between 1998 and 1999. The difference between this value and the one for capital inflows is accounted for by the two kinds of adjustments: -$5.2 billion for currency adjustments and -$73.2 billion for "other." The latter item was explained by a Commerce Department analyst: "In 1999, transaction values were boosted by high valuations in the communications-related sectors of the U.S. equity markets and by substantial premiums, in relation to preacquisition market prices, that foreign investors paid for many of the acquired firms. The downward adjustment reconciled the transaction values of the acquisitions, which are reflected in capital inflows (and would otherwise determine the measured change in position), with the smaller book values that are recorded in the historical-cost position."[4]

The cumulative sum of the annual change in the historical-cost position over time yields the stock of foreign direct investment in the United States on a historical-cost basis—the most commonly cited value of FDI. In 1999, it came to $987 billion.

All three measures of foreign direct investment flows are highly correlated, even though they are based on different concepts and arise from different surveys and methods. Table 8.2 shows the inflows of direct investment using the three measures. Investment outlays is somewhat more sensitive to changing economic conditions because it only covers initial activities; additional investments in existing operations and reinvested earnings are excluded. Japan-financed outlays rose very sharply starting in 1986. They hit a peak of $20 billion in 1990 but then fell off just as quickly in the rest of the decade.

Table 8.2: Alternative Measures of Foreign Direct Investment Flows to the United States, 1980-1999 (billion dollars)

Year	Investment Outlays		Capital Inflows		Change in Position	
	Total	Japan	Total	Japan	Total	Japan
1980	12.2	0.6	16.9	0.9		
1981	23.2	0.6	25.2	3.0	25.7	3.0
1982	10.8	0.6	13.8	2.0	16.0	2.0
1983	8.1	0.4	11.5	1.6	12.4	1.7
1984	15.2	1.8	25.6	4.4	27.5	4.7
1985	23.1	1.2	20.5	3.4	20.0	3.3
1986	39.2	5.4	36.1	7.0	35.8	7.5
1987	40.3	7.0	59.6	8.8	43.0	7.6
1988	72.7	16.2	58.6	17.2	51.4	16.7
1989	71.2	17.4	69.0	18.7	54.2	16.1
1990	65.9	19.9	48.4	18.8	26.0	15.8
1991	25.5	5.4	22.8	12.8	24.2	12.1
1992	15.3	2.9	19.2	4.2	4.0	2.6
1993	26.2	2.1	50.7	2.9	44.3	3.0
1994	45.6	2.7	47.0	6.2	13.3	2.3
1995	57.2	3.6	69.4	6.6	54.9	2.0
1996	79.9	8.8	78.8	11.9	62.5	11.1
1997	69.7	2.3	103.5	10.6	91.8	7.0
1998	215.5	4.9	181.8	7.6	103.9	11.5
1999	282.9	8.0	271.2	9.5	192.9	14.4

Source: Department of Commerce, *Survey of Current Business*.

The decline of Japan's U.S. direct investment was affected by economic conditions in both countries. In fact, direct investments from other countries, which had peaked in the 1988-1989 period, also fell abruptly, mainly due to the U.S. recession at the start of the 1990s. A rush of new investments that outpaced the earlier flows followed the bottom of this trough in 1992. However, the recovery of Japanese direct investment outlays appeared weak in comparison with the resurgence from other countries, led by the traditional foreign participants in the American market—the United Kingdom, Germany, Canada, and Switzerland.

The jump in capital flows from Japan to the United States during the second half of the 1980s made Japanese investors a permanent part of the American economic scene. From a position of only 5.7 percent of all FDI in 1980, the share of Japan's direct investment stock doubled to 10.5 percent in 1985 and doubled again to 21.8 percent in 1990. The subsequent collapse of new flows, plus the resumption of strong activity by other countries, reduced the Japanese share to 15.1 percent at the end of 1999. The erosion in the proportional weight of Japanese companies in the U.S. economy is likely to continue as their FDI position adjusts to long-term forces. However, the absolute value is unlikely to fall back to earlier levels.

Allocation of Japan's American FDI

Not only did the pace of Japanese direct investment in the United States slow dramatically in the 1990s, the sectors favored by investors also shifted. When Japanese companies first started to expand into the American market, they did so largely through exports of consumer and capital goods plus intermediate products used in manufacturing activities. The marketing of these products was supported by sales subsidiaries as well as by warehouse and service facilities. However, new manufacturing establishments of these Japanese importers, which the Commerce Department originally designated in the wholesale trade category, continued to be counted as wholesale activities.

That early experience still shows up in Commerce Department statistics as witnessed in the continuing, though declining, dominance of wholesale trade. (For the allocation of Japanese companies' investment in the American market, see table 8.3.) The government data do not break down each country's wholesale investment figures into product groups, but other information suggests that motor vehicles and electrical goods were the largest; these are among the product groups in which corporate Japan first made its presence felt in the American market. Wholesale trade accounted for two-thirds of the stock of Japanese direct investment in the United States in the early 1980s. Manufacturing was around 15 percent of the total until 1987.

**Table 8.3: Japanese Companies' Distribution of U.S.
Direct Investment Stock by Sector, 1980-1999
(Total in billion dollars, sectors in percent)**

Year	Total	Manufacturing	Wholesale Trade	Banking	Real Estate	Nonbank Financial
1980	4.7	21.9	67.3	13.7	5.6	0
1981	7.7	17.2	64.8	15.3	4.0	0
1982	9.7	16.8	63.3	13.7	4.1	0
1983	11.3	14.2	67.2	12.2	4.5	0
1984	16.0	15.3	60.4	11.5	4.6	3.2
1985	19.3	14.2	61.1	11.2	8.0	0.3
1986	26.8	13.3	51.0	10.1	11.0	7.8
1987	34.4	14.4	47.4	10.6	12.7	8.7
1988	51.1	21.6	36.1	8.5	16.0	11.1
1989	67.3	24.3	31.4	7.4	16.0	14.1
1990	83.1	21.6	31.0	7.1	18.6	10.2
1991	95.1	20.3	28.3	7.1	16.1	9.5
1992	97.8	19.2	33.9	5.6	10.4	15.4
1993	100.7	18.2	35.7	5.4	9.7	15.6
1994	103.0	20.0	34.5	5.1	9.1	16.3
1995	105.0	24.3	32.9	7.3	8.2	19.5
1996	116.1	30.3	30.1	5.7	7.5	15.1
1997	126.5	29.6	32.3	6.0	8.3	13.8
1998	134.6	35.2	26.3	6.5	9.4	12.3
1999	148.9	31.7	33.2	5.0	7.9	11.8

Note: Direct investment stock is measured according to the historical cost basis.
Source: Department of Commerce

Manufacturing assumed greater importance in the post-1985 period as Japanese exporters were forced to cope with the yen's rapid appreciation and actual or threatened U.S. trade protection. Despite the anomaly in the data collection process, the share of wholesale trade in the stock of Japanese investment fell to 30 percent in the 1990s, a level that was matched by a growing manufacturing presence.

By the middle of the 1980s, banking and other financial companies in Japan were exploring opportunities in the U.S. market as deregulation in Japan made such ventures possible. These investments at first supported existing Japanese clients who were operating in the United States. In addition, the financial firms wanted to capitalize on the potential of the American economy. Over the course of a decade, nonbank financial companies, mainly securities brokers, came to represent almost 20 percent of the Japanese money in the United States. However, as problems in the financial sector mounted at home with the rise of bad loans and failing investments, Japanese banks and other financial services companies withdrew from their international operations. After 1995, both the absolute value and the share of Japan's financial services firms in the American market declined.

Real estate investment went through the same process of growth and decline, pushed by the rise and fall of asset prices in Japan. Real estate jumped in importance as the bubble economy perked along in Japan. However, Japan's U.S. real estate position peaked in 1990 and then began a period of long-term decline. By 1999, the share of this once high-profile type of investment represented only about half of its peak value.

The Image of the Japanese Invader

The late 1980s surge of Japanese direct investment fed an American suspicion that corporate Japan was about to take over U.S. business. Largely overlooked is the reality of the 1990s—the almost as quick shrinkage of these takeovers and the retrenchment in some fields such as real estate. A closer look at the 1988-1990 boom years reveals that the U.S. image of an unstoppable marauder with the deepest of pockets was the product of a few huge acquisitions. Table 8.4 shows the largest of the megadeals as compiled by the Department of Commerce in an annual list of publicly identified FDI transactions.

Bridgestone Corp.'s 1988 acquisition of Firestone Tire & Rubber Co. for $2.6 billion typified a strong Japanese industrial company's takeover of a formerly strong but ailing American industrial icon. The 1989 buyout of Columbia Pictures Entertainment Inc. by electronics giant Sony Corp. for $5 billion marked the entry of corporate Japan into the quintessentially American movie industry. The purchase the same year of a controlling share of the Rockefeller Group's Rockefeller Center in the heart of Manhattan by Mitsubishi Estate Co., Ltd. was another indicator of the vulnerability of the American myth. Then, in 1990, the $7.5 billion purchase of MCA Inc. by Matsushita Electric Industrial Co., Ltd. confirmed the "Japanese invasion of Hollywood," as it was portrayed in the press. Japanese interests also acquired the Pebble Beach golf club in California, the home of major American golf tournaments.

People who worried about the "buying of America" ignored the fact that 12 megadeals in the $750 million-plus category occurred in 1988 that involved non-Japanese parents, followed by 11 in 1989 and 10 in 1990. For example, 1989 saw Great Britain's Grand Metropolitan PLC acquire Pillsbury Co. for $5 billion. That deal placed the Burger King fast-food chain under foreign ownership. The hamburger (though named after a German city) is probably even more symbolic of America than is Hollywood.

Table 8.4: Total Japanese Outlays for Acquisitions and New Establishments, and Megadeals Over $750 million, 1988-1990
(billions of dollars)

Year	Total Japanese Outlays	Purchaser	Target	Value
1988	$16.2	Bridgestone	Firestone Tire & Rubber	$2.60
		Nippon Mining	Gould	1.10
		Paloma Industries	Rheem Manufacturing	0.85
		Bank of Tokyo	Union Bank of California	0.75
1989	17.4	Sony	Columbia Pictures	5.00
		Dai-Ichi Kangyo Bank	CIT Group	1.28
		Mitsubishi Estate	Rockefeller Group	0.85
		Fujisawa Pharmaceutical	LyphoMed	0.80
1990	19.9	Matsushita Electrical	MCA	7.00
		Mitsubishi	Aristech Chemical	0.88
		Minoru Isutant	Pebble Beach	0.80

Source: Department of Commerce, International Trade Administration, *Foreign Direct Investment in the United States: Transactions*, various issues.

The megadeals listed in table 8.4—those that made the headlines as well as the ones that escaped the glare of public attention—constituted a large share of new outlays during the boom in Japan's U.S. direct investments: 32.6 percent in 1988, 45.5 percent in 1989 and 46.1 percent in 1990 (the result of just three transactions). As the big deals declined in number, so did the overall volume of Japanese direct investment. By 1994, the last year that the U.S. government published these data, Japanese investors accounted for just a single large $750 million-plus investment out of sixteen. The extraordinary wave in the few years of the late 1980s, spotlighted by megadeals, camouflaged the rather conservative nature of most Japanese foreign investments, direct or otherwise.

Why Did Japan's FDI Surge?

What accounted for the surge of Japanese foreign direct investment worldwide in the second half of the 1980s and its subsequent decline? Addressing these questions requires an examination of several subsidiary issues. Why invest abroad at all? Why invest overseas rather than export goods and services from a domestic base?

Why invest abroad? The simple answer is to earn higher returns than are possible domestically or to diversify an investment portfolio to reduce risk. An investor can expect to earn more abroad than at home if returns in a foreign country generally are higher than domestic returns or, less obviously, if a company possesses a firm-specific asset that enables it to earn sufficient profits in a foreign market even if paybacks in general are not higher there. They can be sufficient, in turn, either because the foreign firm expects higher returns or because it requires lower returns. The bulk of the evidence, though, suggests that, regardless of the nationality of the investor, the main determinant of FDI is the possession of firm-specific assets.

Firm-Specific Assets: Companies often have experience, technology, know-how, or other assets like organizational or marketing skills that are difficult to transfer or sell to others and that can generate returns beyond those available in alternative investments. Richard Caves of Harvard University, who described the concept of "firm-specific assets," notes that no single phrase captures the essence of the term. He suggests as alternatives "proprietary assets" or "intangible assets."[5] If firm-specific assets were transferable at a competitive price, a company would not have to incur the risk of foreign investment; instead, it could license the asset or sell it to another party. Where contracting is feasible and technology is transferable, other methods of selling abroad are possible. Coca-Cola Co., for instance, franchises the right to produce and market its products in many areas around the world where contracts are enforceable.[6]

Why not export rather than invest abroad? The nature of firm-specific assets may indicate why a company chooses not to license or sell its expertise to another business. However, it does not address the issue of why it is profitable to be on the scene rather than to export. A traditional explanation for direct investment abroad is the factor proportion hypothesis. It states that manufacturers integrate production vertically across borders to take advantage of input factor price differences associated with varying relative factor supplies. This explanation was adequate in the years following World War II when the majority of multinational firms were American and much of their investment went to countries with significantly lower labor costs.

However, an emergent feature of the modern global economy—namely, that the United States was well on its way to becoming both the world's largest direct investor abroad as well as the largest destination for foreign direct investment by other countries—forced attention to alternative theories. By 1988, some 70 percent of all direct investment flows occurred among the five biggest industrialized countries.[7] It is difficult to explain such two-way flows on relative cost grounds.

An alternative explanation suggests that manufacturers are more likely to expand production abroad the higher are transport costs and trade barriers and the lower are investment barriers and plant scale economies. Firms should expand across borders when the advantages of access to the destination market outweigh the disadvantages of reduced scale economies. In addition to avoiding transportation costs as an incentive for FDI, being physically close to a market often enhances the feedback of essential demand information and allows the producer to respond more flexibly and quickly than if it were an ocean away.

Another kind of localization advantage is access to specialized skills that are not captured by the traditional factor proportion theory. These skills can be as broad as general engineering capabilities or as narrow as a specific scientific field. The location of many international bioengineering firms in Bethesda, Maryland, near the research campus of the National Institutes of Health testifies to the importance of highly specialized local skills.

Empirical studies find support for all of the cited theories. However, the single most important factor promoting FDI is the existence of firm-specific assets.[8] As noted by Edward M. Graham of the Institute for International Economics and Paul R. Krugman, then at the Massachusetts Institute of Technology, "When U.S. production is undertaken by foreign firms it is typically because the foreigners have firm-specific assets that give them an advantage in management and technology."[9] The two economists go on to say, however, that, within this broad story, "shifts in exchange rates, taxation, and protection all probably play an important role in explaining the timing of this investment." For Japan, exchange rates and the cost of capital played especially important roles in the late 1980s.

Although productivity throughout the Japanese economy in general is considerably below comparable American levels, this situation is not true across the board. Many Japanese companies possess firm-specific assets that allow them to earn higher profits in the United States than their U.S.

rivals do. In particular, Japan's motor vehicle, steel, and electronics industries are estimated to be more efficient than their U.S. counterparts.
The other firm-specific asset that can generate returns elsewhere than in
the home country is a company's brand. Names such as Toyota or Sony,
combined with locational advantages, enabled Japanese manufacturers to
establish competitive operations in the United States and to transfer their
in-house efficiency and branded images to their American subsidiaries.

Rate-of-Return Differentials: In general, the relative cost of capital
fails to explain why direct investments are chosen over investments in financial assets, especially since FDI involves more risks. However, this
argument does not rule out comparative returns as an explanation for
FDI. Even though foreign firms might be no better at production in another country than domestic firms there and have no other special advantage, they might be willing to pay more for an offshore property because they apply a lower profit requirement.[10] As noted in previous
chapters, since the early 1980s, rates of return to capital in Japan were
especially low in comparison with other industrialized countries. Even if
Japan-based businesses earn lower profit rates in the United States than
American investors, it still could be economically rational for Japanese
companies to be there if profits exceeded what could be generated at
home.

Corporate Purchasing Power: In a world of imperfect capital markets,
anything that lowers the costs of assets for foreign firms increases their
purchasing power. Three separate phenomena combined to produce such
an effect for Japan in the late 1980s. Between 1985 and 1989, average
share prices on the Tokyo Stock Exchange (as represented by the Nikkei
index of 225 stocks listed on the exchange's first section) more than tri-
pled. As prices rose, the number of yen that could be raised by floating a
share went up proportionately.

The easy availability of financial capital was only part of the story.
Yen raised in Tokyo had to be converted into dollars to invest in American assets. The yen appreciated sharply in the wake of the fall 1985 Plaza
Accord, which enabled Japanese investors to exchange their currency for
more dollars, leveraging rising Tokyo stock prices. Moreover, the costs
of American assets, as represented by equity prices on the New York
Stock Exchange, were not rising as fast as in Tokyo. In addition, the
October 1987 stock market crash in New York created buying opportunities for foreigners whose own markets had suffered milder declines.

An index number can be constructed to reflect these three links by
dividing the Nikkei stock price index by the yen-dollar exchange rate and
the NYSE composite price index. The resulting figure (indexed to Janu-

ary 1985 equals 100) can be interpreted as the number of shares in New York that can be purchased with the proceeds from floating 100 shares in Tokyo. Another interpretation is that the index is the real exchange rate for assets.

This Japanese corporate purchasing power index tracks outlays for acquisitions and new establishments in the United States remarkably well (see figure 8.2). Purchasing power rose rapidly from 1985 through 1988, held steady for a year, and then collapsed in 1990. The outflow of money for U.S. direct investments followed suit with a short lag. As the Tokyo stock market took a dive in the 1990s while the yen leveled off and the NYSE began to outpace the TSE, the cost of overseas investments went into a tailspin that continued through the end of the decade.[11]

Figure 8.2: Japanese Outlays for U.S. Acquisitions and New Establishments and Japanese Purchasing Power, 1980-2000 (left scale: billion dollars; right scale: index)

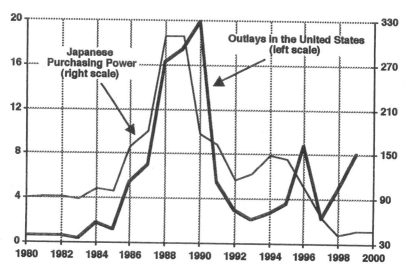

Not all industries will be affected to the same degree by the corporate purchasing power index. A depreciating dollar that makes U.S. assets less expensive for foreigners also raises the dollar costs of parts and other products imported into the United States. Automotive wholesale trade, in particular, suffered a sharp decline in profitability in the first half of the 1990s owing to the weaker dollar.[12]

At the same time, investors expecting the dollar's depreciation to continue might find an incentive to produce in the United States in order to avoid or minimize the expected rise in import costs. Dollar depreciation would be even more important if foreign producers planned to export the output of their factories back home or to third countries. On balance, though, the profitability of foreign affiliates in the United States seems to be little affected by exchange rates. A study conducted by two economists at the Federal Reserve Bank of New York found that positive effects balanced negative ones.[13]

Economists sometimes argue that exchange rate considerations should not influence FDI decisions because returns are earned in the same currency in which investments are made. The price of U.S. assets should not matter in this view, only their rates of return. This argument, which refers mainly to such assets as bonds, is reinforced by reference to the well-known observation that exchange rates behave in the short run like random walks. The implication is that exchange rate changes are unpredictable at least over periods of up to two years or so. Since neither depreciation nor appreciation can be predicted, the prudent response for companies weighing direct investments abroad is to assume that exchange rates will continue at current levels.

This argument breaks down, however, if products made offshore are exported or production inputs are imported or if long-run forces appear to be moving exchange rates in a predictable direction. It also fails if capital markets are imperfect and considerations like the availability of funds influence investment decisions. Real exchange rates also may make a difference if a foreign firm acquires the firm-specific assets of a domestic firm, which the foreigner can then use at home. For example, the target firm may have a technology that will improve the profitability of the acquiring company. Bruce Blonigen at the University of Oregon finds support for such behavior.[14]

Low Profitability of Japanese FDI

Japanese firms presumably faced lower "hurdle rates" in their investment decisions at home in the late 1980s because of the easy availability of funds during the bubble years and economywide low returns. It might follow then that corporate Japan would be satisfied with lower returns on its U.S. investments. That is just what happened. As shown in figure 8.3, returns on Japanese corporate investment in the United States plunged in the 1980s, turning negative for four straight years beginning in 1990. Other foreign investors experienced the same downward shift in their American profitability, but Japan's slide was steeper. Estimates of domestic companies' returns show a decline in U.S. firms' profits in the early 1990s as a result of a weak economy, but the slide was less than 1.5 percentage points, whereas Japanese companies saw a collapse of more than ten percentage points.

**Figure 8.3: Rates of Return on Foreign Direct Investment
in the United States, 1980-1999 (percent)**

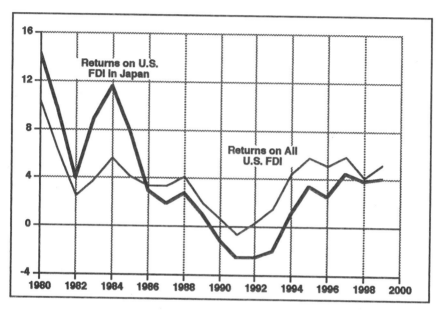

Note: Returns calculated as income paid to owners divided by asset value estimated on historical-cost basis.
Source: Department of Commerce

It should be noted that returns on FDI in the United States as a whole are lower than on American investments abroad or U.S. firms' returns at home. A major reason for the comparatively low profitability of foreign firms doing business in the United States is that they are newer than American firms operating at home or abroad. It takes many years to overcome the costs and attendant problems of a new venture; U.S. multinationals got a big head start on their foreign counterparts in the postwar period. Internal Revenue Service data for large American corporations operating abroad in 1988 and 1989 showed that returns on assets rose steadily from 2.1 percent for companies that were a year old or less to 16.1 percent for concerns that had been in business for twenty-nine to thirty-three years.[15]

Economists at the New York Fed attributed the depressed earnings of foreign firms operating in the United States to their rapid buildup in the late 1970s and the 1980s. In addition, "these companies paid top dollar for underperforming U.S. firms, borrowed heavily, and then spent freely on investment and marketing. As the share of recently acquired firms in the United States rose in the 1980s, aggregate returns deteriorated."[16]

Table 8.5: Return on Assets of Large Domestic and Foreign Firms in the United States by Age of Firm, 1994-1997

	U.S. Firms		Foreign firms		Japanese Firms	
Age:	0-2	3+	0-2	3+	0-2	3+
1994	2.27	2.54	0.79	1.21	0.30	0.93
1995	3.09	2.91	-0.39	1.45	-0.85	0.47
1996	2.07	2.93	0.00	1.64	-0.53	1.14
1997	2.43	2.56	1.06	1.76	1.53	1.50

Note: Profitability is defined as net income before taxes divided by total assets. Total assets were those reported in the end-of-year balance sheets and were net amounts after reduction by accumulated depreciation, accumulated amortization, and the allowance for bad debts.
Source: Department of Treasury, Internal Revenue Service, *Statistics of Income Bulletin*, various.

Analyzing IRS data, this study noted that many foreign ventures do not move out of the red for up to a decade and take longer to break even on their investments. Manufacturing firms became profitable after eight years but companies in the wholesale and retail industries were not earning positive returns even after ten years.

A later study by a staff member of the Commerce Department's Bureau of Economic Analysis repeated this theme. This study was able to use the detailed survey information on individual firms collected by the U.S. government, something that most private economists are not able to do. They defined returns as the sum of profits from current production plus interest paid; rate of return—the ratio of this amount to total assets valued at current cost—averaged 5.1 percent for 1988-1997. (The same ratio based on assets valued at historical costs was 5.7 percent.)[17] Domestic companies earned, on average, 2.2 percentage points more than the foreign-based companies. Differences in the industry mix of companies were not a major reason for the discrepancy, nor was the possibility of shifting profits abroad through transfer pricing. However, the profit gap disappeared for those foreign companies with more than 30 percent of the U.S. market. The gap also narrowed as foreign firms gained U.S. experience, just as earlier studies had found. Unfortunately, the author did not report separate breakdowns by country of ownership.

Other data suggest, however, that Japanese firms have fared worse than the typical foreign company doing business in the United States, even when the age of the firm is taken into account. The IRS analyzes foreign-owned firms based on the tax returns of large companies, defined as concerns having either $250 million in assets or $50 million in sales. These big businesses did somewhat better than the aggregate of all foreign-owned firms. Table 8.5 summarizes these data, which shows that foreign companies performed worse than their domestic counterparts of the same age, and that Japanese companies did even worse. Older firms tend to do better than newer ones, although for Japanese companies, this difference seemed to have disappeared by 1997. The bottom line (literally) of this analysis is that the average Japanese investor has made little money in the United States since the early 1980s.

Case Studies of Two Firms

The recitation of facts and numbers obscures the individual actions of thousands of Japanese companies in their American adventures. These investments were driven by a myriad of influences—the potential for the yen's appreciation, the prospect of Washington-imposed trade barriers, the desire to service longtime Japanese customers operating in the United States, the easy availability of credit at home, the higher returns available in the U.S. market, the costs imposed by operating at a distance, and the opportunity to cash in on a company's special knowledge and expertise. All these motivations and more drove the wave of Japan's U.S. direct investments. Behind each was a unique story of individuals and special situations. Two case studies may put a little flesh on the bare statistical bones.

One involves NKK Corp., an industrial steelmaking giant that built its American entry on its financial, managerial, and technological assets. The other case study is drawn from the other end of the industrial spectrum, women's lingerie. Wacoal Corp. was a rash entrant into Japanese business in the postwar era. It went on to dominate the market at home and subsequently established an international reputation.

NKK Corp.: NKK was among the world's largest integrated steel producers and a technology leader when it acquired 50 percent of the fourth-biggest American steel company, National Steel Corp., in 1984 for approximately three hundred million dollars. The two companies had a relationship dating to when National Steel supplied leading-edge technology to NKK thirty years earlier. By the 1980s, NKK and Japan's other major steelmakers were beginning to eye onshore U.S. operations. Such a presence would give them a way around the trade restrictions that seemed to have become a fixture at the time so that they could service the automotive and other Japanese manufacturers setting up American plants. At the same time in the early 1980s, American steel companies were suffering from declining domestic demand, worldwide overcapacity, and technological inferiority to the industry's leaders abroad. National Steel went private in 1980 and over the next four years cut its steelmaking capacity in half. By the time of the NKK bid, restructuring had restored profitability while the rest of the American steel industry was in the midst of losing billions of dollars.

However, the Japanese investor's close inspection of its new acquisition revealed low efficiency, an inability to meet the quality requirements of potential U.S.-based Japanese customers, rigid personnel practices, and the absence of any recent investment in plant and equipment. Almost immediately, NKK began to put money into new equipment to raise productivity and quality to the desired levels. These investments added up to more than $2 billion, with an estimated half coming from Tokyo along with loan guarantees that peaked at $330 million in 1993.[18] In 1990, NKK upped its stake in National Steel by acquiring another 20 percent of the steelmaker's shares for $147 million. In order to raise additional funds, it offered a 24 percent stake to the public in 1993.

The monetary side of the investment was only part of the problem. The steelmaking culture at National Steel had to change before NKK could even contemplate a semblance of profitability. Industry observers note that head office management and control issues are vital to the success of a foreign investment, but getting the mix of tightness and looseness right is difficult. For ten years, NKK executives deferred to National Steel's domestic managers. Although quality and efficiency improved, largely due to the parent's massive investments in equipment and the introduction of NKK production methods, National Steel still did not perform to the desired standards. In 1994, NKK's chairman moved himself and his family to National Steel's new headquarters in Mishawaka, Indiana, to personally oversee operations.

National then engineered a bold raid on a rival when it hired the entire management team of the U.S. Steel Group's flagship plant in Gary, Indiana, and put the six men in charge of the underperforming company. The new team quickly went to work, hammering out accords with the union and taking steps to boost productivity. However, two years later, with earnings still weak, Tokyo replaced the chief executive with a new assignee from headquarters.

In the meantime, personnel practices had been transformed by guaranteeing employment to workers in exchange for workplace flexibility. Since workers no longer could be laid off to cope with business downturns, sales had to be increased. That, in turn, demanded a closer working relationship between the sales force and the plant—something that National Steel's Japanese managers had done instinctively at home without realizing the changes that this type of cooperation required in the American context.

Eventually, NKK's investments and production changes began to have an impact. The number of man-hours per ton of steel produced at National Steel fell by 50 percent in the decade after 1985, and the proportion of finished steel in the highest quality category more than doubled after the new Japanese chief operating officer took over.

Ten years after NKK bought into it, National Steel achieved profitability for five years straight. However, it then sunk into the red again for the next several years. In the ten years from 1991 to 2000, cumulative net income was a negative sixty-six million dollars. The company's stock was trading at one to two dollars per share in 2000-2001, down from the ten to twenty dollar range at which it had traded in the 1990s. It is doubtful whether NKK ever will break even on the money it has plowed into National Steel, especially with excess capacity in the global market.

Consolidation in the global steel industry did not leave parent NKK untouched. In April 2001, NKK Corp. and Kawasaki Steel Corp., Japan's second- and third-largest producers, announced plans to merge into what would be the world's second-biggest steelmaker. Analysts viewed this merger as good for National Steel because it might give the U.S. company a stronger parent. The alternative of selling the American subsidiary was considered less likely, ironically, because of the low share price, which would produce a huge capital loss for the Japanese parent.[19] However, at the close of 2001, NKK announced that it was negotiating the sale of NKK to U.S. Steel Corp.

NKK's experience with National Steel is not unique, as a glance at the profitability figures in table 8.5 reveals. Money, technology, and operating proficiency are insufficient by themselves to guarantee profitability.

Wacoal Corp.: Wacoal is Japan's largest manufacturer and marketer of women's lingerie and undergarments. Wacoal typifies the group of companies started in the postwar period when Japan's old structures and long-standing business relationships had broken down. It was established in Kyoto in 1949 by the young, brash, and entrepreneurial Koichi Tsukamoto, then twenty-nine years old and three years out of the military. Within a few years of its founding, the upstart signed deals to produce and market jointly American brands entering Japan. Through his U.S. connections, Mr. Tsukamoto gained entry to the big domestic department stores that previously had refused to talk to him because he did not have a longstanding reputation. Although the American ties soon unraveled, they gave Wacoal the legitimacy needed to succeed in Japan's business world.

As production and sales grew, Wacoal drafted a long-range plan for expanding internationally. First, it opened production facilities in Asia. In 1969, the company signed technical and trademark agreements with Teen Form Group, the largest maker of brassieres for American teenagers, and began selling Teen Form products in Japan. It opened a New York branch office in 1977 and issued American Depository Receipts to enable its shares to be traded in the United States on the NASDAQ market. Being publicly traded meant that Wacoal had to adhere to American accounting and disclosure practices, which were stricter than in Japan. A wholly owned subsidiary, Wacoal America, Inc., was established in 1981.

As part of its long-term strategy for developing the American market, Wacoal sought to acquire Olga Co., a producer of high-end intimate apparel, after many years of dealings between the two companies. The heads of the two companies had built up a personal relationship and agreed that the Japanese firm initially would purchase 30 percent of Olga's shares with the remaining 70 percent to be transferred in seven years if business relations between them had deepened sufficiently. Olga's greatest attraction was its 3,000 outlets in department stores and other shops around the United States. Wacoal produced products in its Southeast Asian plants to support this venture. However, in 1982, Olga requested that the deal be terminated.

With this setback to its marketing efforts, Wacoal continued its longstanding discussions with Teen Form, finally acquiring it in 1983. Wacoal America constructed a factory in Puerto Rico in 1985 that complemented the one it had acquired there with its purchase of Teen Form.

Wacoal's product strategy at this time was to aim for the midrange of the bra market, which it saw as an unfilled niche between American-made mass-market products and high-quality European imports. It established in-store boutiques at fifteen major department stores across the country to support its quality image and improve distribution.

However, Wacoal's products at first did not find ready acceptance by American women. Company designers discovered that the physical proportions of American women had greater variability than those of Japanese women. In Japan, for example, the A-cup bra had the largest market share, whereas in the United States, C, D, and DD cups together made up a comparably sized segment.[20] It took Wacoal two years of trial and error as well as a study of U.S. styling methods to work out a line of American products. The company went on to enter the so-called full-figure segment of the market in 1984.

Tomio Taki, the Japanese investor behind designers Anne Klein and Donna Karan, was also on the board of Wacoal—the only noncompany person on the Kyoto company's board. Wacoal moved into a new market segment in 1991 when it signed a licensing agreement with Donna Karan to produce and sell her designer lingerie. The company negotiated a separate agreement with DKNY in 1998, which put Wacoal products in more than eight hundred American department stores. Ms. Karan said that she had been thinking about launching a lingerie collection for several years. However, the technical design and production of lingerie required different skills from the ones her regular contractors possessed. Industry observers suggested that the notoriously meticulous designer had delayed an introduction until she found a manufacturer that could meet her quality standards.[21] Sales began a year later—but not until after considerable internal debate at Wacoal about the company's ability to produce and market a high-end product.

Profits remained elusive throughout the 1980s. Sales were booming, but costs always seemed to outstrip revenues. Part of the problem arose from the fact that Wacoal imported 70 percent of its merchandise from Japan during a period when the yen was rising in value. As a company report noted, "It is not an exaggeration to say that the more products Wacoal America sold, the higher its deficit became."[22] According to Yoshikata Tsukamoto, the founder's son who became president in 1987, the majority of Wacoal head office directors believed the company should pull out of the U.S. market. The father insisted that they had to give it more time to develop. Sales of Wacoal America reached $100 million in 2000 and the company's products were in 1,600 retail outlets. Although details are not published, company reports ascribe an increasing share of parent company profits to the American subsidiary.[23]

As with most overseas ventures, a continuing problem was the choice of leadership. Should it be Japanese or American? Executives in New York and Kyoto debated this issue; finally, an American was chosen as Wacoal America's chief executive officer. In 1991, however, a Japanese executive took over the U.S. subsidiary as chairman, with authority to control costs and achieve profitability. He chose as president an American executive with a financial rather than a production or a marketing background. By the mid-1990s, almost twenty years after establishing an American branch office and fifteen years after opening a U.S. subsidiary, Wacoal finally managed to earn positive returns.

When the founder died in 1998, the company had fifteen overseas subsidiaries with sales of about $1.4 billion. Wacoal America had more than 600 employees and produced in Puerto Rico, Dominican Republic, and Barbados while importing less complex pieces from its Asian plants, especially Thailand. Its experience conforms to the broad statistical story of Japanese direct investment in the United States, but the characters and the details reflect the personality of a single individual, which is often an important part of the picture of Japanese investment in America.

Notes

1. Bank of Japan, *International Investment Position of Japan*. Here and below, yen figures are converted into dollars at the average exchange rate of each fiscal year.
2. Ned G. Howenstine and Rosaria Troia, "Foreign Direct Investment in the United States: New Investment in 1999," *Survey of Current Business* (June 1990).
3. Sylvia E. Bargas, "Direct Investment Positions for 1999: Country and Industry Detail," *Survey of Current Business* (July 2000).
4. Bargas, "Direct Investment Positions for 1999," 63.
5. Richard E. Caves, *Multinational Enterprise and Economic Analysis* (New York: Cambridge University Press, 1996), 3.
6. Edward M. Graham and Paul R. Krugman, *Foreign Direct Investment in the United States* (2nd edition) (Washington, D.C.: Institute for International Economics, 1991), 178.
7. Cited by S. Lael Brainard, "An Empirical Assessment of the Proximity-Concentration Trade-off Between Multinational Sales and Trade," *American Economic Revie*, 87, no. 3 (September 1997): 520.
8. Caves, Multinational Enterprise, 3.
9. Graham and Krugman, Foreign Direct Investment in the United States, 3.
10. This argument is called the cost-of-capital explanation of FDI. See Graham and Krugman, *Foreign Direct Investment in the United States*, 36.
11. For similar findings on the importance of real exchange rates, see Bruce A. Blonigen, "Firm-Specific Assets and the Link Between Exchange Rates and Foreign Di-

rect Investment," *American Economic Review*, June 1997, Table 2, 456.

12. David S. Laster and Robert N. McCauley, "Making Sense of the Profits of Foreign Firms in the United States," *Federal Reserve Bank of New York Quarterly Review* (summer-fall 1994): 54-55.

13. Laster and McCauley, "Making Sense of the Profits of Foreign Firms," 55.

14. Blonigen, "Firm-Specific Assets," 463.

15. Returns were defined as before-tax current profits divided by total assets. John Latzy and Randy Miller, "Controlled Foreign Corporations, 1988," *Statistics of Income Bulletin* (fall 1992): 86.

16. Laster and McCauley, "Making Sense of the Profits of Foreign Firms," 41.

17. Raymond J. Mataloni Jr., "An Examination of the Low Rate of Return of Foreign-Owned U.S. Companies," *Survey of Current Business* (March 2000).

18. Nigel Holloway, "School of Steel," *Far Eastern Economic Review* (October 9, 1997): 70.

19. "NKK, Kawasaki Agree to Merge," *American Metal Market* (April 16, 2001).

20. Wacoal America, Inc., *Tenth Anniversary*, 1991, 17.

21. *Women's Wear Daily*, August 24, 1992.

22. Wacoal America, Inc., *Tenth Anniversary*, 26.

23. "Wacoal Enjoys Booming Business in U.S. Lingerie Market," *Asahi Shimbun*, September 25, 1999.

Chapter 9

Foreign Direct Investment in Japan

Until the late 1990s, foreign investment into Japan was like water flowing uphill. So many legal, regulatory, and economic forces acted to retard the flow that strong counterforces were required to overcome them. This situation began to change in the late 1990s such that, by the end of the decade, foreign funds moving into Japanese investments were as large as those invested in Europe just a few years earlier. Restructuring was the main force altering the pace of FDI into Japan. The increased concern for profitability drove many domestic firms into foreign arms through mergers or buyouts. Indeed, a wave of domestic M&A activity that occurred simultaneously with the increased foreign activity suggests that FDI growth is part of an extensive turnabout in the nature of corporate governance in Japan.

Strong Disincentives to Foreign Investment

Many forces worked against FDI into Japan. For starters, since the early 1980s, domestic savings were more than sufficient for local investment requirements. Moreover, average rates of return on capital had fallen to well below comparable returns in the United States and elsewhere in the developed world. Japan, therefore, was not the place to embark on a broad search for high returns.

A major incentive for foreign direct investment is to locate production in low-cost countries. On these grounds, too, Japan falls short, as its labor costs in manufacturing are among the highest in the world. In 1991, the American Chamber of Commerce in Japan listed the high cost of doing business as the number-one factor inhibiting inward investment.[1]

Another cost-related barrier is the exchange rate. It pays to produce a product for local sale or reexport when the host's currency is depreciating rather than in one with an appreciating exchange rate, which penalizes exports. Again, the incentives act in the wrong direction. The long-term appreciation of the yen favored Japanese production in Europe or the United States, but worked against foreign production in Japan.

An additional disincentive to foreign manufacturing firms is that they often face strong, productive, and technologically advanced Japanese competitors, especially in motor vehicles and certain sectors of the semiconductor and electronics industries. However, this is not the case across the board. Moreover, even where the competition is particularly strong, foreign companies often have products or management techniques that are dominant.

The empirical literature on the motivation for foreign direct investment cites similarities in business practices and culture as positive influences, whereas cultural and physical distance acts as a deterrent. Potential investment targets with "low information costs bulk disproportionately large as destinations for U.S. FDI."[2] The typical overseas expansion sequence for an American company starts with Canada and proceeds to the United Kingdom, Germany, Mexico, Australia, and France. This pattern repeats itself for other countries. French companies go first to French-speaking countries and then to adjacent European neighbors. Australian businesses invest disproportionately in New Zealand. Italian enterprises start with neighboring southern European countries and go on to countries with heavy immigration from Italy. Measured by this yardstick, Japan is light-years away from most advanced countries along many business and cultural dimensions.

The natural impediments noted above would have been sufficient by themselves to retard foreign business, but several additional formal and informal measures reduced it even further. Some of the more important were laws, regulations, and business relations such as widespread cross-shareholding. These barriers, though, are subject to political and economic forces. Deregulation in finance, telecommunications, and retailing opened these industries to new entrants. Long-term relations among Japanese companies act as an additional barrier to newcomers, domestic as well as foreign. For much of the postwar period, such ties were considered to be one of the strengths of the Japanese economy; among other benefits, they provided incentives for a supplier to invest in technology and equipment under the assurance of continued sales. However, globalization trends and increased technological fluidity have weakened many of the advantages of long-term ties as it became less certain that a particular supplier, product, or technology would be needed in the future. Reductions in cross-shareholding motivated by a search for higher returns on assets also are lowering the barriers faced by foreigners. Thus, the same changes to the economic and political environments that are opening the Japanese economy domestically are also producing opportunities for outsiders.

Positive Incentives for FDI in Japan

Notwithstanding the many barriers to direct investment in Japan, positive attractions often overcome the impediments. The most important of these also turns out to be the single most important factor promoting FDI anywhere: firm-specific assets that yield high returns to the company possessing them. FDI occurs when it is difficult to realize these returns by way of exports or licensing other companies to produce the products. A special kind of firm-specific asset is the volume and the quality of a company's research and development, which often produces knowledge that is difficult to transfer to others. Since American companies are the most productive in the world and among the most innovative, their store of specialized knowledge is one of the most powerful sources of advantage in the Japanese market.

Many industries in which American businesses are trailblazers, such as retailing, finance, telecommunications, entertainment, and Internet products had been regulated in Japan; local rivals suffered from high costs and low levels of innovation, which offered opportunities for outsiders with the requisite skills. However, the very factors that kept these industries uncompetitive in Japan also restricted the entry of newcomers with new products and services. As the Japanese government gradually deregulated these parts of the economy, foreign firms were able to take advantage of their specialized assets.

In addition to specialized, difficult-to-transfer assets as a source for

FDI, locational advantage is the other major incentive to establish foreign activities. Being there matters. This situation is obvious where high transportation costs penalize exports from a home country. However, many other locational factors also influence investment decisions. First among these is the fact that Japan's economy is the second largest market-oriented one in the world; its standard of living and industrial capabilities make it an obvious target for American companies. Being better able to service users and consumers is one of the most common reasons for locating in Japan, since often it is necessary to tailor products to local requirements. This consideration also gives rise to the establishment of in-country design and development facilities. Since Japan is the second-biggest spender on R&D behind the United States and is especially strong in industrial technologies, many American companies have located in Japan to take advantage of such skills in both production and research across a broad array of industries and technologies.

Service industries, in particular, find it necessary to locate at the actual place of business. Banks, brokerages, retail operations, or telecommunications providers must bring their foreign specialization to the scene of operations even if most of their staff is local.

Capital, in general, is not scarce in Japan, but risk capital may be in short supply. Deregulation of the financial system and greater competition throughout the economy weakened the so-called main bank system. In these long-term relationships, banks often had private information about their customers that allowed them to take greater apparent risks than an arms-length investor might find comfortable. Banks were expected to finance business ventures and expansions in return for the continued patronage of the corporate client. As these ties weakened in the 1990s and as support for distressed clients waned, companies often were forced to seek outside help; increasingly, this came from abroad. This lesson was brought home when the Fuyo Group, centered around Fuji Bank, Ltd., could not prevent the 1997 collapse of Yamaichi Securities Co., Ltd. or provide financial support in 1999 to Nissan Motor Co., Ltd. Merrill Lynch & Co., Inc. subsequently purchased Yamaichi's retail operations and Nissan found a rescuer in France's Renault S.A.

The last chapter noted that Japan's new direct investment in the United States was closely correlated with Japanese firms' purchasing power over U.S. assets. U.S. investment into Japan, however, does not follow American purchasing power as closely, at least not until the end of the 1990s.

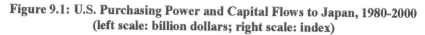

Figure 9.1: U.S. Purchasing Power and Capital Flows to Japan, 1980-2000
(left scale: billion dollars; right scale: index)

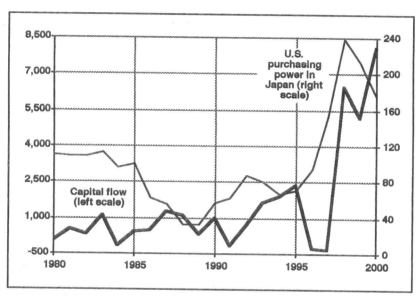

Figure 9.1 plots capital flows from the United States into direct investment in Japan; also plotted is a purchasing power index that is just the inverse of the one from the last chapter. It divides the New York Stock Exchange composite price index by the dollar-yen exchange rate, and divides that by the Nikkei stock price index of the Tokyo Stock Exchange. In parallel with the trans-Pacific figure, this index can be interpreted as the number of shares in Tokyo that can be purchased with the proceeds from floating 100 shares in New York (indexed to January 1985=100). Although, this index was relatively high before 1985, U.S. FDI was minimal. However, when Japanese assets became relatively inexpensive again twenty years later, barriers had fallen sufficiently to allow foreign companies to take advantage of the low prices in Japan, with about a two-year lag.

Data Issues

Japanese government agencies collect and publish two kinds of FDI data. The Bank of Japan collects information on capital flows across the national borders, including FDI, as part of its balance-of-payments record keeping. The Finance Ministry also collects before-the-fact notification or after-the-fact reports on specific cases of incoming and outgoing foreign investment. The MOF's reports and notifications are less comprehensive than either the Commerce Department's Bureau of Economic Analysis figures or the BOJ's. The latter two agencies employ surveys of multinational companies, which are legally required to respond to data requests.

In the first postwar decades, the foreign exchange and foreign trade control law and the foreign investment law required certain cross-country capital flows to be reported and approved in advance; these notifications were the basis of the MOF notifications data. Changes in the foreign exchange control law from "prohibition in principle" to "liberalization in principle" were implemented in 1980. Further liberalization in the following years eliminated controls on capital flows, but a scheme of prior notification was kept in force, which raises problems because they are voluntary. In addition, if plans are not actually implemented or if disinvestment occurs later, this information is not collected. The MOF figures, therefore, show planned, new transactions only and do not include the opening and expanding of branches. Neither does the MOF survey include land purchases. Moreover, the MOF numbers do not count investments of less than thirty million yen; one estimate suggests that up to one-third of all inward transactions are missed by the MOF surveys.[3]

The BOJ overhauled its balance-of-payments calculations and reporting process beginning in January 1996 to bring them into line with the International Monetary Fund's balance-of-payments manual. Before 1996, for example, reinvested earnings were not included because they did not cross national boundaries; subsequently, they have been counted. The recorded stock of foreign investment accumulated before 1996 missed this important component.

The U.S. government collects two broad sets of data on direct investment abroad: (1) international transactions, including direct investment position data; and (2) financial and operating data of U.S. parent companies and their foreign affiliates.[4] Both types of data are grounded in benchmark surveys of all multinational firms every five to seven years.

The first type of data, international transactions and direct investment position information covering bank and nonbank multinationals, are collected in quarterly surveys. They focus on the U.S. parent's share, or interest, in the affiliate rather than on the affiliate's size or scale of operations.

The second kind of information, financial and operating data on the overall operations of U.S. parent, nonbank companies and their foreign affiliates, are collected in annual surveys. These data include balance sheet and income statements, employment and compensation of employees, research and development expenditures, sources of finance, trade in goods, and sales of goods and services. In addition, the gross product (value added) of U.S. parent companies and their majority-owned foreign affiliates is estimated from the reported data. This information covers the entire operations of U.S. parent companies and their foreign affiliates, irrespective of the percentage of U.S. parent ownership.

Direct investment flows passing through offshore financial centers and holding companies can distort the picture of economic activity because the capital flows in the international transactions surveys are attributed to the country of immediate destination. Therefore, financial centers such as Bermuda, or favored holding company locations such as the Netherlands, can loom larger in the FDI position data than warranted by actual production or employment. However, the financial and operating data are always attributed to the country in which the affiliate's physical assets are located or in which its primary activity is carried out. Another difference in the two sources is that the international transactions and position data show only the U.S. contributions of capital whereas the financial and operating data indicate the size of the operation as measured by total assets, sales, employment, or gross product.

In addition to the official statistics on FDI, private sources report on cross-border mergers and acquisitions. It turns out that M&A data are highly correlated with the more comprehensive FDI statistics, even though M&A is only part of the whole. The complete FDI accounting includes new green-field investments, reinvested earnings, new equity investments in established foreign operations, and intrafirm lending, all of which M&A data miss. Nevertheless, M&A information provides one more view of Japan's globalization.

Aggregate Trends

Although the positive forces for FDI in Japan have been growing in relative strength, the flows have been notoriously low by international standards. As recently as 1995, inward FDI was less than 10 percent of outward investment according to the MOF's transactions data. Even if these data were scaled up by one-third to reflect missing information, the disparities would remain. Inward and outward FDI flows are shown in figure 9.2. (Note that the scale for inward FDI in the figure is one-third that for outward-bound funds.) The inward-outward ratio for the United States is over 100 percent; foreigners invest more in the U.S. than Americans invest abroad. The German, British, and French ratios of inward to outward FDI are 36 percent, 70 percent, and 85 percent, respectively.

**Figure 9.2: Japanese Inward and Outward Direct Investment,
1980-1999 (billion yen)**

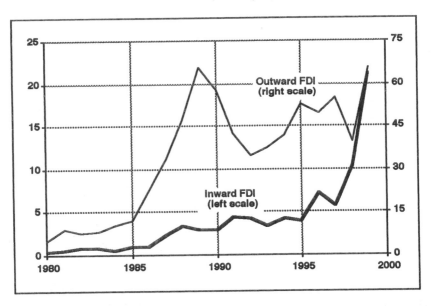

Source: Ministry of Finance

Toward the end of the 1990s, financial liberalization and restructuring of Japanese companies pushed the volume of inward investment closer to international norms. The MOF transactions figures, for example, show 1998 and 1999 activity doubling each year. Table 9.1 shows both the finance ministry's and Bank of Japan's FDI estimates.

The FDI data are buttressed by the count of mergers and acquisitions. Through the early 1990s, only a small number of foreign acquisitions of domestic Japanese firms occurred. Recof Corp., a leading M&A specialist, publishes an annual update on the volume of activity. Its figures showed fewer than twenty annual out-in transactions through the early 1990s (see figure 9.3). Activity jumped to 51 in 1997 and surged to 175 in 2000.

**Table 9.1: Japan's Inward and Outward Direct Investment,
MOF and BOJ Data, 1980-2000 (billion dollars)**

Year	Inward		Outward	
	MOF	BOJ	MOF	BOJ
1980	0.3	0.3	4.7	2.4
1981	0.4	0.2	8.9	4.9
1982	0.7	0.4	7.7	4.5
1983	0.8	0.4	8.1	3.6
1984	0.5	0.0	10.2	6.0
1985	0.9	0.6	12.2	6.4
1986	0.9	0.2	22.3	14.4
1987	2.2	1.2	33.4	20.1
1988	3.2	-0.5	47.0	35.4
1989	2.8	-1.1	65.5	46.2
1990	2.8	1.8	57.7	50.8
1991	4.4	1.3	42.3	31.7
1992	4.2	2.8	35.0	17.3
1993	3.2	0.2	37.3	13.9
1994	4.2	0.9	41.9	18.1
1995	3.9	0.0	52.7	22.6
1996	7.1	0.2	49.7	23.4
1997	5.6	3.2	54.7	26.0
1998	10.2	3.2	39.9	24.2
1999	21.1	12.8	65.5	22.8
2000	29.2	5.8	50.1	20.7

Sources: Ministry of Finance, Bank of Japan

At the same time, mergers and acquisitions among domestic partners also took off. Several forces drove these parallel trends: a search for rescuers of troubled companies; the sale by larger conglomerates of noncore and less profitable business units; the inability or unwillingness of domestic banks to continue lending to troubled clients; the retirement of a generation of owners who had established their businesses in the early postwar period; and the falling prices of assets. By 1998, foreign funds experienced at rescues and turnarounds entered Japan to seek out investment opportunities. According to fund managers, shortages of skilled professionals such as accountants and lawyers limited the number of transactions; the opportunities, they said, were more abundant than could be handled with the available personnel.

Notwithstanding Japan's M&A boom, its value pales in comparison with the United States or the United Kingdom, although it must be noted that these two countries are outliers in any international comparison. Japan's dollar value of inward M&A since 1997, though, is comparable to the European experience of just a few years earlier. This similarity is illustrated in figure 9.4, which shows that Japan's inward M&A in 1999 was equal to Germany's in 1996. Germany's inflow of $238 billion in 2000 was dominated by a single transaction, the British Vodafone Group's takeover of Mannesmann.

**Figure 9.3: Mergers and Acquisitions in Japan, 1986-2000
(number of transactions)**

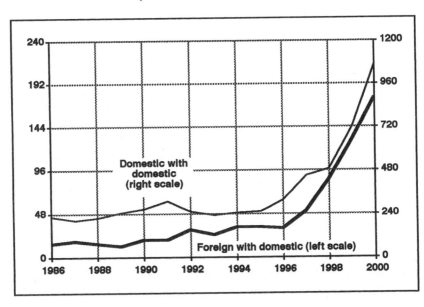

Source: Recof Corp.

The increased rate of foreign investment into Japan is confirmed by all the available data, whether it comes from the MOF or BOJ, or from M&A counts or values. This is not just, or even mainly, a cross-border phenomenon, but follows the shift within Japan toward more disciplined corporate governance as marked by the swelling of domestic M&A. Although FDI was powered in part by international forces, it was enabled by domestic metamorphoses.

The Foreign Direct Investment Position in Japan

The foreign stake in Japan is rather limited relative to the size of the economy as well as to levels elsewhere. The stock of FDI, shown in table 9.2, at the end of 2000 was ¥5,782 billion ($50.6 billion). This amount was less than 2 percent of the value of FDI in the United States as measured on a comparable market value basis. The foreign investment stock was just one percent of Japan's GDP in 2000, versus 30 percent in the United States. In fact, the total foreign position in Japan was less than one-fifth Japan's investment position in the United States.

**Figure 9.4: Value of Inward Mergers and Acquisitions
in Four Countries, 1996-2000
(billion dollars)**

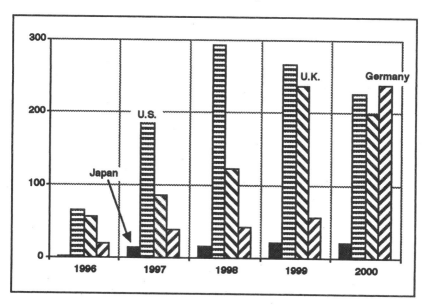

Source: KPMG and Computasoft Research, Ltd.

Part of the reason for the apparently low value of foreign investment in Japan is due to differences in accounting and measurement methods between the United States and other countries. The U.S. Department of Commerce put the year-end 1999 stock of American investment in Japan at $47.8 billion. The Bank of Japan's estimate was ¥1,910 billion ($18.7 billion). Several valuation differences account, at least in part, for this rather considerable inconsistency. Perhaps the greatest difference arises from the fact that the American figures are valued according to historical costs whereas the BOJ estimates are at market value. Although the IMF's direct investment manual calls for market value, only three of the advanced economies in the Organization for Economic Cooperation and Development make this adjustment.[5] The United States does it for its global position, but not for individual countries. The BOJ's adjustments of foreign investment to market value reduced the FDI stock position in the country during the 1990s—the years of greatest inflows—because of sharp falls in the Tokyo stock market indices.

Table 9.2: Foreign Direct Investment Position in Japan,
Selected Countries, 1996-2000
(billion yen)

Country	1996	1997	1998	1999	2000
United States.	1,785.4	1,769.6	1,688.0	1,910.1	1,625.5
France	35.9	37.6	38.9	882.3	949.4
Netherlands	140.2	186.7	159.6	337.1	614.9
Germany	253.0	286.4	233.0	314.4	554.8
United Kingdom.	284.4	324.8	157.5	322.7	424.5
Switzerland	148.2	197.1	178.9	232.9	249.9
Canada	65.2	97.6	77.0	36.7	240.3
Hong Kong	55.2	194.8	98.4	160.7	201.8
Taiwan	6.9	207.4	143.5	152.1	172.2
Australia	2.6	12.0	20.5	25.3	62.1
Sweden	18.5	27.3	35.6	17.4	49.4
Belgium / Luxembourg	18.8	16.6	13.7	1.3	48.5
Singapore	5.2	16.2	26.4	30.4	46.0
South Korea	1.3	7.3	10.8	12.9	12.3
Total	3,472.7	3,518.7	3,013.1	4,713	5,782.1

Source: Bank of Japan

In addition, historical-cost accounting does not adjust to a current-cost basis, which calibrates for changes in the replacement costs of the tangible assets of affiliates. Since the Japanese deflator for investment has actually fallen on the average since 1980, cost adjustments made by the Japanese authorities, but not by the American, would tend to reduce the yen value of investments made over this period. Another source of U.S.-Japan differences is that Japanese data compiled before 1996 did not include reinvested earnings or real estate transactions, which would tend to reduce the BOJ's stock position.

However, currency adjustments are made in all three methods—historical costs, current costs, and market value—to translate affiliates' foreign-currency-denominated assets and liabilities into U.S. dollars.[6] The yen's value relative to the dollar has risen over most of the period since the currency was allowed to float in the early 1970s; consequently, the U.S. adjustment to its historical-cost figures boosted the dollar value of investments in Japan. However, the same exchange rate appreciation also raises the dollar value when Japan's yen figures are converted back into current dollars. Exchange rate changes, therefore, do not explain the discrepancies.

Despite the data problems, the evidence of actual transactions shows a very different Japanese business sector from the one that existed over much of the postwar period. One example is the automobile industry. Of the ten auto and truck producers, six had substantial foreign ownership as of early 2001. General Motors Corp. held 49 percent of Isuzu Motors Ltd., 20 percent of Suzuki Motor Corp., and 21 percent of Fuji Heavy Industries, producer of the Subaru nameplate. Ford Motor Co. held a third of Mazda Motor Corp. and DaimlerChrysler AG owned 34 percent of Mitsubishi Motors Corp. The French auto company Renault S.A. owned a controlling 36.8 percent of Nissan Motor Co. Ltd. and 22.5 percent of its subsidiary Nissan Diesel Motor Co., Ltd. Only Toyota Motor Corp. and Honda Motor Co., Ltd. remained as independent companies, with Toyota controlling more than 50 percent of the shares of minicar maker Daihatsu Motor Co. Ltd. and the leading heavy truck producer Hino Motors Ltd.

According to Japanese corporate law, one-third share ownership gives a blocking vote on boards of directors; if actively managed, this position is equivalent to outright control. Ford, DaimlerChrysler, and Renault have taken command of their subsidiaries' driver seats. Through both capital investment and various forms of cooperation, the Japanese firms have become more integrated with the global industry.

U.S. FDI Experience in Japan

From ninth position in 1980, Japan charged into fourth place in the early 1990s in the league table of countries targeted by U.S. multinationals (see table 9.3). In 1995, the Netherlands overtook Japan as American and other investors poured funds into Dutch holding companies for reinvestment elsewhere. In the same way that American firms incorporate in the state of Delaware because of its lower legal and tax hurdles, multinationals have been basing their international operations in the Netherlands, especially since the creation of the European Union. This trend distorts the direct investment figures since the ultimate destination of the funds is likely to be different from the location of the holding company. For example, according to Japanese statistics, subsidiaries of Canadian and U.K. companies located in the Netherlands expanded their investment in Japan in 1999.[7] If the Netherlands is ignored, the U.S. FDI stock in Japan is the fourth largest.

Table 9.3: U.S. Direct Investment Position in Japan and Other Countries, 1980-2000 (billion dollars)

Year	Total	Japan	Canada	U.K.	Germany	Switzerland
1980	215.6	6.2	45.0	28.6	15.4	11.3
1981	226.4	6.8	45.1	30.3	15.8	12.5
1982	207.8	6.4	43.5	27.5	15.5	12.9
1983	212.2	7.7	44.3	27.6	15.3	14.1
1984	218.1	7.9	46.4	28.6	14.8	14.9
1985	238.4	9.1	46.4	34.0	16.7	16.2
1986	270.5	11.5	50.6	35.4	20.9	16.4
1987	326.3	15.7	57.8	44.5	24.4	19.7
1988	347.2	18.0	62.7	49.5	21.8	18.7
1989	381.8	19.9	63.9	67.7	23.7	21.1
1990	430.5	22.5	69.1	72.5	27.5	25.2
1991	467.8	24.9	68.9	78.1	34.0	25.6
1992	502.1	26.6	68.7	85.2	33.0	28.7
1993	564.3	31.1	69.9	109.2	36.8	33.1
1994	612.9	36.5	78.0	121.3	38.5	34.4
1995	699.0	37.3	83.5	106.3	44.2	36.3
1996	795.2	34.6	89.6	134.6	41.3	30.7
1997	871.3	33.9	96.6	154.5	40.7	30.6
1998	1,000.7	41.4	98.2	183.0	47.7	38.2
1999	1,130.8	49.4	111.1	212.0	50.9	48.8
2000	1,244.7	55.6	126.4	233.4	53.6	54.9

Note: Direct investment position is measured according to historical costs.
Source: Department of Commerce

Based on MOF transactions figures, cumulative U.S. direct investment in Japan since 1950 totaled $50.7 billion as of March 2000, a figure comparable to that from the Commerce Department, despite the many definitional differences.

A different perspective on the scale of U.S. operations is provided by the financial and operating data of U.S. parent companies and their foreign affiliates. These data are collected according to two different definition of FDI based on ownership percentages: 10 percent ownership of an enterprise—the standard definition in the IMF manual; plus a narrower definition that requires majority ownership. Both of these sets of figures are shown in table 9.4. Owners' equity in majority-owned affiliates in Japan was $39.3 billion in 1998, which is not too different from the historical-cost position for that year.

Table 9.4: Financial Data of U.S. Affiliates in Japan, Greater than 10-Percent and Majority Ownership, 1985-1998

Year	Affiliates (number)	Total Assets (bn. $)	Sales (bn. $)	Net Income (bn. $)	Employees (000)	Owners' Equity (bn. $)	Gross Product (bn. $)
Greater than 10-Percent Ownership							
1985	667	63.9	80.2	2.0	329.6	NA	NA
1990	825	155.2	165.0	3.7	402.4	NA	NA
1995	1,008	281.0	214.6	5.7	423.6	NA	NA
1998	1,001	298.5	182.3	4.0	404.2	NA	NA
Majority Ownership							
1985	NA	18.9	28.0	0.9	NA	6.2	NA
1990	489	61.4	61.9	2.1	98.0	14.3	NA
1995	657	191.0	111.2	4.3	141.6	29.6	24.3
1998	683	232.3	103.6	3.1	168.0	39.3	23.6

Source: Department of Commerce

One gauge of American activity in Japan is gross product, which is measured in a way that allows comparisons with gross domestic product. To calculate gross product, purchases from other firms are subtracted from sales. The remainder is the value of the final product that is added by the firm; it comprises payments for so-called factors of production: labor, interest, profits, and indirect taxes. Gross product (or value added) of majority-owned U.S. firms in Japan was $23.6 billion in 1998, enough to rank Japan in fifth place among the targets for U.S. FDI. However, as a proportion of national GDP, Japan's ratio of 0.6 percent is almost at the bottom of the listings, just ahead of Korea, China, and India. Among the advanced economies that have a reputation for hostility to foreign investment, the gross product of American companies in France and Germany was 2.5 percent and 2.6 percent, respectively.[8] Thus, the assertion that Japan has had a low receptivity to foreign presence is consistent with this evidence.

The sales of majority-owned U.S. affiliates in Japan amounted to more than $100 billion in 1998, more than 90 percent of which were in Japan. Exports from the United States to these affiliates added up to over $12 billion, while imports were $2.0 billion.[9] Most of this trade was between affiliates and parents. More broadly, U.S. exports involving U.S. parents and their foreign affiliates accounted for 64 percent of total American exports in 1998. Such a positive association between exports and FDI has been observed frequently. For example, a study by Edward M. Graham of the Institute for International Economics in Washington, D.C., found that exports are positively correlated with FDI. In addition, he notes, "the 'runaway plant' argument is not supported by the analysis" and "the 'pauper labor' argument so often heard in the United States these days is not supported by the results." In contrast to popular beliefs, U.S. direct investment abroad and U.S. imports are more closely associated with high-wage countries than with low-wage economies, Mr. Graham notes.[10] Indeed, the Commerce Department's surveys show that almost 80 percent of the assets of American affiliates are in high-wage countries.

The sectors targeted by U.S. investors in Japan have changed over time. The investment position on a historical-cost basis indicates that the share of the petroleum industry, which was more than 40 percent of the total in the 1970s, already was down to 25 percent in 1980. Figures for 1999 put it under 10 percent. Manufacturing also declined from its high of 52 percent in 1987; its 1999 share at 28 percent was 24 percentage points below that peak.

Services industries gained the most. Wholesale trade and financial services (other than banking but including insurance and real estate) more than doubled their combined shares from 19 percent in 1984 to 43 percent in 1999. Despite the relative gains of services broadly defined, manufacturing still represents the second largest absolute amount of American investment in Japan, with a 1999 value of $13.3 billion.

According to the financial and operating data on parent companies and their foreign affiliates, the distribution across industries of U.S. firms in Japan with greater than 50 percent ownership differs from that in the 10 percent-50 percent range; almost three-quarters of the assets of majority-owned firms were in finance and real estate whereas the minority firms had under 1 percent of their assets in that sector. (See table 9.5.) Minority-owned firms were more likely to be in manufacturing, with two-thirds of their assets committed to that sector.

**Table 9.5: Asset Distribution of American Affiliates in Japan
by Industry and Ownership Share, 1988, 1998
(billion dollars and percent)**

Percent Ownership	Total Assets (bn. $)	Mfg. (%)	Wholesale Trade (%)	FIRE (%)	Services (%)	Other (%)
1988						
> 50%	50.4	30.0	16.9	43.7	1.5	0.7
10-50%	80.5	59.0	7.9	9.6	1.1	2.3
1998						
>50%	232.3	9.9	6.4	72.5	6.3	11.1
10-50%	66.2	67.0	1.5	0.2	6.5	31.3

Note: FIRE: Finance (except banks), insurance, and real estate.
Source: Department of Commerce

The 1998 concentration of majority-owned firms in the financial sector reflects, in part, their date of entry into the Japanese market. Finance opened up only in the late 1990s. American financial services firms had both experience operating in new fields and risk capital, both of which were scarce among domestic competitors. When the foreign investment houses and brokerage firms arrived, those already on the scene had little special advantage in understanding an environment that was changing rapidly.

Why have American companies invested almost $50 billion in Japan? Sales of $100 billion are an insufficient incentive if the returns are not competitive with alternative investments. U.S. companies received $7.3 billion in investment income from Japan in 2000, equivalent to an annual rate of return of 13.1 percent. As figure 9.5 shows, rates of return, calculated as the ratio of income earned from foreign investment to its value on a historical-cost basis, are somewhat lower in Japan than elsewhere, especially in the slow-growth 1990s. The average return from 1980 to 2000 was 10.1 percent compared to the average worldwide figure of 12.2 percent. FDI generated higher returns than the estimated yields on domestic U.S. investment, which averaged 7.8 percent, although measured on a different basis.[11] As measured on a consistent basis through 1990, foreign direct investment by American companies in the ten most important destinations for U.S. capital overseas was more profitable than the return earned at home.[12] In contrast, as described in the last chapter, foreign companies in the United States earn significantly lower returns than do domestic American companies. In short, U.S. companies make more money abroad, including Japan, than the average local company. They earn more abroad than they do at home, and they do considerably better than foreign investors in the United States. American FDI pays.

Figure 9.5: Returns on U.S. FDI in All Countries and Japan, 1980-2000 (percent)

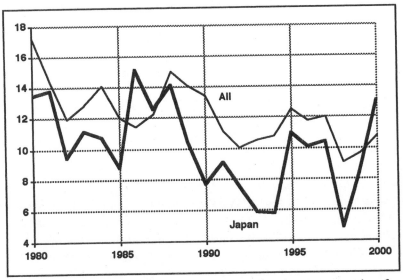

Note: Returns calculated as ratio of income earned on direct investment to value of FDI on a historical-cost basis.
Source: Department of Commerce.

Zooming in for Details

Just where is this money going? Who is doing the investing? What areas are they emphasizing? A review of the Japan Economic Institute's monthly *Japan-U.S. Business Report*, which tracked developments involving Japanese businesses in the United States and U.S. activities in Japan, provides some tentative answers to these questions. I extracted from the pages of the report all instances of direct investment for two periods: the twelve months from April 1996 to March 1997, and the six months from January through June 2000, the last issue of the publication. Because of the growth of FDI in Japan between these periods, the number of cases per year doubled over the four years between the two data samples.

Table 9.6: Cases of U.S. Direct Investment in Japan by Industry, 1996-1997, 2000

	April 1996-March 1997	January-June 2000
Chemicals	21	3
Computers and Peripherals	17	8
Construction and Real Estate	7	9
Electric Machinery	4	3
Financial Services	5	59
Food and Agricultural Products	11	5
Merchandising	17	3
Miscellaneous	28	33
Nonelectric Machinery	9	3
Precision and Medical Equipment	8	6
Semiconductors	18	13
Software and Information Services	54	56
Telecommunications	21	23
Transportation Equipment	3	5
Total	223	229
Of which, Internet related	36	77

Source: *Japan-U.S. Business Report*, various issues

The compilation identified 223 inward investment activities in the first period and 229 in the second. Such activities included opening or expanding a subsidiary, enlarging production capacity, or opening a service center or office. Licensing agreements, distribution relationships, and new product introductions were ignored. Some of these latter actions may have involved the investment of new resources, but it could not be verified with the information available in the original sources. These cases, aggregated in table 9.6 into broad categories, illustrate the broad horizon of U.S. business investment in Japan and the change over the relatively brief period of four years.

Not all of the investments were made by large multinational corporations. Hand-tool maker Zircon Corp., for example, in Japan since 1997, opened a new headquarters in 2000 to extend its customer base beyond do-it-your-self amateurs to professional contractors. In the Internet business sector, Razorfish Inc. jumped into the e-business consulting market in Japan through an equally owned venture with Intervision Inc., a Sony Corp. advertising agency. Especially in the software industry, many of those opening or expanding in Japan were themselves new startups who found Japan either too large a potential market to ignore, or who teamed up with Japanese companies that possessed complementary technologies.

Software had the largest number of transactions in 1996-1997 and the second largest in 2000, when it was outpaced by financial services. The torrent of activity in the financial sector reflected two main influences, deregulation and the great number of distressed Japanese companies that had become tempting targets for investors armed with cash and a willingness to accept risk. The other booming area was almost anything related to the Internet. The American Internet boom of 2000 echoed across the Pacific. In 1996-1997, Internet-related activities were associated with thirty-six transactions (16 percent), mainly in the software and telecommunications sectors; by 2000, they accounted for one-third of all cases, scattered across most sectors. These ventures were at the interface between hardware, software, finance, and telecommunications services, representing the leading edge of American high technology industry. Whether the Internet exuberance proves to be profitable remains to be seen.

Another illustration of U.S. productivity and innovation is in the merchandising sector, where seventeen transactions were recorded in 1996-1997. Retailing penetration covered a wide range, from catalog stores to large discount centers for products as varied as office supplies and sporting goods. In addition to retailers themselves, the construction and real estate sector included several shopping center developments. The American retail scene is one of the most dynamic in the world; its increasing presence in Japan is consistent with this strength. One development that permitted the introduction of larger stores was the progressively liberalized regulatory environment, especially phasing out the Large Retail Store Law. However, by 2000, a good deal of the momentum in this industry had dissipated.

There is no single path to success in Japan, but some patterns exist in the data. A common approach to investment is gradual immersion in the market. A small representative office initiates the process, often as part of a marketing agreement with a Japanese distributor. Later, expansion of this office into a service and support operation may be justified as the volume of business grows. A full-fledged subsidiary, generally responsible for marketing and sales, but sometimes involving local development and production, is a next step. Finally, after the accumulation of sufficient local experience, some companies withdraw from their original joint venture arrangements to go it alone.

Not all investments pay off. There were fifteen withdrawals or downsizings in the earlier period and five in the later. Among the 1996-1997 disinvestments were three delistings from the Tokyo Stock Exchange, plus the sale of a seat on the TSE. In the heady days of the late 1980s when Japan's stock market was skyrocketing in value, a Tokyo listing looked like a good bet. However, the post-1989 stock market collapse and the even greater shrinkage in traded shares reduced the benefits of an active presence on the exchange.

The other withdrawals represent ventures that did not pan out as expected. For several, the market did not develop or competition from other providers was too severe. For example, Hughes Electronics Corp., the parent of DirecTV, Inc., acknowledged defeat in the direct-to-home satellite television services market. At the end of 2000, DirecTV Japan ceased operations after missing all its targets for subscriber growth in the two-plus years it had been in business. In retailing, athletic shoe retailer Footlocker Inc. closed all five of its stores and liquidated its subsidiary in 2000. Several operations closed because of high costs in Japan. In 2000, high costs dictated that H.J. Heinz Inc. close a plant in Utsunomiya, Tochigi prefecture, that had been producing soups and sauces since 1982. Other incidents involved the restructuring operations of longtime American competitors in the Japanese market. Ice cream seller Haagen-Dazs Inc. closed the poor performers among its eighty-four stores in Japan—about 20 percent of the total—and replaced them with better-located shops modeled on the dessert cafe it opened at the start of 1999 in Tokyo's Shibuya district.

Inward Investment and Deregulation

Government regulation at the industry level in Japan has been a major barrier to the entry of new firms, domestic or foreign. Sometimes these restraints are formal, as in insurance and banking. In other cases, though, product standards for health, safety, or quality that deviate enough from those in place elsewhere constitute a barrier to entry. For example, safety standards are a problem in cosmetics because the Japanese list of approved ingredients differs substantially from American and international counterparts; disputes have arisen over aerosols, liposomes, and preservatives. Other regulations were designed explicitly to control domestic competition but have had the effect of limiting foreign entry as well. The monopolies formerly given to the two companies responsible for domestic and international telephone services are examples.

One-quarter of the firms responding to a 1990 questionnaire administered by the American Chamber of Commerce in Japan said that regulatory restrictions limited the types of goods and services they could provide and impeded their penetration of local markets. The response varied dramatically across sectors, though. A full 77 percent of financial firms were affected negatively, but competitors in other areas, such as software, saw no effect.[13] Minister Ryutaro Hashimoto's financial sector "Big Bang" deregulation implemented from 1997 through 2002 created the conditions for the next wave of foreign investment; as shown in table 9.6, financial services had the largest number of transactions in 2000. Indeed, late 2001 Tokyo interviews with one major American financial firm suggested that few formal business barriers remain in place.

Attempts to reduce protective barriers can be counted on to generate powerful political opposition. An example of one such barrier that protected a favored political group was the Large Retail Store Law, enacted by the Liberal Democratic Party in 1956 as the Department Store Law to protect small shopkeepers. The 1956 law reestablished restrictions first enacted in the 1930s that were suspended during the American occupation.[14] It set tight limits on the size of retail establishments. Opening stores with sales floor spaces larger than 1,500 square meters (3,000 square meters in Japan's eleven largest cities) required lengthy and often fruitless hearings before approval commissions dominated by local store owners.

When supermarkets and department stores found ways to get around the size limits, the LDP introduced the Large Retail Store Law in 1974 to eliminate the loopholes. Implementation of the law was assigned to local governments, which introduced their own interpretations. MITI also offered guidance in implementing the legislation. The net result was that even tighter restrictions than stipulated in the law severely curtailed shops over 500 square meters. Even if approval eventually was granted, the process often took a decade or more. Many plans were delayed for so long they were abandoned. Other potential entrants never even made the effort, knowing of the long and bitter fights that would be required.

American retailing giants and the U.S. government also viewed the Large Retail Store Law as a major barrier to entry, especially because many American retailing innovations center on large establishments. Toy retailer Toys "R" Us Inc., when planning its entry into the Japanese market, found the law to be the one major impediment that it could not remove on its own. The company requested U.S. government assistance to bring pressure on the Japanese government in the late 1980s to liberalize the law.

That lobbying coincided with the 1989-1990 Structural Impediments Initiative discussions, where the distribution system was one of six areas targeted for reform. Tokyo eventually agreed to liberalize implementation of the Large Retail Store Law by expanding in phases the sizes of stores requiring approval, establishing transparent approval criteria for larger stores, and setting a time limit of one year for a decision.

The process became routine. The time from first request to groundbreaking for Toys "R" Us fell to eighteen months, which the company said compared favorably with its experience in other countries and with the twelve months required in the United States. The change in the application of this one law allowed Toys "R" Us to open more than one hundred large stores around Japan to become the country's largest toy retailer.

The regulatory change also shifted forever competitive relations among industry participants. Toys "R" Us negotiated directly with Japanese manufacturers; at first, they refused to deal. Only when orders went outside the country and the company introduced the incentive of its worldwide sales did domestic producers begin to talk business. Dealing directly with manufacturers and cutting out layers of middlemen, Toys "R" Us compounded the low costs of its procurement efficiency by offering a much larger variety of products than available in the traditional Japanese store. Moreover, it managed high volumes of sales with computerized transactions and inventory systems linked to product planning and purchasing.

Prices not only fell at the innovating company, Toys "R" Us, but also throughout the industry, as local shops—forced to compete for the first time—formed cooperatives, changed purchasing and selling methods, specialized in particular market niches, and bargained directly with manufacturers that in the past had insisted on maintaining suggested retail prices. Thus, the partial liberalization of the regulations that implemented a single law and the entry of one foreign company transformed an entire industry. Subsequently, merchandising became one of the hot areas for foreign entrants in the Japanese market.

The relaxation of restrictions on large stores had a greater impact on domestic operators than on foreign ones. The number of large stores had been stable between 1985 and 1993, growing barely 1 percent annually despite the booming Japanese economy. From 1993 to 1999, though, more than 1,100 new establishments opened, a 50 percent jump in just six years.[15] In this case, foreign lobbying was able to take advantage of a latent homegrown desire to deregulate; when the new law was implemented, domestic companies were ready to take advantage of their new opportunities.[16]

In most cases, foreign investment barriers were side effects of policies directed toward other goals. Nevertheless, the wave of deregulation that has been proceeding since the 1980s has had a marked impact on FDI. As deregulation proceeds, the presence of foreigners in the Japanese economy can only increase.

Notes

1.   American Chamber of Commerce in Japan, *Trade and Investment in Japan: The Current Environment*, (Tokyo: June 1991), 29.

2.   Richard E. Caves, *Multinational Enterprise and Economic Analysis* (New York: Cambridge University Press, 1996), 52.

3.   David E. Weinstein, *Foreign Direct Investment and Keiretsu: Rethinking U.S. and Japanese Policy* (Working Paper No. 122) (New York: Center on Japanese Economy and Business, Columbia University, June 1996), 5.

4.   Raymond Mataloni Jr., "A Guide to BEA Statistics on U.S. Multinational Companies," *Survey of Current Business* (March 1995).

5.   International Monetary Fund and Organization for Economic Cooperation and Development, *Report on the Survey of Implementation of Methodological Standards for Direct Investment*, March 2000, 44.

6.   Sylvia E. Bargas, "Direct Investment Positions for 1999 Country and Industry Detail," *Survey of Current Business* (July 2000): 57.

7.   "Japan's International Investment Position as of End-1999," *Bank of Japan Quarterly Bulletin* (August 2000): 108.

8.   Raymond Mataloni Jr., "U.S. Multinational Companies, Operations in 1998," *Survey of Current Business* (July 2000): 34.

9.   Mataloni, "U.S. Multinational Companies," 41.

10.   Edward M. Graham, "The Relationship Between Trade and Foreign Direct Investment in the Manufacturing Sector: Empirical Results for the United States and Japan," in Dennis Encarnacion (ed.), *Does Ownership Matter: Japanese Multinationals in East Asia* (London: Oxford University Press, 1997).

11.   Domestic rates of return were calculated as the ratio of profits of domestic non-financial corporations plus net interest to the current-cost value of the net stock of equip-

ment, software, and structures and the replacement cost value of inventories. Daniel Larkins, "Note on Rates of Return for Domestic Nonfinancial Corporations: Revised Estimates for 1960-98," *Survey of Current Business* (June 2000): 16.

12.   Domestic rates of return through 1990 were calculated as the weighted average of the long-term interest rate and the earnings-price ratio of shares. See J. Steven Landefeld, Ann M. Lawson and Douglas Weinberg, "Rates of Return on Direct Investment," *Survey of Current Business* (August 1992): 79.

13.   American Chamber of Commerce in Japan, *Trade and Investment in Japan*, 29

14.   This history is described in Roy Larke, *Japanese Retailing* (New York: Routledge, 1994), chapter 4.

15.   Management and Coordination Agency, Statistics Bureau, *Japan Statistical Yearbook 2001*, table 11.7.

16.   For a description of foreign-domestic links in the negotiations over the law, see: Leonard Schoppa, *Bargaining with Japan: What American Pressure Can and Cannot Do*, (New York: Columbia University Press, 1997), chapter 6.

Chapter 10

U.S.-Japan Relations Viewed through Events Data

Overview

Research on foreign relations based on selected incidents, case studies, or accumulated anecdotes can produce biased selections of information for analysis. Even with the most scholarly of intent, observations based on selected data can reduce the generality of the conclusions. An objective set of comprehensive events data spanning fifty years arguably eliminates many of the biases of other analytical methods. This chapter examines just such an approach.

Events data for the 1948-1997 period provide insight into U.S.-Japan relations in the economic, political, and military spheres across those fifty years. As defined by scholars, an "event" is a discrete occurrence with a beginning and end, an actor and a target; to be considered as an event, the occurrence should possess sufficient prominence to stand out from the background of normal developments. An analysis of more than 4,000 such transpacific records indicates that military events colored the 1950s, political activities characterized the 1960s, and economic issues shaped the U.S.-Japan relationship since the 1970s. In fact, in the 1980s, economic interactions came to dominate bilateral affairs. The expansion of two-way trade between the United States and Japan was the main force making economic events preeminent.

Regardless of the sphere, most U.S.-Japan events are routine, reflecting the many activities that require governmental attention in daily dealings between two of the world's largest economies. Although the number of conflictual events has jumped, especially since the 1980s, the volume and the intensity of cooperative developments have increased even more.

Statistical analysis of the data indicates that neither positive nor negative U.S.-Japan economic incidents have had much effect on bilateral political or military relations. However, political conflict, typically stimulated by random events, appears to produce more economic and military cooperation. One interpretation of this result is that the two governments react to political conflict by working harder to maintain harmony in other parts of the complex relationship.

Evolving Use of Events Data

How may relations between countries be characterized? How, for example, can the following questions concerning dealings between the United States and Japan be answered? Are U.S.-Japan relations strengthening, declining, or suffering from trade frictions; are they marked by cooperation on the security and diplomatic fronts? Are bilateral political and military relations at the mercy of trade disputes, or are American economic interests sacrificed to advance military and political cooperation?

This chapter attempts to address such questions using so-called events data on U.S.-Japan relations that span the fifty years from 1948 through 1997. Before proceeding, though, it may be helpful to discuss the origins of events data and the problems associated with their use, especially since they rarely, if ever, have been applied to analyses of U.S.-Japan affairs.

The use of events data in the study of political science, international relations, and economics began in the 1950s as social scientists in universities and policy analysts working for government agencies and think tanks attempted to apply theories coming from the research community. Case studies of particular events had been the main method for addressing these subjects. However, critics of the case study approach noted that cases usually were selected for their outstanding or unusual properties and, therefore, conclusions based on a limited number of cases were unlikely to be generalizable because of the biases imposed by the selection process itself. As political scientists sought better tests of their theories of intercountry relations, especially those concerning the sources of conflict and war, they turned to collections of comprehensive data on international relations.

One type of information that appeared to satisfy research requirements was the "event." The concept appealed both to diplomats and to historians, who viewed international relations as a series of occurrences—negotiations, protests, agreements, crises, conferences, wars. As scholars tried to distill the data that described these acts into a manageable form, they defined an event as a distinct action with a start and a finish, an initiator and a target, and sufficient prominence to differentiate it from everyday happenings.[1]

The Conflict and Peace Data Bank, a collection used in this chapter, originally was compiled in the late 1960s by Edward Azar in a doctoral dissertation on Middle East conflict. Mr. Azar defined an event as an occurrence between nations that stands out enough from the constant flow of transactions to have been reported by a news source.

Building on his doctoral work, Mr. Azar expanded his data set from its original regional focus to a global range. To enlarge COPDAB, a small army of graduate students at the University of Michigan scanned newspapers and journals from around the world for evidence of intercountry events involving 135 nations; they assigned each event to one of eight issue areas—for example, politics or economics. The researchers also coded each event into one of fifteen cooperation or conflict categories, ordinally ranked by their intensity. The COPDAB data bank eventually incorporated more than 500,000 event records for 135 countries, extracted from seventy periodicals worldwide.

Political science and the study of international relations became more mathematical and data-oriented in the 1960s and the 1970s and the use of events data surged. A survey of fifteen major U.S. international politics journals for the years 1974 through 1986 found events data employed in sixty-one articles.[2] By the early 1980s, more than forty sets of events data were stored at an international depository for political and social research.[3]

As the usage of events data grew, however, it attracted criticism from creators and users as well as from skeptics. Charles McClelland, the originator of one widely used set of data, the World Event Interaction Survey, summarized many of the doubts raised by compilers and critics alike. Events based on public reporting of the news, he said, are likely to be biased by the selection and the suppression of stories by reporters, editors, and media owners. Moreover, since much of the work of international relations takes place in secret, publicly reported events may not represent the real circumstances of world affairs. Even if the reporting is unbiased and complete, the partisan interests of reporters, editors, and data set compilers can distort interpretation. Mr. McClelland accepted the contention that "it is impossible to claim that reports of happenings in international relations are never fabricated, never manipulated, or never concealed."[4]

Nonetheless, he went on to note that world news collection and dissemination have become large-scale, highly organized enterprises. He reasoned that reports appearing in major newspapers and carried by wire services constitute the first version of international history. In addition, participants in secret, closed-door negotiations often have reasons to leak information about the discussions; for instance, they may be motivated by attempts to influence outcomes or to establish their own places in history. Mr. McClelland cited the finding that even intelligence officers derive an estimated 80 percent to 90 percent of their reporting from unclassified sources. Although later revelations and historical scholarship may modify the initial story, "often the current selections, descriptions, and interpretations survive as originally published, or they are modified only slightly to become the conventional 'truth' of history."[5]

Despite this positive review, the critics had made several valid points and funding for and use of events data fell sharply in the 1980s. Work on many data sets was abandoned. COPDAB, for one, ceased to be updated after 1978. However, the growth of computer capabilities and the development of massive on-line news sources such as Lexis-Nexis led researchers to rethink their strategies and to explore methods for exploiting the new capabilities.

A group of international scholars in the early 1990s developed a coordinated research agenda that tried to address the critics while figuring out how to take advantage of the available computer and on-line facilities. The Data Development for International Research consortium received funding from the National Science Foundation to improve existing collections of high-quality events data and to design software to facilitate the generation of such information.[6]

The University of Maryland's Global Events Data System, a DDIR consortium participant, aimed to create a core data set that could be used by various researchers for their own particular requirements. Each data record included sufficient information to code an event and interpret it according to individual interests and questions. The GEDS events framework is based on the older COPDAB approach.

The GEDS project addressed one of the main criticisms of the older methods. Most previous data-gathering efforts used major newspapers like the *New York Times* as their main sources of information. However, editors' selection of each day's stories from a mountain of potential articles imparted a bias to the published news and, therefore, to a database created from that record.

To get around this problem, GEDS used the Reuters World Service, which has news gatherers around the world, usually local reporters, who put stories on the wire for use by editors everywhere. Tapping this source to develop events data removes most of the bias that worried the earlier generation of scholars, although some residual bias may persist in terms of what local reporters find newsworthy.

I acquired all of the 1,479 COPDAB records on U.S.-Japan relations from 1948 to 1978. Through funds provided by an Abe Fellowship grant from the Center for Global Partnership, the GEDS project extracted 2,838 events on U.S.-Japan relations occurring in the years from 1979 through 1997. (Reuters data for the first two months of 1979 were not available.) In all, more than 4,300 observations covering fifty years of postwar experience are available for analysis.

Each COPDAB event was punched into an eighty-column card to create a record that included date, actor and target, a verb indicating the action, and a forty-five-character description of the event. As noted, the COPDAB teams coded events into one of eight issue areas and scored each according to its intensity; this gauge ranged from one for the most cooperative to fifteen for the most conflictual (See the appendix to this chapter for descriptions of the intensity scores.) GEDS researchers compiled events records with the same information, but they increased the number of fields and expanded the descriptions. The text describing U.S.-Japan events averages 500 characters, with some summaries five times that length.[7]

Some scholars insist that events records should be used "as is," without any aggregation, in order to understand the unfolding nature of a negotiation or a crisis. That objective, however, is not the only one that occupies the minds of researchers. A study of U.S. and North Atlantic Treaty Organization relations with Serbia during the Bosnian conflict, for example, used a weekly window to examine the shifting balance of diplomatic behavior and its impact on results.[8] Other studies use monthly or annual events totals. This chapter employs yearly aggregates, which has the advantage of identifying broader tendencies and influences on bilateral ties. Monthly data, on the other hand, would better illuminate diplomatic dynamics as one country reacts directly and immediately to the behavior of the other.

Examples of Events Data

A few examples may give a better feel for the nature of this approach. A COPDAB economic event from October 7, 1969, lightly edited to make the telegraphic style somewhat more readable, states: "Japan agrees with U.S. to lower import controls on some goods." This event was assigned a cooperative value of four. A conflictual economic event with a value of ten occurred March 10, 1970: "U.S. blames Japanese competition for layoffs." Another ten-rated conflictual economic event with Japan as the actor and the United States as the target was dated July 5, 1969: "Japan prohibits U.S. purchase of Sony shares by foreign investor." A political event from June 4, 1972, scored a five on the cooperation scale: "U.S. visit to Japan by Kissinger; discuss U.S. relations, USSR, China."

GEDS event descriptions include much more information than was possible in the abbreviated COPDAB format, although the subject matter often has a haunting familiarity. A mildly cooperative event with a value of seven occurred July 7, 1993:

> U.S. President Bill Clinton called for a tearing down of trade barriers with Japan on July 7. Clinton issued a plea on Wednesday to the Japanese people to join in a "common cause" to tear down trade barriers that not only hurt American workers but drive up prices in Japan. "The persistent trade imbalance ... has hurt the Japanese people, deprived you of the full benefits of a strong economy," he told students at Waseda University. "I would send this message to all of you and to the people beyond the walls here in this hall," Clinton said. "You have a common cause with the people of America—a common cause against outdated practices that undermine our relationship and diminish the quality of your lives." "You are entitled to no less, and it will be a part of your role as a great nation for the foreseeable future to have that sort of open relationship," he said. "We look to Japan to address its own economic agenda with equal vigor, including help with promoting global economic growth and removing both formal and informal barriers to the flow of goods, services and investment," he said.

A more critical economic event with a value of ten took place later that year:

> U.S. Trade Representative Mickey Kantor said he was ready to act if no progress was made in trade negotiations with Japan on October 22. The row comes over what the U.S. says are unfair practices in Japan's construction bidding system. If nothing is done, the U.S. says it would close part of its construction

bidding market to Japan. Earlier in Tokyo, a construction ministry official said Japan was considering an open bidding system for public works projects in a last-minute bid to head off the U.S. sanctions. "We have not made significant progress," Kantor said in a telephone interview. "This has been a seven-year struggle and the November 1 deadline is real." "I would like to compile within this month basic plans to introduce an open, competitive bidding system on projects above a certain value, and to improve the bidding and contracting system of public works based on the principles of transparency and competitiveness," Japanese Prime Minister Hosokawa said.

Trends in U.S.-Japan Relations

Transpacific events have grown in number and changed in character over the decades. Military activities were the most numerous type of event in the 1950s, a reflection of the lingering effects of the American military occupation of Japan plus the later establishment of a formal military alliance between the countries. The annual frequency of events, broken down by type, is presented in table 10.1 whereas figure 10.1 summarizes these trends by decade and type of issue.

The data compilers delineated two kinds of political events. One included only symbolic, verbal, or rhetorical actions. Such activities tended to be statements of intent, expectations, or preferences conveying the subjective aspect of relationships. An extract from a rhetorical event of June 18, 1980, states: "American President Carter voiced his sorrow over the death of Prime Minister Masayoshi Ohira." The second type of political event was action-oriented and encompassed diplomatic activities, negotiations, and other political interactions.

To simplify the data presented in the figure, I combined the original eight issues into four. Symbolic-rhetorical political events were joined with political actions to form a unified "political" category. Four separate issues in the original categories were consolidated into a single "other" category: cultural, scientific, and education issues; physical environment, ecology, and natural resource issues; minorities, human rights, and health issues; and "other" issues. Most of the events in this combined category involve scientific and cultural cooperation.

Over the fifty-year period, economic events accounted for 48 percent of the total. The combined political categories represented about one-quarter. The set of military interactions was next largest with 17 percent.

Chapter 10

Table 10.1: U.S.-Japan Events by Year and Type, 1948-1997

Year	Pol. (Rhetoric)	Pol. (Action)	Military	Econ.	Culture, Science	Environ-mental	Human Issues	Other	Total
1948	0	2	5	6	0	0	0	0	13
1949	0	2	1	1	1	0	0	0	5
1950	1	9	6	9	2	0	5	0	32
1951	2	25	15	10	1	0	1	0	54
1952	2	14	12	14	1	0	7	0	50
1953	1	21	25	11	3	0	0	0	61
1954	0	14	11	12	1	0	2	0	40
1955	1	8	20	10	4	2	0	0	45
1956	0	8	4	9	1	1	0	0	23
1957	4	14	31	7	2	1	9	0	68
1958	2	5	18	6	4	2	1	0	38
1959	1	1	9	3	0	0	0	0	14
1960	2	30	9	8	2	0	2	0	53
1961	0	11	4	19	1	1	1	0	37
1962	4	12	19	10	7	0	0	0	52
1963	0	13	15	25	3	1	0	0	57
1964	1	9	8	5	3	0	0	0	26
1965	2	19	7	3	3	0	0	0	34
1966	2	29	9	15	3	0	0	0	58
1967	1	20	6	9	5	2	0	0	43
1968	3	11	11	15	2	2	1	0	45
1969	1	33	15	31	4	0	1	0	85
1970	3	29	21	35	3	0	0	0	91
1971	3	19	11	29	1	0	0	0	63
1972	0	35	11	12	6	0	0	0	64
1973	1	34	18	36	1	9	0	0	99
1974	0	22	5	9	3	2	0	0	41
1975	3	12	9	5	7	0	0	0	36
1976	0	15	8	4	2	1	0	0	30
1977	0	14	4	32	4	8	0	0	62
1978	0	11	9	38	2	0	0	0	60
1979	0	6	0	19	0	0	0	0	25
1980	6	21	8	10	1	0	1	0	47
1981	0	12	21	22	2	1	0	0	58
1982	0	6	3	5	0	1	0	0	15
1983	0	21	34	41	6	0	1	5	108
1984	0	6	3	24	3	6	0	0	42
1985	0	6	4	24	2	0	0	0	36

Continued on next page.

Table 10.1—*Continued*

Year	Pol. (Rhetoric)	Pol. (Action)	Military	Econ.	Culture Science	Environ-mental	Human Issues	Other	Total
1986	3	8	10	49	3	2	0	0	75
1987	1	43	20	115	2	0	0	0	181
1988	0	18	13	129	21	6	1	1	189
1989	0	31	30	94	30	4	3	3	195
1990	0	17	19	96	20	1	4	1	158
1991	4	21	33	90	4	2	1	0	155
1992	0	26	18	99	8	6	4	0	161
1993	2	46	14	159	1	0	1	0	223
1994	5	48	19	159	7	1	3	0	242
1995	1	78	42	272	26	1	2	0	422
1996	2	73	62	137	12	2	12	0	300
1997	0	47	45	77	6	19	12	0	206
Total	64	1,035	754	2,059	236	84	75	10	4,317

The "other" categories added up to less than 10 percent of the aggregate. Political actions came to the fore in the 1960s as Cold War diplomacy and activities in Vietnam and the People's Republic of China assumed greater importance. With the growth of U.S.-Japan trade and other economic interactions, economic events edged out political activities in the 1970s. This trend accelerated in the next two decades. Economics came to dominate and define affairs between Tokyo and Washington.

The importance of economics as the defining issue in U.S.-Japan relations is underscored by a look at the annual number of political and economic events. Economic events surged during the second administration of Ronald Reagan. From an average of only twenty-six economic events per year in the preceding decade, the number climbed to more than one hundred by the end of 1980s (figure 10.2). The main topics were exchange rates and trade in semiconductors and other electronics products.

The number of events fell off somewhat over the next few years, but rose again in President Clinton's first term to a peak of 272 in 1995. In the following year, economic interactions plunged as the White House declared victory in its self-generated trade war and went on to win a second presidential term.

Political events tended to rise and fall with the action on the economic front; peaks of political activity coincided with economic crests, as revealed in figure 10.2. In fact, the apparent relationship suggested in the figure is not an apparition: the simple correlation between the annual numbers of economic and political events is a highly significant 0.76. Of course, correlation does not indicate causality, a subject that will be discussed further below.

Figure 10.1: Number of Events by Issue and Decade, 1948-1997

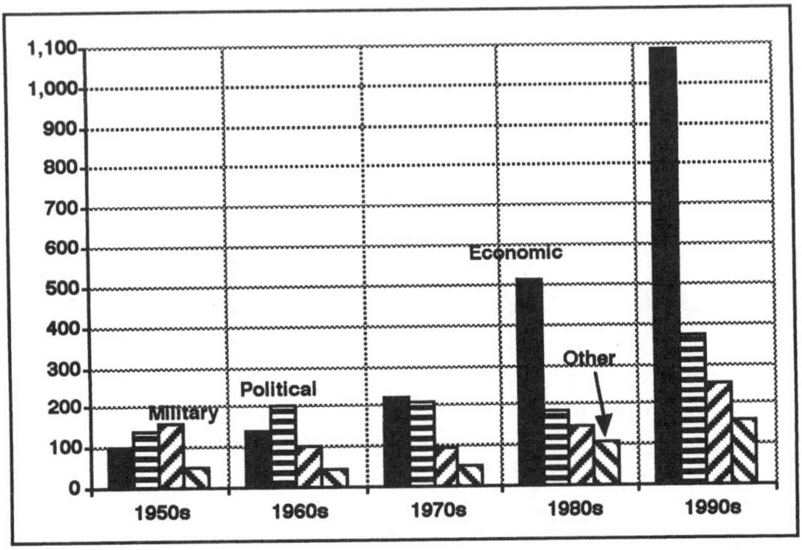

Cooperation and Conflict

With all this action, how well did the overall relationship hold up? A useful tool to examine that question is the cooperation-conflict scale assigned by the data compilers. This ordinal ranking assigns the most cooperative events the value of one and the most extreme conflict (all-out warfare involving extensive death and destruction) a fifteen. On this scale, level eight events are considered neutral.

Different authors have used a variety of methods to portray the trend of cooperation and conflict. Mr. Azar's original fifteen-point scale was intended to provide an ordinal ranking, with a higher number representing more conflict but not necessarily indicating the intensity of an event. Some studies simply use the ratio of cooperative to total events, not considering intensity. Others use the fifteen COPDAB categories to calculate a weighted sum of events for each period.

Figure 10.2: U.S.-Japan Economic and Political Events, 1948-1997

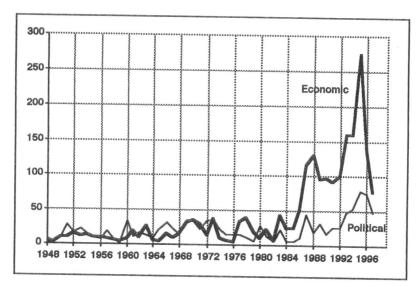

Mr. Azar himself first pointed out that the ordinal rankings provided little sense of the importance of a category. Is the difference between a thirteen and a fourteen, which involve acts of war, the same as that between a nine and a ten, which span verbal actions or other nonviolent acts? He asked a panel of international relations experts and diplomats to assign a relative intensity value to each of his fifteen categories. These values, ranging from 92 to −102, are shown in the appendix description of the categories and are used in the statistical analysis below.

Most bilateral events are routine, dictated by the sheer number of activities necessary to maintain relations between the two countries. As shown in table 10.2, cooperative events, clustered in scale values seven through nine, accounted for more than half of all bilateral affairs described by these data.

Only seven events involved outright clashes that fell into a range of conflict greater than level eleven. All of these were nongovernmental actions by Japanese citizens against American targets. They included violent demonstrations against American bases on Okinawa in the 1950s and 1960s, demonstrations against the U.S. war in Vietnam, and terrorist attacks against U.S. installations. There were only twenty-three nonstate actions in the entire database, representing less than 1 percent of all events.

**Table 10.2: Number of U.S.-Japan Events by Cooperation-Conflict
Scale Values, 1948-1997 (number and percent)**

Scale		Number	Percent
2	(Most cooperative)	14	0.3
3		152	3.5
4		291	6.7
5		331	7.7
6		506	11.7
7		1,627	37.7
8		52	1.2
9		840	19.5
10		401	9.3
11		96	2.2
12		6	0.1
14	(Most conflictual)	1	0.0

Although the incidence of conflictual developments has been increasing, cooperative events have grown even faster. Despite the overwhelming number of recurring transactions between the United States
and Japan and the general tendency toward cooperation, not surprisingly,
it is the occasional conflict that catches the eye of the news media. Table
10.3 aggregates the fifteen-point scale of cooperation and conflict into
four broader categories: high cooperation, cooperation, routine, and conflictual. Routine events are defined as those falling in cooperation-
conflict values seven to nine. Cooperation includes categories four to six,
and high cooperation one to three. Conflictual events are those in categories ten to fourteen.

Figure 10.3 shows the annual average level of the cooperation-
conflict scale for economic events. From the cooperative averages of the
early 1950s, the economic scale moved increasingly toward conflict.
Although the data clearly display a steady march away from cooperation,
the average economic event barely broke through the neutral dividing
line into conflict. Interestingly, after peaking in the late 1980s, the average value declined slightly toward greater cooperation in subsequent
years despite the increasing number of events.

Political events, in contrast to economic activities, exhibited a constant level of cooperation, staying around a value of seven through the
mid-1980s. However, from 1984 onward, the average political event also
became somewhat less cooperative.

Figure 10.3: Average Annual Value of Cooperation-Conflict Scale, U.S.-Japan Economic Events, 1948-1997

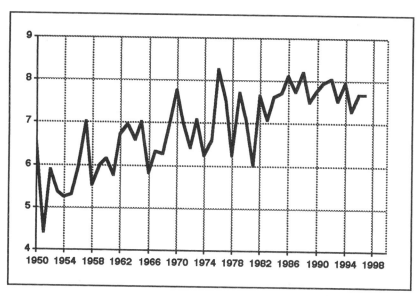

The trend away from cooperation should not be overemphasized. From the 1960s on, the median value for each decade for both economic and political events remained fixed at seven, defined in the codebook as "minor official exchanges, talks, or policy expressions of mild verbal support."

Table 10.3: Number of U.S.-Japan Events by Degree of Cooperation and Conflict, 1948-1997

Years	High Cooperation	Cooperation	Routine	Conflict
1948-1959	47	178	165	53
1960-1969	22	184	224	60
1970-1979	29	238	245	59
1980-1989	28	181	579	158
1990-1997	40	347	1,306	174

Although most activity was—and continues to be—routine, the picture did deteriorate somewhat. Whereas the central 50 percent of economic events in the 1950s and 1960s had cooperative values between four and seven, in the 1980s and 1990s the middle half fell in a slightly less cooperative range of seven to nine. While certainly not the kind of behavior exhibited by warring states, the events indicated a distinct, if mild, cooling of relations.

These points are further illustrated in figure 10.4, which focuses on the number of economic events by decade within the central range of co-operation-conflict values. To simplify the figure, the few observations from the 1940s were excluded, as were the less than 4 percent of events falling into the highly cooperative and highly conflictual categories.

Figure 10.4: Number of U.S.-Japan Economic Events by Decade and Cooperation-Conflict, 1950-1997

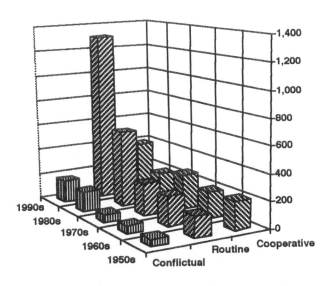

The number of routine economic events rose rapidly over time. Co-operative events increased at a steady pace, while conflictual events jumped in the 1980s and the 1990s. However, routine events came to represent about 75 percent of all economic activity. Although conflictual incidents climbed from only 26 in the 1970s to more than 100 in the next two decades, their proportion in the 1990s was the same as in the calmer days of the 1960s and 1970s. One conclusion that might be drawn from these trends is that most relations between the United States and Japan are routine and nonconflictual, despite the headlines earned by the more contentious issues. Indeed, cooperative events far outnumber conflictual ones.

Untangling Relationships

What drives the frequency of events between the two countries? What factors influence the tenor of the relationship? One response is that as bilateral links have grown—especially in the realms of trade, finance, and direct investment—it takes much more government effort simply to keep up with the innumerable details generated by private matters. The great expansion of routine actions seems to be consistent with that response.

The end of the Cold War might have been expected to cause a decline in military and political interactions. However, such a drop did not occur for political events; table 10.1 indicates an increase—rather than a decline—in military interactions in the late 1980s, a trend that continued into the 1990s. For political and economic events, U.S. imports from Japan are the main influence on both the number and the tone of bilateral relations.

Consider figure 10.5, which shows a plot of the annual cooperation-conflict scale for economic events and U.S. imports from Japan (measured as the ratio of Japanese imports to total purchases from abroad). With a correlation of 0.71 between the two variables, the suggestion of a link is hard to ignore. However, because imports and exports are highly correlated with each other, almost as compelling a figure could be plotted with exports instead of imports as the explanatory variable. In order to disentangle the effects of several forces acting simultaneously, multivariate analysis is required.

Regression analysis was used to determine the influences on the dependent variables. Likely variables that might influence the number and nature of events included:

• Imports, exports, the trade balance, and total trade between the United States and Japan.

• American and Japanese military spending as an indicator of the saliency of cold wars and military conflict.

• The relative sizes of the real American and Japanese economies as a measure of the economic and political importance of Japan on the world scene.

• U.S. unemployment, as a possible index of domestic political sensitivity to trade.

• The political party of the president as a proxy for American domestic political priorities.

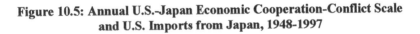

**Figure 10.5: Annual U.S.-Japan Economic Cooperation-Conflict Scale
and U.S. Imports from Japan, 1948-1997**

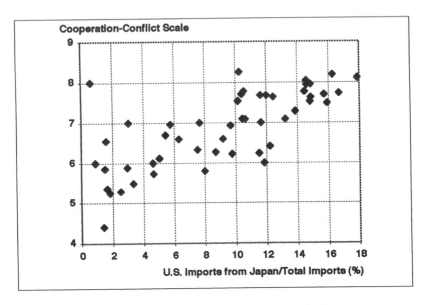

To consider the question of whether economic affairs influence political and military relations or vice versa, the problems created by simultaneity and estimation biases must be addressed. Consider, for example, a situation in which the number of economic events affects the
number of political events, and politics—in turn—impacts economics. A
naive use of statistical regression techniques would produce nonsense.
The intermingled effects cannot be separated unless something more
about the relationships is known. Specifically, factors that work on one
of the dependent variables but not the other must be found.

In order to estimate unbiased coefficients in a system of simultaneous equations, instrumental variables were used in a two-stage, least-
squares procedure. Such indicators as military spending, for example,
might act as proxies for broad changes in international relations. The estimated (rather than the actual) values of political events, based on such
proxies, then were used as independent variables in the other equations.
In addition, lagged values of the other dependent variables were used in
the equation for economic events, thereby disentangling the simultaneity
in the relationships. Independent variables such as military spending (assumed unrelated to economic events) are called instruments or instrumental variables

What Influences the Volume of Activity?

What drives the number of economic events initiated by the United States? (See table 10.4 for the equations on the number of events. Figure 10.6 lays out the linkages graphically among the three types of events.) Confining the estimates to those events in which Washington was the actor allowed a clearer delineation of the domestic factors that may have motivated relations. The first conclusion is that trade, indeed, consistently was a statistically significant influence on the number of events. A rise in total trade was associated with an increased number of economic events; higher U.S. exports decreased the number; and more imports raised the volume.[9] The trade deficit, however, had no impact.

Political activity had a negligible effect on the number of economic events. Military events, however, were positively associated with economic activity; ten more military events produced an estimated three more economic ones.

The number of events in one year is roughly 40 percent of the previous year's number, regardless of the other variables. Thus, a change has a tendency to persist. That finding is not surprising since trade relations are ongoing affairs that do not end with the turning of a calendar page. One lesson from this equation is that the effects of random events on the pace of bilateral economic discussions will linger until time and the intervention of new influences diminishes their impact.

Although the point estimates of the effects vary according to the specific formulation of the equations, we can get an idea of the size of the trade effects on the number of economic events from the first equation in table 10.4. (To calculate the net impact of a variable, the unlagged and lagged coefficients are added together.) A one percentage point increase in imports from Japan as a share of all U.S. imports (say, from the 1997 level of 12 percent to 13 percent) would have contributed two-thirds of an event to the total of forty-seven U.S.-initiated economic events in 1997. A one-percentage point rise in the Japan-bound share of U.S. exports would have reduced the number of events by a more substantial 3.6. A gain in two-way trade with Japan of $10 billion was estimated to generate about 1.3 events. (The value of 1997 two-way trade with Japan was about $210 billion in 1990 dollars.) It is this last variable—the value of real trade—that mainly was responsible for the rise in economic events over the 1980s.

Table 10.4: Equations for U.S.-Initiated Events, 1948-1997

Independent variables	Coefficients	t-statistics	R^2 (adjusted)
Dependent variable: Economic events			0.88
Constant	14.87	1.29	
Economic events (-1)	0.38	1.72	
US-Japan imports/total imports	-5.43	-2.19	
US-Japan imports/total imports (-1)	6.09	2.18	
US-Japan exports/total exports	-4.26	-1.30	
US-Japan exports/total exports (-1)	0.70	0.24	
Total US-Japan trade, 1990 prices	1.51	4.01	
Total US-Japan trade, 1990 prices (-1)	-1.38	-3.25	
Military events (estimated)	0.70	1.47	
Military events (-1)	-0.40	-2.10	
Dependent variable: Political events			0.71
Constant	16.48	2.75	
Political events (-1)	0.27	1.47	
Economic events (estimated)	0.13	2.7	
Military events (estimated)	0.43	1.92	
Military events (-1)	-0.19	-1.92	
Defense spending (1992 prices)	-0.04	-2.07	
Unemployment rate	-0.98	-1.73	
Dependent variable: Military events			0.57
Constant	5.72	1.14	
Military events (-1)	-0.27	-1.73	
Economic events (estimated)	-0.18	-1.71	
Political events (-1)	0.42	3.53	
Political events (-1)	0.48	2.18	
Defense spending/GDP (-1)	0.80	1.47	
President's party	-4.62	-1.73	

Notes: Figures in parentheses represent annual lags; variables designated as "estimated" were generated by instrumental variables; 49 observations.

Turning to the influences on the other types of events, economic actions had a small positive impact on political events. Surprisingly, economics had a strong positive impact on military affairs. Political activity also has a positive effect on the number of military events, with behavior in these two domains tending to move together. American defense spending and the political party of the president, influenced the number of military events. A Democrat in the White House, for example, tends to

Figure 10.6: Relationships Among Number of Events with United States as Actor by Issue Area, 1948-1997

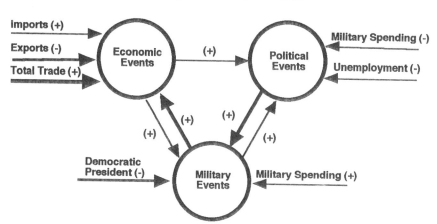

Notes: Arrows indicate direction of effect. Line thickness indicates strength of relationship. Sign indicates positive or negative effect.

reduce the events total by about five annually.

Unraveling Cooperation and Conflict

In order to analyze the intensity of U.S.-Japan relations, cooperative and conflictual events were treated separately as two different kinds of events. They were assigned weights according to Mr. Azar's intensity scale. However, to make the statistical results more intuitive, the conflict scale was redefined to be positive; therefore, a higher positive number indicates greater conflict. These measures are indicators of the total volume of cooperation or conflict in a given year since they combine each event with its intensity. Unlike the analysis of the number of events, which included only those where Washington was the actor, all events were included in this weighted cooperation-conflict analysis.

The annual volume of economic cooperation and conflict is shown in figure 10.7. Several points jump out. The tally of weighted negative events stayed in the range of zero to two hundred until the mid-1980s. In 1985, it increased sharply; similarly, cooperative events jumped at about the same time. Moreover, the two curves appear to track each other. When conflict peaks, cooperation follows with a lag of up to about a year. In fact, the simple correlation between the two variables is 0.85. A possible explanation is that talks on difficult trade issues usually begin on a note of conflict and stay that way until resolution—a positive outcome. Such a relationship between cooperation and conflict does not appear in the political sphere.

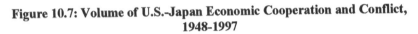

Figure 10.7: Volume of U.S.-Japan Economic Cooperation and Conflict, 1948-1997

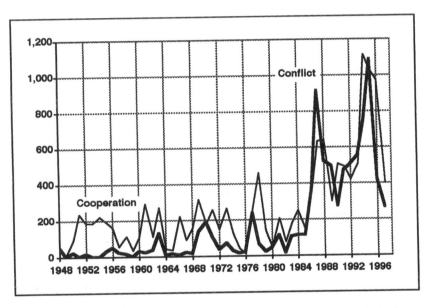

Analyzing the cross-relationships among economic, political, and military cooperation and conflict requires the same statistical techniques applied earlier. The equations appear in table 10.5 and figure 10.8 lays out the relationships estimated in the equations.

As suggested by the curves in figure 10.7, a change in weighted economic cooperation (holding other factors constant) induces about a 60 percent movement in weighted conflict, and vice versa. Trends in exports and imports strongly influenced economic conflict, with U.S. imports from Japan increasing conflict and exports to that country sharply diminishing it. Imports also reduce political cooperation. A Democratic president, on average, is associated with greater economic cooperation.

Table 10.5: Equations for Volume of Cooperation and Conflict, 1948-1997 (weighted by Azar intensity scale)

Independent variables	Coefficients	t-statistics	R2 (adjusted)
Dependent variable: Economic cooperation			0.73
Constant	-135.20	-1.25	
Economic conflict (-1)	0.62	5.17	
Political conflict (estimated)	3.38	2.53	
Political conflict (-1)	0.69	1.34	
President's party	72.02	1.76	
Military spending/GDP (-1)	9.53	1.07	
Dependent variable: Economic conflict			0.80
Constant	24.47	0.26	
US-Japan imports/total imports (-1)	26.45	2.77	
US-Japan exports/total exports (-1)	-65.47	2.84	
Economic cooperation (estimated)	0.61	3.96	
Political conflict (estimated)	4.84	3.41	
Political conflict (-1)	1.97	4.38	
Political cooperation (estimated)	-1.19	3.05	
Dependent variable: Political cooperation			0.60
Constant	-31.48	1.18	
Political cooperation (-1)	0.27	2.56	
Political conflict (estimated)	3.37	5.04	
Political conflict (-1)	0.77	2.94	
US-Japan imports/total imports	-7.08	2.59	
Dependent variable: Political conflict			0.10
Constant	20.96	1.56	
Political cooperation (estimated)	0.20	2.46	
Dependent variable: Military cooperation			0.38
Constant	-47.36	1.14	
Military cooperation (-1)	0.30	2.63	
Political conflict (estimated)	3.24	4.49	

Notes: Figures in parentheses represent annual lags; variables designated as "estimated" were generated by instrumental variables; 49 observations.

Neither unemployment nor imports affected economic cooperation or conflict by themselves. Nor did the cross product of unemployment and imports affect economic cooperation. A possible reason for the absence of a statistical relationship is that imports tend to be strongest and unemployment is low when the U.S. economy is surging, not the most likely time for trade frictions.

The statistical results suggest that political conflict is largely random (the adjusted R^2 of the best equation was only 0.095). A look at conflictual political events lends some support to this interpretation. Political conflicts scaled at ten and eleven on the COPDAB scale included riots associated with the U.S.-Japan security treaty in the 1960s, Japanese unhappiness over delays in the return of Okinawa, American dissatisfaction with Japan's implementation of environmental treaties, and U.S. government reactions to perceptions of closed Japanese markets. Regardless of their origins, these conflicts spilled over into other areas.

Higher levels of political conflict were associated with increased economic conflict. However, political conflict appears to boost cooperation in the economic and military arenas. Recall that we are treating cooperation and conflict as separate phenomena. A hypothetical story that would be consistent with the statistical results might involve tense political negotiations over removal of an American base from Okinawa backed up by tough talk from the State Department on aviation issues. Meanwhile, the U.S. Trade Representative could be especially solicitous to gain Japanese cooperation on World Trade Organization negotiations. In other words, negative political occurrences appear to provoke positive spillovers elsewhere, perhaps as a way of repairing deteriorating relations triggered by domestic or international events.

How well do the equations estimate weighted cooperation and conflict? As noted, political conflict was largely random. However, the other spheres of U.S.-Japan relations were predicted quite well, with some 70 percent to 80 percent of the variance "explained" by the equations.

Why did economic conflict soar in 1994 and 1995? The projected value of economic conflict based on the equation from table 10.4 tracks the main trends quite closely, except for 1987 and 1994, both of which were badly underpredicted by more than 40 percent.

The explanation for the 1994 discrepancy is that American trade relations seem to have been tied more closely to domestic politics in the United States than to bilateral economic affairs. Table 10.6 shows the number of times since 1979 that event summaries mentioned by name the U.S. trade representative, the top American trade policymaker. Since individuals serve as USTR for different lengths of time, the number of mentions per year in office also is indicated.

Mickey Kantor, Mr. Clinton's first trade representative, is the outlier in this compilation. His aggressive attempt to sign trade deals with Japan was intended to demonstrate the difference between the Clinton administration and the previous Bush presidency, about which Mr. Kantor repeatedly asserted, "They negotiate and negotiate and nothing happens." The Clinton-Kantor strategy was to be visibly different and aggressively effective. In 1996, a presidential election year, the Democrats announced in essence that the fight for greater U.S. access to Japan's markets was over and that the administration had won.

Figure 10.8: Relationships Among Volumes of Cooperative and Conflictual Events by Issue Area, 1948-1997

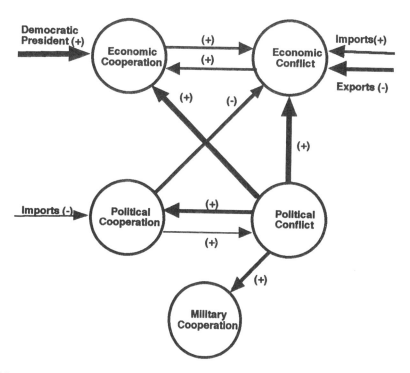

Notes: Arrows indicate direction of effect. Line thickness indicates strength of relationship. Sign indicates positive or negative effect.

With the end of the Cold War, the early Clinton administration believed that the cost of economic friction had fallen. However, the evidence assembled here suggests that economic relations between the United States and Japan had at most a weak influence on political and military ties, cooperative or conflictual both during the Cold War and after. The spillover into other areas of national interest was minimal. Bilateral political relationships swayed economic and military ties but were not affected by them.

**Table 10.6: Number of Times U.S. Trade Representative
Mentioned in Database, 1978-1997**

Trade Representative	Years in Office	Number of Mentions in Database	Mentions per Year
Reubin Askew	1979-1981	0	0.0
William Brock	1981-1985	17	4.2
Clayton Yeutter	1985-1989	70	17.5
Carla Hills	1989-1993	52	13.0
Mickey Kantor	1993-1996	180	55.4
Charlene Barshefsky	1996-1997	41	24.6

These conclusions are econometrically robust. One interpretation is that both Tokyo and Washington attempt to manage domestic and international events that, left unchecked, might dictate the nature of fundamental relations.

Consistency with Other Evidence and Conclusions

A study of U.S. trade protection policy appearing in a leading economics journal came to conclusions roughly consistent with the results reported here. It found that for politically unorganized industries, protection tended to increase with import penetration. Both total employment in an industry and the unemployment rate boosted the likelihood of protection.[10] These results support the notion that trade policy is driven largely by domestic politics.

Marcus Noland of the Institute for International Economics conducted a statistical analysis of the Office of the U.S. Trade Representative to determine the sources of American trade policy actions.[11] He found that for the years from 1984 through 1993, a country's trade balance with the United States was the single most important variable related to the attention paid by USTR to that trading partner. Attention was measured by the number of pages devoted to the country in USTR's annual *National Trade Estimate Report*. However, that measure had no relationship to the other country's trade barriers. A variable designating Japan indicated that more moves were made against it than Japan's economic characteristics seemed to warrant. Additional analysis was undertaken of all formal, unilateral trade measures initiated by the U.S. government to achieve enhanced market access between 1984 and 1993.

Again, a variable for Japan was strongly related to official U.S. actions beyond the prediction of the other variables.

These findings, which are consistent with those reported above, raise a critical question about policy. Economists argue that trade imbalances are not economically meaningful indicators for targeting trade policy actions. However, if imports act as domestic political lightning rods, alerting trade policymakers by their noise and dazzle, and if these moves have no discernible impact on bilateral balances, then the pursuit of such a strategy is doomed to frustration and failure.

Other research on the influence of international relations on trade concluded that close political ties increased trade but that even military disputes failed to reduce it significantly.[12] The results from this review of six countries from 1907 to 1990 are consistent with the evidence from U.S.-Japan relations. Economic issues seem to be isolated from activities on the political, diplomatic, and military fronts.

Trade has its own rationale; trade politics feeds on domestic politics, which can intrude onto the world scene and make life uncomfortable for negotiators. Nonetheless, economic affairs seem to have relatively little lasting effect on other facets of the U.S.-Japan bilateral relationship.

Appendix to Chapter 10

Definitions of Conflict and Peace Data Bank (COPDAB) Scale of International Cooperation and Conflict[13]

1.   (92) Voluntary unification of separate states into one nation.
2.   (47) Major strategic alliance. Fighting a war jointly; establishing a joint military command or alliance; conducting joint military maneuvers; establishing an economic common market; joining or organizing international alliances; or establishing a joint program to raise the global quality of life.
3.   (31) Military, economic or strategic support. Selling nuclear power plants or materials; providing air, naval or land facilities for bases; giving technical or advisory military assistance; granting military aid; sharing highly advanced technology; intervening with military support at request of government; concluding military agreements; training military personnel; or joint programs and plans to initiate and pursue disarmament.
4.   (27) Nonmilitary economic, technological or industrial agreement. Making loans or grants; agreeing to economic pacts; giving industrial, cultural or educational assistance; conducting trade agreements or granting most-favored-nation status; establishing common transportation or communication

networks; selling surplus industrial/technological equipment; providing technical expertise; ceasing economic restrictions; repaying debts; selling nonmilitary goods; or giving disaster relief.

5.   (14) Cultural or scientific agreement or other support (nonstrategic). Initiating diplomatic relations; establishing technological or scientific communications; proposing or offering economic or military aid; recognition of government; visit by head of state; opening borders; enacting or fulfilling friendship agreements; or conducting cultural or academic agreements or exchanges.

6.   (10) Official verbal support of goals, values or regime. Official support of policy; upgrade of legation to embassy; reaffirming friendship; asking for help against third party; apologizing for unfavorable actions or statements; allowing entry of press correspondents; offering thanks for or requesting aid; or resuming broken diplomatic or other relations.

7.   (6) Minor official exchanges, talks or policy expressions and mild verbal support. Meeting of high officials; conferring on problems of mutual interest; visit by lower officials for talks; issuing joint communiques; appointing ambassadors; announcing cease-fires; proposing talks; exchanging prisoners of war; requesting support for policy; or stating or explaining policy.

8.   (1) Neutral or nonsignificant acts for the international situation. Rhetorical policy statements or nonconsequential news items.

9.   (-6) Mild verbal expressions displaying discord in interaction. Low-key objection to policies or behavior; communication of dissatisfaction through third party; failure to reach an agreement; refusal of protest note; denial of accusations; objection to explanation of goals or position; or request for change in policy.

10.   (-16) Strong verbal expressions displaying hostility in interaction. Warning of retaliation for acts; making of threatening demands and accusations; condemning strongly specific actions or policies; denouncing leaders, system or ideology; postponing visits by heads of state; refusing participation in meetings or summits; leveling strong propaganda attacks; denying support; or blocking or vetoing policy actions or proposals in the United Nations or other international bodies.

11.   (-29) Diplomatic/economic hostile actions. Increasing troop mobilization; boycotts; imposing economic sanctions; hindering movement on land, waterways or in the air; embargoing goods; refusing mutual trade rights; closing borders and blocking free communications; manipulating trade or currency to cause economic problems; halting aid; granting sanctuary to opposition leaders; mobilizing hostile demonstrations against target country; refusing to support foreign military allies; recalling ambassador for emergency consultations regarding target country; refusing visas to other nationals or restricting movement in country; expelling or arresting nationals or press people; spying on foreign government officials; or terminating major agreements.

12.   (-44) Political/military hostile actions. Inciting riots or rebellions (providing training or financial aid for rebellions); encouraging guerrilla activities against target country; limited and sporadic terrorist actions; kidnapping or tor-

turing foreign citizens or prisoners of war; giving sanctuary to terrorists; breaking diplomatic relations; attacking diplomats or embassies; expelling military advisers; executing alleged spies; or nationalizing companies without compensation.

13. (-50) Small-scale military acts. Limited air, sea or border skirmishes; border police acts; annexing territory already occupied; seizing material of target country; imposing blockades; assassinating leaders of target country; or material support of subversive activities against target country.

14. (-65) Limited war acts. Intermittent shelling or clashes; sporadic bombing of military or industrial areas; small-scale interception or sinking of ships; deployment of mines in territorial waters.

15. (-102) Extensive acts of war causing death, dislocation, or high strategic costs.

Note: Numbers in parentheses are the weighted intensity scale assigned by Edward Azar to each category.

Notes

1. *International Event-Data Development: Data Development for International Research, Phase II*, ed. Richard Merritt, Robert Muncaster, and Dina Zinnes (Ann Arbor, Mich.: University of Michigan Press, 1993), 2.

2. Merritt, Muncaster, and Zinnes, *International Event-Data Development*, 16.

3. Jack Vincent, "WEIS vs. COPDAB: Correspondence Problems," *International Studies Quarterly* 27, no. 2 (1983): 161.

4. Charles McClelland, "Let the User Beware," *International Studies Quarterly* 27, no. 2 (1983): 170.

5. McClelland, "Let the User Beware," 170.

6. Merritt, Muncaster, and Zinnes, *International Event-Data Development*, 1.

7. Data, field descriptions, coding rules, and the GEDS Manual are available at <http://geds.umd.edu/geds/gedsdata.htm> (2 Jan. 2002).

8. Joshua Epstein and Jon Pevehouse, "Reciprocity, Bullying and International Cooperation: Time-Series Analysis of the Bosnia Conflict," *American Political Science Review* 91, no. 3 (September 1997).

9. The variables were defined as imports from Japan as a percentage of total U.S. imports, exports to Japan as a share of total exports, and the sum of U.S.-Japan exports and imports in real (1990) dollars.

10. Pinelopi Koujianou Goldberg and Giovanni Maggi, "Protection For Sale: An Empirical Investigation," *American Economic Review* 93, no. 5 (December 1999): 1136.

11. Marcus Noland, "Chasing Phantoms: The Political Economy of USTR," *International Organization* 51, no. 3 (summer 1997): 365.

12. James Morrow, Randolph Siverson, and Tressa Tabares, "The Political Determinants of International Trade: The Major Powers, 1907-90," *American Political Science Review* 92, no. 3 (September 1998): 649.

13. John Davies, *The Global Event-Data System, Coders' Manual* (College Park, Md.: University of Maryland, 1998), and Edward Azar, *The Codebook of the Conflict and Peace Data Bank (COPDAB)* (College Park, Md.: University of Maryland, 1982): 36.

Chapter 11

Structural Change and Adaptation

Myths and Realities

A common myth about Japan is that its labor force is immobile and its industry inert. The assertion that Japan's economy is less dynamic than that of the United States appears on the surface to be indisputable. Bogged down by slow growth or outright recession in the 1990s, the Japanese economy frequently is characterized as mature, if not downright decrepit. The American economy, in contrast, has been lauded for innovations in finance and retailing and for new digital technologies. Japan more often than not is criticized (appropriately) for the overregulation, cartels, and collusion that are holding back its productivity. With conventional wisdom congealing in a negative assessment, it may be useful to examine the overall dynamism of that aging creature, especially in comparison with the seemingly ever-youthful American counterpart.

One reason to explore this issue is that policymaking in Tokyo often is influenced by the belief that change is unacceptable to most citizens. Politicians' avoidance of hard-landing solutions to work out the country's problems is due in part to the desire to avoid large, visible disruptions. As will be discussed below, however, the Japanese economy has steadily absorbed structural changes that are at least of the same magnitude as those faced by the United States. The seemingly moribund Japan is more adaptive in many dimensions than its own citizens and leaders realize.

Structural Dynamics: Changing Industry Shares

Economic development has been associated with broad structural shifts from agriculture to manufacturing to services. The shifting demands caused by rising income levels, demographic transitions, changing tastes, and technological change require economic flexibility and structural adaptation. With sufficiently detailed information, it is possible to track the variations of employment and output over the years and to compare them between countries.

One measure of structural transformation adds up the year-to-year changes in industry-specific shares of employment or gross domestic product. Consider a situation where employment in a specific industry (transportation equipment, for example) experienced a plunge in the number of employees that equaled 1 percent of the total labor force of the country; at the same time, the health-services business experienced an increase of the same magnitude. One measure of structural change adds together the values of the changes in both industries (ignoring, in this case, the minus sign in manufacturing). In this example, 1 percent of the workforce crossed industry lines.[1] Generalizing from this example, an aggregate measure of structural change across the whole economy at a specific time would be:

$$S(t) = 100/2 * \sum \{|(E_i(t)/E(t) - (E_i(t-1)/E(t-1))|\},$$

where $S(t)$ is the sum of the absolute percentage changes in employment across all industries between time period $t-1$ and t, E_i is employment in industry i, and E is total economywide employment. The summation of absolute changes is taken across all industries and divided by two to eliminate double counting. Of course, (using the above example) individual workers in the transportation equipment industry would not necessarily have taken jobs in health services. Net transfers across industries plus people moving in and out of the workforce would add up to the measured value. A similar calculation substitutes industry GDP for employment in the above equation.

One problem with this measure is that it is sensitive to the level of detail in the data used to measure the structure of the economy. Narrower categories would produce a larger index of movement because a specific move more likely would cross industry lines. Therefore, in making comparisons, it is important to use similar numbers of categories and industry definitions.

The U.S. Department of Commerce produces statistics on employment and GDP originating in sixty-five industries. Figure 11.1 shows the structural shifts in the U.S. economy from 1948 through 1999 using the measure of change defined in the equation described above. Structural change was relatively high in the immediate post-World War II years as the economy adjusted to the accumulated effects of the depression and the war. Things quickly settled down, though. Since 1960 or thereabouts, employment crossed industry borders at the rate of a bit more than 1 percent per year. GDP has followed the same general path, but that measure of structural change jumped to more than 3 percent in the 1980s, only to fall back to the 1.5-percent level in 1996. The 1990s do not indicate any speedup in change that may be associated with conjectures about a "new American economy."

Figure 11.1: Annual Structural Change in U.S. Employment and GDP Across Sixty-Five Industries, 1948-1999 (percent)

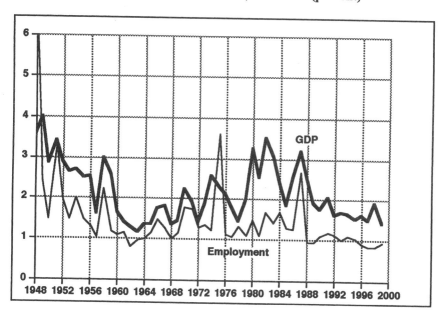

Source: Department of Commerce

The categorization of Japan's GDP is not as detailed as the U.S. breakdown: it covers forty-three industries versus the sixty-five included in the Commerce Department series. In order to make country-to-country comparisons, the U.S. and Japanese data were reaggregated into forty industries based on Japanese definitions. As expected, reducing the number of American groupings yielded slightly smaller measures of structural change, particularly in peak years. The average difference, though, was less than 0.5 percentage points.

Figure 11.2 compares structural change in Japan and the United States based on GDP originating in the forty comparable industries. Except for a spike in 1975, which reflected the recession induced by the first oil shock, changes in Japan parallel the American experience. From 1980 on, in fact, the two curves are virtually indistinguishable. Those who believe that the economy of the United States is more dynamic than Japan's will have to look to other evidence for confirmation.

Figure 11.2: Annual Structural Change of GDP in Forty Industries, Japan and United States, 1970-1999 (percent)

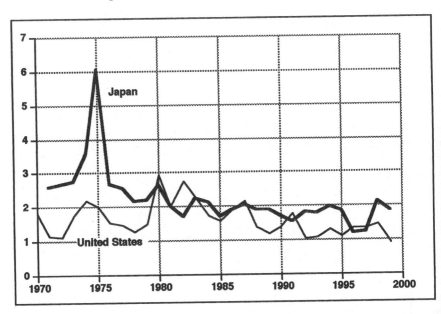

Source: United States, Department of Commerce; Japan: Economic Planning Agency

Employment does not exhibit any less adaptability than does GDP. Employment curves for the two economies are shown in figure 11.3. Japan's employment data are broken down into twenty-five industries; the U.S. figures were reaggregated into the same number of categories. The employment curves lie even closer together than the GDP curves do, with the difference in their average values amounting to less than 0.1 percentage point. For both countries, the spike in 1975 again reflected the response to the 1973-1974 surge in international oil prices.

Figure 11.3: Annual Structural Change of Employment in Twenty-Five Industries, Japan and United States, 1970-1999 (percent)

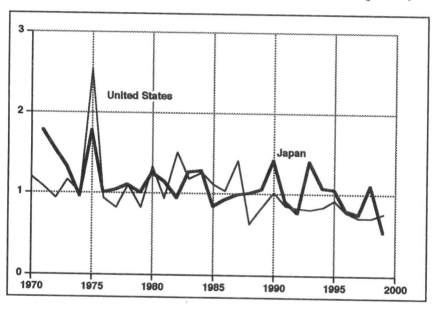

Source: Department of Commerce; Economic Planning Agency

These findings are quite striking and surprising. They indicate a broad similarity in the aggregate pattern of structural change in Japan and the United States. Both economies responded to the immediate postwar environment with a considerable reshuffling of people and production resources and then adapted to the flux of economic life with the same magnitude of adjustment.

A look behind the aggregate pattern, however, reveals important differences between the two economies. Across the forty similarly defined industries, the correlation between the changes in GDP of Japan and the United States over the 1970-1998 period is 0.55, indicating only a loose relationship between the gainers and the losers in each economy. The biggest outliers in the comparison include finance and health services, the GDP shares of which grew in the United States by 4 percentage points and 2.6 percentage points, respectively, but rose in Japan by only 0.7 and 0.6 percentage points.

The GDP share of general government (including national, state, and local governments) in the United States fell by 2.7 points over the 1970-1999 time frame compared with a gain of 0.9 point in Japan. Construction, an industry that in Japan is a noted beneficiary of political favors, jumped by 2.0 percent of GDP while falling 0.7 percent in the United States. Real estate in Japan vaulted an astonishing 5.2 percent of GDP against a more modest U.S. increase of 0.9 percent. In the remaining industries, the movements were more alike. If the four industries with the greatest differences are dropped from the sample, the correlation between GDP changes on the two sides of the Pacific rises to 0.80, suggesting that Japan and the United States have undergone fairly similar structural changes over the past twenty-five years or so for 90 percent of the industries.

The 1975 jump in the curves for Japanese GDP and employment was due mainly to an increase in construction activity as the government resorted to public works to stimulate the economy out of its first postwar recession. The small 1993 spurt in activity also included positive increases in construction. The rise in 1998 also was from a change in construction, but this time in a negative direction as government stimulus programs ended. These spikes reflect the use of public works in Japan as a tool of fiscal policy.

A closer look at the U.S. economy using the full sixty-five-industry breakdown reveals that employment by state and local government grew rapidly from the late 1940s to the 1980s. With the exception of times of military buildup, the number of people working for the federal government fell over most of the same period. By 1960, more people worked for state and local governments than for Washington. During the 1980s, though, state government's share of GDP declined. State and local government shares of GDP and employment were associated with the education demands of the baby boom and its movement through the educational system.

According to these measures of economic dynamism, the United States and Japan are not all that different. Although the growth paths of several sectors diverge, for the most part, the development of the two economies since at least 1955 has been quite similar when measured by shifts in GDP and employment across the full range of industries.

Perhaps the presumed greater dynamic quality of the American economy can be explained—despite its nonappearance in these calculations—by the argument that the industry classifications used in this analysis are too coarse to capture the mutations that occur. The presumed dynamic quality of the American economy may be among firms rather than industries. For example, American retailing is one of the more innovative sectors. Its continuous transformations are illustrated by the competitive dynamics of company sales rankings. A McKinsey Global Institute case study of the retail sector found more than 17,000 failures in the United States in 1994 versus 5,000 in Japan, despite the fact that there are many more smaller retail and wholesale establishments in Japan. An examination of the top ten retailers in different market segments in 1982 and 1992 showed high turnover rates among the biggest U.S. department stores and discounters, with three new department stores and five different discount operations in the top ranks. In Japan, however, the same general merchandise retailers appeared in the top ten over the course of a decade; within the rankings, there were only two shifts of a single place between years.[2]

The long-term growth of income and productivity in Japan demonstrates that the country has adapted successfully to the never-ending shocks and forces impinging on any large economy. This responsiveness shows up at the industry level examined above. If there are basic differences, they must lie at the level of the firm or the individual.

Employment and Changes in GDP

The responsiveness of employment to variations in economic output is one indicator frequently cited as proof of the relative adaptiveness of the American economy. This relationship is illustrated in the top and bottom panels of figure 11.4. The conventional wisdom correctly predicts the two different patterns in the figures: employment follows output more closely in the United States than it does in Japan. The elasticity of employment with respect to real GDP (the annual percent change in job numbers associated with a 1 percent change in output) is 0.53 in the United States, whereas the employment elasticity in Japan is only 0.19.

One reason for Japanese employment stability at the economywide level is that government acts indirectly as the employer of last resort through its public works program. Public works have been important

Figure 11.4: Percentage Changes in GDP and Employment, United States and Japan, 1955-2000

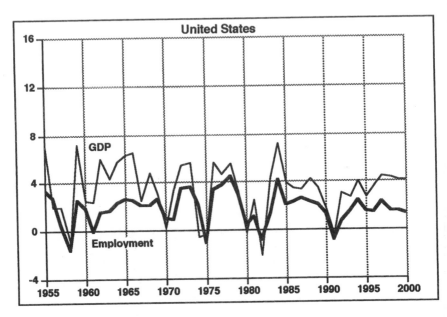

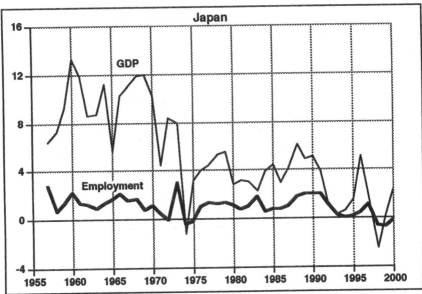

partly because of the weakness of automatic stabilizers in the Japanese public fiscal system.

In many countries, particularly Canada, Germany, and the United Kingdom, unemployment compensation and various welfare benefits rise automatically when the economy turns down. The movement of the government deficit responds quickly and without the need for explicit fiscal policies and decisions. In Japan, however, these automatic stabilizers are not well developed; they never had to be in the past since unemployment and a large welfare burden were not part of the economic structure. The need to use discretionary measures to react to recessionary strains puts greater weight on active fiscal policy and results in a bumpy adjustment process. Because of a political preference for public works and because they are relatively easy to implement quickly to get money into the hands of the public (and the construction companies), this tool emerged as a principal method for stimulation in times of slowdown.[3]

As business turns down in recessions, construction spending increases. These responses are one cause of the stable overall employment levels as well as of the bumps in the structural change curves seen in the figures above.

This evidence, though, points to only one aspect of employment flexibility. It says that American companies as a whole are more likely than Japanese firms to react to changes in demand by hiring and firing workers. However, there are other ways to respond to shifting output. Wage rates and hours also can be altered. A study by the Paris-based Organization for Economic Cooperation and Development is consistent with many others in finding that wages and hours in Japan are markedly more responsive to ups and downs in output than they are in Germany and the United States. From 1960 to 1991, wage rates in Japan were 13 times more affected by employment conditions than was pay in the United States. Hours worked were some 17 percent more adaptive.[4]

Simple correlations between annual changes in real GDP and changes in total employment, average weekly hours worked, and average real hourly earnings lead to conclusions that are similar to those produced by the econometric models used in the OECD study. As shown in table 11.1, the relationship between GDP and employment is quite strong in the United States, with a correlation of 0.73 versus a 0.50 match in Japan. At the same time, neither hours nor earnings in the United States are as closely related to changes in U.S. output.

The conclusion that the U.S. labor market is more flexible and adaptive clearly depends on the measure being used. Nevertheless, the rapidity of employment change in the United States permits a faster response to shifts in demand. Wages and hours adjustments in Japan are constrained by legal restrictions and social norms from fully adapting to severe or prolonged declines in company fortunes. After companies reduce bonuses and overtime hours, reductions in base salaries or the length of the workweek are rarely contemplated. The reluctance to engage in layoffs without the compulsion of imminent business failure prolonged Japan's adjustment process in the 1990s.

Table 11.1: Correlations between Annual Changes in Real GDP and Changes in Employment, Hours, and Real Earnings

Variable	United States	Japan
Employment	0.73	0.50
Average Weekly Hours	0.07	0.40
Average Real Hourly Earnings	0.54	0.69

Notes: The years included in the correlations are: 1948-1997 for GDP and employment in the United States; 1964-1997 for U.S. earnings and hours; and 1955-1998 for Japan's GDP, employment, hours, and earnings. Weekly hours and hourly earnings (for the United States) were lagged one year.

The fact remains that not all companies in Japan are able to avoid layoffs or closure. During the 1990s shakeout, many manufacturing establishments disappeared. According to the Establishment and Enterprise Census conducted by the Management and Coordination Agency, the number of establishments fell in 1996 for the first time since the original census was undertaken in 1947. The decline was 10 percent—a net loss of 86,000 production units—between 1991 and 1996. Employment in manufacturing contracted by 1.2 million, or 8.3 percent, over the same period. The net disappearance of almost 90,000 manufacturing establishments suggests that the gross loss was considerably greater; the creation of new firms partially offset the number of closures in the reported net figures. Where did the people who had worked for these firms go? Many found jobs in the services sector, where total employment jumped by 2.4 million-plus from 1991 to 1996, according to the establishment census.

The apparent stability in the gross employment figures shown in figure 11.5 hides a good deal of churning occurring below the surface. In 1998, for example, employment fell by nearly a half million people (about 0.7 percent of the total) from the year before. However, not all industries lost workers. Across the twenty-five industries into which employment is broken down, four had job gains in 1998, six were stable, and fifteen lost employment. Although the net decline of employees across the entire economy was 450,000, the ups and downs across the twenty five sectors added up to 1.44 million people, or more than three times the net flow.

Political Implications

The employment figures cited above indicate that the job situation in Japan is not as moribund as the popular myths and lifetime employment norms would lead one to expect. Although the slowdown of Japan's economy in the 1990s produced a good deal of political dither and policy muddle, most people who lost their jobs managed to find new ones. Remarkably, the Japanese media paid little attention to the structural changes going on in the economy, highlighted by the significant decline in the number of manufacturing establishments and the accompanying net loss of more than 1.2 million jobs between 1991 and 1996. Apparently, these indications of the economy's flexibility also have gone unrecognized by the public at large. Even people who have been forced to change jobs seem to believe that their personal history does not represent the more general experience.

The evidence belies the notion that people in Japan do not move from job to job or that industries and companies are static. More importantly, it restricts policy choices. In fact, the myth of a rigid economy may be the biggest barrier to political efforts to deregulate and open Japan to achieve more competition and raise productivity. Since these beliefs are so widely held, it may take some time for the reality of Japan's adaptability to reach a level of popular acceptance that could free the political will to proceed vigorously with economic restructuring.

Notes

1.   This measure was developed in Douglas Ostrom, "Postwar Japanese Industrial Policy and Changes in Industrial Structure" (Ph.D. diss., University of Michigan, 1984).

2.   McKinsey Global Institute, *Capital Productivity* (Washington, D.C.: McKinsey Global Institute, June 1996).

3.   Martin Muhleisen, "Too Much of a Good Thing? The Effectiveness of Fiscal

Stimulus," in Tamim Bayoumi and Charles Collyns (eds.), *Post-Bubble Blues: How Japan Responded to Asset Price Collapse* (Washington, D.C.: International Monetary Fund, 1999), 118-28.

4.   Dave Turner, Pete Richardson and Sylvia Rauffet, *The Role of Real and Nominal Rigidities in Macroeconomic Adjustment: A Comparative Study of the G3 Economies* (OECD Economic Studies, 21) (Paris: Organization for Economic Cooperation and Development, winter 1993), 97-100.

Chapter 12

Deregulation in Aviation

Rigid Structure Based on Postwar Law and Regulation

The basic framework for Japan's aviation industry was established by the Civil Aeronautics Law of 1952, which gave the Ministry of Transport the mandate to set routes and fares and approve operators. Japan Airlines Co., Ltd. had been formed the year before. In 1953, the government became the airline's controlling owner by putting up half of its capital. JAL entered the international air transport market in 1954 as Japan's "flag carrier"—the term used at that time to denote a country's designated international airline. While JAL had a monopoly on overseas routes, several companies competed in the small and chaotic domestic market of the early postwar period. Two of them merged in 1957 to form All Nippon Airways Co., Ltd.

The industry was brought under the heavy regulatory hand of MOT with the adoption in 1970 of a cabinet resolution, which was implemented two years later. The so-called 1970-1972 system, also referred to as the "aviation constitution," created a segmented industrial structure built around three companies: JAL, ANA, and Toa Domestic Airline Co., Ltd., the latter formed under official guidance through the merger of two smaller carriers.

Under the 1970-1972 system, JAL had responsibility for international service and a few domestic trunk routes—that is, routes connecting Tokyo, Osaka, Sapporo, and Fukuoka. ANA was assigned domestic trunk routes, local routes, and some short-haul international charter flights. TDA, which merged with several other small carriers to form Japan Air System Co., Ltd. in the 1980s, received local routes and a portion of the domestic trunks. Competition among the three carriers was almost nonexistent.

Near-monopolies on most routes as well as regulated fares allowed MOT to assign unprofitable flights serving outlying islands or small towns to ANA and JAS. The earnings from high-density routes subsidized this far-flung network, parts of which had been established under pressure from influential Diet members looking after their constituents.

The 1970-1972 system was internally consistent. It allowed the three airlines to earn sufficient profits to maintain service to important domestic and international centers. It also provided the cross-subsidization to satisfy other locales. The absence of competition on prices and routes or from the entry of new carriers guaranteed a relatively quiet life for JAL, ANA, and JAS. It also brought high fares and costs that grew increasingly out of line with those of deregulated airlines in the United States and elsewhere. However, forces were brewing on the international front and in aircraft technology that would cause the system to unravel.

Competition Stirs up Domestic and International Markets

Following the late 1970s' deregulation of airline operations in the United States, the White House turned its attention to the international system's cartelized market structure and government price supports. In negotiations over bilateral pacts, the mechanism that governs international aviation relations among most countries, Washington sought more liberal entry and pricing arrangements. Its eventual aim was deregulated international "open skies." Japan was an early target of American negotiators because its 6 percent share of total U.S. international passenger traffic seemed small in comparison with the potential market that could be accessed if fares and routes were liberalized.

Japan's aviation policymakers recognized in the early 1980s that the deregulatory wave ultimately would break over their own shores. They hoped to introduce such reforms as might be desirable at a pace that would allow domestic participants time to adjust to new economic forces created under a freer regulatory regime. Implementation was expected to take decades.

Before this policy could be articulated very clearly, however, a sharp increase in the demand for international cargo flights and the introduction of Boeing Co.'s wide-body 747 aircraft made lower-cost freight traffic technically and economically feasible. MOT opened a small crack in Japan's segmented market structure in 1983 when it granted a license to Nippon Cargo Airlines Co., Ltd., a venture formed by ANA and six major Japanese shipping companies. The appearance of NCA as a competitor to JAL on international cargo routes was the first challenge to the established system.

The crack widened further in 1985 when the United States and Japan began a new round of negotiations over transpacific rights. The agreement that emerged was based on the principle of "balanced expansion." It allowed three new carriers from each country to launch service across the Pacific. To forgo this opportunity would have left Japan faced with a dominant American presence in the all-important U.S.-Japan market. Moreover, by this time, Japan had signed aviation agreements with Australia, France, Great Britain, and other countries that also allowed more than one Japanese carrier to serve those markets.

The logic of the 1970-1972 system made it impractical for Tokyo to open the international market to new entrants and still keep the domestic market tightly regulated. JAL would face stepped-up competition and probably declining revenues and profits without the opportunity to make up the difference elsewhere. Moreover, ANA was losing money on some 70 percent of its domestic flights. New competition on its major, profitable routes would jeopardize the carrier's financial survival.

Unsure of how to handle the potential problem of new Japanese airlines flying international routes, MOT turned to one of its advisory committees. This blue-ribbon panel recommended increased competition in both the international and the domestic markets. The suggested framework allowed for multiple carriers on international routes, new entrants on routes serving domestic city pairs (as warranted by traffic volume), and the privatization of JAL. With these recommendations and the earlier creation of NCA, the old system was swept away by the wave of deregulation that MOT had forecast. It happened, however, years before aviation policy planners had anticipated.

The advisory committee advocated the introduction of "double and triple tracking"—the practice of two or three carriers servicing a particular route—based on passenger volume. MOT implemented this suggestion by declaring that two airlines would be allowed on routes with at least 700,000 passengers per year and three carriers would service routes with more than one million passengers annually. For the first time, JAL, ANA, and JAS faced competition on their most important routes. In return, however, they were permitted into market segments formerly denied them.

In its measured way of promoting a more competitive industry, MOT lowered the hurdles for double and triple tracking in 1992 to 400,000 and 700,000 passengers a year, respectively. In 1996, they were cut further to 200,000 and 350,000.

ANA took advantage of the new opportunities. By 1990, it controlled 10 percent of Japan's international passenger traffic, doubling that share to 20 percent in 1997. JAL did the same in the domestic market, competing with ANA on routes between the densest city pairs and quickly capturing 20 percent of in-country traffic. Its cut of the domestic passenger business hovered at a bit less than 25 percent over the next fifteen years. Meanwhile, ANA's domestic share, which had been around 60 percent before the breakdown of the segmented system, fell to around 45 percent. JAS and a handful of small local carriers shared the remaining one-third-plus of Japanese traffic.

MOT Barriers to Expansion

The market shares of JAL and ANA quickly plateaued in their new operations because of capacity constraints at Japan's major airports. Although both airlines were willing to add flights on existing routes and to inaugurate new ones, the takeoff and landing rights that were required to do so could only be obtained by taking them from some other carrier, a move that would have been considered to be unfair. Thus, the expansion plans of the airlines were strangled and the Transport Ministry's deregulation hands tied.

In fact, though, the shortage of slots was partly the result of the ministry's own policies. MOT's airport construction efforts had been directed at building new airports rather than expanding established facilities in major markets. Pork-barrel politics and the clout of Japan's construction industry were behind this approach.

Every district wanted an airport or a construction contract, and MOT, at the urging of the political leadership, obliged. Consequently, many of the regional airports were underused while others were bumping against capacity ceilings. Furthermore, high usage fees were imposed to raise money to pay for the construction of new facilities. Landing fees at Narita International Airport, for example, were more than three times those at New York's J. F. Kennedy International Airport and almost five times higher than the surcharges at London's Heathrow International Airport.[1]

In 1998, MOT finally shifted gears, instituting a new focus on improvements at major hubs. A ministry spokesman, citing Japan's continued economic slump, reported that an outright ban on new airports was under consideration. Those comments were interpreted as a message to local politicians and officials that the old days were over. However, the ruling Liberal Democratic Party was not yet ready to put a full stop to pouring more concrete on local runways in support of its construction industry clientele.

Money diverted from airport building projects was to be earmarked to offset reduced landing fees at local airports.[2] One reason for using the savings this way was that steep airport charges were motivating airlines to shift flights to cities that are more lucrative and to abandon lower-density routes. Small airports were not the only ones affected by high fees. By early 1999, five foreign carriers had suspended operations at Osaka's Kansai International Airport, and more would depart later in the year. On paper, the September 1994 opening of this engineering marvel, which enabled Japanese and foreign airlines alike to better serve Japan's second-largest city and the surrounding area, went a long way toward resolving the capacity constraint, at least in this populous region. However, in an attempt to recoup part of the huge costs of building the facility, the airport authorities imposed stiff and, ultimately, counterproductive fees.

Another enduring problem is that the capacity that existed was not used efficiently. One reason has been opposition from the air traffic controllers' union over operating procedures that would expand the number of aircraft movements. Another source of delays in implementing procedures that are more efficient appears to be extreme caution on the part of the authorities. However, a third explanation offered by some Transport Ministry staff is that the MOT has tried to protect JAL's preferred position by limiting the number of slots available to competitors.

In the mid-1980s, most airports were open less than thirteen hours a day. Just three airports operated around the clock. Osaka's Itami Airport operated thirteen hours daily but with many restrictions, while Haneda Airport outside Tokyo was open seventeen hours. Local jurisdictions attempting to control noise imposed many of these restrictions, but they were abetted by the controllers' union.

Historically, the Transport Ministry has been unwilling to confront directly the union's objections to longer hours and increased flight frequencies, partly because the officials themselves were not fully committed to greater use of existing capacity. Although the controllers' union explained their reluctance to accept more flights by reference to physical limitations and safety concerns, capacity clearly was greater than was being used. For example, in 1985, Narita International Airport operated about twelve aircraft movements per hour.[3] By 1999, the number had increased to roughly twenty-six per hour. Additional evidence is the fact that at the comparable one-runway Gatwick Airport in London, the hourly rate is between forty-one and forty-six flights.[4]

Despite the slowness in utilizing capacity, in 1999, Narita Airport was the world's second largest freight handler, it ranked nineteenth in terms of takeoffs and landings, and was number eight in passengers—despite its single runway and limited hours of operation.[5] Nevertheless, one informed American expert told me that capacity at Narita appeared to be determined arbitrarily, apparently based more on strategic evaluations of domestic politics and international pressures than on objective criteria. The gradual increase in the intensity of operations illustrates what might be called a Japanese approach to change: deliberate and with sufficient time for everyone to adjust to new arrangements

Revising the Fare Structure

In 1986, MOT introduced a new fare structure based on a standard pricing formula. Published tariffs, which required ministry approval, were built on the notion of average costs plus a "reasonable" profit. Costs comprised both a fixed portion and a variable component based on distance. Fares for flights of a given length were supposed to be the same, regardless of the number of passengers or other factors that might influence costs or demand. A major reason for this approach was that politicians from smaller towns and from Hokkaido in the north did not want their constituents disadvantaged by higher fares than paid by people living in more populous areas.

According to the standard pricing formula, a one-way ticket for the 250-mile flight from Tokyo's Haneda airport to Osaka's Itami was ¥16,350, based on a fixed portion of ¥9,500 and a variable part of ¥27.4 per mile. The calculated one-way fare for the 510-mile trip from Tokyo to Sapporo was ¥23,440. Actual fares were allowed to vary within 10 percent of the standard. Under the 1986 plan, airlines' published ticket prices remained within a few percent of the standard fares for the next ten years.

Beneath this seemingly well regulated surface, however, real competition was having an effect. The introduction of multiple carriers on the most heavily traveled domestic routes coincided with the arrival of new wide-bodied aircraft designed for short to medium hauls. These planes could provide service at a lower cost, but only if they were filled with paying passengers.

Japanese airlines sought to sell seats by negotiating discounts with travel agents. Regulations allowed discounts from standard fares of up to 50 percent on group package tours. Making use of these cut rates, travel agents were able to offer such attractive prices that customers could afford to discard hotel vouchers or any other parts of a deal that they did not need because the air portion alone was worth the total price of the package. Large travel agencies also sold excess capacity to smaller discount agencies, which, in turn, offered the group fares on an individual basis. Taking a lesson from their American counterparts, Japanese airlines offered rebates to travel agencies that sold more than an agreed number of seats.

While the airfares included in the group tour packages fell within guidelines set by MOT authorities, the rebated tickets and the individual discounted fares did not. The ministry, however, seemed unwilling to enforce its pricing regulations, possibly because Japan's Fair Trade Commission had become interested in cartel arrangements among the airlines. A former JAL managing director told me that around 1988, when ANA was offering discounts on several of its routes, he had called an ANA official to get together to discuss the discounting in order to avoid "excessive competition." The JAL executive was quite surprised about a week later to receive calls from the JFTC warning him about the penalties of collusion in setting prices. When he complained to MOT about this "meddling" from the JFTC and requested the Transport Ministry to get the antitrust watchdog off his back, MOT officials told him that there was nothing that they could do, that the JFTC was an independent body. Although JAL had higher costs than ANA, it was forced to compete with the discounted prices.

Rewriting International Aviation Agreements

Competition was being felt in the international arena as well. The 1952

U.S.-Japan air transport services agreement had been written at a time when domestic and international aviation markets were thoroughly regulated and cartelized. The pact, which included such concepts as control of capacity, required government approval for most changes. In the first half of the 1980s, U.S. aviation negotiators insisted repeatedly during bilateral talks that Washington could name any American carrier to fly routes to Japan. The Japanese team responded that free entry went well beyond the original intent of the agreement, adding that any new entrants that might be designated should not have the full rights granted to the "incumbents" named in the 1952 document.

A memorandum of understanding that Washington and Tokyo concluded in the spring of 1985 created two classes of carriers on each side. One consisted of incumbents with relatively unrestricted rights to fly to designated gateway cities in the other country and beyond. The second group was made up of new entrants. Their operations were constrained by explicit agreements on beyond rights. Schedule approvals as well as slot constraints also limited their activities.

In the United States, intense domestic competitive pressures following deregulation had forced American carriers to lower their costs. The efficiencies gained in domestic operations carried over into the international markets. Between 1978 and 1985, the average revenue per passenger mile of American carriers on both domestic and international routes dropped 25 percent. As costs and fares fell and as traffic expanded, U.S. airlines were able to take advantage of their ability to gather large numbers of passengers at domestic hubs; this concentration of passengers at a single point allowed the carriers to take advantage of high capacity utilization, which reduced costs and enabled the airlines to offer low fares on international routes. Japanese airlines were forced to meet these fares if they wanted to carry passengers overseas.

The lowest-cost company flying between two countries generally sets ticket prices on international routes. These often are American, although Singapore Airlines and other carriers jockey for that position in Asia. As in the domestic case, Japanese airlines first competed through travel agents rather than by offering lower fares directly to passengers.

By 1993, the discrepancies between published tariffs and the international fares available through travel agents were so large that, according to industry consensus, some action was needed to bring the figures into alignment. An off-season, round-trip coach trip between Tokyo and Los Angeles, for instance, could be had for 80 percent below the published standard tariff. Several estimates made at the time indicated that, depending on the route and the season, as many as 50 percent to 80 percent of all travelers were paying less than the standard fares.[6] When Tokyo introduced new international fare rules in April 1994, authorized discount fares for individuals fell by 60 percent, "nearing current market prices" in MOT's view.[7]

The fall 1994 opening of Kansai International Airport serving the Osaka area further undercut MOT's international pricing scheme. With the added capacity, ticket prices fell as much as 40 percent, according to MOT calculations. This fresh source of pricing pressure expanded the threat to the new system of international fares that had been put in place only months earlier.[8]

International Pricing Pressures Affect Domestic Market

With the advent of lower international fares, Japanese tourists were flocking to foreign locations rather than to more distant resorts at home. A golfing holiday in Guam or Hawaii, for example, could be a better deal than the same type of vacation on Okinawa. In January 1994, MOT announced that it would introduce legislation in the Diet to allow discounts of up to 50 percent on domestic fares for "strategic business reasons." Moreover, in an important break with past practice, the lower rates did not require explicit MOT approval; an airline simply needed to notify the ministry of its fares. The rules, implemented in December 1994, allowed carriers to respond more quickly and flexibly to competition.

The Transport Ministry could not, however, easily abandon its oversight role. Officials stated that the purpose of this round of deregulation was "to stimulate demand, not to get into a dumping war." They added that MOT would not accept a situation in which discounts resulted in a drop in total revenues. "If sales decline due to a particular discount, we may issue an administrative order to stop the discount."[9]

Standard fares quickly became the exception on both domestic and international flights as customers sought out discounts, either from the airlines themselves or from travel agencies that specialized in low-priced tickets. Figure 12.1 depicts the revenues per passenger-kilometer that ANA and JAL received on domestic routes—that is, the actual amount of money collected by the two airlines, undisguised by regulation, formula, or published list prices. Also shown are the average yields for American carriers on their domestic routes, converted into yen using the purchasing power parity for each year. The use of purchasing power parity instead of exchange rates makes it possible to present fares in terms of the relative costs and prices of both countries.

As early as 1986, ANA's average yield was ¥22 per passenger-kilometer, which would have produced a Tokyo-Osaka ticket price of ¥8,866, or about half the standard price according to MOT's formula. By 1999, JAL's average price was around ¥15 per passenger-kilometer and ANA's about ¥2 higher. A striking feature of figure 12.1 is that the fares of Japan's two biggest carriers were nearing those of American airlines by the end of the decade.

Figure 12.1: Domestic Passenger Yields on Japanese Airlines and Average U.S. Domestic Yields (yen per revenue passenger kilometer)

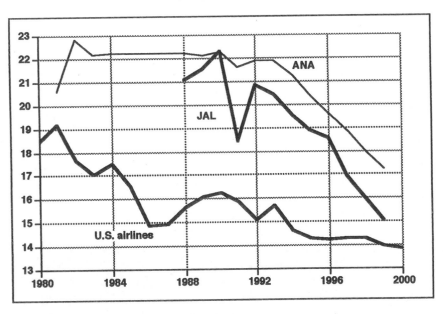

Note: Dollars converted to yen at annual average purchasing power parities.
Sources: Companies' annual reports; U.S. Air Transport Association.

ANA's annual report for the year ending March 31, 1995, illustrates the difference between the surface (*tatemae*) and the *honne* or reality of airfares. Early in the report, ANA proudly observes that its discounted, four-week advance-purchase ticket for Tokyo-Osaka travel cost only ¥10,500, or an average of ¥26 per kilometer, handily beating the Shinkansen bullet train fare of ¥14,430. However, not even midway through the report, in statistical tables describing its nationwide domestic passenger volume and revenues, the airline offers figures that, employing a bit of quick arithmetic, indicate average domestic yields of ¥20.4 per passenger-kilometer. This not only was more than 20 percent below the touted discount fare to Osaka but also below the ballyhooed fares to Hiroshima and Yamagata from Tokyo: ¥22.5 and ¥31.7 per kilometer respectively.

Figure 12.2 presents the same type of information for international yields. In this case, however, American revenues are converted into yen using exchange rates rather than purchasing power parity. Japanese carriers competing in international markets have to compete on the basis of market exchange rates. Consequently, such a comparison shows the real pressures confronting JAL and ANA. The remarkable development evident here is the convergence of Japanese and American prices. Although this comparison does not necessarily reveal anything about relative efficiencies, it does underscore the vicious competition in the international aviation market.

Figure 12.2: International Passenger Yields on Japanese Airlines and Average U.S. International Yields (yen per revenue passenger kilometer)

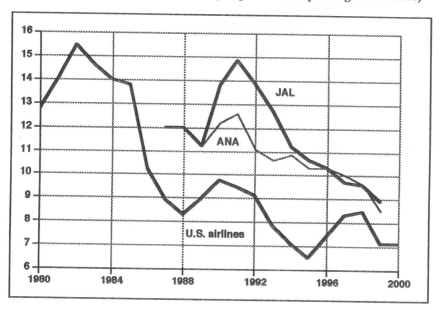

Note: Dollars converted to yen at average annual exchange rates.
Sources: Companies' annual reports; U.S. Air Transport Association.

With falling prices as a backdrop, MOT introduced in April 1996 a new fare structure based on the notion of standardized costs like all its pricing schemes since 1970. Published fares could be as much as 25 percent below the standard, which acted as a price cap. Even if a carrier reduced its standard fares by the maximum 25 percent, though, the results still would be considerably above the average fare actually collected. Nonetheless, this approach permitted discounts on a much broader and deeper scale, including time-of-day and time-of-year discounting, advance-purchase discounts, and group discounts. Individuals who booked directly with airlines rather than through travel agents could receive discounts of up to 50 percent, but they also paid the maximum fares for travel during Golden Week (which extends from late April through early May) and at other peak times.

The Japanese media treated the new fares as price increases because the average standard fare rose by about 1 percent. Surprisingly, news accounts said little about the availability of discounts and mentioned nothing about the fact that actual fares typically were only about half the list prices. Even Japan's leading business newspaper, *Nihon Keizai Shimbun*, headlined the change and began its story with the assertion, "rather than deflate prices, deregulation of airline ticket prices in Japan is sending sky-high fares even further aloft."[10]

Travel agents took note of the actual pricing situation, however, since the new discount fares offered directly to individuals by airlines could be even lower than the group fares arranged by travel companies. Such a shift in pricing power obviously benefited JAL and ANA. By selling tickets directly to passengers, the airlines could avoid paying commissions. Since 70 percent to 80 percent of all tickets were sold through travel agents, reducing these numbers would strengthen carriers' bottom lines.

One problem with the individual discounts offered by the airlines, though, was that their numbers were small and no one, not even travel agencies, knew how many were available. In addition, these fares came with restrictions that limited their applicability. Group discounts through travel agencies that later were resold to individuals had greater appeal to many customers. Taking advantage of group discounts, the travel service units of fifteen major firms, including Nippon Steel Corp., Nippon Telegraph and Telephone Corp., and Honda Motor Co., Ltd., teamed up with Japan's largest discount travel company, H.I.S. Co., Ltd., to purchase domestic and international tickets. These were made available to company employees for business travel and were sold to the public.[11]

New pricing pressures emerged in January 1998, when the United States and Japan concluded a far-reaching agreement that removed all restrictions on transpacific flights by two passenger airlines and one all-cargo carrier from each country. The pact also granted these companies liberal or unrestricted rights to fly beyond the other country to regional markets. Equally important, as many as four other U.S. airlines were permitted to fly up to ninety new weekly passenger frequencies to Japan. Moreover, two new entrants providing passenger service were to be allowed in the market from each side, one immediately and another by 2000.

This sudden increase in transpacific capacity was bound to have a major impact on prices. To fill the extra seats, international discounts proliferated, pushed mainly by Japan's low-price travel agencies. Although it sold some discounted tickets, Japan's largest travel agency, Japan Travel Bureau, Inc., generally had stayed out of this market. However, as JTB saw that discounters regularly were selling approximately 30 percent of overseas tickets, it decided to join the game. The company announced in early 1998 that it, too, would market low-price tickets at its 634 branches and affiliates.

A New Runway and New Airlines

Despite the considerable loosening of MOT regulations governing fares and routes, capacity constraints at Tokyo's Haneda and Narita airports and at Osaka's Itami limited carriers' flexibility. Additional flights to accommodate the increased volume of passengers drawn by lower prices could not be contemplated as long as the number of flights through the nation's main airports was fixed. Likewise, the entry of new airlines into both the domestic and the international market was all but impossible.

The 1994 opening of Kansai International Airport was intended to increase takeoff and landing slots in the Osaka region since the airport, built on a man-made island in Osaka Bay, could be operated with fewer noise and air pollution restrictions. MOT aviation authorities had planned to close Itami in due course, but local business interests pressured the government to preserve the older facility. It continued to handle mainly domestic flights. Most of Itami's international flights were transferred to Kansai, which had been planned as a hub linking international and domestic flights. The decision to keep Itami open not only foiled this plan but also made transfers in Osaka between international and domestic flights an ordeal of several hours. However, the new airport did relieve congestion in the Osaka area.

A new offshore runway at Tokyo's Haneda Airport opened in early 1997. This facility allowed forty or so additional takeoffs and landings a day as well as round-the-clock operation because its isolated location reduced the noise impact on surrounding areas. In September 1996, MOT aviation policymakers alluded to the possibility of assigning some of the extra Haneda slots to new users, possibly for late-night connections from Kansai or Sapporo. One of the people most interested in these comments was Hideo Sawada, the president of H.I.S. He had concluded that for a new carrier to be viable, the one necessary requirement was access to slots in the Tokyo area.

Mr. Sawada had attended a German university and, as a student, had traveled extensively in Europe and Africa. In 1980, at the age of twenty-nine, he founded H.I.S. and pioneered the practice of purchasing large blocks of group tour seats directly from carriers and reselling them to individuals. H.I.S. and other discount travel agencies routinely negotiated with airlines to buy blocks of seats that number in the thousands. Such transactions transfer the risk of holding unsold seats from an airline to a travel agency, which can be stuck with excess inventory or be forced to sell below cost if demand does not match expectations. MOT rule makers had not contemplated this kind of middleman-wholesaling. The practice turned out to be instrumental in bringing down the ministry's elaborate regulatory structure. H.I.S. went public in 1995. A year later, it was Japan's second-largest travel agency behind industry leader JTB.

In December 1995, Mr. Sawada and a venture capitalist friend, Junichi Okawara, met with several other like-minded colleagues to plan a new carrier, eventually named Skymark Airlines Co., Ltd. By then, MOT policies on fares and multiple tracking seemed to presage a general willingness to consider more radical liberalization moves. Messrs. Sawada and Okawara had first discussed starting an airline in 1991, but at that time, the feasibility of such a venture seemed to be near zero. In the mid-1990s, they sensed new currents in the air, especially after MOT officials had intimated in the fall of 1996 that they would change the procedures for allocating slots at an expanded Haneda.

According to subsequent comments by the Aviation Bureau's Katsuhiko Nawano, MOT indeed was inviting responses from potential new entrants. "We had been hearing rumors that companies like Toyota, which has to shuttle its employees between plants, wanted to enter the market. When I heard of Skymark, I thought, 'finally.'" Mr. Okawara later reported that when he asked about the possibility of getting Haneda slots for a start-up, Mr. Nawano told him, "I am pro-deregulation, so go for it."[12]

The press got wind of the Skymark venture while the entrepreneurs still were working out the details. Consequently, the group was forced to go public with its intentions in October 1996, before a business plan was fully developed. The initial strategy called for a Tokyo-Sapporo fare that was half the standard ticket price. The group took as its models America's Southwest Airlines Co., which had grown into a low-cost alternative in the U.S. market, and Great Britain's Virgin Atlantic Airways Ltd., which combined low fares and high levels of service on international routes.

Skymark's strategy was to avoid as many fixed operational costs as possible, especially while the airline still was new. It would lease rather than buy aircraft, outsource maintenance, and use the H.I.S. network of travel offices as a sales force and reservations management system. Furthermore, it would be a no-frills operation, eliminating meals and such amenities as warm towels and newspapers from its in-flight services. Finally, since Japanese pilots are among the highest paid in the world, foreign pilots would be hired to save on personnel costs.

Skymark had attracted initial investments from Mr. Okawara, who later became its president, H.I.S., Japan's top leasing firm, Orix Corp., cellular phone retailer Hikari Tsushin, Inc., and Masao Ogura, former chairman of Yamato Transport Co., Ltd., the country's biggest door-to-door package delivery service. This lineup of investors included several companies and individuals that earlier had gone head-to-head with Japan's regulatory authorities. They brought to Skymark their experience in dealing with the bureaucracy in addition to their money and their commitment.

A new aviation regime clearly was in the works. Shortly after the Skymark announcement, several other groups declared their intent to get into the industry. At the end of October 1996, Hokkaido's largest poultry processor, speaking for a local business consortium, unveiled plans to form a new carrier. Hokkaido International Airlines Co., Ltd. (nicknamed AirDo) would bring low-cost transportation services to Japan's northern island, the lack of which, the backers said, had stifled regional growth. The following month, a group of Okinawa firms under the leadership of the Naha-based Bank of the Ryukyus, Ltd. disclosed its idea of launching service between Okinawa and Osaka and Fukuoka.

Skymark was licensed in July 1998 and inaugurated service with a single plane in September. It contracted for maintenance work with ANA, which insisted that the relationship was strictly a business deal on which it made a profit. The new carrier also used ANA's airport personnel to run its check-in counters. ANA staff simply changed uniforms for their shifts at the Skymark gate.

Instead of competing with Air Do on the Tokyo-Sapporo run, Skymark started off with three daily round-trip flights between Tokyo and Fukuoka at a fare of ¥13,700, or half the regular price on that route. Its initial plans included moderate price increases after a year or so, by which time it would have established itself as a reliable alternative to the major players. Skymark added a second plane and in April 1999 inaugurated new routes linking Osaka to Fukuoka and to Sapporo. In December 1998, Air Do launched three daily round-trips between Sapporo and Tokyo, charging ¥16,000 one way, or 36 percent less than the standard fare of ¥25,000.

Around this time, the business press in Japan finally took notice of the fact that the actual fares paid by many travelers were averaging around 65 percent of the standard fares. Analysts started to wonder how the new carriers could survive if all they had to offer were low fares. JAL, ANA, and JAS had several advantages. They possessed established brand names and offered convenient schedules throughout the day. Because they operated hundreds of aircraft, a problem with one plane would not disrupt the entire flight lineup. Perhaps most important, the Big Three went head-to-head with the newcomers by dropping prices to the same levels as those of the entrants on competing flights.

Skymark's load factor, the proportion of available seats occupied by paying passengers, was a highly satisfactory 70 percent in its first month of operation and climbed to a spectacular 90 percent in November 1998. The load factors of ANA, JAL, and JAS on the Tokyo-Fukuoka route had been 60 percent, but they fell below 50 percent after the start-up's debut. Moreover, Skymark's Boeing 767-300 planes each were fitted with thirty-seven more seats than the same aircraft flown by ANA.

The honeymoon ended for Skymark in early 1999. By April of that year, its load factor had dropped to about the same level as that of its competitors, under 60 percent, which was below its break-even point. Nevertheless, the company stated that it would keep its low introductory fares and not raise them as originally planned.

ANA was able to lift its load factor through discounts, but more than 70 percent of its passengers on routes that competed with Skymark had purchased tickets that cost less than half the normal fare. In June 1999, Skymark's load factor fell to 46 percent, forcing a hike in its Tokyo-Fukuoka fare by ¥2,300 to ¥16,000 to make up for the declining revenues. The airline's newer route between Osaka and Fukuoka also experienced a declining load factor, which had dropped to 40 percent by mid-

1999. However, when its competitors ended their discount war for the summer holiday season, Skymark's occupancy rate bounced back up to 85 percent.

A top executive of Air Do described to a Sapporo business audience in May 1999 some of the trials of starting a new airline in what had been a highly regulated industry. Despite MOT's desire to promote new services, policymakers could not easily shake the habits of the past fifty years. At first, the ministry tried to convince the carrier that it should confine its operations to Hokkaido. When Air Do refused to consider that course, MOT requested that the airline's Sapporo-Tokyo fare be raised about 10 percent (also refused) and that the company calculate its break-even point at a 65 percent load factor, the standard among established companies.

Air Do had planned to hire six pilots to fly a like number of daily one-way flights, which would have given the airline more than enough reserves. MOT required that it hire sixteen pilots. When Air Do tried to lease a plane from Cathay Pacific Airways Ltd., the Hong Kong airline said that it would do so only if it got approval from JAL, which it did not receive. Air Do finally was able to find a willing partner in Australia's Ansett Worldwide Aviation Services, the world's third-largest aircraft leasing company.

Air Do's initial load factor was above 80 percent, but the Hokkaido airline suffered from the same competitive counterattacks as Skymark did, and its load factor fell to 45 percent in June 1999. The carrier received a major infusion of cash in February 1999 to help carry it over the inevitable money-losing initial period when Kyocera Corp. invested ¥500 million, becoming the largest shareholder with more than a 10 percent ownership stake. Air Do's other main investors included thousands of Hokkaido businesses and individuals. Moreover, it was actively supported by local governments, which directed their employees to use the new carrier. Still, some analysts wondered how far regional enthusiasm could go in supporting an airline flying into the headwinds of ever-stronger competitive forces.

For its part, Skymark launched a business-class service in April 1999 at the fixed price of ¥8,000 above the regular fare; it also introduced a half-price child's ticket. To generate even more revenues, the carrier leased the sides of its planes for advertising and offered various product promotions to passengers. Not to be outdone, Air Do introduced a fare of ¥8,000 fare for people under the age of twenty-two and special fares for disabled passengers.

Maintenance remained a problem for the start-ups. Skymark's contract with ANA was jeopardized when a major cost-cutting drive at the larger airline caused staff reductions and ANA claimed that it no longer had the capacity to service the newcomer's aircraft. Air Do had a similar arrangement with JAL, which, after a time, also expressed reluctance to help its new rival. In April 1999, the Transport Ministry stepped in, warning the bigger companies not to cut off service and ignore "ministry guidance."[13]

Skymark and Air Do faced sizable hurdles in their attempts to compete in what emerged as an almost completely deregulated Japanese market. After raising their load factors in the summer of 1999, full-scale price competition resumed. In April 2000, Skymark announced that it was canceling the three daily flights on each of its routes linking Osaka with Fukuoka and Sapporo. However, the carrier said that it would increase daily operations between Fukuoka and Tokyo's Haneda when new slots become available.

Mr. Okawara, one of Skymark's founders and top executives, left to form a regional airline, Fair Inc., which planned three daily flights between Osaka and Sendai. ANA stated that it would assist the new firm with sales, maintenance, and crews. Fair's business plan explored a new model: to fly small aircraft to local airports and concentrate on business travelers who otherwise would have to make connections at metropolitan airports. Given its focus on serving smaller airports, Fair would not compete directly with the three big carriers, which would make it easier to gain their cooperation.

Other start-ups also were announced, but little was heard from them after their first press releases. Through the end of 2001, only three new companies actually began service: Skymark, Hokkaido International Airlines, and Fair Inc.

These carriers may or may not succeed. By the close of 2001, Skymark was flying only a single route. Air Do was in serious financial trouble, existing on the hope of continued subsidies from Hokkaido government agencies.

Indeed, the American experience included several failures. However, some U.S. start-ups did find a business plan that worked. As a new sense of experimentation appeared in Japan's skies, attempts to try out different approaches continued to be hamstrung by the shortage of slots at Japan's major airports. Many experts questioned whether any carrier in Japan could succeed without concentrating on Tokyo. Fair Inc. is operating under a different model that will perhaps prove the truth or falsity of that theory.

A continuing problem of the start-ups is the large amount of capital required to get even a small fleet of aircraft into the air, organize maintenance capabilities, and create marketing and distribution channels. The Japanese start-ups have been operating with the barest of capital investments, hoping to grow fast enough to generate additional capital. However, the deregulation that allowed their entry also forced the existing fliers to compete more vigorously and to reduce costs. Competition is having the desired outcome, pushed along by the new entrants. Unfortunately, they may not survive long enough to enjoy the fruits of their competitive pressures.

Complete Price Deregulation in 2000

In February 2000, a revised Civil Aeronautics Law, passed by the Diet in June 1999, went into effect. It eliminated regulations on domestic airfares and gave airlines a free hand in determining their routes and flight frequencies. The revamped law follows a 1998 cabinet decision to eliminate supply management in the transportation business more generally.

ANA was first out of the hangar with an announcement of a new pricing structure. Interestingly, the top domestic carrier's regular, unrestricted, nonpeak fares were 15 percent higher than the previous standard fares. At one time, MOT officials were fond of pointing out that published fares in Japan were lower than full fares in the United States. Usually left out, however, was any reference to the fact that more than 90 percent of American travelers buy tickets at discounts that average 65 percent off list prices, but range as high as 90 percent.

The benefit of maintaining high published fares is that it gives airlines more pricing flexibility. ANA projected in its announcement that 95 percent of its customers would be able to take advantage of discounts compared with the 70 percent who were doing so before February. As an experiment, the airline introduced a superdiscounted fare for ten specified days in a two-month period, when all seats not purchased during the reservation period (two months before the flight date) would be priced at a flat ten thousand yen on every domestic route ANA serves. Other domestic airlines came up with fares and discounts comparable to ANA's, but each had a different wrinkle. JAL, for example, offered 15 percent off any trip booked over the Internet. It predicted that 80 percent of its passengers would take advantage of the lower prices.

The changed regulatory environment resulted in new problems for the start-ups, however. Air Do said that it would offer reduced prices on two of its six daily flights. Skymark suggested that it may have to do some discounting from its all-the-time low fares, but the carrier was reluctant to make this move since the simplicity of its fare structure was one of its selling points.

ANA's superdiscount program was so successful that it was repeated. The carrier also introduced discounts on routes that competed with high-speed Shinkansen (bullet train) rail services. This move was recognition of the fact that on many of Japan's most heavily traveled corridors, most people go by train. Rather than just competing for an established group of air travelers, the company planned to target the bulk of medium-distance travelers who frequented the bullet trains.

Remaining Slot Issues

As has been discussed, insufficient takeoff and landing capacity at Japan's major airports affects the vitality of both the international and the domestic airline business. The January 1998 U.S.-Japan bilateral aviation agreement contemplated a large number of extra flights by Japanese and American carriers alike. Access to Narita International Airport was the plum for all parties.

Many aviation experts figured that Narita can increase daily flights by 25 percent or more, notwithstanding its single runway and the limited hours of operation imposed on the facility by noise and environmental restrictions. However, even assuming that Narita's air traffic controllers could be persuaded to handle more flights, it was apparent that the desired number exceeded the airport's theoretical capacity.

A second runway planned for Narita, expected at the time of the U.S.-Japan aviation agreement to be completed in 2000, would increase slots by some two-thirds; that could satisfy most of the latent demand. Moreover, airport authorities also managed to find underutilized slots at Narita—for example, capacity that had been set aside for trips by the royal family and high government officials, or slots used intermittently by domestic and foreign companies for seasonal peaks. These also were open for redistribution. In all, Narita managers came up with 202 extra takeoff and landing slots; they authorized seventy to eighty additional flights a day.

Work on Narita's second runway ran into a major snag in April 1999 when holdout landowners refused to sell property in the middle of the construction site. MOT abandoned the projected 2000 opening date and settled on a new plan to build a shorter runway, one that bypassed the unavailable land. The start of service on the second runway was scheduled for June 2002, in time for the World Cup soccer matches to be held jointly in Japan and South Korea.

Meanwhile, the new runway at Haneda became operational in the summer of 2000. The number of flights there increased to 351 a day from 320, a third more than planned two years earlier. Studies of Haneda's air traffic control system persuaded airport authorities that additional flights could be squeezed out of the facility. They set a target of 377 daily flights for July 2002.

The key issue was how to divide the new capacity. MOT rejected the idea of auctioning the slots because of fears that one major carrier would grab all of them and gain a near-monopoly on traffic at Haneda. At the same time, though, the ministry was criticized for using a nontransparent allocation system, one that can be abused. In fact, slot assignments are among the few aviation regulatory functions still under the Transport Ministry's control.

To remove some of the arbitrariness of this process, an advisory committee developed a point system based on airline operations and how well carriers served the public interest. The thirty-one new slots for 2000 were allocated according to this new formula. Japan's start-ups received seventeen of them.

Restructuring Costs and Finances

The covers of the English-language versions of JAL's and ANA's annual reports for FY 1998 summarize the main internal problems facing Japan's two biggest airlines. JAL's publication carried the caption, "A More Competitive JAL Group." The ANA headline read, "Action—A progress report on ANA's restructuring plan." JAL has made the greatest strides toward reducing its unit costs from levels that even its chief executives acknowledged were among the world's highest. Since three-quarters of the airline's revenues come from foreign operations, the strength of the yen has colored cost comparisons with foreign carriers, but even in dollar terms, JAL's achievements are significant.

JAL reduced total costs by 30 percent between FY 1990 and FY 1998; labor costs shrank by an even larger 40 percent. Unfortunately, yields fell even faster, by 35.5 percent on the airline's most important international routes and by 29 percent on domestic operations. The International Civil Aviation Organization calculates standardized cost data for the world's major carriers. It shows JAL's costs falling to forty-eight cents per available ton-kilometer in 1998 from sixty-eight cents in the early 1990s. The new cost structure is within shouting distance of United Airlines' 44.2 cents for 1997.[14]

JAL became more efficient in the usual ways. For example, it reduced ground staff by more than a third since 1991. In addition, it hired flight attendants on a contract basis only and at wages considerably below the old standard. The company had planned to cut costs further by using foreign staff, but MOT intervened, arguing safety issues. JAL also formed a low-cost subsidiary to fly vacationers to Southeast Asia, hiring cabin crew in Thailand and pilots in Ireland, Great Britain, and elsewhere. The foreign pilots are based in Hawaii, and the attendants return to Bangkok on their days off, which is more cost-effective than basing staff in Japan.

A money-losing hotel chain, expanded during the "bubble economy" years of the late 1980s, was sold off, with JAL taking a one-time charge. It applied its available cash flow to reduce debt by ¥350 billion by 2002 in order to cut interest expenses.

ANA has not been as ruthless as JAL in trimming staff, but the carrier did provoke a pilot strike on its international routes in 1998 when it tried to revamp a guaranteed payment scheme, whereby pilots were assured of at least sixty-five hours of pay a month regardless of their actual working time. ANA has been more successful in reducing unneeded capacity by delaying deliveries of planes and moving some equipment to a low-cost subsidiary. The carrier focused on flying more passengers through aggressive fare cuts and by taking advantage of its new incumbent status on transpacific flights, where it gained the same route flexibility as JAL. During the East Asian financial and economic crisis that began in mid-1997, ANA was able to increase its service to several American destinations. At the same time, membership in the United Airlines-led Star alliance gave ANA important code-sharing relations that boosted transpacific sales over those of other segments.

In late 2001, JAL and JAS announced that they would merge their two companies by 2004. The primary motivation for the consolidation was to cut costs. With a 48 percent share of the domestic market, the merged carriers would have just about the same share as ANA.

Deregulation with Japanese Characteristics

The restructuring efforts of Japan's airlines indicate that deregulation and increased competition are having a predictable effect. Japan's high-cost, inefficient, and high-price aviation industry is now only a memory of the old regulated system. As competition heats up even more with the opening of new slots at major airports, the pressure only will get fiercer. To date, no Japanese carrier has called it quits, but that may not be true in the future.

One of the lessons that can be drawn from the aviation experience is that substantial change can be produced by small, but sustained, actions. The trend toward deregulation has moved forward by large and small steps that, cumulatively, have wrought considerable change. This approach to reform seems to be compatible with Japanese social values and political processes. The following list summarizes the main regulatory changes since 1952:

- 1952: Civil Aeronautics Law passed; MOT prescribes routes, fares, and airlines; manages supply-demand balance.
- 1970, 1972: Cabinet approves segmented industry structure; MOT implements plan in 1972.
- 1983: New cargo airline authorized for U.S. service.
- 1985: 1972 system abolished; international routes opened to all carriers conditional on bilateral agreements; domestic triple tracking introduced on routes with one million passengers annually; double tracking with 700,000 passengers.
- 1986: Standard pricing formula introduced reflecting average costs and distance.
- 1992: Triple tracking lowered to 700,000 passengers, double tracking to 400,000.
- April 1994: New international price structure allows deep discounts on group tours and individual inclusive tours.
- January 1996: Triple tracking reduced to 350,000, double tracking to 200,000.
- April 1996: A new domestic fare system bases maximum on distance and standard costs with 25 percent variation; up to 50 percent discounts allowed; carriers only required to notify MOT, not seek advance approval.
- October 1996: H.I.S. Co. announces plan for new low-cost airline, stimulated by MOT September decision to allocate new Haneda slots to newcomers.
- October 1996: Hokkaido business group plans airline for Hokkaido-Tokyo routes.
- October 1996: MOT says it will not require new entrants to comply with existing fare system and will remove price floors.
- March 1997: MOT announces end of domestic entry restrictions in FY 1999.
- April 1997: MOT lifts entry barriers at Haneda; double and triple tracking system is abolished.
- April 1997: MOT allocates slots at Haneda to new entrants; allows flexibility

in deciding routes.
• March 1998: Cabinet calls for ending capacity controls in aviation as part of broader deregulation measures.
• February 2000: Civil Aeronautics Law, revised in June 1999, allows airlines to set domestic fares, routes, and frequencies.

Among the indicators of a deregulated industry are falling prices and rising output. In the eleven years following the ending of strict regulation, from 1987 to 1998, JAL's domestic yields fell by 3.1 percent annually and ANA's came down 2.25 percent. For comparison, yields in the United States in the decade after deregulation in 1978 declined an inflation-adjusted 2.6 percent annually. Japan's domestic and international passenger traffic, as measured in passenger-kilometers, shot up 7.1 percent per year and 8.2 percent respectively, despite the onset of recession and slow economic growth for most of that period. American domestic and international growth in the ten years after 1978 was a bit slower at about 6 percent.

Competition on U.S.-Japan routes is shown in figure 12.3, which plots the number of passengers on scheduled airlines flying between the two countries. Until 1985, the numbers were evenly split between the two countries. As international fares charged by American airlines came down (see figure 12.2), the market share shifted to U.S. shores. When Japanese companies started to compete more effectively in 1994 and later, their share jumped sharply.

This evidence on fares and passenger traffic indicates that deregulation in Japan was not hollow. Prices and quantities behaved as one would expect under a liberalized regime. However, the process was distinctly Japanese. Based on U.S. experience, transport ministry officials decided in 1980 that deregulation was on the agenda. Given their desire for predictability, combined with a sense of fairness to allow everyone time to adjust, they planned a time horizon of decades. In fact, a combination of technology plus foreign and domestic pressures hurried the turnabout to twenty years, which was ahead of the MOT schedule. Clearly, this two-decade process was not at all similar to the American experience, which took only a few years.

The search for consensus stretched out the time to add a second runway at Narita to more than a quarter century. The authorities also avoided direct confrontation with the air traffic controllers, but over a decade or two they were able to increase flight frequencies by substantial amounts at the major airports. This demonstration of patience is a far cry from President Ronald Reagan's firing of American air traffic controllers in 1981 to break a strike. Nevertheless, despite the MOT's deliberate reduction of regulatory authority, it could not completely abandon old habits when it offered guidance to JAL restricting its hiring of foreign flight attendants or to ANA on not ending its maintenance contract with Skymark. ANA's difficulty in reducing employment is a reminder that lifetime employment is difficult to abandon, despite the economic pressures to reduce costs. Nevertheless, the airlines are getting their costs down, although the process may seem to be extended in some American eyes.

Figure 12.3: Passengers on Routes between Japan and United States, Japanese and American Airlines, 1976-1998 (millions)

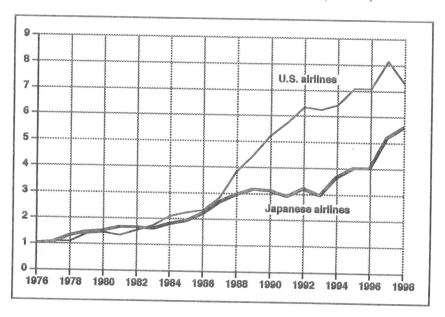

Source: U.S. Department of Commerce, I-92 database.

One case is insufficient to draw general conclusions, but at least in aviation, deregulation is occurring—with Japanese characteristics. Manifest fairness, time to adapt, reluctance to engage in confrontation, and difficulty in abandoning employees and others in long-term relations are all attributes of this example. However, it may not always be possible to manage change in such a civilized way, especially if the lineup of economic and political forces were to be less favorable.

Notes

1.   Alexandra Harney, "Airlines Get That Sinking Feeling Over Japan," *Financial Times,* November 30, 1999.
2.   "Transport Ministry to Cut Landing Fees at Local Airports by One-Third," *Nikkei Weekly,* August 10, 1998.
3.   "Japan's Cautious Airline Deregulation: How Far Will It Go?" *Oriental Economist,* June 1985.
4.   Patrick Killen, "A Tale of Two Airports, or Three," *Journal of the American Chamber of Commerce in Japan,* February 2000, 16.
5.   "Narita Second in Air Cargo Volume in 1999," *Japan Times,* February 24, 2001.
6.   "System Is Sought to Cut Air Fares, End Discount War," *Japan Times,* June 16, 1993.
7.   "New Fare Rules May Hurt Discounters," *Japan Times,* February 23, 1994.
8.   "Kansai Warming," *Aviation Week & Space Technology,* January 23, 1995.
9.   "Fare Rules Loosened for Domestic Flights," *Nikkei Weekly,* December 5, 1994.
10.   "Unfettered Air Fares Fly Higher," *Nikkei Weekly,* February 26, 1996.
11.   "Nippon Steel, NTT, Others to Sell Discount Air Tickets," *Nikkei,* August 4, 1997.
12.   Sandra Sugiwara, "Japan's 1st No-Frills Airline Steers to Uncharted Territory," *Washington Post,* February 10, 1997.
13.   "New Airlines Face Pressing Maintenance Issue," *Nikkei,* April 9, 1999.
14.   "Japan Airlines Rights Itself Through Cost Cuts," *Nikkei Weekly,* February 7, 2000. The cost per available ton-kilometer measures how much it costs to carry one metric ton—including plane, passengers, fuel, and cargo—one kilometer.

Chapter 13

Is Japan an Outlier?

Japan Is Different; All Countries Are Different

It is evident that Japan has many distinctive characteristics that make it different from other countries. Among some Japanese scholars, *nihonjin-ron* is a branch of study that examines Japanese attributes and celebrates Japan's presumed uniqueness. Elsewhere, the feeling is widespread that, especially in the spheres of economics and business-government relations, Japan's style of capitalism differs—certainly from the American variety and, less assertively, from the economies of other developed nations.

The assertion of significant differences between American and Japanese economic behavior focusing on business-government links is a foundation of revisionist writers on the Japanese economy. In 1986, for example, financial writer Karel van Wolferen described as fiction "the premise maintained by the United States and Europe that Japan belongs with them in that loose category known as capitalist free-market economies."[1] James Fallows, in a widely cited 1989 article in the *Atlantic Monthly*, underscored his assertion of difference by noting that proponents of *nihonjinron* agreed with foreign critics of Japanese economic policy "that the institutions and values of modern Japan are highly unusual."[2]

It does not require a great deal of research to discern that Japan differs from the United States and from other advanced nations operating according to capitalist norms. Indeed, most countries are quite different from each other. An American visitor to Canada, the closest nation to the United States in most dimensions of comparison, quickly recognizes different institutions, politics, values, business behavior, and government-economic relations.

The economic effect of the U.S.-Canada border and its proxy for other differences was the subject of a study published in the *American Economic Review*. These two countries were chosen for several reasons: trade between them is relatively free, they share a very long border with few natural barriers, the majority of Americans and Canadians speak English, and the two countries have similar cultural and political traditions. These conditions suggested fewer cross-border restrictions between the United States and Canada than would be found in most other similar cases.

Examining the border's effect on the prices of similar goods, the authors found that the cost of moving products between the United States and Canada was equivalent to adding transportation expenses of a distance between 1,780 and 75,000 miles. They concluded that, "despite the relative openness of the U.S.-Canadian border, the markets are still segmented."[3]

The presence of economically significant variations between countries as close as the United States and Canada suggests the need for caution when drawing conclusions about differences between other nations. That countries differ is obvious. What is less obvious is the extent to which the economics and the government-business relations of Japan differ, over what dimensions, and compared to whom.

Hints in Some Studies

Several researchers have compiled data on a large number of countries across many dimensions of economic and government behavior. For example, economists studying development recently have come to focus on institutions and governance as important preconditions for growth. They have collected measures of the quality of government and the nature of government-economic relations to support this research.

One such study by economist Paolo Mauro generated data for sixty-eight countries on legal systems, bureaucracy and red tape, and corruption. Surveys probed investors' assessments of conditions in the relevant country. Indices for the three variables were defined as follows:[4]

> Legal system and judiciary: efficiency and integrity of the legal environment as it affects business, particularly that of foreign firms.
>
> Bureaucracy and red tape: the regulatory environment foreign firms face when they seek approvals and permits and the degree to which it represents an obstacle to their operations.
>
> Corruption: the degree to which business transactions involve corruption or questionable payments.

The three separate indices were averaged to produce a "bureaucratic efficiency" index. According to this ranking, Switzerland, Singapore, and New Zealand held the top three positions; the United States ranked fifth. Japan was in thirteenth place, sandwiched between Hong Kong and Belgium. In terms of bureaucratic efficiency, Japan was not very different from other advanced industrial nations. At the bottom of the surveyed sixty-eight countries were Indonesia, Iran, Haiti, and Zaire.

One of the first conclusions apparent from this preliminary examination is that when comparisons are broadened to include a range of nations at various stages of economic and institutional development, Japan falls within the general experience of rich countries. This effect becomes even more obvious when the sample of countries is enlarged and the number of variables is increased.

Consider, for example, a regularly updated index representing "economic freedom" for 103 countries compiled by the Fraser Institute, a Canadian economic think tank. In *Economic Freedom of the World, 1975-1995*, the information was organized within seventeen subindices grouped in four sections: money and inflation, government operations and regulation, government expropriation and discriminatory taxation, and restraints on international exchange. The average overall ranking placed the United States in third place behind Hong Kong and New Zealand and ahead of Switzerland and the United Kingdom. Japan ranked ninth, between Australia and the Netherlands. The last three places belonged to Zaire, Iran, and Somalia. Again, according to the Fraser Institute report, Japan's brand of capitalism is not very different from that of other advanced nations.[5]

However, to say that Japan is not very different begs the question of significance among differences. Moreover, the use of averages and indices may mask meaningful variations at a more detailed level. In addition, several statistical questions intrude into the discussion. For example, many of the variables mentioned above are highly correlated among themselves; should we adjust for the, perhaps, obvious notion that an efficient judicial system and low degree of corruption seem to go together. In other words, is there a dependence among the various measures that may exaggerate the apparent closeness of advanced countries? These issues will be addressed below.

Is Japan an Outlier?

To assess whether Japan really is an outlier, eleven separate studies were reviewed. They included information on forty-six individual variables; the studies covered a range of different countries, from forty-six to one hundred fifty. (The sources and data descriptions are presented in the appendix to this chapter.) The analytical problem is to find a way of dealing with scores of variables in a way that helps to answer the questions of "how different," "how close," or "how far."

A statistical artifact that exaggerates the similarities between Japan and the United States could bias the results of the various studies referred to above. The indices are averages of separate subindices. For example, ten main variables are averaged to come up with a summary index of economic freedom. Moreover, each of the ten variables were, themselves, averages of two or more underlying variables that were normalized and averaged to produce the subindex. For example, a variable labeled "taxation" was produced from the average and marginal tax rates on corporate and personal incomes. Thus, the averaging process could be homogenizing underlying differences.

To illustrate this problem, consider two variables from the Fraser Institute's data used to compile its measure of economic freedom: the ratio of government expenditures to GDP and the marginal tax rate. Since the ratio of government expenditures to GDP in Japan is relatively small, it warrants a relatively high index value of eight, whereas high marginal tax rates generate an index value of two. The United States is just the reverse, with values of three and seven. Although transpacific differences across these variables are relatively large, their average values are the same: five for each country.

One way to deal with this problem is to calculate a multidimensional distance among variables for each pair of countries. Such an indicator makes use of the Pythagorean theorem that the distance between two points is the square root of the sum of the squares of the distances measured along each of the separate dimensions.[6] This so-called Euclidean distance can be used to measure any number of dimensions or variables. The Euclidean distance between the two variables in the above example is 7.07, the square root of $(8-3)^2 + (2-7)^2$. The simple average of the two variables shows the countries to be the same.

Euclidean distances between the United States and the 102 other countries in the sample were calculated in this way across all seventeen of the Fraser Institute economic freedom variables based on standardized variables with means of zero and a standard deviation of one. The results for the closest countries to the United States are shown in table 13.1. The top ten on the list, in addition to the United States, includes the United Kingdom and four other closely associated countries—colonies or former constituent parts of the United Kingdom. Japan falls between Canada and Ireland on the list. The results of the same exercise also are given for Japan as the point from which distance is measured. In this case, the United States is the nearest to Japan, followed by Australia.

Table 13.1: Distances of Nearest Fifteen Countries from the United States and Japan Based on Seventeen Economic Freedom Variables

Rank	Country	Distance from United States	Country	Distance from Japan
1	United States	0.00	Japan	0.00
2	New Zealand	1.49	United States	3.24
3	United Kingdom	1.80	Australia	3.36
4	Australia	2.04	Spain	3.38
5	Switzerland	2.79	Korea	3.55
6	Canada	2.93	Ireland	3.58
7	Japan	3.24	New Zealand	3.69
8	Ireland	3.24	Netherlands	3.78
9	Panama	3.34	France	3.81
10	Germany	3.43	United Kingdom	3.83
11	Costa Rica	3.46	Canada	3.91
12	France	3.50	Belgium	4.13
13	Spain	3.58	Switzerland	4.16
14	Denmark	3.74	Italy	4.20
15	Taiwan	3.79	Finland	4.26

Source: James D. Gwartney, *Economic Freedom of the World, 1975-95* (Vancouver, British Columbia: Fraser Institute), 1996.

In addition to considering each of the surveyed studies separately, it is possible to combine them for a more comprehensive view. As samples were combined, however, unmatched data across them caused the number of observations to fall. For example, one study may have data on Malawi but not on Yemen, while another has Yemen but not Malawi. In such an instance, neither country would appear in the joined sample. All forty-six variables extracted from the eleven studies were used to define distances among countries, although comprehensive data were available for just twenty-five nations (see table 13.2). Again, the United Kingdom, Canada, Australia, and Japan follow the United States. Other Northern European countries trail in close order. The same pattern is repeated when distances are measured from Japan.

Table 13.2: Distances from the United States and Japan Based on Forty-Six Variables from Eleven Studies

Rank	Country	Distance from United States	Country	Distance from Japan
1	United States	0.00	Japan	0.00
2	United Kingdom	3.88	United Kingdom	4.86
3	Canada	4.04	Canada	5.16
4	Australia	4.39	Spain	5.30
5	Japan	5.51	Australia	5.32
6	France	6.26	United States	5.51
7	Finland	6.68	France	5.61
8	Sweden	6.88	Finland	6.10
9	Netherlands	6.90	Netherlands	6.18
10	Spain	7.20	Chile	6.26
11	Norway	7.24	South Korea	6.55
12	Austria	7.46	Austria	6.59
13	Chile	7.64	Norway	6.96
14	Malaysia	8.18	Sweden	7.08
15	Singapore	8.61	Malaysia	7.25
16	South Korea	9.07	Singapore	7.71
17	Israel	9.21	Israel	8.54
18	Greece	10.38	Thailand	8.66
19	Thailand	10.77	Greece	8.78
20	Turkey	11.48	Turkey	9.68
21	Philippines	11.59	Philippines	10.26
22	Brazil	12.20	India	11.08
23	India	13.20	Venezuela	11.20
24	Venezuela	13.22	Brazil	11.36
25	Indonesia	13.58	Indonesia	11.68

A potential criticism of the above distance measures is that many of the variables are correlated with each other. Rather than forty-six different dimensions, the tables could be reporting the same ones several times, possibly biasing the results. To take account of this possibility, a so-called factor analysis was performed on the set of original variables. This statistical process combines the variables into a smaller set based on the linear relationships among the original variables. The factors are calculated to be statistically independent of, or uncorrelated with, each other. Because of the missing data problem noted above, not all the variables could be included in the factor analysis. Dropping the six variables with the fewest number of observations allowed the analysis to proceed among the remaining forty variables. Eight factors were extracted; the four most important were selected for calculating distance measures among the countries.[7] The main results of the distance measures based on the four factors are shown in table 13.3. Again, the same patterns are observed as in the other tests. Japan ranks among the Anglo-Saxon economies in terms of its distance from the United States, and the same group of countries is closest to Japan.

Table 13.3: Distances of Nearest Ten Countries from the United States and Japan Based on Four Factors and Forty Variables

Rank	Country	Distance from United States	Country	Distance from Japan
1	United States	0.00	Japan	0.00
2	New Zealand	0.38	United Kingdom	0.43
3	Australia	0.81	Canada	0.61
4	Switzerland	0.95	Ireland	0.62
5	United Kingdom	1.08	Taiwan	0.98
6	Japan	1.38	Australia	0.98
7	Canada	1.48	New Zealand	1.29
8	Chile	1.79	Malaysia	1.34
9	Norway	1.86	Switzerland	1.34
10	Denmark	1.90	United States	1.38

Factor analysis can be revealing when it uncovers patterns among the variables that have an intuitive interpretation. Sometimes a poetic imagination is helpful in revealing the patterns but the four factors calculated above demonstrate a straightforward structure. The first factor, accounting for 40 percent of the variance among the variables, was heavily weighted toward variables associated with efficient and competent government. Such variables as low red tape, an efficient legal system, the rule of law, absence of corruption, guarantees of property rights, and a high level of democracy were important. Other contributory variables to this factor were associated with minimal levels of government intervention in the economy in areas such as regulatory barriers to business and wage and price controls. The second factor depended heavily on a few variables dealing with small government: low taxes and government spending. The third most important factor was influenced mainly by open trade and foreign capital flows. The fourth factor was related to market price-setting mechanisms: unregulated credit markets, creditor rights, few price controls, and low inflation.

Interestingly, the first factor (related to good governance and limited regulation) highlights one area that some critics of Japan assert characterizes that country—excessive economic regulation. However, when compared across many countries and over several different dimensions of economic behavior, Japan does not seem to be strikingly out of line with the experience of other advanced countries. On just this one factor, the United States is in second position, between New Zealand and Switzerland. Japan falls a bit further down between Finland and France in twelfth place. Its relative position reflects some common intuitions, but it is not notably out of place among the advanced economies.

One additional test perhaps can reveal more of the underlying structure among the countries and variables. The techniques so far have required that many observations be dropped from the statistical analysis because of missing data. In the next test, U.S. data are correlated with the same variables of each of the other countries. The correlation coefficient then becomes the measure of the closeness of each country to the United States. The defect of this measure is that the correlation may be based on different sets of variables; however, the countries nearest the United States, according to this measure, include data for most variables. In order to retain statistical significance, at least twenty variables were required for a country to be included in this analysis.

Table 13.4, shows the fifteen countries nearest and furthest from the United States in terms of correlations. Correlations tell the same story as distances and factors. Japan falls just after the Anglo Saxon countries in its closeness to the United States. The bottom countries on the list also tell a revealing story. When people say that the Japanese economy and government are different, they appear to have forgotten such countries with ineffective governments, planned economies, or nonmarket systems as Haiti, Syria, Tanzania, or Russia.

Table 13.4: Correlations between the United States and 102 Countries: Fifteen Most Positive and Fifteen Most Negative Correlations

Rank	Country	Correlation	Variables
1	United States	1.00	46
2	New Zealand	0.90	40
3	United Kingdom	0.88	46
4	Canada	0.87	46
5	Australia	0.84	46
6	Switzerland	0.76	40
7	Japan	0.76	46
8	Denmark	0.75	40
9	Ireland	0.72	40
10	Germany	0.69	45
11	France	0.68	46
12	Netherlands	0.66	46
13	Taiwan	0.66	40
14	Hong Kong	0.64	45
15	Finland	0.64	46
88	Nicaragua	-0.55	34
89	Egypt	-0.55	46
90	Venezuela	-0.56	46
91	Nepal	-0.57	23
92	Congo	-0.58	27
93	Algeria	-0.62	35
94	Chad	-0.63	26
95	Burundi	-0.64	23
96	Tanzania	-0.66	28
97	Syria	-0.71	27
98	Haiti	-0.73	27
99	Russia	-0.76	21
100	Zaire	-0.77	28
101	Iran	-0.82	27
102	Somalia	-0.85	20

Japan and the U.S. Really Are Different, Aren't They?

Why is the widespread view that Japan is "different" not supported by the data? In fact, for a handful of variables, such as marginal tax rates and the ratio of government expenditures to GDP, the U.S.-Japan gap is significant. However, these variables are not what most people usually mean when they refer to differences.

What about, for example, foreign direct investment? The flow of FDI into Japan has been only a few percent of the investment into the United States or Europe. On a scale of one to five, with one being the least restrictive, the Heritage Foundation's index of economic freedom rated Japan a three and gave the United States a grade of two. Hong Kong, Singapore, and Israel, among others, got perfect scores of one. Concerning Japan, the study's authors noted: "The close relationship between government and businesses, however, continues to impede foreign investment because some businesses and government agencies collude to make it too costly."[8] This evaluation, together with other considerations, yields a grade for Japan that is lower than the one for the United States but higher than that for many other countries.

Turning to an evaluation of governmental variables, Raymond Gastil, one of the first political scientists to attempt a systematic survey of political rights, devised a scale of one to seven to measure political and civil liberties, with one signifying the highest degree of freedom.[9] His measure of democracy gave the United States a one and Japan a two. This assessment can be compared with the seven assigned Laos or the six for the Ivory Coast.

A point to draw from these examples is that the world of economic-government behavior is rather broad. What may look like deviant behavior when viewed from a limited perspective is seen to be less extreme when the bands of possibilities are widened.

In a simple two-way, U.S.-Japan comparison across the forty-six variables analyzed here, the values for the two countries were equal in seventeen instances, Japan came out "better" or less regulated and more free on seven, and the U.S. figure was better for twenty-two indicators. In this match, American actions are more market-friendly on almost half the measures, while Japan outranks the United States across only 15 percent of the indices. This finding is consistent with the widespread notion that America's market is more open than Japan's and that government in the United States is less intrusive.

Other measures of economic activity could be chosen that would emphasize the differences between the United States and Japan. For example, two components of the subindices of a World Bank property market database consider residential mobility and housing floor space per person. Residential mobility—defined as the percentage of all households that moved during the past year—can be considered an indicator of the range of choices available to people. High mobility is a sign that people are able to move easily in response to changes in circumstances. According to this measure, Americans have by far the greatest mobility with 26.5 percent of all households moving in any one year. Relocations in Japan are less than a third as frequent at 7.1 percent, which puts Japan at the median level of the forty-seven countries in this sample.

The same pattern appears concerning residential floor area per person. The United States is in first place with a figure of 739.5 square feet per person—50 percent greater than number-two Norway and more than four times larger than Japan's 170.1 square feet. The Japanese figure, though, is slightly above the median of 155 square feet per person. In both examples, the differences among countries are large and in the expected direction, but it is the United States that falls outside the range of global experience.

Differences in the expected direction, actively sought, are not hard to find. For example, studies of individualism versus collective values and behavior find that American behavior is solidly individualistic and that the United States is, in fact, an outlier, even with respect to other similarly inclined societies. The same results put Japan, as expected, squarely in the middle of collectivist societies. However, various studies indicate that "as countries like Japan become more affluent, they also tend to become more individualistic."[10]

When a variety of phenomena is considered, the possibilities for variations in behavior are amplified. However, we will have to await those studies that systematically examine a greater number of micro-level performance indicators to determine whether Japan continues to be situated as close to American values as it is in the present review of the evidence.

The Convergence Hypothesis

The ordering of the countries in the tables suggests that the distance measures may be associated with a country's affluence. This speculation is borne out by comparing a country's real GDP per capita with the distance from the United States, calculated by any of the methods discussed above. Such a plot is shown in figure 13.1 for the one hundred countries having both a correlation as reported in table 13.4 and an estimate of real GDP per capita (plotted on a logarithmic scale in the figure). The correlation of 0.84 indicates that the relationship is far from random. Furthermore, Japan's point is quite close to the predicted value, meaning that its behavior is more or less what would be expected, given its income level.

Figure 13.1: Correlations with United States and One Hundred Countries in Relation to Real 1985 GDP per Capita in Dollars

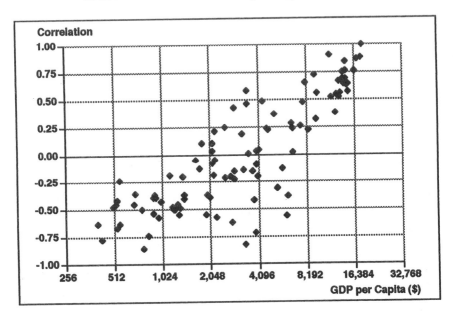

What accounts for the relative similarity of economic institutions among more affluent countries? The weight of the data suggests that Japan fits in the cluster of nations usually considered to subscribe to Anglo-Saxon capitalist norms. Far from being an outlier or significantly different, Japan comes as close to the behavior patterns and the experience of the United States, Canada, and the United Kingdom as any other country in the sample of observations considered here. However, the data point to something deeper; it suggests the hypothesis that if a country wants to get rich, it should mimic the institutions and behavior of affluent economies. Within narrow limits, per capita income seems to be strongly related to these institutional variables.

This deductive conclusion is illustrated by figure 1.1 in the first chapter, which plots annual GDP growth rates averaged over ten-year periods as a function of real GDP per capita. The important point for present purposes is that the variability of income growth among the richest countries is quite low. One could infer from this observation that the institutions of rich countries produce consistent long-term growth. The gains from imitation and catching up have been left behind, and the contributions from rapid rates of investment largely have been exhausted. What seems to occur is that wealthier nations develop roughly equivalent institutions to achieve roughly the same results. In other words, countries are rich because they have adopted institutions that work and that are broadly similar. Japan is not an outlier in this process.

A substantial body of literature examines the existence and the possible causes of institutional convergence. One school of thought contends that advanced industrial countries tend toward common ways of organizing economic life. Suzanne Berger describes this so-called convergence hypothesis as follows:[11]

> In this view, competition, imitation, diffusion of best practice, trade, and capital mobility naturally operate to produce convergence across nations in the structures of production and in the relations among economy, society, and the state. Variations may be found from country to country because of different historical legacies. But such distinctions fade over time.

The convergence hypothesis is not without critics. One common theme is the resilience of diverse national systems and modes of capitalism. Detailed comparisons, for example, between labor relations in France and Germany, banking relations in Germany and the United States, and production methods in Japan and the United States support the national diversity argument.

However, in just the few years since the publication of the book from which these observations were taken, economic and political forces have broken down many of the resilient modes of behavior in both Germany and Japan that were touted to support nonconvergence. In particular, the opening of financial markets—in Japan through deregulation and in Germany through the impact of the European Union—appears to be shifting business attitudes toward considerations of profitability and away from relational transactions and the nurturing of an array of company stakeholders; in other words, the differences among these diverse modes of capitalism seem to be growing narrower.

Convergence Is Not Inevitable

Despite the apparent coming together of economic behavior across nations, such movement is not inevitable. A review of the convergence of income and productivity concludes:[12]

> Statistical evidence does not confirm any general and secular trend toward eco-

nomic convergence in productivity and standards of living. Such convergence is restricted to the small club of nations that have been able to invest sufficiently in productive investment, infrastructure, and education. . . . Even within developed or rich countries, the long-run evolutions of Great Britain and Argentina remind us that decline is always a possibility and that convergence is never automatic, but is associated with the choice and implementation of an adequate strategy, given a changing international regime and radical changes in technologies.

Nor does convergence occur in a single direction. The United States is an implicit object of comparison. However, in terms of production methods, for example, the greater movement over the past twenty-five years has been that of the United States in the direction of Japan.

Convergence certainly is not automatic for Japan, although its main lines of economic development have brought it closer to the Anglo-Saxon model. Whether it can continue to evolve in a more market-oriented direction is a political issue that will be fought out in coming years. Thus, the question of whether the differences between Japan and the United States will diminish further must remain unanswered. However, it appears that the divergence is not as great as first and even later impressions might suggest.

Appendix: Data Sources and Definitions

Raymond Gastil, *Freedom in the World: Political Rights and Civil Liberties, 1986-1987* (New York: Greenwood Press, 1987). Data available from the World Bank, <www.worldbank.org/research/growth/ddeale.htm> (June 24, 2000).
One variable for 148 countries:
Measure of democracy.
James D. Gwartney, *Economic Freedom of the World, 1975-95* (Vancouver, British Columbia: Fraser Institute), 1996.
Seventeen variables for 103 countries:
Average annual growth rate of money supply during the last five years minus potential growth rate of GDP.
Standard deviation of annual inflation rate during the last five years.
Freedom of citizens to own a foreign bank account domestically.
Freedom of citizens to maintain a bank account abroad.
Government general consumption expenditures as a percent of gross domestic product.
Role and presence of government-operated enterprises.
Price controls, or the extent that businesses are free to set their own prices.
Freedom of private businesses and cooperatives to compete in markets.
Equality of citizens under the law and access of citizens to a nondiscriminatory judiciary.
Freedom from government regulations and policies that cause negative interest rates.
Government transfers and subsidies as a percent of GDP.
Top marginal tax rate and income at which it applies.

Use of conscripts to obtain military personnel.

Taxes on international trade as a percent of imports plus exports.

Difference between official exchange rate and black market rate.

Actual size of trade sector compared with expected size based on econometric estimates.

Restrictions on freedom of citizens to engage in capital transactions with foreigners.

Kim Holmes, Bryan Johnson, and Melanie Kirkpatrick eds., *1997 Index of Economic Freedom* (Washington, D.C.: Heritage Foundation, 1997).

Ten variables for 150 countries:

Trade policy: average tariff rates and nontariff trade barriers.

Taxation: average and marginal corporate and individual tax rates.

Government intervention in the economy: government consumption as a percent of GDP, plus the extent of government-owned enterprises.

Monetary policy: inflation rate.

Capital flows and foreign investment policy: restrictions on and treatment of foreign investors.

Banking: openness, regulation of, and restrictions on banking system to compete and provide services.

Wage and price controls: degree to which markets or government sets wages and prices, including minimum wages and utility pricing.

Property rights: degree to which private property is a guaranteed right, including the probability of expropriation and the adequacy of courts and the legal system to protect private property.

Regulation: ease or difficulty in opening a business and keeping it open, including production limits, quotas and corruption.

Black market: existence and size of black markets, smuggling and illegal workers.

Institute for Management Development, *World Competitiveness Yearbook 1998* (Lausanne, Switzerland: Institute for Management Development, 1998).

One variable for forty-six countries:

Competitiveness index based on domestic economy, internationalization, government, finance, infrastructure, management, science, and people.

Philip Keefer and Stephen Knack, "Institutions and Economic Performance: Cross-Country Tests Using Alternative Institutional Measures," *Economics and Politics* 7, no. 3, (November 1995). Data available from the World Bank, <www.worldbank.org/research/growth/ddeale.htm> (January 8, 2002).

One variable for 115 countries averaged for 1982 to 1995:

Corruption: likelihood that high government officials will demand special payments and that illegal payments are generally expected throughout lower levels of government in the allocation of import and export licenses, foreign exchange, tax assessments, and credit.

Paolo Mauro, "Corruption and Growth," *Quarterly Journal of Economics* 110, no. 3 (August 1995).

Three variables for sixty-eight countries:

Legal system and judiciary: efficiency and integrity of legal environment as it affects business, particularly foreign firms.

Bureaucracy and red tape: regulatory environment foreign firms must face when seeking approvals and permits and degree to which it represents an obstacle to business.

Corruption: degree to which business transactions involve corruption or questionable payments.

Schlomo Angel and Stephen K. Mayo, *Enabling Policies and Their Effects on Housing Sector Performance: A Global Comparison* (Habitat II Conference) (Istanbul, Turkey: June 1996).

Six variables for fifty-two countries obtained from World Bank, *Global Survey of Housing Indicators of 1990* (unpublished):

Property rights index: compiled from items on restrictions on land and housing transactions, squatting, and land registration.

Housing finance regime: level of development of institutional and regulatory environment of housing finance system.

Housing subsidies index: involvement of public sector in demand or supply subsidies.

Property infrastructure index: government spending on roads, water, sewers, drainage, and electricity, plus such other indicators as commute time and housing affordability.

Regulatory regime index: measures impact of land-use flexibility, zoning, and building code regulations as well as bureaucratic flexibility and efficiency.

Industrial organization index: includes monopolization index of construction industry, restrictions on obtaining building materials and skilled worker availability.

Political Risks Services, Inc., *International Country Risk Guide* (Syracuse, N.Y.: various years). Data available from the World Bank, <www.worldbank.org/research/growth/ddeale.htm> (January 8, 2002).

One variable for eighty-one countries:

Rule of law.

Transparency International, *1998 Corruption Perception Index* (Berlin: Transparency International, 1998).

One variable for eighty-five countries compiled by combining data from at least three and up to seven international surveys:

Corruption perception index: relates to perceptions of degree of corruption as seen by business people, risk analysts and general public.

World Bank, *World Development Report 1998/99*, (Washington: World Bank, 1999), 181.

Three variables for forty-nine countries, 1995-1996:

Creditor' rights: based on automatic stay on assets of distressed company, continuance of management, and priority of secured creditors.

Shareholders' rights: based on five indicators of shareholders' ability to protect value of their assets.

Enforcement: based on an assessment of the law and order tradition in the country and on the ability of government to unilaterally modify a contract.

World Economic Forum, *Global Competitiveness Report 1998 (Geneva: World Economic Forum, 1999).*

Two variables for fifty-three countries:

Competitiveness index: compiled from eight subindices on openness, government, finance, infrastructure, technology, management, labor, and institutions.

Executive opinion survey: survey measures opinions of leading business executives about country in which they operate concerning the country's competitiveness and comparative strengths and weaknesses. More than three thousand executives in fifty-three countries responded.

Notes

1.   Karel G. van Wolferen, "The Japan Problem," *Foreign Affairs* 65, no. 2 (spring

1986): 292.

2.   James Fallows, "Containing Japan," *The Atlantic Monthly* (May 1989): 48.

3.   Charles Engel and John Rogers, "How Wide is the Border?" *American Economic Review* 86, no. 5 (December 1996): 1123.

4.   Paolo Mauro, "Corruption and Growth," *Quarterly Journal of Economics* 110, no. 3 (August 1995): 684.

5.   James D. Gwartney, *Economic Freedom of the World, 1975-95* (Vancouver, British Columbia: Fraser Institute, 1996).

6.   If X_i represents the value of variable i for country X, and Y_i is the value of variable i for country Y, then the Euclidean distance between X and Y across all variables is: $[\sum_i (X_i-Y_i)^2]^{0.5}$.

7.   All eight factors explained 80 percent of the variance among the variables. The top four factors explained 66 percent.

8.   Kim Holmes, Bryan Johnson, and Melanie Kirkpatrick eds., *1997 Index of Economic Freedom* (Washington, D.C.: Heritage Foundation, 1997), 255.

9.   Raymond Gastil, Freedom in the World: Political Rights and Civil Liberties, 1986-1987 (New York: Greenwood Press, 1987).

10.   Daniel Goleman, "The Group and the Self: New Focus on a Cultural Rift," *New York Times*, December 25, 1990.

11.   Suzanne Berger, "Introduction," in *National Diversity and Global Capitalism*, ed. Suzanne Berger and Ronald Dore (Ithaca, N.Y.: Cornell University Press, 1996), 1.

12.   Robert Boyer, "The Convergence Hypothesis Revisited: Globalization but Still the Century of Nations?," in Berger and Dore, *National Diversity and Global Capitalism*, 57-58.

Chapter 14

America's Images of Japan

The Importance of Images

A 1991 analysis of the Japanese attack on Pearl Harbor in a Central Intelligence Agency journal illustrated the lessons learned since 1941 in how to evaluate intelligence information. After listing thirteen intelligence failures relating to Pearl Harbor, the author noted the importance of deeply held images as "the greatest hazard by far." A particular problem, he pointed out, was "the profound, widely held indifference or disdain with which many American experts viewed the Japanese and their capabilities."[1]

The same journal had published another article on Pearl Harbor, classified as secret, twenty-six years earlier in which the author similarly concluded, "We failed to foresee the Japanese assault largely because we were influenced by a faulty stereotype." The writer went on to note, "These stereotypes constitute the intelligence officer's greatest peril because he cannot escape their influence. . . . Although he may shut out invalid elements that he is aware of, as he reviews his materials he is bombarded by the stereotypes' other elements. . . . He is thus inevitably and to some degree unwittingly more or less under the influence of ideas that he might consciously reject." The notion that images lying beneath the layers of conscious thought govern a person's thinking processes is an

insight that was key to the research described below. But just as insight-
ful was this analyst's recognition that facts and logic did not always govern the thinking of those held up as exemplars of careful thought: "The
American view prior to Pearl Harbor was ambiguous and shot through
with inconsistencies. At the extremes it ran contrary to observed data and
to common sense."[2]

Although the catalog of American images of Japan has grown more
extensive in the intervening years, today's images are held just as deeply
now and shared even more widely among Americans than they were a
half century ago. They still have the power to influence policy, politics,
and public discourse, even when they are contrary to observed data and
even though a person might consciously reject them.

An important research task now is to understand contemporary
American thought structures related to Japan. It was for this reason that
Japan's Ministry of Foreign Affairs commissioned a study, on which this
chapter is based, to ascertain the set of images that Americans hold about
Japan and their subsequent dynamic interactions. The research was conducted in collaboration with Dr. Robert Deutsch, then with EBR Consulting, Inc. of Vienna, Virginia. The goal was to get behind the attitude
surveys and opinion polls to learn how Americans convert information
about Japan into personal perceptions and meanings. The research effort
centered on the proposition that there are no direct links between events,
media messages, and public opinion, but that these all are filtered
through images.

The research effort comprised two approaches: applying a theory of
image creation to analyze focus groups in six American cities; and reviewing television news programs dealing with Japan from 1983 to 1995
from the point of view of narrative style rather than content analysis. Before discussing the results of these efforts, it may be useful to consider
the process of image creation and its contribution to thought processes.

The Structure of Image and Metaphor

Images operate at many levels. At an obvious level, readily available
thoughts reference selected events from the immediate environment.
Using symbolic reasoning, the mind integrates such information with
long-standing assumptions and expectations.

A more primitive level of thought is responsible for basic assessments that occur rapidly and automatically, before conscious or deliber-

ate cognition. A primary example is the evaluation of other—that which is different from self. The other is assessed primitively and emotionally as familiar or novel, as friend or foe. Aspects of familiarity are evaluated immediately. "Is it like me? Am I comfortable with it? Do I know what to expect?" The resulting images are often self-referencing. This process involves an intimate and inescapable interaction between an individual's sense of personal identity and an evaluation of qualities or traits in others.

Massachusetts Institute of Technology professor John Dower in his study of the wartime images and metaphors separately held and promoted by the Anglo-American powers and Japan noted, "Both sides reveal more about themselves than about the enemy they are portraying. Certainly, no one views a documentary film such as *Know Your Enemy—Japan* decades later to learn about the Japanese in the war; they do so mainly to learn about the Americans." Mr. Dower discovered something about ideological and overt discourse taking place in the heat of war that was obvious in our study fifty years later. In Mr. Dower's words, "Speakers, viewers, listeners alike (so long as they were all on the same side) generally took these statements seriously, and there is much to be learned here in retrospect about language, stereotype, and the making of modern myths."[3]

After being confronted with new data, people quickly leave the world of objective information and move into the realm of symbols and metaphors, transforming the new information into personal meaning by bringing it into line with preexisting emotional sentiments and images. Images are not fantasies totally divorced from "reality," but, like the patterns on a shoreline, are constructed gradually from succeeding waves of new bits of data overlaid on old memories and impressions.

Metaphorical thinking is a method the mind uses for making sense of new information. Metaphor connects objects or events that are not usually associated with each other. The word "metaphor" derives from the Greek root "to transfer," "transport," or "carry;" it is the figure of speech in which a name or descriptive term is transferred to some object different from, but analogous to, that to which it is properly applied. In a metaphor, one thing is likened to another with the understanding that the two are not the same. The resulting mutation produces an emotional reaction, which gives the metaphor power and meaning. This power to convey emotional truth through metaphor was one of the great discoveries of the ancient storytellers and mythmakers. Metaphor is one of the classical figures of speech, but it also describes literally a primary method that the mind uses to process information. Metaphors are neither true nor false in the sense of conveying analytical truth, but they "fit" in that they synthesize disparate experiences.

The use of metaphor offers a person a way to overcome the unknown by applying familiar concepts to describe the new. Novel associations based on partial similarities can generate a cognitive process that produces new insights. Applying a metaphor, in fact, can change the way people perceive and understand the world. This method of assimilation also produces one of the most common mental biases—confirmation bias, or the tendency to admit as evidence only those ideas that support preexisting and deep-seated beliefs.

Although metaphor can generate understanding, its power has hidden dangers, especially when people forget that they are using metaphors. Delusion is possible as well as insight. People can be lulled into associating the metaphor's linkages to reality and imagining that the attributes held by one of the objects in the metaphor are held by the other. As suggested by the 1960s intelligence analyst quoted above, people may be unwittingly under the influence of ideas that they would reject consciously. Therefore, an important goal in understanding American images of Japan is to reveal and make conscious the underlying metaphorical thinking.

Focus Groups as a Tool to Uncover Metaphors

The research problem is to find techniques that get past the surface thoughts to the underlying metaphorical level of thinking. Attitude surveys and opinion polls generally fail to do this because they touch only the outermost layers of thought. When polls do tap deeper thought processes, often a limited range of preestablished responses are allowed, and these do not reveal the line of thinking leading to metaphors.

Research on thought processes suggests that the methods of eliciting and analyzing images and metaphors should not violate the boundaries of spontaneously occurring speech, which surveys do. To allow such speech, we used focus groups as the primary analytical device. These small groups participated in intensive discussions lasting several hours. Their structure encouraged the spontaneous, fortuitous quality of natural conversation. Speakers could orient their statements to an ongoing dialogue. Later evaluations of the taped focus group sessions allowed the analyst to search for overtones in dialogue, intonation, cadence, and hesitation that contribute to the meaning of words. Interspersed between standard methods of speech were less conscious forms of discourse that could be analyzed for embedded meaning; among the latter are: ellipses, asides, slips of the tongue, idioms, puns, double entendres, and metaphors.

Focus Group Mechanics

In 1994 and 1995, three groups of ten people each were selected in each of six cities: Washington, Detroit, Seattle, Tampa, Houston, and Los Angeles. Two more Washington sessions were held in mid-1998 to determine if there had been significant shifts in peoples' views. The members of the groups were chosen to be demographically representative of the local area as characterized by gender, race, ethnicity, age, and education. Also, in Washington, each group included members with U.S. government connections; several individuals in Detroit were selected who had an association with the automobile industry; and in Seattle, focus group members with ties to Boeing and Japanese-owned companies were included. The Tampa and Houston groups were designed to exclude people who had moved to the area from major metropolitan areas; the preferred members were people who had grown up in the area. Excluded from all groups were people with extensive experience with Japan or Japanese; according to prior focus group encounters, such individuals would be likely to dominate the discussions because of their special knowledge. However, several participants had visited Japan for business or vacation purposes, and others had regular contacts with Japanese in their locales.

The first three cities were chosen because of their obvious surface characteristics. In Washington an "inside the Beltway" attention to national and international politics and news presumably sensitized residents to ongoing political disputes with Japan. The "Motor City's" experience vis-à-vis competitive Japanese automobile imports offered an opportunity to speak to those whose local views about Japan may have been shaped from predominantly negative experiences. Seattle, in contrast, was doing well economically, partly due to strong links to Japan through trade and local Japanese investments; in addition, Seattle residents had much greater opportunity to deal with Japanese personally through their work or social activities. Tampa and Houston represented cities without identifiably strong links to Japan, positive or negative.

Focus group participants were invited for dinner, followed by discussions on a subject not yet known to them in a facility whose surroundings and decor were intended to convey the seriousness of the effort. During dinner, Dr. Deutsch, the session coordinator, had an opportunity to put the participants at ease. The sessions lasted three hours, about twice as long as a usual focus group session. Invariably the participants were surprised when the session ended, commenting that the three hours had gone by so quickly. Following the session, the members were paid for their participation.

In the introductory part of the session the coordinator pointed to a one-way mirror at one end of the conference room and mentioned that members of the research team might be observing from behind the mirror. After being informed of this, participants often waved and smiled at the mirror and then promptly appeared to forget about it. Each session also was videotaped, with each participant asked to sign a release. The tapes allowed the analyst to view repeatedly the session behaviors, noting not only what people said, but how they said it, including nonverbal behavior and responses from other participants (for example, smiles or nods).

The sessions began with the coordinator handing out blank cards and requesting, "Write down the first thing that comes into your mind when you hear 'Japan.'" This was the first mention of Japan heard by the group. The next forty-five minutes or so were spent in free discussion of this first question. Another approach to eliciting views was a request to make a story about what the world would be like during the next decade if the only two countries were the United States and Japan. The session leader's principal roles involved listening quietly and encouraging people to reach beyond triteness and cliche to a level of deeper thought.

Main Focus Group Findings

The uniformity of American images about Japan is striking across demographic variables. Participants in each city tended to have a different surface coloration to their views, based on the data generally available in their locale. Nevertheless, the deeper reactions or indications of thought processes were much less variable. Each individual, of course, had different things to say, but the montage of views heard from group to group and city to city was remarkably similar. The overarching tone of their comments revealed that there exists a widespread, general undercurrent of negative sentiment regarding Japan in the American mind. Across all locales metaphorical thinking linking economics and war, as related to

Japan, appeared to produce images that, in turn, drive the entire public opinion process.[4]

The great value of the Houston and Tampa groups was that they allowed observations of images in locales that are not focused on Japan. Having fewer immediate topics and direct data on which to attach their images and sentiments, they revealed their feelings about Japan through more direct references to their images of themselves and America. The findings in these cities, when related to the observations in the other cities, revealed that much of the negative sentiment regarding Japan results from the fact that Americans see their presumed shortcomings more clearly when reflected in a mirror of what they imagine to be Japanese behavior.

Many of the focus group conversations can be summarized as a plot in which America was in an economic battle with Japan, and America had lost. The 1998 follow-up sessions found most of the same images revealed earlier, but with less emotion attached to them. Evidence of how the self-referencing was used to define the Japanese was contained in such comments as: "Japan is constantly strategizing." "They are never laid-back." "They think long term." In contrast, these Americans think of themselves as easygoing, spontaneous, fixed on the short term; consequently, strategic, long-term thinking in a fundamental way is considered un-American. Focus group members asserted the proposition that they have more freedom to act in an individualistic, carefree way. When others are presumed to follow opposite behavior, the impact can be unsettling, even frightening, especially when Americans suspect that they themselves should be following suit.

Focus group participants consistently talked first about Japan as a business machine. An only slightly abbreviated list of first responses describing Japan included cars, electronics, industrious, efficient, productivity, products, products are everywhere, buying up America. A 45-year-old woman from Seattle echoed the general sentiment: "In my mind, they make it so there is only room for business." A 32-year-old woman in Tampa said: "In business, they do whatever it takes. They are taught from an early age; it's in their culture. It doesn't matter if it's Sony, Lexus, or whatever."

The responses indicated how pervasive and invasive Japanese cars and electronics are in American markets, households, and psyches. A 58-year-old Washington, D.C., man put it this way: "They are always with us." This does not mean that Americans are quaking with anxiety and fear as they think about Japan, but when the subject comes up they seem uneasy, worried. Putting together an amalgam of the comments, the reasoning pattern seems to go like this: (1) "Everything to them is business." (2) "They are always preparing for the future." (3) "They are capable of anything." (4) "We must be on guard, they always have a hidden agenda."

Implied in the American perceptions of Japan is a sense of current Japanese and past U.S. technological expertise. For example, "We bombed them to smithereens and look what they have achieved." In a different vein that also draws on World War II images but in a different context is the comment: "Japan is extremist and fanatical, and they are willing to suffer like we are not." Admiration, respect, and revulsion vie for predominance. One Detroit focus group member put the issue in terms of high respect and extreme wariness: "Because Japan is capable of anything, they are an unknown quantity."

The injunction, "We must be on guard," corresponded to a widespread feeling from the focus groups that, because the United States defeated Japan and dropped atomic bombs on two of its cities in World War II, "Japan is out to get back at us." Self-reference was seen as a powerful motivator of this view. When a young man in Los Angeles in one of the final sessions repeated, "Japan is out to get back at us," something heard perhaps a dozen times in other cities, the moderator probed more deeply and pushed him about just what was meant. The one word response was, "Hiroshima." When probed again about what that meant, the young man responded, "If they had done that to us, we would be out to get back at them."

One of the striking commonalities was the almost exclusive use of the word "they" when speaking about Japan. For example, in a Washington, D.C., session a Virginia man said, "They bought Rockefeller Center," noting his disapproval of the "disappearance" of an American symbol of wealth and achievement. Although some participants referred directly to Sony Corp.'s 1989 acquisition of Columbia Pictures Entertainment Inc., one person generalized, "They are buying Hollywood, too." An even more general echo concluded, "They are buying up all of L.A."

The attributes Americans assign to the Japanese seem to be attached to diffuse ideas about Japan as a monolithic culture. One Washington participant stated, "Their orientation to business and their tough business style is a culturally learned thing. They can't help it."

Related to the impersonal pronoun "they" is the idea of the faceless Japanese. Few, if any, Japanese politicians, business people, or other personalities are known to Americans. When they are seen on television, they are not recalled. One Japanese sociologist conducted a poll in the

United States and asked people what Japanese person or persons were most familiar to them. The most common responses included Bruce Lee, Godzilla, and Yoko Ono. When this question was repeated in the focus groups, we heard similar responses. When challenged that Bruce Lee is not Japanese and that Godzilla is a cinema creation, a common response went something like this: "It doesn't matter if they are not Japanese. They *are* Japanese." Further probing elicited these common threads: "They are bent on destruction and cannot be stopped."

Impressions of Japan among the focus group members quickly moved from the realm of what they considered to be objective information (cars, real estate, movie monsters) and entered the domain of metaphor. The transition frequently was represented by a sequence that proceeded from, "They are buying up all of L.A." to "That's what Japan does: they invade and conquer." Comparisons uniformly were developed that linked World War II memories and images of present day commerce.

World War II Linkages to Today's Business Activities

People from all the groups used Pearl Harbor to create a metaphor between the "sneak attack" nearly fifty-five years ago and what they perceived as the Japanese economic threat today: "Then, as now, America was caught unprepared." "Their kamikaze loyalty to the emperor has been replaced by loyalty to Toyota. Now they use Toyotas instead of battleships, but they are still fighting a war." "They took our lives in 1941. In 1981 they took our livelihoods." "We ripped their military from them, so now they replace their soldiers with industrial might." "They are superachievers. There is not a middle ground with them. They will go all the way. It's their culture. They push everything to the limit until it explodes. They blew our car industry right out of the water."

The economics-as-war metaphor provides a potent sense and direction to thought. It is the web that snares all manner of mental associations into an organized whole and brings the past into the present. For example, the Learning Channel on cable television presented a series titled "Ancient Warriors," which told of past military techniques and successes. The television listings provided by the channel summarized separate programs in the series, such as "The Arabs' mobility was a decisive factor in their ability to conquer Persia," and "The Celts' military success lay in their use of finely made weaponry and skilled chariot tactics." The only program listing that brought forward an ancient military skill to the present was the one that focused on Japan. "The unswerving loyalty of the samurai warrior influences modern-day corporate Japan."[5] Yet, there was nothing in the program about contemporary Japan.

The words behind the metaphor are often potent in their simplicity, shared meaning, and emotional directness. Terms like "war," "invade," "sneaky," and "aggressive," when incorporated in metaphor, mangle fact and logic. This process is illustrated in "derailments of thought," which express what is latent in the mind. A dialogue from Detroit is typical.

Charles:	The Japanese are just sneaky. It doesn't matter if it's Pearl Harbor or anything else. They are just sneaky. They toured our Ford assembly plant and took pictures of things they weren't supposed to.
Moderator:	If they were allowed to go to these places and were not told to refrain from picture taking, then why is that sneaky?
Jim:	They're sneaky. They will just walk right up to you and do it. Have you ever been to Hawaii? They will just push you right off the sidewalk.
Moderator:	Then you are talking about this particular "sidewalk" behavior.
Jim:	They are still sneaky, too. They will copy everything you get, refine it, and then take you over.
Charles:	Exactly!

The process of metaphorical linkages is illustrated by the following discourse by a 22-year-old woman. "Japan is very efficient. Their methods of rice production are very advanced. They know how to get the most from something. That's what they will do: they will come here and leave America barren and dead." This woman began with what she believed to be facts drawn from her exposure to things about Japan: rice eaters, efficient production, exports, U.S. investments. She then generalized from these fact-based statements to opinion. The generalization enabled her to apply the rice/efficiency metaphor to other domains that were completely independent of the original focus. Although this particular refrain did not appear in every focus group, it occurred enough times that it was inserted in an interim research report. When I appeared on a television talk show some months later, a caller used almost the same words: "Japanese steel producers are very efficient. They bought the plant I worked in, increased production, and then fired everyone and stripped the plant. They left us barren and dead." My first reaction was inappropriate laughter and the thought that the caller had read the research report.

Once swept up with notions of "Japan as invader, conqueror," people do not have far to leap to the conclusion, "They will take over." In some cases, their conclusion was that such a fate already has occurred: "They have taken over. We lost." Probing the meaning of this assertion elicited, "We're not the best anymore, we're not number one." This sentiment was most blatant in Houston but was also heard in Tampa and Detroit.

The groups in Los Angeles, in contrast, tended to be somewhat different. In general, the California focus group participants held most of the same sentiments about Japan, but with one major difference—the defeatist tone was absent. The participants there did not blame Japan for America's problems and often expressed a nuanced view of their feelings toward Japan.

The notion of Japanese society as ritualistic and closed appeared with regularity. As an example, the comparison between Japanese and Chinese restaurants came up several times. Many people expressed some anxiety in a Japanese restaurant. "Should I bow, take off my shoes? Will I eat things wrong?" The unfamiliar ritualism of the activity was unsettling, and the speakers suggested that the restaurant made it that way. The contrast with Chinese restaurants was revealing. "The family of the proprietor is sitting around the place and helping out. Babies are crying. The establishment may not be as clean, but it has an inviting, comfortable feeling. If someone eats things the wrong way, everyone laughs good-naturedly rather than stares disapprovingly."

The sentiments that people express about a closed society illustrate that the primary reason that people say, "Japan is a closed market" is that they have a prior notion, "Japan is a closed society." News topics are used to justify an argument, but they appear not to be the foundations of the argument's creation. The accumulation of data in everyday life, over decades or even centuries, is more important than current events in producing contemporary images of Japan.

Ambivalence and Mirror Images

The 200 Americans in the six cities and twenty focus groups were not as uniformly negative as it may appear from the above description. Indeed, the discourse had two sides that conflicted. Participants related positively and negatively to Japan. One speculation is that they exaggerated the negative and demonized Japan in order to resolve their own ambivalence. By emphasizing one element and diminishing the other, dissonance or conflict could be minimized.

One strongly positive response was that participants view the Japanese as their kin in a mutual commitment to democracy, capitalism, and modernism. This is in stark contrast to their picture painted about other Asian nations in general. The Americans in the groups also exhibited a basic desire for supportive, friendly relations with Japan. In the stories made up by the focus groups about a future in which only Japan and the United States exist, the overwhelming preference was for the two countries to "live happily ever after."

Among the examples of ambivalence resolved in a negative manner were consistently complimentary descriptions of the Japanese as hardworking, which then quickly was associated with being disciplined. In the American context, the notion of discipline seems to have a negative connotation, being antithetical to freedom. Focus group participants moved from the idea of being disciplined to being efficient. Efficiency was attached to a whole subterranean system of negative associations: regimented, obedient, blindly following orders. At the end of this chain often came the assertion, "Japanese are like robots." In contrast, the group members described Americans as disorganized, chaotic, and individualistic.

In another case of ambivalence, participants viewed Japan's group orientation as a beneficial and enviable attribute, something that is missing in the heterogeneous, mobile, and individualistic American society. They then associated these qualities with nationalism, bullying, and uncompromising behavior. This sequence led on to "ritualistic and unfeeling," which linked back to robotic. The same dynamic applied when people talked of Japan as ritualistic, unchanging, and "different from America where everything is new every day." A Virginia woman summed up these feelings, "Japan is closed, the Japanese are closed, the whole thing is impenetrable . . . and they're coming this way. We better watch out."

Another source of ambivalence and conflict is the mix of pride and complicity that Americans feel about having helped Japan in making its economic miracle. Since the American occupation of Japan after World War II, Americans have thought of Japan as a junior America. When Japan exerts its own strivings, the "parents" say, "We helped make them what they are today and look at what they do to us." The sense of betrayal is palpable.

Ambivalence is also present over the atomic bombings of Hiroshima and Nagasaki. While most focus group participants approved the use of the bombs as a means to end the war, many also expressed guilt and remorse over the catastrophic destruction.

In most of the sessions, after the first five to ten minutes of discussion of such attributes of the Japanese as hardworking and efficient, the direction of the conversation inevitably turned to the United States. (This happened with such regularity that I began to time how long it would take this switch to materialize.) Emphasizing their ambivalence, participants would say, "That's the way we used to be: hard working, community-oriented, devoted to family." A middle-aged Tampa man declared, "My picture of Japan is what America was in the 1950s: strong work ethic and family values. Now we're lazy, slack, too lenient. Japan is what we were. We lost because we lost what we were."

Interspersed with descriptions like "unfair trade practices" and "business invasion" there lay a recurrent characterization of America as the addicted consumer and Japan as the willing supplier. "We are spoiled. As Americans, we are accustomed to abundance—the abundance of things, the abundance of choices. The more we have, the more we want. 'Right now' is the only time frame we live in. We expect so much. We want everything now, right now. Hurry, hurry, hurry! And Japan produces everything we want. They make it, we want it." A Houston man reiterated, "We're angry at ourselves and we can't stand Japan for making us see that. We know our shortcomings through our reflection looking at them."

News Coverage of Japan

When participants were asked how they knew what they had just expressed, the usual answer was, "It was on the news," or "I saw it in a documentary." Sometimes the respondents could point to a specific item to back up their assertions, but more often, the reference was a vague, "I saw it on TV," or "I read it in the newspaper."

Having heard this repeated reference to the news media in the early focus groups, we decided to investigate the role of television in the American image of Japan. The Vanderbilt Television News Archives provided all the nightly news spots mentioning Japan that had been broadcast by the ABC, CBS, and NBC television networks from 1983 to April 1995. The number of such news stories peaked at 117 in 1989 at the height of the bubble economy in Japan, which coincided with the large flow of Japanese capital to the United States. An earlier peak occurred in 1985 connected to the fortieth anniversary of Hiroshima. Between 1989 and 1995, the frequency of network news stories about Japan fell to less than one-third of the 1989 figures.

Since news writers, producers, correspondents, and news program anchors are all part of the same broad American society tapped for the focus groups and since the sentiments about Japan were shared so widely among the participants, it should not be surprising that the focus groups and the news media tell the same stories, using the same metaphors.

In analyzing the media reports, the main focus was on the form and the structure of the words and images that made up the complete story, not just on the objectivity of the content. News segments can be objective and relevant while still implying other kinds of images. Often the implication is carried by a single word framing a story, by a montage of pictures and voice-overs, by the clash between the story proper and its conclusion. One example out of hundreds concerns an ABC story on January 9, 1995, dealing with the export of American apples to Japan. Peter Jennings introduced the story: "For years and years Japanese farmers and their accomplices in government have thrown up every roadblock. . . ." In fact, it did take decades to negotiate this particular market opening, but the use of the word "accomplice" is reserved in American speech for criminal or conspiratorial behavior: a person who helps another in a crime or wrongdoing. Framing the story in this way establishes the context for whatever may follow by alerting the viewer to expect criminal behavior.

The major themes in the U.S. news coverage of Japan include:

Japan is different; it has a self-image of uniqueness and superiority.
    Japan is better than the United States.
    Japan is insensitive, harsh, and ruthless.
    Japan is a rigid and obsessively controlling nation.
    Japan, the invader, seeks to dominate.
    Japan is fanatical, in work and in war.
    Japanese are sneaky, lying, unfair, cheaters.

These themes are apparent in the following extracts.

NBC (November 14, 1985) Topic: Japanese Sing Sinatra's Song, "My Way."
The story shows Japanese trying to sing the song, "My Way," made famous by Frank Sinatra. This light-hearted piece has an ominous-sounding ending as anchor Tom Brokaw says: "Of course, while we are all laughing, they are learning our language. And who will have the last laugh?"

NBC (March 28, 1987) Topic: Semiconductors
The story is about U.S.-Japan trade conflict in semiconductors, but the image is of cars being loaded on a dock. The use of visuals showing an invasion by cars

being shipped from Japan, regardless of the actual story, is quite common.

NBC (June 16, 1990) Topic: Japan Invades American Baseball
The story line is that Japan has invaded minor league baseball in Salinas, California, which has invigorated play there. Further commentary states: "The Japanese players are tireless, fanatic. Baseball is no longer as American as apple pie."

The insidious quality that can be part of unconscious metaphorical linkages is illustrated by a four-part series aired by CBS News in May 1983 called "The Japaning of America." The producer's goal was to present an objective view of the complex relationships between the two countries. As an individual who is described as favorably disposed toward Japan and Japanese culture, he expressed considerable surprise when reviewing parts of his programs some thirteen years later to find the very elements of stereotype evident in much of the rest of American television. Excerpts from this series includes:

CBS (May 17, 1983) "The Japaning of America, Part 1"
This segment begins, "In World War II we beat Japan; now we petition it to open its markets." Pictures are shown of the Japanese surrendering aboard the USS Missouri.

Bob Simon (narrator): "Japan lost World War II. It would never challenge the U.S. again, at least on the battlefield. After the war, we told Japan to abandon its military and concentrate on economics. They did everything we told them to and that's the problem: a $21 billion trade surplus. Not since Russia launched Sputnik have Americans felt so threatened."

President of Harley Davidson: "U.S. industry is being attacked and destroyed by the Japanese."

Simon: "In one economic battleground after another they are hitting us and hitting us hard, sometimes pushing us right out of the ring. (Pictures of sumo wrestlers are shown.) And now they are beating us in computer chips, the crucial high-tech industry of the future. So they are threatening us, they are crippling our industry, and we hate them. Right? Well, not quite. Sushi and Japanese fashion are very popular in America."

(Pictures of U.S. autoworkers smashing a Japanese car are shown.)

U.S. autoworker: "They are not playing the game the way everyone else is."

Simon: "They have captured our markets, but they have captured something else: our imagination. (Pictures of a Japanese puppet theater are shown.) The culture of a nation on the make, a rising star; watch them and wonder: are they as good as we are? Are they possibly better?"

Joseph Papp (theater producer): "If anything will kill us one day, if we buckle under, it will be because we feel we weren't as successful as somebody else. I tell you, that psychology is the most devastating."

Simon: "They have captured our imagination and a bit of our self-consciousness as well. We have all become a soft touch for Sonys, Datsuns, and Japanese chic."

The story switches to Colorado and Zen archery.

Simon: "Americans are asking, can we find the answers in Japan?"

Archery teacher: "One must polish one's mind."

American: "In bonsai I have found a harmony America may have lost. Elegance, simplicity, tranquility."

Simon: "Everything the Japanese touch becomes more beautiful."

(Picture shown of autoworkers smashing a Japanese car.) "The darker side of the Japaning of America. Watch tomorrow."

CBS, (May 18, 1983) "The Japaning of America, Part 2"
This segment opens with pictures of Zen archery. Simon talks about targeting: the Japanese approach to Zen archery and industrial policy. The picture cuts to an exterior view of the Ministry of International Trade and Industry in Tokyo and then to an interior room.

Picture with voice-over: "Is this the board room of the Trade Ministry in Tokyo or is it the war room of Japan's economic offensive?"

Motorola president: "Japan's imperial ambitions may not be a thing of the past. The Japanese are moving towards dominance." As these words are spoken, pictures are shown of a phalanx of Japanese pedestrians moving toward the viewer.

The CBS "Japaning of America" programs include most of the themes heard in the focus groups and seen in the media over the intervening period: the economics-as-war metaphor, America in decline, Japan dominant, the "otherness" of Japan, the ambivalence produced by admiration of Japanese culture combined with anxiety and fear over its presumed superiority.

In general, U.S. television news spots on Japan give little information to help people understand the political, historical, or cultural context of U.S.-Japan relations. Even in the economic issues that dominate public discourse, there is almost no economic analysis. The big picture context is missing; when the "Japaning of America" series tried to remedy this situation, it suffered from many of the same defects as many of its less ambitious competitors, despite garnering high praise for the network.

Why does the media portray Japan the way it does? This study did not attempt to provide a definitive answer, but the results of this research suggest that it would be an error to assume that the editorial choices of words and images are made consciously. Media folks are simply part of the "folk." Their imaginings of Japan are similar to those heard in the focus groups from people who often were as intelligent, educated, and informed as the staff at the television networks putting the programs together. It is clear, though, that the stereotypes and cliches about Japan spoken by the average men and women in the focus groups were the same that the media were reaffirming, which created a self-reinforcing, exaggerated spiral.

Consistency with Other Studies

The findings from these focus groups and the media analysis are quite consistent with many other studies that have examined the same phenomena with somewhat different methods. One study looked at bias in titles and subtitles in three of the leading news magazines, *Newsweek, Time,* and *U.S. News and World Report* from 1988 through 1991. Titles were chosen as the unit of analysis because they are designed to lure the reader into the article. They frame the contents and provide an emotional lead-in to the story. No matter how objective the text may be, the title establishes a context for the reader. Bias was assigned to a headline if it fell into any of several categories. War metaphor bias existed when war terms, such as "invade," "fortress," or "foe," were used inappropriately to describe other behavior. Anxiety bias was intended to capture the idea of American decline amid Japanese ascendance. Stereotype bias pertained to those attributions of traditional Japanese culture that were out of context; for example, even though the *Atlantic* magazine was not included in the study, its use of a sumo wrestler on the cover to illustrate an article on "containing Japan" could be an example of stereotype bias. Humanity bias was considered if any word or phrase was intended to "erase the human face of the Japanese people." Finally, monolith bias referenced words that removed individual name distinctions and substituted "Japan" for, say, "Sony."

Roughly, one-third of all titles was designated as biased according to the study criteria, with little variation among the different magazines. The rate fell steadily over the four years, however, with 51 percent deemed to be biased in 1988 and only 25 percent in 1991. Out of the total number of biased items, anxiety bias accounted for almost 40 percent; monolith bias was second with 28 percent, and war metaphors came in third with 18 percent. The most significant finding was that the rate of bias declined sharply with the importance of the headline. Among magazine cover titles, 54 percent were biased, and the numbers went steadily down: cover subtitles, 46 percent; table of contents, 42 percent; article title, 38 percent; article subtitle, 31 percent.[6]

Charles Burress, a journalist at the *San Francisco Chronicle*, came up with similar findings in a master's degree project study. Mr. Burress examined the appearance of monolith bias in the treatment of foreign acquisitions of American entertainment companies. He had noted the frequency of the headline "Japan Invades Hollywood" to describe the actions of one Japanese company buying a single American company. When Matsushita Electric Industry Co., Ltd. announced its intention to buy out MCA Inc. in 1990, the *New York Times* played the news on the first page on two days. One day's headline read, "Japanese Expected to Take Over Another Major Hollywood Studio," and the other said, "MCA Agrees to Japanese Buyout." Mr. Burress asked the reasonable question, did these headlines exhibit a type of bias or just a newspaper convention in reporting on activities of foreign companies? An answer to this question was available without too much trouble. In 1990, Pathe Communications Corp. of Italy took over MGM/United Artists. Five years earlier Rupert Murdoch's News Corp. of Australia had purchased 20th Century Fox. Of the nineteen headlines in the *New York Times* that mentioned the MGM/UA deal, all referred to Pathe. None mentioned the company's home country or even continent. According to Burress' headline count of the Fox deal, none of the seven mentioned Murdoch's home country and most mentioned the purchaser by name. One argument that has been offered as to why Japanese names are not used is that they are unfamiliar to American readers. However, few corporate names are likely to be better known than Sony. And in Mr. Burress' eyes, "Even Matsushita is better known than Pathe."[7]

The finding of bias in headlines contrasts with studies that find objectivity greater in the contents of news articles. One study by Stanley Budner and Ellis Krauss looked at the comparative U.S. and Japanese newspaper treatment of three major stories in the late 1980s. The stories were the U.S.-Japan FSX fighter aircraft development program, the purchases of Rockefeller Center and Columbia Pictures by Mitsubishi Estate

Co., Ltd. and Sony, respectively, and U.S.-Japan negotiations on the Structural Impediments Initiative. The study concluded that coverage "appears to have been both balanced and objective." Overall, American coverage tended to be more balanced and objective than the Japanese version, the authors said. They based their determination of balance on an analysis of the articles' structure, which they assessed according to whether one side, two sides, or no sides of an argument were presented. This approach assumed that controversy or argument was the central characteristic of a story, and that balance hinged on whether the different sides in an argument are cited. Interestingly, the authors noted that "the arguments most frequently cited in American stories seemed to emphasize a concern about Japanese behavior as threatening the economic well-being of the United States combined with fear of an actual or potential American decline."[8]

Anthropologist Sheila K. Johnson took yet another approach in her sensitive and thoughtful examination of American attitudes toward Japan as viewed in books that dealt with Japan as their central theme and that were on the *New York Times* best-seller lists from 1941 to 1973. This time span is considerably longer than any of the other studies cited here and it occurs during World War II and before waves of imports came crashing on American shores. Her findings, therefore, are particularly interesting because they give a glimpse of what Americans were thinking when Japan still was struggling to accomplish its postwar reconstruction.

The book begins with the line, "It seems that Americans have always been ambivalent about Japan." The second sentence is just as revealing: "Commodore Perry's men found the Japanese to be 'the most polite people on earth'; yet Perry was deeply frustrated by what he considered to be their outright lies, evasions, and hypocrisy."[9] Ms. Johnson notes that themes, regardless of when they emerge, have a tendency to persist. This occurs even when new themes contradict the old ones.

To get a sense of what the wartime public was seeing about Japan at the movies, Ms. Johnson examined a report produced by the Office of War Information on American film. According to the OWI analysis, "Germans were gentlemen with whom it was possible to deal as equals. As soldiers, they were efficient, disciplined, and patriotic; the bureau was unable to find a scene in which the Germans were morally corrupt or delighted in cruelty. . . . Japanese soldiers were pictured as less military than their German counterparts, and were almost universally cruel and ruthless. Japanese were short, thin, and wore spectacles. They were tough, but devoid of scruples. In almost every film showing American-Japanese battles, the enemy broke the rules of civilized warfare."[10]

One of the themes that Ms. Johnson addresses is the emotional power produced by portraying people as individuals. An example was Pappy Boyington's surprise best-seller, *Baa Baa Black Sheep*, an ungrammatical and poorly written story about his experience as a prisoner-of-war of the Japanese. "His relatively favorable impression of the Japanese stems in part from the fact that as a fighter pilot he dealt with Japanese Zero and bomber pilots on one-to-one basis," Ms. Johnson wrote.[11] His habit of viewing Japanese as individuals persisted after he was shot down, captured, and treated badly. In Ms. Johnson's words, he "always distinguished between 'good Japs' and 'bad Japs.'"

Another of the best-sellers, John Hersey's *Hiroshima,* was notable for the technique that Mr. Hersey explicitly used to arouse empathy among Americans—a focus on individuals. "It is easier to identify with six recognizable individuals than to feel for the plight of faceless thousands," Ms. Johnson wrote in describing the Hersey novel. "In the wake of this individuation, there of course came feelings of American guilt; there is an enormous difference between dropping a bomb on an enemy target and dropping a bomb on Miss Toshiko Sasaki." Ms. Johnson reflected, however, on the possibility that the combination of positive and negative feelings leading to ambivalence may not produce feelings of affection. "Paradoxically, our guilt feelings may also cause us to dislike Japanese more. We not only tend to avoid people who make us feel guilty, we also tend to 'project' our own feelings of guilt, so that the victim becomes transformed into an accuser whom we can then hate for accusing us."[12]

Ms. Johnson also reviewed magazines. From the very beginning of the postwar period, there were articles arguing against the strengthening of the Japanese economy; these competed with articles promoting the urgency of reconstruction. Ms. Johnson cited a report from *Fortune* magazine in 1947 that many American business leaders were "denouncing General MacArthur's efforts to rehabilitate the Japanese economy, particularly those parts of it that competed with American manufacturers before the war." That same year, the *New York Herald Tribune* reported, according to Ms. Johnson, "It had been hoped, particularly among textile manufacturers in this country, that Japan would be kept down, if not eliminated, as a competitive factor. Ceramic interests are reported to have raised a $200,000 propaganda fund to prevent the Japanese from 'stealing the bread out of American mouths.'"[13]

A major image transformation in the postwar period accompanied the improving quality of Japanese products. The widespread, often accurate, prewar and early postwar view that Japanese products were "cheap, shoddy, and gimcrack" evolved into the equally valid view by the 1970s that they were reliable, precision-made, and well designed. Both the real and the perceptual transformation coincided with Japanese exports of products previously considered as peculiarly American, such as automobiles and consumer electronics, or as the hallmark of advanced manufactured goods, such as cameras that competed with the best German models. Along with the products came articles "explaining" the Japanese export success. Ms. Johnson noted that as early as 1970, a *Fortune* magazine headline referred to Japan's "export blitz" and "a powerful government-business complex dubbed 'Japan Inc.'" To the surprise of no one who had listened to the 1995 focus groups on Japan, the 1970 *Fortune* article quoted by Ms. Johnson carried similar references to a Japanese "export drive . . . taking on the overtones of a relentless conspiracy to invade and dominate every vital international market."[14] Many of today's images were already in place, using the same metaphors, before "Japan" invaded Detroit, Hollywood, and midtown Manhattan and before America's own sense of decline in the 1980s.

Conclusions

The focus group research has some obvious analytical holes. It is not comparative; do other countries excite different responses among Americans? The study was confined to the United States; do other nationalities, such as Canadians, have similar views? The study did not consider the knowledge base of the respondents; would elites have different images? Nor was there a detailed examination of the formation of the image structures; do children of different ages have other kinds of responses? The focus groups were conducted in the mid-1990s and 1998; did the experience of Japan's economic stagnation reverse earlier views of dominance and inferiority? The list of additional questions is endless. Nevertheless, this research did find a set of images across the country that was consistent with the findings of other studies. Focus groups conducted several years after the first set incorporated the new experience of almost a decade of Japanese economic stagnation and several years of an expanding American economy. Nevertheless, the same themes repeated themselves, with perhaps a lowered note of anxiety.

One conclusion is that image and metaphor are not shaped often by data and logical analysis. Rather, as Mr. Dower notes in the wartime context, the depiction of self and enemy "serves to remind us of how much the professional and popular mind was shaped then as now by quick, disjointed images and impressions—by headlines, photographs, newsclips, and cartoons; by symbolic items and events such as cinema samurai, . . . the Rape of Nanking, Pearl Harbor, and the Bataan Death March; by catch phrases (divine emperor, world conquest, kamikaze); by sweeping racial cliches (regimented, treacherous, fanatic, bestial)." He further observed, "What passes for empirical observation is revealed to be permeated with myth, prejudice, and wishful thinking."[15]

A related, important conclusion is that the structure of today's image and metaphor is not shaped by today's events, but develops as a complex and poorly understood consequence of the gradual accumulation of impressions that predate any single individual. The eddies, currents, and layers in this pool of images incorporate the rush of many streams. None seem to disappear, but they do not remain unchanged, either. Pearl Harbor, Hiroshima and Nagasaki, and Rockefeller Center become landmarks of the mind as well as designations of real places and events. An economic slowdown in Japan or a revival in America's belief in itself is not likely to change Americans' images of Japan in the short run. Perhaps, in the end, it is only the raising of these images into the realm of conscious discourse that will allow a more complete examination that deals in less emotional and more rational terms.

Notes

1.   Harold Ford, "The Primary Purpose of National Estimating," *Studies in Intelligence* (fall 1991) (unclassified), 75.
2.   A. R. Northridge, "Pearl Harbor: Estimating Then and Now," *Studies in Intelligence* (fall 1965) (declassified June 24, 1994), 65-66.
3.   John Dower, *War Without Mercy: Race and Power in the Pacific War* (New York: Pantheon Books, 1986), 27-28.
4.   For a critical discussion of the economics-as-war metaphor see, "Competitiveness: A Dangerous Obsession," *Foreign Affairs* (March/April 1994). Mr. Krugman debunks the trade-competitiveness-war metaphor, which is common in popular discussions about trade issues, particularly in U.S.-Japan relations.
5.   "TV Week," *The Washington Post*, March 26-April 1, 1995.
6.   Japan Pacific Resources Network, "Media Biases in Covering Japan," *JPRN Monograph* 010, (October 4, 1993) Oakland, Cal., 24, 30.
7.   Charles Burress, "Yellow Peril Between the Lines: The American Press Covers Japan," Master's project, University of California at Berkeley, Graduate School of Journalism, August 30, 1995, 11.
8.   Stanley Budner and Ellis Krauss, "Newspaper Coverage of U.S.-Japan Fric-

tions," *Asian Survey* (April 1995) 342-46.

    9.   Sheila K. Johnson, *American Attitudes Toward Japan, 1941-1975* (Washington, D.C.: American Enterprise Institute, 1975), 1.

    10. Johnson, American Attitudes Toward Japan, 18.

    11. Johnson, American Attitudes Toward Japan, 24.

    12. Johnson, American Attitudes Toward Japan, 33, 38.

    13. Johnson, American Attitudes Toward Japan, 48.

    14. Johnson, American Attitudes Toward Japan, 101.

    15. Dower, *War Without Mercy*, 13, 28.

Chapter 15

Revisionism Revisited

Revising America's View of Japan

Revisionism, as it refers to theories about Japan's political-economic system, is about the evolution of a set of ideas that were generalized and applied far beyond their original provenance. Theories of economic development in backward economies in the late nineteenth and early twentieth centuries, exemplified by Germany and Japan, formed the basis of this school's analysis of Japanese practices through the 1970s. In a kind of freeze-dried view of history, the same institutions and processes identified as critical to Japan's stellar economic advancement are said to continue to determine the way things are done there today. Nothing changes, assert revisionist writers. Don't be fooled by surface movement; underneath everything remains the same.

The model that the architects of revisionism derived from Japan's experience has relevance to other audiences for two reasons. First, the methods presumed to have worked in Japan to produce its economic miracle through the 1970s and its alleged competitive trade threat since then have been recommended as appropriate economic policy for developing countries as well as for the United States. Second, the assumptions about Japanese behavior found in revisionist writings informed American trade policy in President Clinton's first term.

297

The more influential revisionist writers, whose work appeared in the latter half of the 1980s and the early 1990s, include journalists James Fallows and Karel van Wolferen as well as former Reagan administration trade negotiator Clyde Prestowitz. They were preceded by then University of California professor Chalmers Johnson and his 1982 historical, political-economic study of what he and others have labeled the central institution in Japan's economic development—the Ministry of International Trade and Industry. *MITI and the Japanese Miracle* provided the intellectual foundations for the more popular writings of the other authors and for Mr. Johnson's later essays. Its combination of scholarly insight and provocative findings also stimulated a great deal of further academic research that tested many of the hypotheses advanced by the originator of revisionism.

Enough time has passed since the revisionist books and articles were published that their hypotheses, predictions, and assertions can be assessed with less emotion than governed their first appearance. This chapter will focus on the authors named above and concentrate on their discussions about Japan, particularly those related to economic issues. Mr. Johnson and other members of the revisionist school unquestionably produced insights about the operation of Japan's state bureaucracy. Their generalizations are more problematic.

Japanese Capitalism Is Different

Revisionism, according to its intellectual founder Chalmers Johnson, "refers to the observation that Japan has a political economy different from that of the Anglo-American countries in terms of institutions, the role of the state, and the weight of economic nationalism."[1] He contrasts this view with those of "orthodox, academic American economists" who maintain that Anglo-American patterns define capitalism, including the Japanese variety, and that economic rationality ought to, and does, motivate business and state policy and behavior. Since Mr. Johnson and his colleagues claim that Japan differs from the alleged norm, they are said to be revisionists of the standard view.

Mr. Johnson's analysis begins with the observation that, since Japan was a late developer, circumstances required the state to take an activist role in overseeing and guiding economic behavior. Japan is a "capitalist development state" as opposed to a "capitalist regulatory state," such as the United States and other early developers. The Japanese style of capitalism, therefore, is different from that espoused and practiced in the United States and other Western economies.[2] Most important, the central role of the state is not the maximization of consumer values—the guiding star of liberal Western economies—but the pursuit of economic nationalism.

The roots of economic nationalism go back to the Meiji reforms of the 1870s when the state led industrialization in order to defend the country against Western imperialism. However, Mr. Johnson moves beyond the Meiji reforms in his notion of the concept. "Japanese pursue economic activities primarily to achieve independence from and leverage over potential adversaries rather than to achieve consumer utility, private wealth, mutually beneficial trade, or any other objective posited by economic determinists."[3]

The revisionist understanding of Japan's industrialization in the nineteenth century is extended to Japanese behavior in the twentieth century, with considerable continuity ascribed to the postwar period. Mr. Johnson's scholarly work takes the story up to the 1970s, but he and others in the revisionist camp maintain that the same basic system continued through the end of the century. This system, they insist, was the source of Japan's enviable economic growth and the model for the other countries participating in the Asian economic miracle.

This model is further extended and generalized by the notion that Japan's development approach is applicable to most nontotalitarian, underdeveloped states. Even more, revisionists explicitly suggest that many elements of the Japanese system are appropriate to the United States and other developed countries.

Alexander Gerschenkron:
Economic Backwardness and Late Development

The intellectual source of the model of Japanese economic development adopted by Mr. Johnson came from the concept of late development—industrialization that occurred after the early examples of Great Britain and the United States. The primary name associated with these ideas is that of Alexander Gerschenkron, the Harvard University economic historian who specialized in Russian and European development. In a seminal article published in 1952, Mr. Gerschenkron speculated that there may be regularities in development among those countries that followed the original industrial economies. He noted that "the development of a backward country may, by the very virtue of its backwardness, tend to differ fundamentally from that of an advanced country."[4] The rapid speed of industrialization and the organizational structure of industry, in particular, seemed to show considerable differences from more advanced countries.

Although Mr. Gerschenkron expressly denied detailed knowledge of Japan in the formulation of his hypothesis, it appeared to him that the Meiji Restoration had served the purpose of removing the barriers to development. Once this occurred, large-scale industrialization on a broad front would allow the potential benefits "to become sufficiently strong to overcome existing obstacles and to liberate the forces that made for industrial progress."[5]

This process happened often enough that Mr. Gerschenkron was able to speak of "industrial revolution" when development took off in a "sudden, eruptive way."[6] His description predated Japan's postwar economic miracle. It suggests that developmental spurts already were sufficiently common to be incorporated into a theory of development.

Fourteen years after publishing his first essay on economic backwardness, Mr. Gerschenkron summarized his further thoughts and research as well as the findings of others stimulated by his original essay. He listed several outcomes that he believed were associated with the development of an economically backward country: the more likely was its industrialization to start discontinuously; the greater was the emphasis on producer goods as against consumer goods; the larger was the part played by special institutional factors designed to increase the supply of capital to nascent industries and to provide them with better informed entrepreneurial guidance; and the more pronounced were the coerciveness and the comprehensiveness of these special institutional factors.[7]

Mr. Gerschenkron's Harvard University colleague, economics professor Henry Rosovsky, set out to test the backwardness theories on the Japanese experience. He noted that government was "Japan's institutional instrument for rapid industrialization." However, only "if national and international comparative advantages were lacking, and if the particular economic activity was deemed a developmental imperative, did the government dominate the picture." Japan's military requirements supplied that imperative. "In fact, it was present during almost the entire period of modern Japanese economic development."[8]

Chalmers Johnson: The Capitalist Developmental State

Mr. Johnson's explanation of Japanese behavior is rooted in the concept of late development. According to his formulation, late developers require a conscious political decision to industrialize. Mobilization regimes force their economic priorities on society. "The two fundamental types of such mobilization regimes are the Leninist-Stalinist totalitarian model and the Bismarckian-Meiji authoritarian one. Both involve social goal setting, forced saving, mercantilism, and bureaucratism."[9] The second model, the capitalist developmental state, is based on market-conforming methods. It uses the market to implement its goals. Mr. Johnson notes that this process is infinitely more efficient than its communist rival but not as efficient as the ideal market economy. He declares, however, that the capitalist developmental approach is much more effective in achieving its societal goals than its market competitor.

At the center of Mr. Johnson's model of Japanese development is a covert, elite establishment that perpetuates itself through a conservative alliance. It promoted national pride to motivate the spirit of development and to deflect attention away from constitutional development. Through 1945, imperialism was the motivational influence; in the postwar period export promotion and competition for market share supplied substitutes for imperial expansion and war. The elite state bureaucracy set the goals of the society, "but in order to implement the goals, they must enter the market and manipulate and structure it so that private citizens responding to the incentives and disincentives make the market work for the state."[10]

According to Mr. Johnson, the government gave greatest precedence to industrial policy—to establishing a structure of domestic industry that enhanced international competitiveness. In addition to looking after the industrial structure, the state may intrude into the detailed operations of individual enterprises to improve them. The Ministry of International Trade and Industry was the "pilot agency" that faced the concrete challenges of originating and implementing industrial policy. The chief duties of this bureaucracy were to identify and choose the industries to be developed, select the best means of rapidly developing the targeted industries, and supervise competition in the designated strategic sectors to guarantee their economic health and effectiveness. Commenting on MITI's view of markets, Mr. Johnson says that, despite a commitment to free enterprise and markets, Japanese industrial planners were convinced that market forces alone never would produce the desired results.[11]

Mr. Johnson's historical overview of MITI describes the unplanned nature of an evolving system. After a harrowing struggle that spanned the challenges of Manchurian development in the 1930s, mobilization in wartime, destruction in its aftermath, and the vast structural changes of the immediate postwar period, the system came to a full flowering in the 1955-1975 period. Only looking backward did the participants in this process come to the conclusion that they had produced a theory of development.

The MITI system of industrial policy, Mr. Johnson argues, grew out of Japan's particular history. He warns of the dangers of attempting to generalize and adapt Japanese institutions and policies. Despite this caution about the hazards of emulation, a few pages later in his *MITI and the Japanese Miracle,* the author suggests that other developing societies might match, if not replicate, the preconditions and "apply the model of the Japanese high-growth system to use as a guide for its own application." By the last page of the book, Mr. Johnson proposes that, to meet their long-term requirements, "Americans should perhaps be thinking about their own 'pilot agency.'"[12]

Having described the operation of a covert, elite state bureaucracy that planned and implemented industrial policy for nationalistic rather than economic goals, Mr. Johnson extends this characterization in his later writings on American and Japanese policies. Thus, he argues, Japan's form of capitalism is different from America's and that of other Western countries. Japan does not respond to economic forces in its external behavior because it is not governed by economic goals. Case in point: despite the yen more than doubling in value in the post-1980 period, Japan's trade surplus continues to build. As a mercantile power, Japan uses state action to export the greatest possible quantity of its own manufactures and to import as little as possible.[13] Although Japan is immune to changes in its economic environment, Mr. Johnson maintains that policymakers deliberately foster the illusion of change.

The problem for America, says Mr. Johnson, is that Japan's foreign economic policy—based as it is on genuine mercantilism—is predicated on "protecting its domestic market, overcharging domestic consumers, and using the overcharges to subsidize exports, and predatory pricing abroad to destroy competitors." He ends his 1990 article on trade and revisionism from which the just-cited material is drawn by declaring that the United States must emulate or match Japan's accomplishments in government-business relations, industrial policy, and industrial organization "or go the way of the USSR"[14]

The founder of the revisionist school extends and intensifies some of these ideas in a 1993 article. For example, he expands the notion of deliberate illusion, stating that "Japan's economic strategy implies indirection, disinformation, and deception in order to defeat the nation's economic competitors."[15] He explicitly says that the historically based nature of economic nationalism continues to be the fundamental principle of Japan's government-guided capitalism. Mr. Johnson also reiterates the need for a U.S. industrial policy, given that the "high-growth economies of East Asia have demonstrated that the state can be a critically important contributor to the success of market economies." He recommends, too, that the United States adopt a results-oriented trade policy. This, he claims, is the logical conclusion to draw from the differences between the United States and Japan, where state guidance prevails, the effects of economic forces are weak, the bureaucracy never changes, exports are an imperative, and the trade surplus will not disappear. Such a policy would recognize the underlying reality, Mr. Johnson asserts.[16]

Karel van Wolferen: The Headless State

Karel van Wolferen, a Dutch financial journalist and a longtime resident of Japan, describes the Japanese state as one without a head; it is missing a center of accountability. "No person or group holds a mandate to make binding decisions for all of Japan's institutions as part of a national effort."[17] The subtitle of his 1989 book, *The Enigma of Japanese Power: People and Politics in a Stateless Nation,* makes this point. The headless state is bound to be a problem for the United States because its prime minister and other power figures "are incapable of delivering on political promises they may make concerning commercial or other matters." There is "no room for an accommodation to foreign wishes or demands."[18]

Mr. van Wolferen's other main points largely follow Mr. Johnson's. For example, he also emphasizes the different kind of capitalism found in Japan: "Far from beating the West at its own game, it might not be playing the Western game at all." Later he adds: "It is a fiction that Japan belongs in the category known as capitalist, free-market economies."[19] Its political and economic behavior is meant to accomplish aims that are fundamentally different from those assumed by the United States. Moreover, Mr. van Wolferen argues, barring some great upheaval, Japan is unlikely to change because that would entail the breakup of the bureaucracy-business partnership that forms the heart of its system.

Mr. van Wolferen develops these points in a 1990 article but adds the twist of Japanese omnipotence and a United States that is close to help-less. He reiterates his earlier point that any Japanese government commitments gained through bilateral negotiations are "unlikely to provide Americans with the opportunities they hoped to gain." This outcome will lead to American frustrations, but any indications that the special relationship between the two countries may be endangered will "give greater purpose to Japan's further frantic economic expansion." He underlines the notion of conspiracy with the revelation that the "Ministry of Finance coordinates the important international moves of financial institutions operating in informal cartels." Those "are essentially in the business of national security. International domination in as many industrial areas as possible is part of an uncoordinated and never delineated yet powerful campaign to make the world safe for Japan."[20]

A powerful government presence that directs international conspiracies is difficult to reconcile with a headless state. He tries to introduce some consistency by suggesting that "parallel operating groups" are the source of economic vitality, but also a great weakness. It is the highly developed institutional memories of the participants and their intricate but informal methods that preserve order.

The threat to the United States is so powerful, maintains Mr. van Wolferen, that even if it greatly improved its competitiveness by doing everything suggested by American analysts—balance the budget, increase savings, improve investment—"the United States would still face an often hopeless competition against Japanese manufacturers and banks." This longtime Japan observer also states that American negotiating demands that irritate Japan "must take into account a newly emerging and intimidating right-wing force . . . with a network of sympathizers reaching into the press, the universities, and the ruling party."[21]

The problem that this system generates for the United States is left unclear in Mr. van Wolferen's later writings. To some degree, it did not have to be defined because Americans already had absorbed the idea that a problem existed. All that Mr. van Wolferen had to do was to allude to it, and readers could summon up their own images to fill in the gap. In the 1986 article where he introduced the "Japan problem," the issues were somewhat clearer. It was not just the bilateral trade deficit that was the difficulty, but that "if present trends are allowed to continue, they will eventually lead to the gradual loss of industrial capacity in the United States."[22] Moreover, legislators, driven by their constituents, could end up wrecking the international trading system in attempts to protect the United States from unstoppable Japanese imports.

Is it possible for the United States to deal with a fundamentally incompatible, conspiratorial, Hydra-headed, potentially fascist nation that hopelessly outcompetes us and for which there is not even an address to send a letter of complaint? Mr. van Wolferen suggests that the U.S. government first must unambiguously recognize the enormity of the problem it confronts. However, his 1990 article trails off into a fuzzy proposal to completely overhaul multilateral trading institutions. Perhaps, given Mr. van Wolferen's description of Japanese behavior, nothing concrete can be done. However, in his earlier article he suggested that the United States learn from Japan's predilection for cartels and impose fixed import commitments or else unilaterally restrict U.S. imports of Japanese goods, an approach that is similar to Mr. Johnson's call for managed trade.

James Fallows: Learning from Japan and Asia

Intrigued by the economic dynamism of East Asia, James Fallows, also a journalist, took himself and his family to Japan and Malaysia for a three-and-a-half-year stay in the late 1980s to understand and report on developments in Asia. This sojourn resulted in several articles and a book, the titles of which explain his point of view. A major article, "Containing Japan," attempted to alert Americans to the threat posed to the mutually beneficial U.S.-Japan relationship by the "one-sided and destructive expansion of Japan's economic power."[23] The only solution, in both countries' interests, is somehow to limit this force.

Mr. Fallows' 1994 book, *Looking at the Sun*, refers to the brilliance that is Japan and East Asia. Because their economic successes can be blinding and the reasons behind those achievements so confounding, Americans avert their eyes because it is painful to contemplate and comprehend the meaning of the Asian experience. Mr. Fallows urges his readers to view the situation directly and to learn from it.[24]

What is there to learn from Japan and East Asia? Mainly it is the importance of promoting production over consumption and the use of industrial policy to accomplish that task. A central conclusion of Mr. Fallows is that the East Asian system, including repression of the individual, has "made the whole society, including its business sector, function more effectively than most in the West." Further, the system's success creates American dependence and vulnerability. "It is clearly better to have more control over the decision yourself—or by people subject to the constraints of your political system and social mores," Mr. Fallows writes. Because Japan has had more power to push its economy in the direction it wants, the United States is being pushed in directions it does not like.[25]

Mr. Fallows cites the importance to Japanese thinking of German economist Friedrich List with his emphasis on national economic power rather than the consumer welfare of Adam Smith's economics. Whereas the Anglo-American economic objective is the materialistic one of raising living standards, the Asian goal is political, with national power as an end. Moreover, the Anglo-American model views unpredictability and surprise as the ever-present traits of economic life. Free and fluid markets are the chosen means for dealing with unpredictability in contrast to attempts to outwit markets by "picking winners." The Asian system, Mr. Fallows asserts, mistrusts markets as a method for determining economic direction.[26] In order to promote various aims and values, industrial policy was both necessary and effective for the developing Japanese and East Asian states.

Mr. Fallows describes industrial policy as government support for and encouragement of certain industries in the form of steering more money toward them than the market otherwise would provide. The government also sets conditions, rules, incentives, and standards to increase the chances that the additional money has the intended effect. However, specific operational decisions are undertaken by businesses motivated by competitive market forces.[27]

Trade policy, says Mr. Fallows, should implement industrial policy. He recommends that the United States move away from its ideal, free trade approach to one that recognizes its leverage and that aims at Asian sensibilities about the way things work. The clearest example of this approach in his view was the "expectation" expressed in a side letter to the 1986 U.S.-Japan semiconductor trade agreement that foreign products would represent 20 percent of chip sales in Japan. The goal was a target, not a process, that would make Japan become "open" or "fair." That agreement worked in Mr. Fallows' estimation. The more traditional American approach—"cajoling, negotiating, holding hands, waving sticks, and all the while asking for 'openness' and 'change'—leads nowhere economically."[28]

Focusing on the "Japan problem," Mr. Fallows picks up the idea of Chalmers Johnson that developmental states follow certain imperatives that are inimical to U.S. interests. "Conflict arises from Japan's inability or unwillingness to restrain the one-sided and destructive expansion of its economic power."[29] Specifically, Japan's uncontrolled, unbalanced growth threatens America's ability to pay the costs of global leadership. "If Japan cannot restrain the excesses of its own economy, then the United States, to save its partnership with Japan, should impose limits from outside." As indicators of excess and imbalance, Mr. Fallows notes Japan's large overseas investments but high prices at home, its export successes together with suppressed domestic consumption, and a continuing trade surplus in the framework of an appreciating currency.

As did Mr. Johnson, Mr. Fallows uses this last point as an indictment of the economics profession. "Classic free-trade analysis has proved virtually useless in predicting how Japan's trade balance would respond to a rising yen." Even so-called market-opening measures illustrate adversarial trade tendencies. Reduced barriers to beef imports, he maintains, led to greater sales of U.S. beef ranches, not American beef. "Japan and its acolytes, such as Taiwan and Korea, have demonstrated that in head-on competition between free-trading societies and capitalist developmental states, the free traders will eventually lose."[30]

Clyde Prestowitz: America's Lost Economic War

Following a five-year stint as special counselor on Japan affairs to the secretary of commerce, Clyde Prestowitz resigned in 1986 to devote himself to a book detailing his perceptions of the changing American relationship with Japan. The message was simple. The United States had been in an economic war with Japan; America lost. He describes this debacle in vivid imagery. "There were no military weapons and no armed troops. There were casualties but no blood; tears, but no one missing in action. It was an economic rather than a military defeat, partially self-inflicted, and partially at the hands of friends and allies among which Japan was foremost."[31]

Mr. Prestowitz elaborated some familiar themes. "Few, if any, American companies can compete with the Japanese in the areas the latter deem important. . . . The Japanese government views industrial performance as akin to national security and pours enormous energy into ensuring that its industry is the world leader. . . . The United States does not view industry as a matter of national security as Japan does. . . . The United States and Japan have fundamentally different understandings of the purposes and workings of a national economy. . . . Japan has focused on production and dominance of key industries that will enhance its strategic position."[32]

Writing in 1987, Mr. Prestowitz bemoaned the accelerating decline of the U.S. economy. In 1984, he notes, Pentagon studies had pointed to the increasing vulnerability and withering technological capability of the defense establishment. More broadly, Americans did not understand that the demands of world power require capabilities in certain industries and key technologies. Such action is not in response to a military threat, which can be comprehended, but to Japan's challenge. When U.S. industries have declined in the face of Japanese competition fostered by government policies aimed at achieving industrial leadership, "our government leaders have agonized over what to do. They have hesitated to enforce U.S. trade laws even in cases of clear violation." Moreover, argued Mr. Prestowitz, the United States has not learned anything from Japanese successes. "The U.S. government has not attempted to change any structure of a whole industry to achieve the strategic power that dominance in that industry would confer."[33]

With respect to trade policy, the former trade negotiator proposed that the United States always go for results with Japan. These can include the revision or the passage of a law, a market share, or a specific amount of sales—anything concrete. Negotiators also require credible threats to attain results. Mr. Prestowitz offers the semiregulated international civil aviation industry as an example of how to compete with Japan more generally. "We give x number of flights a week to Japan, and they give us x number of flights in return. It is not an open market; but within the reciprocal framework, a great deal of competition takes place."[34]

America Was Ready for Revisionism

The revisionist writings fell on fertile ground. The United States had witnessed the undeniable fact of Japan's precedent-making economic development. Tidal waves of made-in-Japan products seemed to dominate every American market entered. The apparent inability of domestic companies to match the designs and the prices of their Japanese counterparts spoke to a worrying flight of competence among U.S. producers. By the late 1980s, the volume of Japanese capital flowing into the country suggested that Dai-Ichi Kangyo Bank, Ltd., the largest bank in the world at that time as measured by assets, might become the Toyota Motor Corp. of the 1990s. The ostensible threat to this country's prosperity from Japanese products and finance was compounded in American eyes by Japan's unfairness, evident in its attempts to block U.S. competitors from breaking into Japanese markets. The revisionists had the explanations for the seeming predicament as well as the responses.

Several strands came together to weave this fabric of American anxiety and—even—fear. The strongest strand was the Japanese economic miracle, which excited curiosity and analysis in the United States, as academics sought to explain the sources of this unprecedented phenomenon. Harvard University professor Ezra Vogel's 1979 book, *Japan as Number One,* established a genre of studies that sought to teach the country about the sources of Japanese growth and to apply them to the United States. Although U.S. gross national product per capita in 1979 still was some 50 percent greater than Japan's (measured at purchasing power parity), the comparable figure in 1955 was 500 percent. Clearly, something was going on in Japan to review and perhaps copy.

While Japan's amazing growth was underway, another development was emerging that would have an even greater impact on the American psyche. The nature of production was proceeding through evolutionary change at Toyota, led by production chief Taiichi Ohno. Twenty years of persistent development coalesced to produce a production revolution. In 1965, Toyota already was 50 percent more productive than the average American company was, after adjusting for differences in vertical integration, capacity utilization, and employee hours.[35] By 1983, Toyota and Nissan Motor Co., Ltd., the automotive industry's number two, produced approximately twice as many vehicles per employee as their American counterparts (again after making various adjustments to the raw data). Mr. Ohno rightfully could join Eli Whitney and Henry Ford as an exemplar of revolutions in manufacturing.

Americans first became aware of these production developments in the mid-1970s, as higher gasoline prices drove automotive buyers to seek smaller, more fuel-efficient cars. At first, the Japanese models did not impress U.S. customers. By the 1980s, however, Toyota and the other major Japanese vehicle companies had adapted their designs to American preferences. The cumulative results of productivity and quality advances propelled the new models to a 20 percent or so share of the American car market.

Other Japanese automotive companies and their suppliers and then other industries learned the Toyota system. In the 1980s, made-in-Japan cars, television sets, machine tools, electronics components, and other consumer and producer products became ubiquitous companions to Americans at home and at work. Earlier in the postwar period, invasions of Japanese textiles and steel had disrupted familiar production and purchasing patterns. Now the same thing was happening to the icons of American technological know-how and prosperity.

As Japan's newly efficient producers were preparing to enter export markets big time, the U.S. dollar was becoming overvalued. Driven by an American demand for funds to satisfy an economy that was investing more than it was saving, the dollar was an estimated 25 percent higher than inflation differentials in export goods would have warranted.

As if a deficiency of American savings was not enough to drive up the dollar, savers in Japan had more than they wanted to invest in their own economy. Japanese growth was downshifting to a more sedate pace. With growth falling, industry's need for capital investment declined. Household savings, which had fed the demand for capital throughout the postwar period, remained at high levels. At first, government budget deficits absorbed the difference between high household savings and diminished corporate demand for investment purposes, but by 1980, Tokyo had reduced its deficit. The residual savings consequently were available to flow to the rest of the world. Coincidentally, this export of capital had become feasible with the breakdown in the early 1970s of the postwar Bretton Woods fixed exchange rate system and the subsequent liberalization of Japanese capital controls.

The supply of yen on world currency markets, combined with the shortage of dollars in the savings-deficient United States, drove up the dollar. At its high in 1985, the real value of the dollar was 65 percent above its 1978 low. The high-priced dollar strengthened the competitiveness that Japanese exporters had gained through their production efficiency. U.S. imports from Japan surged. From 1978 through 1986, U.S. imports from Japan jumped from $24.5 billion to $80.8 billion. The transpacific trade deficit for those same years climbed from $11.6 billion to $54.3 billion. U.S. car imports from Japan, a bare 34,441 units in 1965, soared to almost one million units in a decade and reached 1.9 million by 1980, representing 21 percent of U.S. sales.

The other defining event for U.S.-Japan relations was the "economic bubble" that seized Japan from roughly 1986 through 1990. During this period, land and stock prices skyrocketed by more than 300 percent. The real cost of raising capital on the Tokyo Stock Exchange fell into negative territory. Financial capital flowed abroad, mainly to the United States, as Japanese investors sought profitable opportunities to reinvest their burgeoning paper wealth. U.S. Treasury bills were a favored parking place, but real estate and corporate investments made headlines when well-known American properties fell under Japanese control. To many Americans, it looked as though the country was up for sale.

The economic forces driving the *tsunami* of Japanese exports to and investments in the United States created anxieties among Americans about the economy's overall competitiveness. In fact, some American products that had dominated the postwar scene at home and abroad gradually had lost their competitiveness as productivity and design advances elsewhere overtook American producers. However, this was not true of the full range of domestic products and services.

The high-priced dollar did its part to render otherwise solid U.S. products unsellable in foreign markets. But Japan's government and companies on the other side of the Pacific played a significant role in turning Americans' anxieties into anger because of what most people interpreted as unfair practices that kept competitive American products out of Japanese markets. Such practices included long-term business relations, exclusionary arrangements among companies, collusion, nontransparent administrative guidance by government agencies over business activities, regulated industries, and explicit government interpretation of rules that denied entry to U.S. goods. Emblematic of the high-visibility fairness issue was the prohibition of American aluminum baseball bats on safety grounds and French skis on the pretext that Japan's snow was different from France's. What was difficult enough to understand and accept on economic grounds was converted by clumsy but routine Japanese behavior into widespread suspicion and distrust.

Revisionist views and the swelling emotions directed toward Japan as well as America's earlier negotiating experience colored U.S. trade strategy toward Japan in the first Clinton administration. Administration officials were swayed by the revisionist rhetoric. Japan was different; it did not respond to economic forces; the Japanese government coordinated economic activity; collusion, conspiracy, and a headless state prevented Washington from gaining a meaningful response from Tokyo. It was not surprising, therefore, that previous negotiations had failed to produce results. "We negotiate and negotiate and nothing happens," was the cry from U.S. Trade Representative Mickey Kantor.

The approach that came out of the revisionist model of Japanese behavior was to negotiate specific targets or indicators of trade progress, with sanctions to be applied if these were not attained. It then would be up to Japan to decide, in its own inscrutable way, just how these results would be accomplished. However, that was a Japanese problem. America just wanted to be dealt into the game and be assigned its fair share of the pot.

It did not take long for reactions from Japan and elsewhere, including those of many Americans, to cause this initial conception to be watered down. However, for two years or so it produced a troubled relationship with Japan. Eventually, the United States realized that its diplomacy in Asia required Japan's active cooperation. Since one part of the White House's results-oriented policy was intended to demonstrate to the electorate that the Clinton team could get tough with Japan on market access, the approaching 1996 presidential election gave Mr. Clinton the opportunity to declare victory.

Assessing Revisionism

The revisionist model can be assessed by posing several questions. Does it accurately describe Japanese behavior in the postwar period extending up to today? Does it apply to developing countries more broadly? Is it applicable to developed countries like the United States? And how well do some of the predictions hold up in light of subsequent experience?

Before tackling these questions, it should be noted that the revisionist authors produced valuable evidence about the functioning of Japan's state bureaucracy. Mr. Johnson's description of MITI opened an entire subject for additional research. Mr. van Wolferen's portrayal of a fragmented government drew attention to the inadequacy of the assumptions about the operation of state power in Japan. Messrs. Fallows and Prestowitz gave their readers inside views of a dynamic Asia and the workings of American trade negotiations. It is the conclusions and the generalizations of these writers that are problematic.

The machine tool industry, for example, was the exemplar strategic industry. From the 1930s, it was an explicit target of the different phases of industrial policy. However, according to a study of this industry, "none of MITI's machinery policies was successful. In the period of planning and financial support, output objectives had no effect on industry performance, while government loans did not generate economic expansion. The cartelization phase did not reduce firm entry or market volatility, nor did it rationalize production. . . . Numerical control development and export success were not the result of government or private efforts to coordinate production and marketing abroad. . . . In no single instance did MITI's policies lead to anticipated market outcomes."[36]

The machine tool study indicates an inherent problem in the approach used by Mr. Johnson. Examinations of internal operations and selected case studies do not answer the questions of whether policies actually were implemented as planned and whether the results were different from what otherwise might have occurred. It is one thing to say that MITI had a policy. It requires a good deal more evidence and analysis to say that the relevant strategy was effective and necessary.

One compilation of all of MITI's policies from 1967 through 1971 showed overall agreement within the ministry on broad objectives but inconsistencies in the detailed plans of MITI's bureaus. Such a wide array of targets was proposed that any sense of strategic purpose was undermined. The author compared a statistical analysis of the actual growth of favored industries with counterfactual projections of how these industries might have grown without policy interventions. The industries were chosen based on those characteristics deemed to be important by MITI strategists: high income elasticity, technological progress, knowledge and information intensity, and import substitution. Virtually no evidence of shifts in output in the desired directions could be identified.

An analysis then was performed on two lists of industries, the favored group as identified in MITI documents, and those that industrial policy planners felt should grow slowly or decline. When the actual historical record was compared with a policy-neutral simulation, the out-of-favor industries seemed to grow faster than did the targeted ones. The author concluded by noting that "industrial policy in the sense of a fully integrated, consistent approach to industrial structure has not really been tried. To a substantial degree, this is clear even from an examination of what policymakers have said. Those who have studied Japanese policy and found that policy to be effective have failed to consider the interindustry effects of policy and to be comprehensive in considering the relative size of different factors affecting a given industry."[37]

Gary Saxonhouse of the University of Michigan examined MITI's leadership in an important new industry, biotechnology, in the decade to 1985.[38] MITI targeted biotechnology as a knowledge-based industry that could replace resource- and labor-intensive heavy industries. Despite this identification, the government had trouble taking major, overt steps to aid the industry because of tight budgets. In 1984, for example, Tokyo allocated roughly $35 million to biotechnology compared with the U.S. government's $522 million. Moreover, a large proportion of the Japanese funds went to energy research, aid to companies in the structurally depressed chemicals, pulp and paper, and textile industries, and to the traditional area of fermentation.

Some observers believed that simply listing biotechnology as a targeted industry would act as a guide to Japanese business and finance to move into this new area. However, no new firms had entered the market by 1985 compared with 111 new American companies and 108 established firms that had branched out into this field. Moreover, equity markets had raised $1.5 billion for small U.S. biotechnology firms. The four largest established Japanese firms spent less than $100 million on biotechnology R&D through 1985; total estimated private R&D was about

$400 million, 15 percent less than the expenditures of just the top four U.S. firms. In every industrial policy objective usually attributed to MITI, its plan for biotechnology did not produce results.

Princeton University's Kent Calder examined the ability of Japanese government industrial policymakers to allocate credit strategically. He found that they lacked a wide-ranging ability to shape the financial system to their vision of priorities, although they did play an important role in orchestrating the early postwar recovery and the heavy industrialization of the next decade. After 1970, though, broader market forces intruded with increasing persistence to undermine the position of industrial policy planners. Mr. Calder concluded that state-directed credit allocation was successful only when a relatively unusual configuration of characteristics prevailed: state power was centralized; the private sector was disorganized; domestic and international interventions were limited; and credit demand was greater than supply at prevailing interest rates. This was achieved most clearly during the 1946-1954 period.[39]

Examinations of whether Japan's approach to economic intervention should be recommended to other developing countries have produced a mixed record. The World Bank, for one, has conducted numerous studies on just this question, with some of the work financed by a Japanese government that was suspicious that the multilateral development agency may have a bias against industrial policy. Much of this research was brought together in the World Bank's 1997 *World Development Report*. The document noted that Japan's postwar development of the steel, coal, machinery, and shipbuilding industries illustrated the rationale for intervention—as well as the stringent institutional prerequisites for success. It concluded, "pursuing this style of investment coordination presupposes levels of public and private institutional capability that are beyond the reach of most developing countries." A warning also was attached: "Implemented badly, activist industrial policy can be a recipe for disaster."[40] Illustrative of the World Bank's ranking of industrial policy among all the functions performed by government is that this subject rates only four pages out of the report's 167 pages of text.

It is not that World Bank economists consider government unimportant. "An effective state is vital for the provision of the goods and services—and the rules and institutions—that allow markets to flourish and people to live healthier and happier lives. Without it, sustainable development, both economic and social, is impossible."[41] Essential functions include establishing a foundation of law, maintaining a nondistortionary policy environment, and investing in basic social services and infrastructure.

These seemingly routine tasks are extremely complex, however, and tax the capabilities of most governments. Some analysts speculate that an important source of modern Japan's economic growth was its heritage from the Tokugawa Shogunate of a capable civil service, a functioning bureaucracy, and a fairly literate society. On closer examination, therefore, the main contribution of the Japanese state could be its competence in the mundane job of getting the fundamentals right and not in the more heroic role of choosing and nurturing strategic industries.

A bit of evidence used by revisionist writers to demonstrate that economic forces just do not work in Japan is that its huge trade surplus persists, even though the yen has appreciated more than 100 percent in value against the dollar since the gap between exports and imports first appeared in 1980. The reason for the yen's run-up in real terms over the long term is because of Japan's current account surplus, not in spite of it. Revisionist writers have cause and effect backward. The capital outflow associated with a current account surplus builds up assets abroad. These assets generate income that flows back to the home country and drives up the price of its currency. The reverse has been happening to the value of the dollar. Therefore, the persistence of Japan's surplus in the face of an appreciating currency means that economic forces are working just as predicted by theory.

Likewise, the appreciating yen produced the results predicted by standard, Anglo-American economics on Japan's trade volumes (which adjust nominal values for price changes). In the ten years after 1986, when the yen went up sharply in the aftermath of the previous fall's Plaza Accord, import volume soared 100 percent. Exports, in contrast, grew in real terms by just 24 percent.

Some of the other predictions put forth by the revisionist school fare about as well as the notion of missing economic forces. Mr. Fallows commented that the United States should not expect much from the liberalization of beef imports. In fact, U.S. beef shipments to Japan rose from $356 million in 1985 to $1.7 billion ten years later.

Many of the revisionist writings had the misfortune to appear in the late 1980s, just as Japan's economic bubble was at its height. Predictions made at that time of unrelenting production growth and investment expansion at home and abroad often were based on simple extrapolation—an always-dangerous approach to forecasting. Ten years after the publication dates of Mr. Fallows' "Containing Japan" and Mr. van Wolferen's "The Japan Problem Revisited," production remained at or below the levels of the earlier period. Likewise, Mr. Prestowitz's lost economic war takes on a different hue from a later perspective. In retrospect, many of the points made in the cited books and articles were reflective of America's image of itself rather than the result of a clear-eyed vision of Japan.

What should be made of proposals that the United States seriously consider the adoption of some form of Japan-style industrial policy? This is not the place to review the many arguments about industrial policy. Nonetheless, it should be noted that industrial policy might not have been as important for Japan's strong economic performance as proponents of this view have claimed. Japan up to the 1970s, like East Asian countries in the nest two decades and the America of Alexander Hamilton (prominently cited for his promotion of industrial policies), was small and backward. Small size permits policies denied to large countries. A small country, for example, can take advantage of the global trading system; however, if all countries or just the big ones were to do the same, the system would be destroyed.

This "fallacy of composition" is an easy trap to fall into when one has an overly narrow focus. American policy since 1945 has recognized the primacy of the system of free trade. Successive administrations, Democratic and Republican alike, have worked consistently to achieve that goal (despite occasional backsliding), with the understanding that temporary advantage should be eschewed in return for the greater long-term gains from openness. This is not a strategy based on vague moral principles or a peculiar brand of economics, as argued by Mr. Fallows, but one grounded in naked self-interest.

Backwardness provides the dubious luxury of having others to follow. A guide is immensely valuable. Neither Alexander Hamilton nor Japanese planners faced much uncertainty in identifying iron and steel and shipbuilding as worthwhile industries because they had precedents. (Both countries since have faced numerous political obstacles in moving out of these nineteenth-century industries.) The Japanese government has proved to be an incompetent player when technology and markets are fluid and changing rapidly. The difficulties faced when a nation reaches the technological frontier are different in kind from those produced by backwardness. Japan, as the most advanced Asian economy, illustrates the pitfalls. Although it demonstrated truly miraculous gains in productivity during its nearly century-long period of economic catch-up, the last quarter-century tells a different story. The evidence for the generalization and transference of the economics of backwardness suggests that the revisionists' ideas require revising.

Notes

1.   Chalmers Johnson, "Introduction," in *Japan: Who Governs?* (New York: W.W. Norton, 1995), 12.

2.   The next chapter explores the notion of differences among economies.

3.   Johnson, "Comparative Capitalism: The Japanese Difference," in *Japan: Who Governs?*, 105.

4.   Alexander Gerschenkron, "Economic Backwardness in Historical Perspective," in *Economic Backwardness in Historical Perspective* (Cambridge, Mass.: Harvard University Press, 1966), 7.

5.   Gerschenkron, "Economic Backwardness in Historical Perspective," 11.

6.   Gerschenkron, "Economic Backwardness in Historical Perspective," 10.

7.   Gerschenkron, "The Approach to European Industrialization: A Postscript," in *Economic Backwardness*, 354.

8.   Henry Rosovsky, *Capital Formation in Japan: 1868-1940* (Glencoe, Ill.: The Free Press, 1961), 102-104.

9.   Johnson, "Social Values and the Theory of Late Economic Development in East Asia," in *Japan: Who Governs?*, 45.

10.   Johnson, "Social Values and the Theory of Late Economic Development in East Asia," 46.

11.   Chalmers Johnson, *MITI and the Japanese Miracle: The Growth of Industrial Policy, 1925-1975* (Stanford, Cal.: Stanford University Press, 1982), 19, 27, 315.

12.   Johnson, *MITI and the Japanese Miracle*, 306, 314.

13.   Johnson, "Trade, Revisionism, and the Future of Japanese-American Relations," in *Japan: Who Governs?*, 71.

14.   Johnson, "Trade, Revisionism, and the Future of Japanese-American Relations," 89, 95.

15.   Johnson, "The Foundation of Japan's Wealth and Power," in *Japan: Who Governs?*, 98.

16.   Johnson, "The Foundation of Japan's Wealth and Power," 111-112.

17.   Karel van Wolferen, "The Japan Problem Revisited," *Foreign Affairs*, fall 1990, 49.

18.   Karel van Wolferen, *The Enigma of Japanese Power: People and Politics in a Stateless Nation* (New York, Alfred A. Knopf, 1989), 6.

19.   van Wolferen, *The Enigma of Japanese Power*, 2, 6.

20.   van Wolferen, "The Japan Problem Revisited," 45, 48.

21.   van Wolferen, "The Japan Problem Revisited," 50-51

22.   Karel van Wolferen, "The Japan Problem," *Foreign Affairs*, spring 1986, 288.

23.   James Fallows, "Containing Japan," *Atlantic Monthly*, May 1989, 41.

24.   James Fallows, *Looking at the Sun* (New York: Pantheon Books, 1994), 19.

25.   Fallows, *Looking at the Sun*, 412, 422.

26.   Fallows, *Looking at the Sun*, 208.

27.   Fallows, *Looking at the Sun*, 445-446.

28.   Fallows, *Looking at the Sun*, 450.

29.   Fallows, "Containing Japan," 41.

30.   Fallows, "Containing Japan," 42-44, 54.

31.   Clyde Prestowitz, *Trading Places: How We Allowed Japan to Take the Lead*

(New York: Basic Books, 1988), 6.

32. Prestowitz, *Trading Places*, 13.

33. Prestowitz, *Trading Places*, 19, 22.

34. Prestowitz, *Trading Places*, 322, 324.

35. Michael A. Cusumano, *The Japanese Automobile Industry: Technology and Management at Nissan and Toyota* (Cambridge, Massachusetts: Harvard University Press, 1985), 299.

36. David Friedman, *The Misunderstood Miracle: Industrial Development and Political Change in Japan* (Ithaca, New York: Cornell University Press, 1988), 72.

37. Douglas Ostrom, "Postwar Japanese Industrial Policy and Changes in Industrial Structure" (Ph.D. diss., University of Michigan, 1984), 274-275.

38. Gary R. Saxonhouse, "Industrial Policy and Factor Markets: Biotechnology in Japan and the United States," in Hugh Patrick (ed.), *Japan's High Technology Industries* (Seattle: University of Seattle Press, 1986).

39. Kent Calder, *Strategic Capitalism: Private Business and Public Purpose in Japanese Industrial Finance* (Princeton: Princeton University Press, 1993), 14-15.

40. World Bank, *World Development Report, 1997: The State in a Changing World* (New York: Oxford University Press, 1997), 73-74.

41. World Bank, *World Development Report*, 1997, 1.

Chapter 16

Long-Term Prospects

Japan as OK

In the early 1990s, I attempted to project the broad lines of Japan's future economic development. The conclusions drawn in 1992 held up fairly well, although in retrospect, some of the details clearly were flawed. That report concluded:[1]

> Many of the characteristics that have qualified Japan's economic performance as an economic miracle are now in the midst of a transformation that is moving Japan from its outlier position among advanced economies to a more regular member of the league. . . . Because of the structural changes now occurring, a new phase of even slower growth over the next decade or more is highly likely. . . . In terms of economic growth rates, investment, productivity, and capital flows to the world, Japan is becoming a "regular" country, not quite the economic or financial superpower proclaimed by those who were dazzled by the fireworks of the late 1980s.

In fact, Japan's economy barely eked out an annual real per capita gain of 1 percent during the 1990s. In contrast, the inflation-adjusted rise in the 1980s averaged 3.5 percent a year. The "miracle" years of the 1960s produced growth rates in the double-digit range. In 1950, Japan's economy ranked seventh in the world on the basis of absolute gross domestic product and thirty-fourth in terms of per capita real GDP.[2] Subse-

319

quent development transformed Japan into the world's second-largest capitalist economy and placed it among the leaders in output per person.

Given such a dramatic metamorphosis in the second half of the twentieth century, what are the country's economic prospects for the next decade or so? The answers start from the observation that Japan is a developed, rich country that possesses the habits, institutions, rules of conduct, and politics of a successful nation. It is a society that works, and works well.

In 1979, Harvard University professor Ezra Vogel wrote one of the most popular foreign books ever published in Japan: *Japan as Number One: Lessons for Americans*.[3] Some fifteen years later, recognizing the many problems then besetting the Japanese economy as well as the possibility, according to the World Bank, that growth of China's aggregate output had moved that country into second place, I titled a report, *Japan As Number Three*.[4] Now, considering the economy's prospects for the next decade or two, perhaps a fitting epigram might be, *Japan as OK*.

Japan will not collapse like Rwanda or Haiti; rich countries do not do that. At the same time, it will not expand at the rate that it managed in the 1960s; rich countries do not behave that way, either. Instead, long-run real per capita growth will average around 1 percent to 2 percent a year. The higher number, sustained over decades, would qualify as a miracle for a rich country like Japan. It would mean a doubling of output per person every thirty-five years, or each generation. Growth at the lower end of the range could cause troubles—political, if not economic—because, under these circumstances, encouraging productive change by paying off economic losers would be difficult. Nevertheless, for a rich nation, 1 percent average annual growth is not a disaster, even if it is somewhat short of dynamic and even if it does mean a gradual slippage in Japan's relative international ranking.

These predictions are based on three empirical observations noted in earlier chapters: the relationship between growth and income levels, the similarity of Japan's institutions and government-economy links to those of the United States and other rich countries, and the relative adaptability of the economy to change. This trio of observations does not follow from theory; instead, it is based on pattern-recognition.

Low Growth Variability among Rich Countries

The first such regularity comes from observations reported in the Penn

World Table, a compilation of national economic accounts for 152 countries over forty years. Expenditures are denominated in a common currency so that real quantity comparisons can be made, both between countries and over time.

**Figure 16.1: Ten-Year Real GDP/Capita Growth and GDP/Capita
(percent and 1985 dollars at purchasing power parity)**

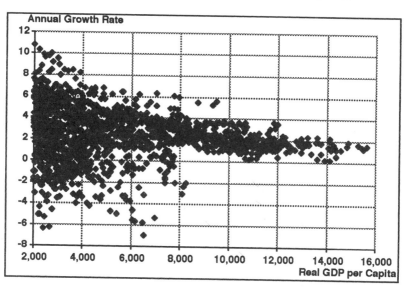

Source: Penn World Table, 5.6

The long-term relationship between growth and real per-capita income that had been described in the first chapter is repeated here in figure 16.1. Several conclusions flow from this scatter plot of global experience. First, high-speed growth occurs only among less-affluent countries, which are clustered at the left side of the figure. However, being poor is no guarantee of strong economic performance. Every collapsing country with negative growth was also a low-income nation.

Japan, though, is no longer a poor country. The essential point to be drawn from this chart for Japan's economic prospects is that among richer countries, growth rates converge. Variance declines as per capita GDP increases. Among the richer nations to the right side of the figure, the annual expansion rate over ten-year periods averaged under 2 percent. New Zealand's stagnation during the 1980s put it at the low end. Japan postwar history followed the pattern of other rich countries, with the economy sliding steadily down its growth curve until it fell below the average in the 1990s. From this perspective, Japan is not likely to fall apart—or to grow much above 2 percent a year for extended periods.

Japan's Institutions Similar to Anglo-American

The second set of observations derives from comparisons of Japan and other countries, as described in chapter 13. There are similarities among developed economies that assist in projecting Japan's future. However, before applying this experience, it is necessary to ask whether Japan is so different as to militate against comparison for prediction purposes; or is it sufficiently similar that we can be comfortable in placing the Japanese experience within the broader pattern.

To begin, it should be patently obvious to any observer that Japan is different from any other economy. The ability to discern differences, however, really is beside the point. It should be apparent that most countries are quite different from each other. Less evident is the extent to which Japan's economy and its government-business relationship are distinct; just as important is the basis for comparison.

To assess the degree of differences or similarities between Japan and other countries, I collected and analyzed eleven separate studies that included information on forty-six variables covering forty-six to one hundred fifty countries. (The variables and their sources are described in the appendix to chapter 13.) The problem is to find a way to deal with scores of variables in order to answer the questions: How different? How close? How far?

One approach involves calculating a multidimensional distance among variables for each pair of countries. Such an indicator makes use of the Pythagorean theorem that the distance between two points is the square root of the sum of the squares of the distances measured along each of the separate dimensions. In this case, a dimension is the same as a variable. This so-called Euclidean distance can be used to measure any number of dimensions or variables. (Variables were standardized to have a mean of zero and a standard deviation of one to avoid the inadvertent biasing of results that could result from arbitrary measurement scales.)

A second approach to measuring difference across an array of different dimensions is to calculate the so-called principal factors that may underlie the variables and then compute the distance between each country's group of factors, rather than between the original variables as in the first approach. Factor analysis is a statistical approach that can be used to analyze interrelationships among a large number of variables and to explain these variables in terms of their common underlying factors. The statistical approach condenses the information contained in the original variables into a smaller set of dimensions. The factors may be thought of as capturing the essence lurking behind a combination of variables.

The results of factor analysis often can be interpreted by examining the relations between the original variables and the way they are combined into factors. Four principal factors emerged from the forty-six original variables. The first factor, accounting for 40 percent of the variance among the variables, was strongly associated with efficient and competent government. The second factor dealt with small government as measured by taxes and government spending. The third most important factor was influenced mainly by open trade and foreign capital flows. The fourth was related to market price-setting mechanisms.

In a third approach, U.S. data are correlated with the same variables of each of the other countries. The correlation coefficient then becomes the measure of the closeness of each country to the United States.

Table 16.1 reports the results of the different approaches. It shows the distance of the nearest countries to the United States as ranked by the three methods. Not surprisingly, all methods rank the Anglo-Saxon heritage countries closest to the United States. Perhaps what is surprising to those who believe that deep differences separate Japan from this group is that Japan also is a member. A similar pattern appears when distances are measured from Japan.

It turns out that the distance measures, calculated by any of the methods discussed above, are associated with a country's affluence. Figure 13.1, for example, demonstrated a tight link between real per capita GDP and the correlation of a country's variables with those of the United States. Here, I take apart the factor analysis of chapter 13 to show the relationship between the first factor and income. As noted above, this factor corresponds to efficient and effective government with relatively low levels of intervention in the economy. Figure 16.2 compares real per capita GDP with the value of that factor. The correlation of 0.9 indicates that economic success is associated with effective, but relatively nonintrusive government.

What accounts for the similarity of economic institutions among more affluent countries? The data suggest the following hypothesis: If a country wants to get rich, it should mimic the institutions and behavior of rich economies. Similarity to the United States, as defined by the variables used in this analysis, is related to wealth. The implication is that wealthier nations have developed roughly equivalent institutions to achieve roughly the same results. In other words, countries are rich because they have adopted institutions that work and that are not too different from each other in a global comparison. Scholars can talk about German corporatism or British communal values or Japan's development state, but the institutions of these countries are qualitatively more similar to each other than to those of Somalia, Iran, Nicaragua, or Nepal—countries that are at the greatest institutional distance from the United States.

Table 16.1: Countries Ranked Closest to United States According to Three Distance Measures

Rank	Distance Based on 46 Variables	Distance Based on Four Principal Factors	Correlations Between Country Variables
1	United States	United States	United States
2	United Kingdom	New Zealand	New Zealand
3	Canada	Australia	United Kingdom
4	Australia	Switzerland	Canada
5	Japan	United Kingdom	Australia
6	France	Japan	Switzerland
7	Finland	Canada	Japan
8	Sweden	Chile	Denmark
9	Netherlands	Norway	Ireland
10	Spain	Denmark	Germany
11	Norway	Ireland	France
12	Austria	Finland	Netherlands
13	Chile	Taiwan	Taiwan
14	Malaysia	Netherlands	Hong Kong
15	Singapore	Israel	Finland

Although the different approaches to comparing Japan and other countries came up with essentially the same result, it could be argued that the selection of the original studies and variables predetermined the outcome. Serious issues remain concerning this approach, including the following:

- Obviously countries differ. Despite Japan's similarities to the United States at one scale of observation, there must be variables that distinguish it from Anglo-American patterns at different scales? At what level of resolution do significant distinctions appear?

- Has Japan changed over time with respect to similarities or differences? If so, have these changes affected economic performance?

- The observation that a country's real GDP per capita is related to its similarity to the United States is based on a cross-section at a specific time. Does this relationship extend over time? As countries become more or less like the United States, do they grow relatively richer or poorer?

• What does the pattern of behavior among rich countries tell us about policies that poorer countries might want to adopt? What are the specific dimensions of national and business governance that are related to getting rich? Are there lessons for developing countries from Japan's convergence toward rich-country norms?

These questions suggest the need for more research into how to measure differences among countries and into cross-national institutional convergence.

Figure 16.2: Relationship between First Principal Factor from Factor Analysis and Real per Capita Income
(1985 dollars at purchasing power parity)

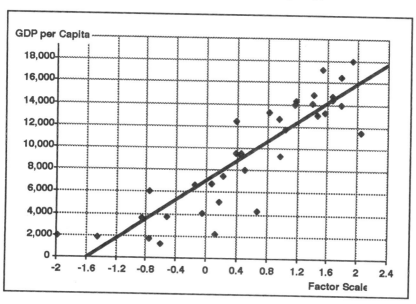

Structural Adaptation

Despite frequent and appropriate criticism of Japan for overregulation, rigidity, and collusive behavior, its economy has produced structural changes that are at least of the same magnitude as those in the United States. A seemingly moribund Japanese economy is as adaptive as the assertedly more flexible United States. This section borrows findings reported in chapter 11 on structural adaptation. Figure 16.3 compares structural change in Japan and the United States based on GDP originating in the forty comparable industries. As described in chapter 13, the employment curves lie even closer together than do the GDP curves.

Figure 16.3: Annual Structural Change of GDP in Forty Industries, Japan and United States, 1970-1999 (percent)

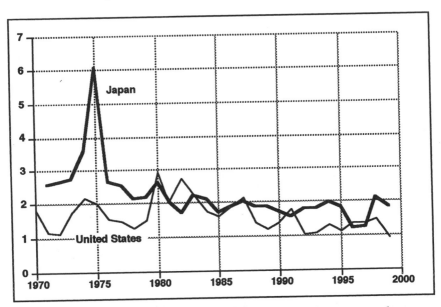

Every modern economy is bombarded moment by moment by unexpected shocks produced by innumerable events: floods, storms, strikes, politics, regulatory changes, legal decisions, war. Supply and demand are never still; tastes, fashions, technology, products, and attitudes shift in a neverending kaleidoscope of reconfiguring relations. The long term, also, reveals demographic transformations, economic growth and maturation, the evolution of institutions and political structures, and secular trends in the physical environment. The point of this litany is to suggest that economic structure must adapt to these changes or be left in the wake of those that do. It is instructive that Japan progressed from being a relatively undeveloped country in the 1930s and 1940s to its present status among the largest and richest. This evidence should suggest that its economy has been successful in mutating to meet a barrage of small and large shocks. Year-to-year changes in industry-specific shares of employment and GDP provide an informative indicator of economywide adaptability.

Both countries restructured at the industry level with comparable amounts of reshuffling of output and employment. Japan was not a noticeable laggard in its flexibility, at least compared with the United States. If adaptability is a mark of a successful modern economy, Japan meets this criterion.

Change Japan-Style

History suggests that rich countries grow within fairly well defined limits. In order to attain a high level of income in the first place, nations must have in place institutions and practices that allow markets to work effectively within an appropriate government-established infrastructure. Just such a framework has allowed Japan's economy to adapt to an always-shifting environment. However, the preservation of these achievements is not automatic. It requires constant struggle on both the political and economic fronts. When shocks occur, especially if they are multiple, the struggle can continue for many years before effective policies are put forward and implemented by bold governments in the face of considerable opposition.

Japan's economy is in the midst of adapting to major changes. For example, in 2000, there were 1,635 mergers and acquisitions among domestic firms, according to industry specialist Recof Corp. In 1990, the figure was 754, and in 1986 only 260. Foreign concerns buying domestic firms totaled 175 in 2000 compared with just 11 in 1989. Similarly, KPMG LLP calculated that the amount of foreign money going into Japanese acquisitions reached more than $20 billion annually in 1999 and 2000, up by more than a factor of ten from earlier in the decade.

Deregulation in industries as diverse as finance and air transport is producing markets that have become as free and open as America's. Nevertheless, how this process has unfolded has implications for the future. Take air travel, for instance. As related in chapter 12, deregulation has proceeded with a distinctive Japanese cast. Deregulation of the air transport industry took more than twenty years. A search for consensus required more than a quarter-century to open a much-needed second runway at Narita International Airport. Regulators avoided a direct confrontation with the nation's go-slow air traffic controllers, but over the course of a decade or two, they were able to increase flight frequencies substantially at major airports. Moreover, Japan's major airlines are reducing their costs to internationally competitive levels, although the process may seem protracted. Slowness in reducing bloated airline payrolls is a reminder that lifetime employment is difficult for corporate Japan to abandon despite economic pressures from all sides to cut costs.

A similar story could be told about the privatization of Japan's nationalized industries in the 1980s. Japan Tobacco nominally was privatized in 1985. However, shares in the company were not sold to the public until 1994. Sixteen years after conversion to a private corporation, the government still held two-thirds of the company. In the meantime, the numbers of one of the most important pressure groups opposing privatization, tobacco farmers, fell from close to 100,000 to fewer than 25,000. Foreign competition in both leaf and cigarettes compelled JT to be more cost conscious, which means, ultimately, to buy tobacco at the lowest possible price. All of these changes occurred over a period measured in decades. At the end of this period, perhaps by 2005, Japan Tobacco will be a fully privatized company. This twenty-year process is another example of privatization with Japanese characteristics.

The story of Japan Tobacco was repeated for the other government-run corporations privatized in 1985. At the end of 2001, the government still held 44.5 percent of Nippon Telegraph and Telephone, 12.5 percent of Japan Railroad East, 41.5 percent of Japan Railroad West, and 39 percent of Japan Railroad Central.

Managing change in such a civilized manner may not always be possible, especially if the lineup of economic and political forces becomes less favorable. In the time that it takes to open markets Japan-style, the world moves on. For example, Japanese airlines are struggling to lower costs and increase efficiency almost a quarter-century after their American counterparts faced the same challenges. In the meantime, U.S. carriers adopted new business approaches that leave the Japanese industry at a disadvantage. In the future, it may not be sufficient to deregulate according to a schedule that fits Japanese sensibilities.

Japan's Economic Prospects

In the end, whether a developed nation grows at 1 percent a year or 2 percent does make a difference. The higher number suggests a vigorous economy; the lower one indicates stagnation. The costs of a graying society are tolerable at the faster rate, but an enormous burden at the scaled-back one. Slow growth itself is an impediment to beneficial changes. Deregulatory initiatives, for example, that cause unemployment while generating greater efficiencies and new opportunities are less likely to be implemented when growth is slow.

Sharply higher productivity is the way out of the slow-growth trap. Unfortunately, the intense competition that seems to stimulate firms to create new efficiencies is lacking in many areas of Japan's economy. The McKinsey Global Institute, the research arm of management consultant McKinsey & Co., Inc., estimates that Japanese manufacturers that compete internationally are 20 percent more productive than their American counterparts. Manufacturing and services firms that are domestically oriented are only 63 percent as efficient. Economywide, capital in Japan generates approximately 40 percent lower returns than in the United States or Western Europe. The productivity gap for labor is 31 percent. McKinsey estimates that overall productivity of the entire economy is one-third below the American level.[5]

At the risk of repetition, raising productivity and returns to capital are the keys to a faster-expanding Japan. Other advanced countries have demonstrated the possibilities. In air transport, for example, numerous business models already tested by the world's airlines are available for consideration. If, from its present productivity position 33 percent behind the United States, Japan were to catch up over the next twenty years, it would add 1.4 percent a year to its GDP growth rate

These examples are intended to demonstrate the utter feasibility of accelerated GDP gains in Japan. One factor holding up the necessary moves is the myth of stability. The belief that change is both unprecedented and unwelcome is widespread. Remarkably, the Japanese media has paid little attention to the structural changes that actually occur on a regular basis, highlighted by the disappearance of some 86,000 manufacturing establishments between 1991 and 1996 and the accompanying net loss of more than 1.2 million jobs. These and other indicators of the economy's flexibility apparently also have not been recognized by the public. Even people who have been forced to change jobs seem to believe that their personal history is unshared by others.

The evidence belies the notion that people do not move from job to job in Japan and that the country's industries and companies are static. More importantly, such thinking restricts policy choices. The myth of a rigid economy has been a major barrier to freeing the country from its political inhibitions.

However, the implication of Japan being a modern, rich, developed economy is that it responds to the forces acting on it through democratic political processes. Japan is a democracy. Its political parties respond to new demands. Politicians know how to count, especially votes and financial support. The Liberal Democratic Party, in particular, has remained in power for the better part of fifty years because of its ability to develop policies that responded to shifting conditions. However, the size of the LDP's traditional support groups has been shrinking because of demographic changes, urbanization, and the growth of the white-collar service sector. Consequently, the forces for political change are present and growing. The selection of Junichiro Koizumi as prime minister in 2001 while espousing policies antithetical to the interests of traditional LDP clients is an illustration of this change.

Nevertheless, political and economic influences can operate at the unhurried pace of continental drift. Social scientists are as incapable as geologists of estimating when or whether the accumulating stresses will be relieved by violent shaking or by gradual accommodation. Nevertheless, ten years time could establish a new political-economic base that favors a more open economic system, coalesced around a political party that represents progressive economic interests.

Nevertheless, the intervening process can be marked by hopeful starts followed by disappointing setbacks. It can take longer to achieve a reformed political system and restructured economy than many foreign observers would find acceptable. Japan, though, did not arrive at its position among the largest, richest, and most productive economies by accident. The virtues that brought it this far also establish the foundation for the future.

Notes

1.   Arthur J. Alexander, "Japan's Economy: A Transformation?" *JEI Report*, no. 11 (March 20, 1992): 1, 10.

2.   Country rankings were derived from the Penn World Tables, described in Robert Summers and Alan Heston, "The Penn World Tables (Mark 5): An Expanded Set of International Comparisons, 1950-1988," *Quarterly Journal of Economics* 106, no. 2 (May 1991): 327-368.

3.   Ezra Vogel, *Japan as Number One: Lessons for Americans* (Cambridge, Mass.: Harvard University Press, 1979).

4.   Arthur J. Alexander, "Japan As Number Three: Long-Term Productivity And Growth Problems In The Economy," *JEI Report*, no. 17 (April 29, 1994).

5.   McKinsey Global Institute, *Why the Japanese Economy Is Not Growing: Micro Barriers to Productivity Growth* (Washington, D.C.: July 2000), Executive Summary.

Bibliography

Acs, Zoltan, David B. Audretsch, and Maryann P. Feldman. "Real Effects of Academic Research: Comment." *American Economic Review* 82, no. 1 (March 1992).

Adams, James D. "Fundamental Stocks of Knowledge and Productivity Growth." *Journal of Political Economy* 98, no. 4 (August 1990).

Alexander, Arthur J. "Japan's Economy: A Transformation?" *JEI Report*, no. 11 (March 20, 1992).

————. Japan As Number Three: Long-Term Productivity And Growth Problems In The Economy." *JEI Report*, no. 17 (April 29, 1994).

Allen, Polly Reynolds. "The Economic and Policy Implications of the NATREX (Natural Real Exchange) Approach." In *Fundamental Determinants of Exchange Rates*, edited by Jerome L. Stein. Oxford, England: Oxford University Press, 1995.

American Chamber of Commerce in Japan. *Trade and Investment in Japan: The Current Environment*. Tokyo: June 1991.

American Metal Market. "NKK, Kawasaki Agree to Merge." April 16, 2001.

Ariga, Kenn, Giorgio Brunello, Yasushi Ohkusa, and Yoshihiko Nishiyama. "Corporate Hierarchy, Promotion, and Firm Growth: Japanese Internal Labor Market in Transition." *Journal of the Japanese and International Economies* 6, no. 6 (December 1992).

Asahi Shimbun. "Wacoal Enjoys Booming Business in U.S. Lingerie Market." September 25, 1999.

Aviation Week & Space Technology. "Kansai Warming." January 23, 1995.

Azar, Edward. *The Codebook of the Conflict and Peace Data Bank (COPDAB)*. College Park, Md.: University of Maryland, 1982.

Bank of Japan Quarterly Bulletin. "Japan's International Investment Position as of End-1999." (August 2000).

————. "Japan's Balance of Payments for 1999." (May 2000).

Bargas, Sylvia E. "Direct Investment Positions for 1999: Country and Industry Detail." *Survey of Current Business* (July 2000).

Bayoumi, Tamim, et al. "The Robustness of Equilibrium Exchange Rate Calculations to Alternative Assumptions and Methodologies." In *Es-*

timating Equilibrium Exchange Rates, edited by John Williamson. Washington, D.C.: Institute for International Economics, 1994.

Berger, Suzanne. "Introduction." In *National Diversity and Global Capitalism*, edited by Suzanne Berger and Ronald Dore. Ithaca, N.Y.: Cornell University Press, 1996.

Blonigen, Bruce A. "Firm-Specific Assets and the Link Between Exchange Rates and Foreign Direct Investment." *American Economic Review* (June 1997).

Boyer, Robert. "The Convergence Hypothesis Revisited: Globalization but Still the Century of Nations?" In *National Diversity and Global Capitalism*, edited by Suzanne Berger and Ronald Dore. Ithaca, N.Y.: Cornell University Press, 1996.

Brainard, S. Lael. "An Empirical Assessment of the Proximity-Concentration Trade-off Between Multinational Sales and Trade." *American Economic Review* 87, no. 3 (September 1997).

Branstetter, Lee. *Are Knowledge Spillovers International or Intranational in Scope? Microeconomic Evidence from the U.S. and Japan.* Working Paper 5800. Cambridge, Mass.: National Bureau of Economic Research, October 1996.

Budner, Stanley, and Ellis Krauss. "Newspaper Coverage of U.S.-Japan Frictions." *Asian Survey* (April 1995).

Burress, Charles. "Yellow Peril Between the Lines: The American Press Covers Japan." Master's project, University of California at Berkeley, Graduate School of Journalism, August 30, 1995.

Calder, Kent. *Strategic Capitalism: Private Business and Public Purpose in Japanese Industrial Finance.* Princeton, N.J.: Princeton University Press, 1993.

Caves, Richard E. *Multinational Enterprise and Economic Analysis.* New York: Cambridge University Press, 1996.

Clark, Robert L., and Naohiro Ogawa. "Employment Tenure and Earnings Profiles in Japan and the United States: Comment." *American Economic Review* 82, no. 1 (March 1992).

Crawcour, Sydney. "Economic Change in the Nineteenth Century." In *The Cambridge History of Japan, Vol. 5, The Nineteenth Century*, edited by Marius Jansen. Cambridge, England and New York: Cambridge University Press, 1989.

Cusumano, Michael A. *The Japanese Automobile Industry: Technology and Management at Nissan and Toyota.* Cambridge, Mass.: Harvard University Press, 1985.

Darby, Michael R., and Lynne G. Zucker. *Star Scientists, Institutions, and the Entry of Japanese Biotechnology Enterprises.* Working Paper 5795. Cambridge, Mass.: National Bureau of Economic Research, October 1996.

Davies, John. *The Global Event-Data System, Coders' Manual.* College Park, Md.: University of Maryland, 1998.

De Long, J. Bradford, and Lawrence H. Summers. "Equipment Investment and Economic Growth." *Quarterly Journal of Economics* 106, no. 2 (May 1991).

Dower, John. *War Without Mercy: Race and Power in the Pacific War.* New York: Pantheon Books, 1986.

Dunne, Timothy, Mark Roberts, and Larry Samuelson. "Patterns of Firm Entry and Exit in U.S. Manufacturing Industries." *RAND Journal of Economics* 19, no. 4 (winter 1988).

Eichengreen, Barry. "Historical Research on International Lending and Debt." *Journal of Economic Perspectives* 5, no. 2 (spring 1991).

Engel, Charles and John Rogers. "How Wide is the Border?" *American Economic Review* 86, no. 5 (December 1996).

Epstein, Joshua, and Jon Pevehouse. "Reciprocity, Bullying and International Cooperation: Time-Series Analysis of the Bosnia Conflict." *American Political Science Review* 91, no. 3 (September 1997).

Fallows, James. "Containing Japan." *The Atlantic Monthly* (May 1989).

———. *Looking at the Sun.* New York: Pantheon Books, 1994.

Ford, Harold. "The Primary Purpose of National Estimating." *Studies in Intelligence.* (fall 1991) (unclassified).

Frankel, Jeffrey. "On the Mark: A Theory of Floating Exchange Rates Based on Real Interest Differentials." *American Economic Review* 69, no. 4 (September 1979).

Frankel, Jeffrey, and David Romer. "Does Trade Cause Growth?" *American Economic Review* 89, no. 3 (June 1999).

Friedman, David. *The Misunderstood Miracle: Industrial Development and Political Change in Japan.* Ithaca, N.Y.: Cornell University Press, 1988.

Gastil, Raymond. *Freedom in the World: Political Rights and Civil Liberties, 1986-1987.* New York: Greenwood Press, 1987.

Geroski, P. A. *Market Dynamics and Entry.* Cambridge, Mass.: Blackwell, 1991.

Gerschenkron, Alexander. "Economic Backwardness in Historical Perspective." In *Economic Backwardness in Historical Perspective*, edited by Alexander Gerschenkron. Cambridge, Mass.: Harvard University Press, 1966.

———. "The Approach to European Industrialization: A Postscript," In *Economic Backwardness in Historical Perspective*, edited by Alexander Gerschenkron. Cambridge, Mass.: Harvard University Press, 1966.

Goldberg, Pinelopi Koujianou, and Giovanni Maggi. "Protection For Sale: An Empirical Investigation." *American Economic Review* 93, no. 5 (December 1999).

Goleman, Daniel. "The Group and the Self: New Focus on a Cultural Rift." *New York Times* (December 25, 1990).

Gollop, Frank M., and James L. Monahan. "A Generalized Index of Diversification: Trends in U.S. Manufacturing." *Review of Economics and Statistics* 73 (1991).

Goto, Akita. "Statistical Evidence on the Diversification of Japanese Large Firms." *Journal of Industrial Economics* 29 (March 1981).

Graham, Edward M. "The Relationship Between Trade and Foreign Direct Investment in the Manufacturing Sector: Empirical Results for the United States and Japan." In *Does Ownership Matter: Japanese Multinationals in East Asia,* edited by Dennis Encarnacion. London: Oxford University Press, 1997.

Graham, Edward M., and Paul R. Krugman. *Foreign Direct Investment in the United States.* 2nd ed. Washington, D.C.: Institute for International Economics, 1991.

Gwartney, James D. *Economic Freedom of the World, 1975-95.* Vancouver, British Columbia: Fraser Institute, 1996.

Hall, Maximilian J. B. *Financial Reform in Japan: Causes and Consequences.* Northampton, Mass.: Edward Elgar Publishing Co., 1998.

Hanada, Mitsuyo. "The Principle of Competition in Japan's Personnel System." *Japanese Economic Studies.* (winter 1988-89).

Harney, Alexandra. "Airlines Get That Sinking Feeling Over Japan." *Financial Times* (30 November 1990).

Hashimoto Masanori, and John Raisian. "Employment Tenure and Earnings Profiles in Japan and the United States: Reply." *American Economic Review* 82, no. 1 (March 1992).

Heston, Alan, and Robert Summers. "The Penn World Table (Mark 5): An Expanded Set of International Comparisons, 1950-1988." *Quarterly Journal of Economics* 106, no. 2 (May 1991).

Holloway, Nigel. "School of Steel." *Far Eastern Economic Review.* October 9, 1997.

Holmes, Kim, Bryan Johnson, and Melanie Kirkpatrick, eds. *1997 Index of Economic Freedom.* Washington, D.C.: Heritage Foundation, 1997.

Hori, Shintaro. "Fixing Japan's White-Collar Economy." *Harvard Business Review* (November-December 1993).

Hoshi, Takeo, Anil Kashyap, David Scharfstein. "The Role of Banks in Reducing the Costs of Financial Distress in Japan." *Journal of Financial Economics* (1990).

Howenstine, Ned G., and Rosaria Troia. "Foreign Direct Investment in the United States: New Investment in 1999." *Survey of Current Business* (June 1990).

International Monetary Fund and Organization for Economic Cooperation and Development. *Report on the Survey of Implementation of Methodological Standards for Direct Investment.* Washington, D.C.: International Monetary Fund, March 2000.

Ito, Takatoshi. "Short-Run and Long-Run Expectations of the Yen/Dollar Exchange Rate." *Journal of the Japanese and International Economies* 8, no. 2 (June 1994).

Jaffe, Adam B. "Real Effects of Academic Research." *American Economic Review* 79, no. 4 (December 1989).

Jaffe, Adam, and Manuel Trajtenberg. *International Knowledge Flows: Evidence from Patent Citations.* Working Paper 6507. Cambridge, Mass.: National Bureau of Economic Research, April 1998.

Jaffe, Adam, Manuel Trajtenberg, and Rebecca Henderson. "Geographic Localization of Knowledge Spillovers as Evidenced by Patent Citations." *Quarterly Journal of Economics* 108, no. 3 (August 1993).

Japan Pacific Resources Network. "Media Biases in Covering Japan." *JPRN Monograph* 010. Oakland, Calif.: Japan Pacific Resources Network, October 4, 1993.

Japan Times. "New Fare Rules May Hurt Discounters." February 23, 1994.

———. "Narita Second in Air Cargo Volume in 1999." February 24, 2001.

———. "System Is Sought to Cut Air Fares, End Discount War." June 16, 1993.

Johnson, Chalmers. *MITI and the Japanese Miracle: The Growth of Industrial Policy, 1925-1975.* Stanford, Cal.: Stanford University Press, 1982.

Johnson, Chalmers, ed. *Japan: Who Governs?* New York: W.W. Norton, 1995.

Johnson, Sheila K. *American Attitudes Toward Japan, 1941-1975.* Washington, D.C.: American Enterprise Institute, 1975.

Katz, Richard. *Japan, The System That Soured: The Rise and Fall of the Japanese Economic Miracle.* Armonk, N.Y.: M.E. Sharpe, 1998.

Killen, Patrick. "A Tale of Two Airports, or Three." *Journal of the American Chamber of Commerce in Japan* (February 2000).

Kim, Jong-Il, and Lawrence J. Lau. "The Sources of Economic Growth of the East Asian Newly Industrialized Countries." *Journal of the Japanese and International Economies* 8, no. 3 (September 1994).

Klein, Burton F. *Dynamic Economics*. Cambridge, Mass.: Harvard University Press, 1977.

Landefeld, J. Steven, Ann M. Lawson and Douglas Weinberg. "Rates of Return on Direct Investment." *Survey of Current Business* (August 1992).

Larke, Roy. *Japanese Retailing*. New York: Routledge, 1994.

Larkins, Daniel. "Note on Rates of Return for Domestic Nonfinancial Corporations: Revised Estimates for 1960-98." *Survey of Current Business* (June 2000).

Laster, David S. and Robert N. McCauley. "Making Sense of the Profits of Foreign Firms in the United States." *Federal Reserve Bank of New York Quarterly Review* (summer-fall 1994).

Latzy, John, and Randy Miller. "Controlled Foreign Corporations, 1988." *Statistics of Income Bulletin* (fall 1992).

Lichtenberg, Frank. *R&D Investment and International Productivity Differences*. Working Paper No. 4161. Cambridge, Mass.: National Bureau of Economic Research, 1992.

Lichtenberg, Frank, and Bruno van Pottelsberghe de la Potterie. *International R&D Spillovers: A Reexamination*. Working Paper 5668. Cambridge, Mass: National Bureau of Economic Research, July 1996.

MacDonald Ronald, and Jun Nagayasu. "On the Japanese Yen-U.S. Dollar Exchange Rate: A Structural Econometric Model Based on Real Interest Differentials." *Journal of the Japanese and International Economies* 12, no. 1 (March 1998).

Maddison, Angus. "Standardised Estimates of Fixed Capital Stock: A Six-Country Comparison." In *Explaining the Economic Performance of Nations*, edited by Angus Maddison. Brookfield, Vt.: Edward Elgar Publishing Co., 1995.

———. "Ultimate and Proximate Growth Causality." In *Explaining the Economic Performance of Nations*, edited by Angus Maddison. Brookfield, Vt.: Edward Elgar Publishing Co., 1995.

Management and Coordination Agency, Statistics Bureau. *Japan Statistical Yearbook*. (Tokyo: Management and Coordination Agency, various years).

Mansfield, Edwin. "Academic Research Underlying Industrial Innovation: Sources, Characteristics, and Financing." *Review of Economics and Statistics* 77, no. 1 (February 1995).

———. "Industrial Innovation in Japan and the United States." *Science* 241 (September 30, 1988).

Mark, Nelson C. "Exchange Rates and Fundamentals: Evidence on Long-Horizon Predictability." *American Economic Review* 85, no. 1 (March 1995).

Marston, Richard C. "Real Exchange Rates and Productivity Growth in the United States and Japan." In *Real Financial Linkages among Open Economies*, edited by Sven W. Arndt and J. David Richardson. Cambridge, Mass.: MIT Press, 1987.

Mataloni, Raymond J. Jr. "A Guide to BEA Statistics on U.S. Multinational Companies." *Survey of Current Business* (March 1995).

———. "An Examination of the Low Rate of Return of Foreign-Owned U.S. Companies." *Survey of Current Business* (March 2000).

———. "U.S. Multinational Companies, Operations in 1998." *Survey of Current Business* (July 2000).

Mauro, Paolo. "Corruption and Growth." *Quarterly Journal of Economics* 110, no. 3 (August 1995).

May, Robert M. "The Scientific Wealth of Nations." *Science* 275 (February 7, 1997).

McCauley R. N., and S. A. Zimmer. "Explaining International Differences in the Cost of Capital." *Quarterly Review,* Federal Reserve Bank of New York (summer 1992).

McClelland, Charles. "Let the User Beware." *International Studies Quarterly* 27, no. 2 (1983).

McKinnon, Roland I. "The Rules of the Game: International Money in Historical Perspective." *Journal of Economic Literature* 31, no. 1 (March 1993).

McKinsey Global Institute. *Service Sector Productivity.* Washington, D.C.: McKinsey Global Institute, 1992.

———. *Manufacturing Productivity.* Washington, D.C.: McKinsey Global Institute, 1993.

———. *Capital Productivity.* Washington, D.C.: McKinsey Global Institute, June 1996.

———. *Why the Japanese Economy Is Not Growing: Micro Barriers to Productivity Growth.* Washington, D.C.: McKinsey Global Institute, July 2000.

Meredith, Guy, and Menzie Chinn. *Long-Horizon Uncovered Interest Rate Parity.* Working Paper 6797. Cambridge, Mass.: National Bureau of Economic Research, November 1998.

Merritt, Richard, Robert Muncaster, and Dina Zinnes, eds. *International Event-Data Development: Data Development for International Re-*

search, Phase II. Ann Arbor, Mich.: University of Michigan Press, 1993

Morrow, James, Randolph Siverson, and Tressa Tabares. "The Political Determinants of International Trade: The Major Powers, 1907-90." *American Political Science Review* 92, no. 3 (September 1998).

Muhleisen, Martin. "Too Much of a Good Thing? The Effectiveness of Fiscal Stimulus." In *Post-Bubble Blues: How Japan Responded to Asset Price Collapse,* edited by Tamim Bayoumi and Charles Collyns. Washington, D.C.: International Monetary Fund, 1999.

Narin, Francis. *Linkage between Basic Research and Patented Technology.* Haddon Heights, N.J.: CHI Research, August 14, 1996.

Narin, Francis, Kimberly Hamilton, and Dominic Olivastro. "The Increasing Linkage between U.S. Technology and Public Science." *Research Policy* 26 (1997).

National Science Board. *Science & Engineering Indicators—2000.* NSB-00-1. Arlington, Va.: National Science Foundation, 2000.

Nikkei. "Nippon Steel, NTT, Others to Sell Discount Air Tickets." August 4, 1997.

————. "New Airlines Face Pressing Maintenance Issue." April 9, 1999.

————. "Credit Co-Op Failures Soar Over Past Five Years." October 20, 2000.

Nikkei Weekly. "Transport Ministry to Cut Landing Fees at Local Airports by One-Third." August 10, 1998.

————. "Fare Rules Loosened for Domestic Flights." December 5, 1994.

————. "Unfettered Air Fares Fly Higher." February 26, 1996.

————. "Japan Airlines Rights Itself Through Cost Cuts." February 7, 2000.

Noland, Marcus. "Chasing Phantoms: The Political Economy of USTR." *International Organization* 51, no. 3 (summer 1997).

Northridge, A .R. "Pearl Harbor: Estimating Then and Now." *Studies in Intelligence* (fall 1965) (declassified June 24, 1994).

Ohkawa, Kazushi, and Henry Rosovsky. *Japanese Economic Growth.* Stanford, Calif.: Stanford University Press, 1973.

Organization for Economic Cooperation and Development. *Structural Adjustment and Economic Performance.* (Paris: OECD, 1987).

————. *OECD Economic Surveys: Japan, 1996-1997.* (Paris: OECD, 1997).

————. *Main Science and Technology Indicators.* (Paris: OECD, 2001).

Oriental Economist. "Japan's Cautious Airline Deregulation: How Far

Will It Go?" June 1985.

Ostrom, Douglas. "Postwar Japanese Industrial Policy and Changes in Industrial Structure." Ph.D. diss., University of Michigan, 1984.

Pack, Howard. "Endogenous Growth Theory: Intellectual Appeal and Empirical Shortcomings." *Journal of Economic Perspectives* 8, no. 1 (winter 1994).

Pigott, Charles. "International Interest Rate Convergence: A Survey of the Issues and Evidence." *Federal Reserve Bank of New York Quarterly Review* 18, no. 4 (winter 1993-1994).

Prestowitz, Clyde. *Trading Places: How We Allowed Japan to Take the Lead.* New York: Basic Books, 1988.

Rodrik, Dani. "Understanding Economic Policy Reform." *Journal of Economic Literature* 34, no. 1 (March 1996).

Romer, Paul M. "The Origins of Endogenous Growth." *Journal of Economic Perspectives* 8, no. 1 (winter 1994).

Rosovsky, Henry. *Capital Formation in Japan: 1868-1940.* Glencoe, Ill.: The Free Press, 1961.

Sarno, Lucio, and Mark Taylor. "Official Intervention in the Foreign Exchange Market: Is It Effective and, If So, How Does It Work?" *Journal of Economic Literature* 39 no. 3 (September 2001).

Saxonhouse, Gary R. "Industrial Policy and Factor Markets: Biotechnology in Japan and the United States." In *Japan's High Technology Industries*, edited by Hugh Patrick. Seattle, Wash.: University of Seattle Press, 1986.

———. "What Does Japanese Trade Structure Tell Us About Japanese Trade Policy." *Journal of Economic Perspectives* 7, no. 3 (summer, 1993).

Schoppa, Leonard. *Bargaining with Japan: What American Pressure Can and Cannot Do.* New York: Columbia University Press, 1997.

Shimazaki, Toson. *Before the Dawn (Yo-ake Mae).* Translated by William Naff. Honolulu, Hawaii: University of Hawaii Press, 1987.

Stein, Jerome L. "The Natural Real Exchange Rate of the US Dollar and Determinants of Capital Flows." In *Estimating Equilibrium Exchange Rates*, edited by John Williamson. Washington, D.C.: Institute for International Economics, 1994.

Sugiwara, Sandra. "Japan's 1st No-Frills Airline Steers to Uncharted Territory." *Washington Post* (February 10, 1997).

Summers, Robert, and Alan Heston. "The Penn World Table (Mark 5): An Expanded Set of International Comparisons, 1950-1988." *Quarterly Journal of Economics* 106, no. 2 (May 1991).

Taylor, Mark. "The Economics of Exchange Rates." *Journal of Eco-*

nomic Literature 32, no. 1 (March 1995).

Thornton, Daniel L. "Tests of Covered Interest Rate Parity." *Federal Reserve Bank of St. Louis Review* 71, no. 4 (July-August, 1989).

Tilton, Mark. *Restrained Trade: Cartels in Japan's Basic Materials Industries.* Ithaca, N.Y.: Cornell University Press, 1996.

Triffin, Robert. *The Evolution of the International Monetary System: Historical Reappraisal and Future Perspectives.* Princeton Studies in International Finance No. 12. Princeton, N.J.: Princeton University Press, 1964.

Turner, Dave, Pete Richardson and Sylvia Rauffet. *The Role of Real and Nominal Rigidities in Macroeconomic Adjustment: A Comparative Study of the G3 Economies.* OECD Economic Studies, 21. (Paris: OECD, winter 1993.

van Ark, Bart, and Dirk Pilat. "Cross-Country Productivity Levels: Differences and Causes." *Brookings Papers on Economic Activity: Microeconomics* no. 2 (1993).

van Wolferen, Karel G. "The Japan Problem." *Foreign Affairs* 65, no. 2 (spring 1986).

———. *The Enigma of Japanese Power: People and Politics in a Stateless Nation.* New York, Alfred A. Knopf, 1989.

———. "The Japan Problem Revisited." *Foreign Affairs* 69, no. 1 (fall 1990).

Vaporis, Constantine. "To Edo and Back: Alternate Attendance and Japanese Culture in the Early Modern Period." *Journal of Japanese Studies* 23, no. 1 (1997).

Vincent, Jack. "WEIS vs. COPDAB: Correspondence Problems." *International Studies Quarterly* 27, no. 2 (1983).

Vogel, Ezra. *Japan as Number One: Lessons for Americans.* Cambridge, Mass.: Harvard University Press, 1979.

Wacoal America, Inc. *Tenth Anniversary.* (1991).

Washington Post. "TV Week," March 26-April 1, 1995.

Weinstein, David E. *Foreign Direct Investment and Keiretsu: Rethinking U.S. and Japanese Policy.* Working Paper No. 122. New York: Center on Japanese Economy and Business, Columbia University, June 1996.

Wolff, Edward N. "Capital Formation and Productivity Convergence Over the Long Term." *American Economic Review* 81, no. 2 (June 1991).

Women's Wear Daily. August 24, 1992.

World Bank, *The East Asian Miracle: Economic Growth and Public Policy.* New York: Oxford University Press, 1993.

————. *World Development Report, 1997: The State in a Changing World*. New York: Oxford University Press, 1997.

————. *World Development Report, 1999: Entering the 21st Century*. Washington, D.C.: World Bank,1999.

————. *World Development Indicators*. Washington, D.C.: World Bank, 2000

Wren-Lewis, Simon, and Rebecca L. Driver. *Real Exchange Rates for the Year 2000*. Washington, D.C.: Institute for International Economics, 1998.

Yamamura, Kozo. "Toward a Reexamination of the Economic History of Tokugawa Japan, 1600-1867." *Journal of Economic History* (September 1973).

Zucker, Lynne, and Michael Darby. "Present at the Biotechnological Revolution: Transformation of Technological Identity for a Large Incumbent Pharmaceutical Firm." *Research Policy* 26 (1997).

————. *Capturing Technological Opportunity via Japan's Star Scientists: Evidence From Japanese Firms' Biotech Patents and Products*. Working Paper 6360. Cambridge, Mass.: National Bureau of Economic Research, January 1998.

Zucker, Lynne, Michael Darby, and Marilynn Brewer. "Intellectual Human Capital and the Birth of U.S. Biotechnology Enterprises." *American Economic Review* 88, no. 1 (March 1998).

Index

All Nippon Airways Co., 229-32, 235, 237-40, 243-53
asset-price bubble, 2, 7, 12, 109, 250; and bad loans, 10; and investment, 5, 28, 65, 101, 111; and revisionist writers, 315; and United States, 146, 152, 285, 310
Azar, Edward, 191, 215-16

balance of payments, 95-97, 109, 112, 126
Bain & Company, 43
Bank of Japan, 7, 99; and exchange rates, 96; and FDI data, 167, 170, 173
big bang (financial), 9-10, 184
biotechnology, 86-88, 313
Boyington, Pappy, 292
Branstetter, Lee, 85, 91
Bretton Woods, 94, 310
Bridgestone Corp., 146
Budner, Stanley, 290, 294
Burress, Charles, 290, 294

Calder, Kent, 314, 318
Canada, 89, 225; and FDI, 139, 143, 164; similarity to Japan and United States, 256, 259-66
capital stock, 5, 27-29, 46, 62, 67-68, 74, 109
Caves, Richard, 114, 148
CBS News, 287
Central Intelligence Agency, 273
CHI Research, 81, 83, 91
Clinton, William, 194, 197, 210-11, 297, 311-12

Cold War, 79, 197, 203, 211
Columbia Pictures Entertainment, 146, 280
Conflict and Peace Data Bank (COPDAB), 191-94, 198, 210, 213-16
convergence hypothesis, 265, 271
corporate governance, 16, 163, 172, 325
covered interest rate parity, 122-23
current account, 68, 93-102, 111-13, 126-27, 132, 135-36, 315

Dai-Ichi Kangyo Bank, 308
DaimlerChrysler, 175
De Long, Bradford, 55, 62, 74
Deutsch, Robert, 274
DirecTV, Inc., 183
diversification, 52-53
Dodge, Joseph, 24
Dower, John, 275, 293-95

economic miracle, 4-5, 12, 23-24, 37, 40, 57, 68, 284, 297-300, 309, 319-20
Economic Planning Agency, 8, 74, 220-21
Euclidean distance, 259, 271, 322
events data, 189-93
exchange rate, 97, 107, 111-12, 115-39, 150, 152, 160, 164, 167, 175, 269, 310
exports, 116, 144, 178, 215; and balance of payments, 96-97; and exchange rates, 120-21, 126-28, 136-37; and FDI, 164-66, 178; and Japanese economic growth,

About the Author

Dr. Arthur Alexander was president of the Japan Economic Institute in Washington, D.C., from 1990 to its closing in 2000; he conducted research on the Japanese economy, industry, technology, and innovation. In that capacity, he testified often before the U.S. congress on Japanese economic issues. He is a visiting professor at Georgetown University and has taught at George Mason University, the Johns Hopkins University School of Advanced International Studies, the University of California, Los Angeles, and the Rand Graduate School. Dr. Alexander grew up in Carbondale, Pennsylvania. He received a B.S. degree in engineering and industrial management from the Massachusetts Institute of Technology, an M.Sc. in economics from the London School of Economics, and a Ph.D. in economics from Johns Hopkins University. From 1968 to 1990, he conducted policy research at the Rand Corp. in Santa Monica, California, where he first specialized in Soviet affairs, including research and development, weapons acquisition policies, and defense decisionmaking. He also worked on U.S. R&D policy and defense economics. His research on Japanese issues in the 1980s included studies on trade in services, legal markets, innovation, and defense industry. Dr. Alexander was a research associate at the International Institute for Strategic Studies in London and a member of the U.S. Army Science Board. He has received an award from the Japanese Minister of Foreign Affairs for his work in promoting research on Japan.